Strategic Survey 2009
The Annual Review of World Affairs

published by

Routledge
Taylor & Francis Group

for

The International Institute for Strategic Studies

The International Institute for Strategic Studies
Arundel House | 13–15 Arundel Street | Temple Place | London | wc2r 3dx | UK

Strategic Survey 2009
The Annual Review of World Affairs

First published September 2009 by **Routledge**
4 Park Square, Milton Park, Abingdon, Oxon, ox14 4rn

for **The International Institute for Strategic Studies**
Arundel House, 13–15 Arundel Street, Temple Place, London, wc2r 3dx, UK

Simultaneously published in the USA and Canada by **Routledge**
270 Madison Ave., New York, NY 10016

Routledge is an imprint of Taylor & Francis, an Informa business

© 2009 The International Institute for Strategic Studies

DIRECTOR-GENERAL AND CHIEF EXECUTIVE Dr John Chipman
EDITOR Alexander Nicoll

ASSISTANT EDITOR Dr Jeffrey Mazo
CONTRIBUTING EDITOR Jonathan Stevenson
MAP EDITORS Sarah Johnstone, Jessica Delaney
EDITORIAL Dr Ayse Abdullah, Katharine Fletcher, Carolyn West
DESIGN/PRODUCTION John Buck
ADDITIONAL MAP RESEARCH Catherine Micklethwaite
CARTOGRAPHY Steven Bernard

COVER IMAGES Press Association; iStockphoto.com/Simon Smith
PRINTED BY Bell & Bain Ltd, Glasgow, UK

This publication has been prepared by the Director-General of the Institute and his Staff, who accept full responsibility for its contents, which describe and analyse events up to 30 June 2009. These do not, and indeed cannot, represent a consensus of views among the worldwide membership of the Institute as a whole.

British Library Cataloguing in Publication Data
A catalogue record for this book is available from the British Library

Library of Congress Cataloguing in Publication Data

ISBN 978-1-857-43526-9
ISSN 0459-7230

Contents

Strategic Geography (after p. 212)

Index of Regional Maps

Events at a Glance

July 2008–June 2009

July 2008

2 **Colombia:** Ingrid Betancourt, former presidential candidate held captive for six years, and 14 others are freed in a military operation in which Colombian soldiers trick FARC rebel captors into releasing hostages without a shot being fired.

4 **China:** First regular flights begin between China and Taiwan

7 **Afghanistan:** Car bomb kills 41 people, including two Indian diplomats, outside Indian Embassy in Kabul.

8 **Czech Republic:** US and Czech governments sign agreement on basing missile-tracking radar in Czech Republic.

9 **Iran:** Iran test-fires missiles, including the *Shahab*-3 which could reach Israel.

13 **United States:** US Treasury announces measures to provide financial support to Fannie Mae and Freddie Mac, which together account for about half of the US mortgage market.

   Afghanistan: Nine American soldiers killed in battle with Taliban fighters at outpost in eastern Afghanistan.

16 **Israel/Lebanon:** Lebanese militia group Hizbullah hands over bodies of two Israeli soldiers killed in 2006 in return for release of five prisoners and remains of 200 dead Lebanese and Palestinian fighters.

19 **Iran:** William Burns, US State Department's third-ranking official, takes part in Geneva talks between Iranian and European negotiators on Iran's nuclear programme.

21 **Serbia:** Radovan Karadzic, Bosnian Serb wanted for 13 years on war-crimes and genocide charges, is arrested in Serbia and taken to The Hague to face trial.

21 **China/Russia:** Agreement signed in Beijing ends last remaining border dispute between China and Russia, covering two river islands.

22 **India:** Government wins vote of confidence in parliament, clearing the way for civil nuclear agreement between India and the United States.

26 **India:** Sixteen bombs explode in western city of Ahmedabad, capital of western state of Gujarat, killing 45 people, a day after seven bomb blasts in southern city of Bangalore, killing one person.

29 **United States:** Government scientist Bruce Ivins dies after taking an overdose as prosecutors prepared to indict him in connection with anthrax attacks which killed five people in 2001.

30 **Israel:** Prime Minister Ehud Olmert announces plans to resign in September to fight allegations of corruption.

Turkey: Constitutional Court narrowly decides not to shut down ruling AK Party, following case accusing party of Islamist and anti-secular activities. In June, the court had overturned a government move to lift a ban on women wearing headscarves in universities.

Ethiopia/Eritrea: UN Security Council votes to end peacekeeping operation on border between Ethiopia and Eritrea, following withdrawal of Eritrean support for the mission.

August 2008

1 **Georgia:** Skirmishes escalate in South Ossetia, breakaway province of Georgia. South Ossetian President Eduard Kokoity accuses Georgia of attempting to start a war.

4 **China:** Sixteen policemen are killed in grenade attack on border post in Kashgar, Xinjiang province. Two ethnic Uighurs are executed for the crime in April 2009.

6 **Mauritania:** Troops seize power, deposing President Sidi Ould Cheikh Abdallahi in a coup.

7 **Georgia:** War breaks out in South Ossetia. Georgian forces attack Tskhinvali, capital of South Ossetia, hours after announcing a ceasefire meant to end several days of skirmishes. Tskhinvali is bombarded with rockets and artillery shells. On 8 August, Russian troops move into South Ossetia via the Roki Tunnel. Thousands of South Ossetians flee to North Ossetia, part of Russia. On 9 August, Russian troops move to take control of Tskhinvali, and Russian aircraft bomb the Georgian town of Gori and its military base. Russian forces advance towards Gori. In Abkhazia, Georgia's other breakaway region, local forces attack the Georgian-controlled Kodori Valley area. Russian forces move into Abkhazia. Russian warships take positions off the Georgian Black Sea coast. Russian troops move beyond Abkhazia and enter the Georgian towns of Zugdidi and Senaki. US President George W. Bush says Russia's invasion

of Georgia is 'unacceptable in the twenty-first century'. On 12 August, Russian President Dmitry Medvedev, after meeting French President Nicolas Sarkozy, says Russia will end campaign under a six-point deal. Abkhaz forces capture the Kodori Valley area. In Tbilisi, Sarkozy secures the agreement of Georgian President Mikheil Saakashvili to a modified peace plan. Russian troops occupy Gori and its military base. Russia says this is permitted under the deal, which foresees 'additional security measures'. Bush calls on Moscow to withdraw and orders the US military to provide humanitarian aid to Georgia. Aid begins arriving in US Air Force transport aircraft and later in US Navy warships. On 26 August, Russia formally recognises the independence of Abkhazia and South Ossetia – a decision that is widely condemned. On 8 September, Russia agrees to withdraw its troops from Georgian territory surrounding South Ossetia and Abkhazia. The pull-out is to be completed when European Union monitors are deployed by 1 October. Georgia says 295 Georgians were killed during the crisis – 186 soldiers and 109 civilians.

18 **Afghanistan:** Ten French soldiers are killed in Taliban ambush east of Kabul.

Pakistan: President Pervez Musharraf resigns after nine years in power, as opponents prepare to impeach him. On 9 September, he is succeeded by Asif Ali Zardari, leader of the Pakistan Peoples Party and the widower of former Prime Minister Benazir Bhutto.

20 **Poland:** US and Poland sign agreement to site US interceptor missiles in Poland.

21 **Pakistan:** Suicide-bomb attack kills 63 people outside Pakistan's main munitions factory, near Islamabad.

28 **DR Congo:** Fighting breaks out in Democratic Republic of the Congo between rebels led by Laurent Nkunda and government forces. Clashes escalate over succeeding months, displacing over 200,000 people.

September 2008

1 **Japan:** Prime Minister Yasuo Fukuda resigns after a year in office. On 24 September, Taro Aso, former foreign minister, is elected by parliament to succeed him.

7 **United States:** Government takes mortgage institutions Fannie Mae and Freddie Mac into public ownership.

13 **India:** Bomb blasts kill about 20 people in Delhi.

15 **China:** Government says two babies have died as a result of contamination of milk powder with melamine, a toxic chemical. By January 2009, 296,000 children have fallen ill, companies have been prosecuted and have offered apologies, and two people have been sentenced to death.

United States: Investment bank Lehman Brothers files for bankruptcy after the US government declines to rescue it following heavy losses in the mortgage-securities market. Bank of America buys Merrill Lynch, another investment bank that had suffered heavy losses. Government takes control of insurance company AIG, which faced huge losses on contracts insuring holders against debt defaults. Interbank-lending rates rise sharply as banks doubt each others' credit. Stock markets fall sharply. Central banks inject large amounts of money into the money markets to boost liquidity. On 18 September, planned acquisition by Lloyds Bank of HBOS, another UK bank, is announced. On 19 September, US Treasury Secretary Henry Paulson announces plan for $700bn programme to buy impaired mortgage assets from banks to improve their balance sheets. The plan requires congressional approval.

17 **Yemen:** Attack on US Embassy in Sana'a, Yemen, leaves 19 dead, including six attackers.

20 **Pakistan:** Truck bomb destroys Marriott Hotel in Islamabad, killing 53 people, including the Czech ambassador.

21 **South Africa:** President Thabo Mbeki resigns after nine years in office. The African National Congress (ANC) party had withdrawn support following a judge's conclusion – later overturned by the Supreme Court of Appeal – that he interfered in the prosecution for corruption of ANC President Jacob Zuma, earlier his rival. Charges against Zuma were later dropped.

25 Sixth largest US bank, Washington Mutual, is seized by government, placed into receivership and sold to JPMorgan Chase. On 29 September, government announces that fourth largest US bank, Wachovia, is to be forcibly sold to Citigroup, though it is eventually sold to Wells Fargo. Banks in Belgium, United Kingdom, Germany and Iceland receive emergency support from governments. Ireland guarantees all deposits in six Irish banks.

Somalia: Somali pirates capture the *Faina*, a Ukrainian vessel carrying a cargo of Soviet-era tanks and ammunition. The US and other navies blockade the ship. It is released on 6 February 2009 after payment of a ransom.

October 2008

3 **United States:** Congress passes $700bn bank-bailout bill after House of Representatives had initially rejected it. Stock markets continue to fall sharply.

8 UK government announces £400bn bank-rescue plan under which it will take up to £50bn of equity stakes in banks, double short-term central-bank loans to boost banks' liquidity and provide up to £250bn in loan guarantees. Central banks around the world announce coordinated reductions in interest rates, and these are later followed by further cuts. Germany, France, Switzerland, the Netherlands, Russia, Spain, Italy, Sweden and other European countries announce emergency measures to support banks. So do the United Arab Emirates, Qatar and Hong Kong. Iceland nationalises largest three banks. On 14 October, President Bush announces $250bn plan to purchase stakes in US banks; nine large banks agree to the government buying shares in them.

United States: President Bush signs US–India civil nuclear cooperation agreement into law following passage by US Congress.

11 **North Korea:** United States removes North Korea from list of state sponsors of terrorism as part of an agreement ending deadlock in talks. Pyongyang agrees to some inspections and to resume disabling its Pyongyang nuclear plant.

14 **Canada:** Early general election called by Prime Minister Stephen Harper strengthens the position of his Conservative Party in parliament, but does not give it an absolute majority.

26 **Israel:** Tzipi Livni, leader of ruling Kadima party, says she is unable to form a coalition government, setting the stage for a general election to be called.

27 **Sudan:** Five Chinese oil workers are killed after being kidnapped.

International Monetary Fund announces emergency loans for Hungary and Ukraine because of effects of financial crisis. It has also made a loan to Iceland and is in talks with Pakistan and Belarus.

30 **India:** Series of bomb blasts kill 81 people in northeastern state of Assam.

November 2008

2 **Azerbaijan/Armenia:** Presidents Ilham Aliyev of Azerbaijan and Serzh Sargsyan of Armenia sign agreement aimed at resolving dispute over Nagorno-Karabakh after meeting with Russian President Dmitry Medvedev.

4 **United States:** Barack Obama defeats John McCain to win the US presidency in an election in which the Democratic Party is overwhelmingly successful. Obama, the first African-American US president, wins 52.9% of the popular vote and gains nine states from the Republican Party. The Democrats gain seven Senate seats with one further seat disputed. This gives them a total of 56 seats with two independents leaning towards them. The Democrats gain 21 seats in the House of Representatives, winning 257 out of 435 seats.

8 **New Zealand:** Centre-right National Party defeats incumbent Labour Party in general election and John Key becomes prime minister.

9 **Indonesia:** Three Islamic militants convicted of the 2002 Bali bombings which killed 202 people are executed by firing squad.

China: Government, facing sharp fall in exports, announces RMB4 trillion ($585bn) stimulus package to boost the domestic economy.

10 **Maldives:** Newly elected President Mohamed Nasheed announces plans for investment fund to buy land elsewhere in the region to provide a home for Maldivians in case global warming causes sea levels to rise and swamp the low-lying islands that make up their country.

14 G20 leaders, meeting in Washington to discuss global financial and economic crisis, agree to take further action to stabilise financial markets and stimulate

economies, as well as to reform financial markets. Figures from many countries show contracting economies, rising unemployment and sharply falling inflation. Governments continue to announce stimulus measures.

15 **Somalia:** Supertanker *Sirius Star* is hijacked by Somali pirates 450 nautical miles off the coast of Kenya. It is released on 9 January 2009 after payment of a ransom.

25 **United States:** Federal Reserve announces $800bn of support for markets in mortgage securities and consumer loans.

26 **Thailand:** Anti-government protests escalate as protesters occupy Bangkok's main airport and stop flights.

India: Terrorists attack multiple targets in Mumbai, including the Taj Mahal and Oberoi Hotels, the main railway station and a Jewish centre. Some of them hole up in the two hotels until 29 November, when security forces complete their operation against them. By the end of the incident, 175 people are dead, including nine militants. One militant is arrested. He is identified as being from Pakistan and is later charged with murder and other offences. The boats in which the group made their journey from Pakistan are traced. India's home minister resigns. On 8 December, Pakistani security forces attack a camp used by Lashkar-e-Tayiba, a Kashmir militant group said to have carried out the Mumbai attack, and arrest the group's operational chief.

27 **Iraq:** Iraqi parliament approves agreement with United States under which American forces will withdraw to bases from mid 2009 and leave Iraq completely by end 2011.

28 **Nigeria:** Violence between Christians and Muslims breaks out in central Nigerian city of Jos following local elections. Some 400 people are killed.

December 2008

1 **United States:** President-elect Obama nominates Hillary Clinton as secretary of state and asks Robert Gates to remain as secretary of defense, with James Jones, former NATO commander, nominated as national security adviser. Timothy Geithner is treasury secretary and Lawrence Summers is director of the National Economic Council.

8 **Somalia:** European Union begins its first naval operation, patrolling waters off Somalia to deter and stop acts of piracy.

14 **Iraq:** Iraqi journalist throws his shoes at US President Bush during press conference in Baghdad.

15 **Thailand:** Parliament votes Abhisit Vejjajiva to be prime minister amid continuing political chaos following removal of two previous prime ministers.

16 **Somalia:** United Nations Security Council adopts Resolution 1851 authorising states to carry out land-based operations in Somalia against piracy, and calling

for deployments of ships and aircraft and for the seizure of pirates' boats and weapons.

23 **Guinea:** Army officer Captain Moussa Camara seizes power following death of President Lansana Conté, who had led the country for 24 years.

26 **China:** Chinese naval task force of two destroyers and a supply ship leaves to undertake anti-piracy patrols off Somalia, in the Chinese navy's first military operation outside the Pacific Ocean.

27 **Israel/Palestine:** Israel launches aerial attacks on Gaza, killing over 225 people. Israeli air strikes and Palestinian rocket attacks continue in the following days, and on 3 January Israel begins a ground offensive into Gaza. Air and ground attacks continue until 17 January, when Israel declares a ceasefire. More than 1,400 Palestinians are killed in the offensive.

29 **Somalia:** Abdullahi Yusuf Ahmed, president of the Transitional Federal Government, resigns after parliament refused to back his sacking of the prime minister. On 31 January, MPs, meeting in Djibouti, elect Sheikh Sharif Ahmed, seen as a moderate Islamist, as president.

29 **Bangladesh:** Following a two-year period of military-controlled caretaker government, general elections result in landslide victory for the Awami League, of which the leader, Sheikh Hasina, becomes prime minister.

January 2009

1 **Ukraine:** Russia cuts off gas supplies in price dispute, severely disrupting supplies to several European countries. A price agreement is signed on 19 January.

Pakistan: US air strike in South Waziristan reportedly kills Usama al-Kini, Kenyan-born al-Qaeda operative believed to have planned destruction of Marriott Hotel in Islamabad.

2 **Sri Lanka:** Army captures northern town of Kilinochchi, the de facto capital of territory previously held by Tamil Tiger rebels, as it continues to press northwards.

3 **Ghana:** Opposition candidate John Atta Mills wins run-off election and becomes president, defeating Nana Akufo-Addo and succeeding John Kufuor.

13 **Somalia:** Ethiopian troops withdraw from Somalia, two years after intervening to oust Islamist militias and support the transitional government.

22 **United States:** President Barack Obama, two days after entering office, orders the closure of the Guantanamo Bay detention centre within a year and of CIA detention centres in other countries.

22 **DR Congo:** Rebel leader Laurent Nkunda is arrested in Rwanda, after Rwandan and Congolese troops launch a joint operation against Rwandan Hutu rebel forces in the DRC. Following Nkunda's offensive towards the Congolese town

of Goma, which displaced hundreds of thousands, Nkunda's chief of staff had switched the allegiance of their rebel group to fight with government forces against the Hutu militias, and the two governments had reached an agreement under which Rwandan troops were allowed into the DRC to hunt the militias.

28 **Sri Lanka:** Human-rights organisations express concern about 250,000 people trapped amidst the fighting as the area controlled by Tamil Tiger rebels shrinks.

February 2009

3 **Iran:** Iran launches domestically produced satellite into orbit.

6 **Pakistan:** A.Q. Khan, who ran a network trading nuclear-weapons technology, is freed from house arrest.

10 **Israel:** Election gives previously ruling Kadima party 28 seats in Knesset, and Likud 27. President Shimon Peres asks Benjamin Netanyahu, Likud leader, to form a coalition government. On 30 March, he reports success and his government is sworn in on 31 March.

12 **Space:** Two satellites collide above Siberia, creating a large amount of space debris. The accident, involving a US privately owned *Iridium* communications satellite and a defunct Russian *Cosmos*, was the first collision between two intact satellites.

13 **United States:** Congress passes $787bn economic stimulus package, including tax cuts and spending increases intended to boost jobs.

Zimbabwe: Nearly a year after parliamentary elections, President Robert Mugabe swears in a unity government following a power-sharing deal with Morgan Tsvangirai, who becomes prime minister. On 6 March, Tsvangirai's wife is killed and he is injured in a car crash, said to be an accident, although the cause is later questioned.

14 **Saudi Arabia:** King Abdullah dismisses head of religious police and the most senior religious judge in a government reshuffle. He appoints the first female deputy minister.

15 **Venezuela:** President Hugo Chávez wins a referendum abolishing limits on the terms of the president, state governors and National Assembly members.

17 **Afghanistan:** US President Obama announces plans to send 17,000 additional troops to Afghanistan.

China/Russia: Russia and China sign agreement under which China will lend $25bn to Russian oil and pipeline companies and Russia will supply 300,000 barrels of oil a day for 20 years.

25 **Bangladesh:** A mutiny at the Dhaka headquarters of the Bangladesh Rifles border guards is put down. The incident leaves 74 people dead, mostly officers.

March 2009

2 **Guinea-Bissau:** President João Bernardo Vieira is assassinated by soldiers hours after the army chief of staff is killed in a bomb explosion. Elections are scheduled.

3 **Pakistan:** Gunmen attack bus carrying Sri Lanka's cricket team to a match in Lahore, killing six policemen and a driver, and injuring several players. All the attackers escape.

4 **Sudan:** International Criminal Court in The Hague issues arrest warrant for Sudanese President Omar al-Bashir, accusing him of war crimes and crimes against humanity in Darfur. Sudan expels 10 foreign aid agencies.

8 **United Kingdom:** Two soldiers shot dead outside army barracks in Northern Ireland. Dissident Irish republicans are believed to be responsible. Two days later, a policeman is shot dead.

11 **France:** President Nicolas Sarkozy announces France's return to the military command structure of NATO after 43 years.

14 **Somalia:** Two Japanese destroyers leave port to carry out anti-piracy patrols off Somalia.

16 **Pakistan:** Chief Justice Iftikhar Chaudhry reinstated along with all remaining judges suspended by former President Musharraf in 2007. The decision by President Asif Ali Zardari is a victory for opposition leader Nawaz Sharif.

17 **Madagascar:** Opposition leader Andry Rajoelina, with the backing of the military, seizes power from President Marc Ravalomanana. Unrest and protests follow.

30 **Pakistan:** Gunmen storm police academy in Lahore and hold it for eight hours. 18 people, including eight militants, are reported killed.

Sudan: *Time* magazine reports that Israeli jets in mid January destroyed a convoy of trucks in Sudan carrying arms to Hamas militants in Gaza.

April 2009

1 **Albania/Croatia:** Albania and Croatia formally become members of NATO.

US/Russia: Presidents Obama and Medvedev agree to pursue reductions in nuclear arsenals and to negotiate new arms-control treaty.

2 G20 leaders, meeting in London, agree to boost resources of International Monetary Fund, tighten regulation of financial institutions and establish a Financial Stability Board.

3 **Malaysia:** Najib Razak becomes Malaysian prime minister following the resignation of Abdullah Badawi.

5 **North Korea:** North Korea launches long-range rocket over Japan. It claims to have put a satellite into orbit, but there is no evidence for this. Following international criticism of the launch, Pyongyang expels inspectors from the International Atomic Energy Agency and says it is restarting its nuclear programme.

13 **Cuba:** US President Obama relaxes restrictions on Cuban-Americans travelling to Cuba.

16 **United States:** Obama administration releases four memoranda from 2002 and 2005 authorising interrogation techniques that could be used by Central Intelligence Agency. Obama says no CIA employee will be prosecuted for role in interrogations. One memo said that Khalid Sheikh Mohammed, an al-Qaeda operative, had been waterboarded 183 times.

22 **South Africa:** African National Congress wins 65.9% of votes in National Assembly elections, and on 9 May its leader Jacob Zuma becomes president.

23 **Turkey/Armenia:** Armenia and Turkey agree on a framework aimed at normalising relations, following long dispute over killings of Armenians in 1915.

27 **Mexico:** Cases of H1N1 'swine' flu, a virus which had spread in Mexico, are discovered around the world. Mexico introduces measures intended to curb its spread. On 29 April, World Health Organisation raises pandemic alert level to five, below the highest level of six. By 25 May, WHO has counted 12,515 cases and 91 deaths, of which 80 were in Mexico. By 11 June, number of confirmed cases nears 30,000 including 144 deaths, and WHO declares a global pandemic, the first in 41 years.

May 2009

7 **Pakistan:** Army launches offensive against militants in Swat Valley and neighbouring areas. Hundreds of thousands of people flee the fighting.

12 **Afghanistan:** US Defense Secretary Robert Gates ends assignment of General David McKiernan as head of international forces in Afghanistan after only 11 months, appointing General Stanley McChrystal, former special-operations chief, in his place.

16 **India:** General-election results strengthen the Congress party's hold on power, and give the United Progressive Alliance, the Congress-led coalition, a narrow majority in parliament. Leftist parties and the Hindu nationalist Bharatiya Janata Party suffer losses.

18 **Sri Lanka:** Government forces overrun last remaining rebel-held territory and kill Velupillai Prabhakaran, leader of the Tamil Tigers. On 19 May, President Mahinda Rajapaksa declares that the 26-year civil war is over and calls for an end to ethnic and religious tensions.

18 **Myanmar:** Opposition leader Aung San Suu Kyi goes on trial in prison, accused of violating the terms of her house arrest. An American, apparently uninvited, had swum across a lake to her house.

22 **South Korea:** Roh Moo-hyun, South Korean president from 2003 to 2008, kills himself after allegations of receiving bribes.

24 **Mongolia:** Tsakhiagiin Elbegdorj of Democratic Party wins presidential election, defeating incumbent Nambaryn Enkhbayar.

25 **North Korea:** North Korea carries out underground nuclear explosion, more powerful than its first such test in 2006, and also conducts a series of short-range missile launches. South Korea announces it will join the Proliferation Security Initiative, US-led group of which members stop and search suspicious cargoes. North Korea says it will no longer be bound by the 1953 armistice that ended the Korean War, and that it will respond militarily if its ships are stopped. On 8 June, two American reporters who were arrested near North Korea's border with China are sentenced to 12 years in a labour camp. On 12 June, UN Security Council unanimously condemns the nuclear test and imposes tougher sanctions including inspection of North Korean cargo and ban on sales by North Korea of heavy and small arms.

June 2009

1 **United States:** General Motors, automaker, files for bankruptcy protection from creditors, to whom it owes $172bn. Under a restructuring plan, the US government will own 60% of the company, and Canada 12.5%.

3 **Cuba:** Organisation of American States votes to lift 47-year suspension of Cuba's membership.

4 **Egypt:** US President Obama calls for a new beginning in relations between the United States and the Muslim world, seeking to end the 'cycle of suspicion and discord'. Though the US bond with Israel was unbreakable, construction of Jewish settlements in the West Bank must be halted and Israelis must accept Palestine's right to exist. There should be no nuclear arms race in the Middle East and 'no system of government can or should be imposed upon one nation by any other'.

7 **Lebanon:** Parliamentary election is won by March 14 Alliance coalition led by Saad al-Hariri, with 71 out of 128 seats, defeating Hizbullah-led March 8 Alliance. On 27 June, Hariri is appointed prime minister-designate and asked to form a government.

9 **United States:** Treasury allows 10 US banks to repay $68bn of bailout funds advanced under the Troubled Asset Relief Program. The group includes JPMorgan Chase, Goldman Sachs and Morgan Stanley, but not Citigroup or Bank of America.

9 **Pakistan:** Truck-bomb attack on Pearl Continental Hotel in Peshawar kills 18 people.

11 **Bermuda:** Four Uighurs from western China are released from the US detention centre at Guantanamo Bay and resettled in Bermuda.

Kosovo: NATO ministers agree to reduce size of peacekeeping force in Kosovo from 14,000 troops to 10,000, but do not set a firm timeline.

12 **Iran:** Mahmoud Ahmadinejad is declared re-elected as Iranian president with 63% of votes cast. However, opposition candidates – in particular Mir Hossein Mousavi who came second in the published results – do not accept the figures, and widespread protests follow. The demonstrations are the largest since the 1979 Islamic Revolution. Although they are non-violent, a number of people are killed. Hundreds of people are arrested. Foreign leaders express concern. Iran imposes restrictions on foreign media. A limited recount of votes is ordered, but Supreme Leader Ali Khamenei says the elections were valid and warns opposition leaders to halt protests.

14 **Israel:** Israeli Prime Minister Netanyahu says he would accept a Palestinian state, but only if it was demilitarised and acknowledged Israel as the Jewish homeland.

16 **Yemen:** Bodies of three abducted foreigners, two Germans and a Korean, are found, while six more kidnap victims are missing.

20 **Iraq:** Bodies of two Britons, kidnapped while working in the finance ministry in Baghdad in 2007, are released and identified. The fate of three more Britons taken hostage at the same time is unknown.

22 **Russia:** Yunus-bek Yevkurov, President of Russian Republic of Ingushetia, is seriously injured by a car bomb.

23 **Kyrgyzstan:** Government reverses decision to close Manas air base, used by the US since 2001, after Washington agrees to triple the rent and make other payments to aid Kyrgyzstan's development.

28 **Honduras:** President Manuel Zelaya is ousted in a military coup and flown to Costa Rica. He had sought to hold a referendum on constitutional change allowing him to stand for re-election, and had fired the head of the army, who opposed holding such a vote. Roberto Micheletti, Congress speaker, is installed as interim president.

30 **Iraq:** US military patrols of Iraqi streets end after six years.

Chapter 1

Perspectives

Never has the world been so caught up in a single country's democratic process as it was in the election of Barack Obama as president of the United States in November 2008. It was not only the American public that was affected by the words and phrases that defined his campaign, such as 'hope', 'change', and 'yes we can'. Many people across the world, it seemed, were impressed by his rhetoric and looked forward to a new beginning. The election of America's first black president was surely a momentous event, not only for America but for the wider world as well.

For Obama, an important challenge was to begin to restore American prestige following the battering that it had taken under eight years of President George W. Bush – a period marked by American unilateralism and a response to the 2001 terrorist attacks that was widely judged to have provided fuel to America's enemies. As it turned out, however, this was not the most urgent problem Obama faced. For he came to office amidst a financial and economic crisis that had begun in the United States, convulsed the world's money and stock markets and dramatically curtailed economic activity to the extent that global output was forecast in 2009 to contract for the first time since the Second World War. In 2008, US government rescues brought the world's largest insurance company, AIG, as well as the two largest real-estate mortgage companies, into public ownership. To these were added in 2009 the bankrupt automaker General Motors. Many of the world's biggest banks, which had suffered huge losses from rash lending that was blamed for triggering the crisis, were being kept in business by massive official support. By mid 2009, while output had declined sharply and prospects remained highly uncertain, the enormous amount of money pumped into economies by governments and central banks appeared to have warded off the danger of descent into a 1930s-style global depression.

Obama's biggest initial task was thus to push through a domestic economic stimulus package. The large fiscal deficit that he inherited from Bush, and its inevitable sharp expansion because of the recession and stimulus spending, threatened to limit the options for change available to him even as he took up his post. Although he inherited the crisis, its effects seemed bound to create political difficulties for him. Nevertheless, the recession also played well into his desire to tackle the world's problems in a more multilateral and consultative manner than had his predecessor: plainly, it was everybody's crisis, and the world needed a healthy America to emerge from it. In his inauguration address, Obama said he detected a 'sapping of confidence across our land; a nagging fear that America's decline is inevitable, that the next generation must lower its sights'. Such apprehensions have been felt not only in America: indeed, for several years some countries have been seen to adopt strategic hedges precisely against the possibility that the United States might never be the power it once had been.

> **The world needed a healthy America to emerge from the crisis**

Notwithstanding the recession, Obama embarked on an ambitious programme to reverse America's course. He announced plans to close the Guantanamo Bay detention centre and secret American prisons abroad, and banned the use of interrogation techniques involving torture. He sought, in a speech in Cairo, to rebuild trust in the United States among Muslims around the world. He called on Iran to enter a dialogue, without demanding that it first halt the enrichment of uranium. He began a new effort to resolve the Israel–Palestine dispute, adopting a harder line towards Israel. He set out a new strategy embracing both Afghanistan and Pakistan, and sent more troops to Afghanistan. He agreed with China on expanding bilateral dialogue and with Russia on mutual cuts in nuclear-weapons stockpiles. He relaxed restrictions on travelling to and doing business with Cuba. And at home, he set out to reform the health-care system, and sought to treat the poor state of the economy as a foundation for, rather than as an obstacle to, his plans for change.

It was far too early to assess the likely success of his agenda. Many of its elements were long-term projects. It was far from automatic that

Washington's new open approach would be reciprocated in other capitals – and indeed, initial reactions from other capitals were reserved. There was no evidence to suggest that Obama would not be hard headed in his dealings with other countries, or that he expected anything other than a careful calculation of interests by all parties with whom he might deal. But his approach contained political pitfalls: the American right was vitriolic in casting him as weak, naive and apologising for America. And he was vulnerable to awkward dilemmas, such as how to treat Iranians' protests against an allegedly rigged presidential election when he wished to begin a dialogue with the victor.

The year to mid 2009 provided plenty of evidence of the perennial nature of the security challenges to be confronted. In August 2008 a brief war was fought between Georgia and Russia, which sent troops across its border as Georgia attacked Tskhinvali, capital of the breakaway region of South Ossetia. While the conflict sent shivers through countries that had been members of the Soviet bloc, it caused only a temporary deterioration in relations between Moscow and the West – although relations were already poor following a period of confrontational assertiveness from Moscow, which vociferously opposed plans for the location of American anti-missile systems in Europe and objected to Washington's promotion of NATO membership for Georgia and Ukraine.

The threat of terrorist violence emanating from Pakistan was vividly demonstrated when a group of ten attackers went on a 60-hour rampage in Mumbai, India's business capital. Militants also escalated a campaign of terrorist attacks within Pakistan, which included the destruction of the Marriott Hotel in Islamabad. While the country's political establishment continued to be torn by disputes, the threat of extremist violence was growing steadily, and the army was heavily deployed. International forces in Afghanistan, swelled by an increase in American troops, sought to repel Taliban fighters, many of whom came across the border from Pakistan. Battles were being fought in rugged areas of Afghanistan where for centuries it had been difficult for any group or power to exert or maintain control. It was increasingly difficult to see how the West's eight-year-old intervention could achieve more than modest goals – and it was not evident that there was a clear vision of what the goals were. A mass of foreign governments, militaries, aid agencies and non-governmental organisations was involved in an insufficiently coordinated effort to build stability around an Afghan government that appeared fundamentally inadequate for the task. Washington's aim in sending more troops seemed to be to prepare the ground, as in Iraq, for an eventual substantial drawdown. It appeared inevitable that negotiations must be held with individuals and groups wielding power on the ground, in the hope of approaching realistic – if less than optimal – solutions.

The threat of nuclear proliferation remained ever present. North Korea's international relations, which had advanced in a series of agreements, lurched backwards in an all-too-familiar series of events, including a nuclear explosion, test launches of missiles, and the resumption of processing of fuel rods to recover plutonium at its Yongbyon plant. Iran's uranium-enrichment programme continued apace, and Obama's call for dialogue with Tehran was, in effect, put into abeyance by the protests that erupted in June 2009 when President Mahmoud Ahmadinejad was swiftly declared re-elected by a 2:1 margin over challenger Mir Hossein Mousavi. The latter's supporters, believing that a massive fraud had been perpetrated, staged huge demonstrations, but violence and threats were employed in an effort to quell public dissent.

The perceived threat from Iran was made much of by the new right-wing government of Israel. But Prime Minister Benjamin Netanyahu failed to persuade Obama that this must be addressed ahead of peace in the Middle East. Instead, Washington added new vigour to its quest for a two-state solution to the Israel–Palestine dispute and told Israel to stop building settlements in the West Bank. Israel had previously attracted heavy criticism for a brutal assault on the Gaza Strip, which was controlled by the Palestinian militant group Hamas.

Several landmarks were reached over the past year. The 26-year civil war in Sri Lanka ended as the army captured all territory controlled by Tamil Tiger rebels. American soldiers ceased to patrol Iraqi streets as a 2008 Status of Forces agreement between Iraq and the United States was implemented, with full withdrawal scheduled for the end of 2010. A unity government was installed in Zimbabwe. Piracy off Somalia prompted the deployment of ships to the Horn of Africa from a large number of countries, including China, Japan, South Korea, Iran, the United States and European countries. While the durability of all these developments was questionable, each was remarkable. But the year to mid 2009 was notable primarily for two events: the election of Barack Obama, and the near-collapse of the world's financial system. Each of these would have large ramifications, many of which are yet to unfold.

America relaunched

The years following the Cold War had seen the United States cast first as the sole superpower and then as the largest power in a 'multipolar' or 'non-polar' world. Its decision to carry out a primarily military campaign against terrorist groups had exposed the limits of what America's military potency could achieve – and thus had undermined its strategic power. The United States had clearly lost traction in its efforts to deal with some of the world's major threats, such as Iran's nuclear programme and Middle East peace. The rise of China and Russia's renewed assertiveness were posing longer-term questions about the global balance of power. And to cap it all, in 2008 its enormous financial markets were brought to their knees.

It might be tempting for some to believe that all this signalled America's inevitable and quick decline – and over the long term, it seems logical that the relative position of the United States could not remain what it was immediately after the collapse of the Soviet Union. But the very attention paid around the world to the election of Barack Obama showed that America was far from being just another power. Moscow, for example, still saw the United States as orchestrating the encirclement of Russia by NATO; when Obama met Vladimir Putin in July 2009, he was subjected to an hour-long private monologue from the Russian prime minister. It was still to Washington that friends and enemies alike looked. Adversaries such as North Korea wanted above all to engage Washington on their terms. Rivals in regional struggles looked to it for crucial support. Allies and friends still wanted it to be the ultimate guarantor of security and prosperity. For most leaders, relations – good or bad – with the American administration were a test by which they were judged. Virtually all, from their different perspectives, wanted Washington to be less ineffectual in its international relations than it had been in the previous eight years.

So the night of 4 November 2008 was one of extraordinary significance far beyond America. Voters had elected not just the next Democratic president, but an African-American, an orator whose heralding of a new beginning seemed much more than a politician's routine promise. An opponent of the Iraq invasion, his approach to the world would be fundamentally different to that of Bush.

In his victory speech in Grant Park, Chicago, Barack Obama said: 'It's been a long time coming, but tonight, because of what we did on this day, in this election, at this defining moment, change has come to America'. Across the country, people spilled on to the streets in celebration. The election was indeed a defining moment not only because of what might be to come, but also because of what had just past. The presidency of George W. Bush had been hit by another defining moment, the 11 September 2001 terrorist attacks on the United States. The loss of 3,000 innocent people was bound to begin a dark period for America, and would have taxed any president severely. Bush, however, was found wanting; his declaration of a 'global war on terror' offered legitimacy to the perpetrators, and al-Qaeda's leaders were not brought to justice; his invasion of Iraq was a costly, hubristic error that gave violent extremists a recruiting tool and enhanced the strategic position of Iran. As the election approached, millions of Americans faced losing their homes in the financial crash, and the economy was sliding into recession. Even though Bush's eight years had until 2008 been a period of prosperity, they were a bleak time. Habitual Republican voters showed their disillusionment in helping to elect Obama.

The new president had emphasised his desire to heal the bitter divisions in American politics. These came to the fore in the election campaign with John McCain's surprise choice of Sarah Palin as his vice-presidential candidate. The virtually unknown governor of Alaska, who espoused traditional conservative values and called herself 'your average hockey mom', was selected to boost McCain's standing with the right wing of the Republican Party, for whom he was not an obvious choice as candidate. Perhaps even McCain was unnerved by the visceral responses of Republican audiences as the self-styled 'pit bull' took the fight to Obama, accusing him of 'palling around with terrorists' – though her evident lack of knowledge of world affairs may, in the end, have made her a liability to McCain. Obama had long seen a new vision for America in which the Red State–Blue State divisions brought out by Palin could be bridged. In his Chicago victory speech, Obama said: 'Let us resist the temptation to fall back on the same partisanship and pettiness and immaturity that has poisoned our politics for so long'. Yet in Obama's first months, there was little sign of blossoming bipartisanship. Obama's efforts to bridge party lines in addressing the economy's troubles met stony opposition. The Republican right, epitomised by the radio commentator Rush Limbaugh, gave him no quarter. Obama was attacked by former Vice President Dick Cheney for making Americans less safe.

Obama's fresh approach to foreign affairs would similarly take time to bear fruit. He abandoned the phrase 'global war on terror', saying instead in his inauguration address that America was at war against 'a far-reaching network of violence and hatred'; and he wasted no time in announcing the planned closure of the Guantanamo Bay detention centre. He made it clear that he did not wish the United States to be in the business of imposing democracy on other countries. In most areas, however, the real differences were in tone and energy rather than policy. Not surprisingly, much of his attention, and that of Secretary of State Hillary Clinton, was focused on the troubled region from Palestine to Pakistan. The problems were still the same as those confronting the previous administration, and advances would be no easier to achieve. Indeed, there was reason to think that the situation could worsen as Islamist militancy spread in Pakistan, the conflict in Afghanistan was stepped up, Iran entered a period of domestic instability, and the likelihood of Israeli military action against Iran increased. It remained to be seen whether violence in Iraq would grow following the withdrawal of American troops from the streets. Gulf Arab countries, in view of the multiple possible scenarios that could affect their interests, were likely to continue to hedge their bets. Nor would it be easy to achieve the concrete steps that Obama had so far set out: for example, the closure of Guantanamo Bay and an end to Israeli settlements in the West Bank. His Cairo speech, therefore, had to be seen as the beginning of a protracted effort to change attitudes in the Muslim world.

> **The real differences were in tone and energy rather than policy**

His approach inevitably involved much more realpolitik than the absolutist, 'with-us-or-against-us' stance of the Bush administration. It involved careful calculation of the strategic interests of the United States, and at least tacit acknowledgement that America did not have the answer to all problems. This opened him to criticism in a political environment in which the demands of the 24-hour news cycle had become so pressing. During the demonstrations in Iran, for example, he said the violence was 'outrageous' but insisted that 'it is up to Iranians to make a decision about who Iran's leaders will be'. Nevertheless, he was accused by Ahmadinejad of meddling in Iranian affairs. When violence broke out between minority Uighur Muslims and Han Chinese in the western Chinese province of Xinjiang, Obama again called for an end to violence but refrained from assigning blame. Following a military coup in Honduras, where President Manuel Zelaya had been seeking constitutional changes to extend his term, Obama made clear that Washington supported his reinstatement because he was the democratically elected leader, even though he had been a strong critic of the United States – Zelaya was a close ally of Venezuelan President Hugo Chávez.

Obama was undoubtedly aware that, momentous as his election was, progress on the international front would be difficult and at best incremental. It would also be bound up in the handling, by his own and other governments, of the financial and economic crisis.

From boom to bust

The transformation of the world's economic fortunes from steady growth to rapid contraction was an extraordinary reversal. While periodic recessions are normal events, the suddenness of the collapse from boom to bust was caused by an even more extraordinary seizing-up in financial markets. For a few weeks in September and October 2008, the world stared into an abyss: it feared the wiping out of savings, the wholesale collapse of banks and businesses, an end to normal means of doing business. It seemed unthinkable that today's interconnected, high-technology world could be plunged into a new Great Depression, but this was a clear danger.

That these dire eventualities did not occur was due to the rapid and substantial actions of governments and monetary authorities. But, with banks for a time unable to lend to each other in the money markets because they did not trust each others' creditworthiness, it was a close shave. And the residual effects were serious enough: at mid 2009, large parts of financial systems were still operating under government control or with official support; bank lending remained severely constrained; and with demand having collapsed and confidence shattered, economic activity had gone into steep decline. According to the International Monetary Fund (IMF), the global economy contracted at an annual rate of 6.25% in the fourth quarter of 2008, compared with 4% growth in the third quarter. The rate of decline in advanced economies was an unprecedented 7.5%, and falls in the first quarter of 2009 were almost as large. Unemployment rates were rising sharply, and budget deficits were widening because of lower tax revenues and higher spending, especially to offset the effects of joblessness. Many countries, from large to small, faced financial difficulties, especially those east European nations that had taken on hard-currency debts as they made an incomplete transition to open markets, and whose currencies fell as investors deserted them. The IMF, whose role had been declining, found itself in demand again and agreed financial rescue packages for Ukraine, Hungary, Iceland, Pakistan, Latvia, Belarus, Serbia, Romania, Mongolia and Bosnia. A number of large industrialised countries, including the United States, the United Kingdom and Spain, faced the prospect of very large government borrowing requirements for years to come.

Illustrating the sudden downturn, at mid 2009 most of the world's shipping lines were operating at well below capacity and more than 700 cargo ships were reported to be moored off Singapore, waiting for business. While the fall in activity was expected to bottom out during 2009, economic prospects remained extremely uncertain. According to the IMF, the global economy will contract by 1.3% in 2009, the first annual decline since the Second World War, and will show a weak recovery of 1.9% in 2010. The worst-affected countries were in the industrialised world, particularly those heavily dependent on exports. Japan was forecast to show a 6.2% contraction in 2009, Germany 5.6% and the United States 2.8%. Newly industrialised Asian economies, heavily dependent on manufacturing exports, were badly hit. China and India were still estimated to show growth in 2009 although the pace, at 6.5% and 4.5% respectively, would in each case be about half the level of two years before.

The recession that began in 2008 followed a decade of exceptional prosperity, marked by strong growth in developing and middle-income countries. Exports to the developed world contributed importantly to their growth, and some built up large foreign-exchange reserves, much of which were invested back into industrialised countries. By 2008 – even before the financial crisis reached its climax – there were strong signs that the global economy was due for a correction: oil prices had risen to $140 a barrel, and there was little spare oil; food prices had also been driven to record highs, with some supply constraints appearing. It was commonly said by economists that unsustainable imbalances had developed, with high savings rates in exporting surplus countries financing a debt-fuelled import boom in the industrialised world. In the United States, in addition to ballooning consumer debt, the borrowing requirement of the government had risen sharply as the tax-cutting Bush administration oversaw a swing from budget surplus to large deficit.

The turmoil in financial markets was thus a trigger for the global recession rather than its fundamental cause. But, as often happens in financial crashes, it cruelly exposed the vulnerabilities of countries, companies and individuals whose financial foundations were less than solid. The financial crisis made the recession far steeper than it might otherwise have been, and may make recovery slower.

The problems of the financial markets had their origins in the global savings–debt imbalance. The exceptional liquidity created by the foreign funds pouring into the United States made for cheap money, which in turn financed a consumer bonanza. A real-estate lending boom, seeking ever more customers, increasingly targeted Americans with poor credit records (so-called 'sub-prime' borrowers). Large volumes of unwise loans were made partly because of a boom-time belief that real-estate prices could not fall, and partly because banks were packaging mortgage loans and selling them on as securities to other banks and investors. Provided the loan was sold on, the original lender was freed of the credit risk; the priority was to create a saleable asset rather than to make a loan subject to criteria of creditworthi-ness. Banks, seeking to maximise profits, had set up 'structured investment vehicles' – part of a so-called 'shadow banking system' – to hold and trade such securities, but did not provide them with adequate capital as insurance against losses. The mood, with stock markets hitting ever-greater highs, was typical of that prevailing before many of the financial disas-ters with which history is peppered.

> **The mood was typical of that prevailing before many of history's financial disasters**

When real-estate prices began to fall in 2006, the entire edifice became vulnerable. Because loans of differing qualities had been packaged together, it became very difficult to put a price on mortgage securities. The vehicles all collapsed and banks were forced to make large provisions against losses on bad loans: by August 2008, write-offs by American and other banks had exceeded $500 billion, of which the banking giant Citigroup accounted for $55.1bn, the investment bank Merrill Lynch $51.8bn and UBS of Switzerland $44.2bn.

This, however, proved to be merely the preamble. A spiral was in progress in which financial institutions increasingly doubted each other's creditwor-thiness. The rates that they charged each other for loans rose, with the effect that a growing number of banks were having difficulty in obtaining day-to-day funding. Assets that they held could not be priced. In addition, markets in derivative products, which typically allow traders to 'hedge' or protect against losses, had grown huge – including an essentially unregulated busi-ness in insurance against debt defaults. Rather than reducing risk, the effect was to create more large exposures to losses, and to transmit risk and insta-bility throughout the world's financial system. Investment banks, which had been at the forefront of innovation in developing new financial instruments and traded heavily in markets, were especially exposed. Following the collapse of the investment bank Bear Stearns in March 2008, tensions built, write-offs mounted and central banks took measures to maintain liquidity in the money markets.

The crisis came to a head in September 2008. In rapid succession, the US government took control of Fannie Mae and Freddie Mac, mortgage institutions that together held or guaranteed $5 trillion of mortgage debt; Merrill Lynch was sold to Bank of America; the investment bank Lehman Brothers filed for bankruptcy on 15 September after the government declined to mount a rescue and no buyer could be found; AIG received an $85bn government rescue loan (subsequently expanded) and was taken into government ownership; Washington Mutual, the sixth-largest US bank, was seized by regulators and sold; and Wachovia, the fourth largest, was rescued. In the United Kingdom, where banks specialising in real-estate lending had also run into problems, HBOS was rescued by a takeover bid from Lloyds. In Germany, Hypo Real Estate was rescued by the government and other banks. Iceland's banking system collapsed and was nationalised. Central banks took further exceptional measures to provide liquidity to banks and to try to ensure that banks' corporate customers were not starved of funds. US Treasury Secretary Henry Paulson announced a $700bn 'Troubled Assets Relief Program' to buy bad assets from banks to improve their balance sheets.

These measures to save the banking system were unprecedented in their scale and speed. But they were insufficient. Confidence in and between banks was not restored. In the United States, there was strong political opposition to Paulson's bailout, which was initially rejected by Congress – and in any case, the Treasury scheme seemed impracticable because of the difficulty of putting a fair price on the troubled assets. Most importantly, the government's decision not to rescue Lehman Brothers – though not much criticised at the time – came to be seen as questionable because trillions of dollars worth of Lehman-related transactions were open in the financial markets and the parties to them were left exposed to losses. Investments traditionally seen as safe were thrown into question. World stock markets went into free fall.

The tide began to turn on 8 October with the British government's announcement of a rescue package which, for the first time, addressed the fundamental underlying problem: that banks did not have enough capital – money put aside to guard against risks. Previously, government measures had treated the crisis as being one of ensuring adequate liquidity – ready funds – to banks. But the failures and rescues that had already occurred indicated that the problem was really one of solvency. Gordon Brown, the British prime minister, announced a £400bn rescue package under which the government would provide up to £50bn of equity capital to banks and £250bn of loan guarantees to help banks lend to each other, and would double to £200bn the amount of short-term loans available from the Bank of England, the central bank. On the same day, central banks throughout the Western world announced coordinated cuts in official interest rates. Within a week, the UK had spelled out which banks would receive equity injections

> **Financial Armageddon had been averted**

– in effect, putting some of them under government control – and Paulson had altered his plan, forcing nine American banks to accept government equity stakes and capital injections totalling $250bn. Other countries took similar steps.

Financial Armageddon had been averted. With many banks in effect on life support, trust began to be restored and conditions in the banking markets became easier. Some of the banks that had received financial support were able to repay it by mid 2009. But banks remained undercapitalised, and still had large amounts of bad debt on their books. These facts continued to overhang the markets, and Paulson's successor, Timothy Geithner, later sought to revive the idea of buying bad loans from banks, this time with private-sector support. He also put banks through 'stress tests' to determine how much additional capital they needed. The size of such needs was indicated by the IMF's April 2009 *Global Financial Stability Report*, which estimated that total write-downs on the US financial sector's loans and securities between 2007 and 2010 would reach $2.7tr, a loss rate of 10% of the sector's total outstanding assets. Of the total, $1.8tr would be write-downs of real-estate debt. In Europe, the total write-down figure over the same period was expected to be $1.2tr, representing a lower 5% loss rate. The IMF estimated that to return to levels of leverage (equity as a proportion of assets) that had been normal in the 1990s, US banks would need to raise $500bn more capital, Eurozone banks $725bn and UK banks $250bn. These demanding targets indicated the scale of the problem still remaining. They meant that bank lending was likely to remain constrained and risk averse for some time to come, and that recovery from recession in the US and Europe could therefore be slow.

The workings of the financial markets may seem remote from high politics and strategic affairs. The two worlds, in recent decades, have rarely intersected. Indeed it had sometimes been remarked that business and finance were sailing ahead regardless of the world's many threats and problems. Yet here was a crisis that veritably brought the two worlds together: leaders of rich countries were faced with the prospect of the widespread and long-term loss of prosperity; global balances of power could be altered; countries which had felt themselves fully committed to free markets found that the role of the state remained vital; and poor countries, many of which had made progress in recent years, faced a severe reverse. Presenting the US intelligence community's annual threat assessment in February 2009, Dennis Blair, director of national intelligence, said: 'the primary near-term security concern of the United States is the global economic crisis and its geopolitical implications'. Emerging countries would suffer a wave of economic problems and would require further support. 'Roughly a quarter of countries in the world have already experienced low-level instability such as government changes because of the current slowdown.' America's allies and friends would be unable 'fully to meet their defence and humanitarian obligations'. While Blair's remarks were open to question – for example about the definition and significance of the instability detected, and the direct linkage to security – they served to underline the importance of the financial crisis.

The immediate challenges posed to leaders in the developed world were highly political. Millions of American families were facing foreclosure on their home loans. Collapsing demand for goods and services brought immediate job losses in many countries, beginning in the financial sector itself. Investors had suffered sharp falls in the value of their portfolios. Fingers were pointed at governments and regulators who had failed to stop banks from taking risks that had turned out to endanger the entire system. Bankers were the object of popular opprobrium, cast as paying themselves huge salaries and bonuses while taking the world to the brink of disaster – and then having to be saved by the taxpayer. To cap it all, many countries faced a period of austerity because government finances would be under far greater strain.

It was, however, to the credit of governments around the world that they utilised the lessons of John Maynard Keynes, the twentieth-century British economist who advocated government intervention to boost demand. He developed his theories while observing the Great Depression of the 1930s, to which government responses to the 1929 Great Crash significantly contributed. In the present case, the primary focus of governments has been to avoid this outcome, and therefore many took substantial measures to boost demand. In February 2009, Obama secured Congressional approval for a $787bn stimulus bill, after China had launched a $585bn stimulus package in November. Many other countries took similar measures. By mid 2009, it seemed that, even though the recession was severe, these actions had prevented an even worse decline and created the conditions for recovery.

If a 1930s-type depression had been avoided, the crisis still left a number of broader questions:

- Was the death knell for capitalism being sounded? It was clear that the previous decade had produced extraordinary excesses. A chief executive of Merrill Lynch, ousted in 2007 after the bank had suffered its first 'sub-prime' write-offs, received a $160 million retirement payment – just one example of pay awards that attracted criticism. As the crisis broke, European leaders were quick to attack what they called 'Anglo-Saxon' capitalism. President Nicolas Sarkozy of France said: 'self-regulation to solve all problems, it's finished. Laissez-faire, it's finished. The all-powerful market that is always right, it's finished.' As governments nationalised companies to rescue them, it was indeed a fact that the state was suddenly playing a bigger role in Western countries. And in the following months, the United States, the European Union and individual European countries began moves to impose tighter regulation on financial services. However, there was no sign yet that the crisis would cause a basic shift away from capitalism and towards state control. While this remained a possibility, tendencies towards yet-bigger government were likely to be countered by the need to cut public spending to rein in budget deficits. Regulation posed dilemmas: was the primary concern to better regulate individual banks, or to guard against 'systemic' risks – exposures that could bring down the system and not just a bank? If a bank was 'too big to fail', it was argued, then it was too big. But setting a limit on size was difficult. These arguments were being thrashed out at mid 2009.
- Will the crisis accelerate America's decline? Some seemed anxious to believe this. Peer Steinbrück, Germany's finance minister, said: 'the world will never be as it was before the crisis. The United

States will lose its superpower status in the world financial system.' But events did not bear out this assertion. In fact, money poured into the United States as its government securities continued to be seen as the safest haven. Swap arrangements made by the Federal Reserve ensured that other countries were able to retain access to dollars and thus to carry out their normal business. America's banking system may have been paralysed and all but bankrupt, but the crash showed the enormous resources that the United States could bring to bear to deal with the situation. Thus, far from ending America's financial dominance, the crisis emphasised it. However, the longer-term effects on America's position remained open to question. Much would depend on America's ability not only to recover but to deal with a yawning fiscal deficit. Failure to reduce the US government's record borrowing requirements could lead to funding difficulties and significant problems in the years to come.

- Will the economic balance of power shift towards China and India? The recent rapid growth of these two countries meant that a long-term shift was already under way. Since both the Chinese and Indian financial systems are still to some extent protected and insulated, they escaped the worst of the stress seen elsewhere. Both countries are forecast to show growth in 2009, though they have certainly been affected by the global downturn. The sharp fall-off in China's exports showed how closely its economic per-formance was tied to that of the United States. Not only is China highly export dependent, but it also holds some \$700bn of US Treasury debt and thus has an important interest in maintaining the value of US investments and the dollar. Chinese Premier Wen Jiabao expressed concern about 'the safety of our assets' but also made clear that China would act to preserve international financial stability. Suggestions came from Beijing for alternatives to the use of the dollar as the predominant reserve currency. But any such ideas would require the development of deep and liquid markets in non-dollar securities to provide alternatives to US markets – and these would take a long time to mature. The Chinese and American economies were therefore likely to be intimately linked for years to come. This would limit China's ability to produce rapid endogenous growth unless it were to take further long-term measures to boost domestic demand and unlock the high savings held by Chinese people.

- What would be the effect on poorer countries? One feature of the global recession was the collapse in the price of oil from over $140 to below $40, although it later stabilised at $60–$70. Food prices also fell from their highs. These changes helped developing countries, for whom fuel and food formed a significant proportion of costs. But the decline in demand and prices also hurt countries dependent on commodity exports. The severe troubles encountered by Russian financial markets as a result of the crisis represented the price for failure to diversify the economy away from oil and gas exports. In addition, developing countries saw a dramatic decline in investment inflows. The developing world thus faced severe challenges as a result of the crisis.

- Will the crisis change the way in which the world is governed? World leaders understood that restoration of global confidence would be a vital element in ensuring economic recovery. The need to show a united front – and one that encompassed more than just the industrialised world – prompted the holding of two summit meetings within the framework of the G20, which had previously been little used. Fundamental differences of view, for example between those who favoured big stimulus packages and those who favoured much tighter regulation of financial markets, inevitably made for anodyne communiqués. However, the G20 offered a new platform for countries such as China, Brazil and India and thus was an advance towards giving newly emerging powers a greater voice in world affairs – a desire for this had already been seen in agitation for reform of the United Nations Security Council and of the shareholding structure of the IMF and the World Bank. However, the G20 format – in fact, there were well over 20 leaders around the table at the April summit in London – was also regarded as too big to be effective. Therefore, it remained to be seen whether the G20 concept would be advanced further or whether it would be adapted. Meanwhile, the crisis had produced both triumphs and failures of cooperation. The actions of central banks showed how international crisis management should be conducted. European governments, however, engaged in unseemly competition to protect themselves: a decision by the

Irish government to guarantee all deposits in its banks was a case in point. Efforts within the framework of the European Union were for the most part ineffectual.

The financial crisis of 2008 was a truly remarkable event, a classic financial accident of global proportions. The world's leaders were tested, and mostly hit upon the correct responses. They could not avert the worst recession since the 1930s, but the outcome could have been a great deal worse. At mid 2009, large risks and challenges remained: it was by no means certain that financial dislocations would not recur, since banks remained fundamentally weak; economic recovery was likely to be slow; and many countries would face financial and economic problems for some time to come.

Realism and risk

At mid 2009, much was uncertain in world affairs. While Obama's 'realist' approach to foreign policy was well understood, and welcome to most after what had gone before, responses were not predictable. Obama, indeed, saw the limits of America's ability to impose its views on others. Economies and government finances were weak in many countries, and the prospects for recovery were shaky. Even apart from the crash of financial markets, events over the past year offered reminders of the potential of the unpredictable: for example, the upsurge of political unrest in Iran, and the global outbreak of the new H1N1 'swine flu' strain of influenza. Most ominously, there was concern that Israel could launch a military strike on Iran's nuclear installations in spite of Washington's refusal to condone such a move – an event that could have very large consequences.

Yet Obama was certainly aware that the effort to restore America's standing would be a long-term one. It would be carried out on a multitude of fronts, among which he would be more successful in some that in others. The dangers of nuclear proliferation, the struggles of the Middle East and the threat of Islamic militancy could not be dealt with by one president of one country. The vivid message of the financial crisis, however, was that America continued to be of vital importance to other countries, including its putative rivals as pre-eminent powers.

Chapter 2

Strategic Policy Issues

Countering Modern Terrorist Threats

Over the past decade terrorism has, through the emergence of al-Qaeda and
related groups, attained a transnational dimension which has elevated it in
some eyes to the status of a global strategic threat. Whether it merits this
status is a subject of continuing debate. But there can be no question that the
response of the United States to the perceived threat from al-Qaeda has exercised a significant impact on the geopolitics of the early twenty-first century.
US President George W. Bush's reactions to the 11 September 2001 attacks on
the United States, and in particular his declaration of a 'global war on terror',
largely defined his presidency. His successor, President Barack Obama, was
left with a substantial foreign-policy legacy to manage, particularly in regard
to relations with the Islamic world.

While arguments about the scale and strategic nature of the threat from
terrorism will continue, a primary task for intelligence agencies and security
forces remains countering the dangers that present themselves around the
world. Terrorist threats continue to centre around the narrative presented by
al-Qaeda and related Islamist extremist groups, which claim that Islam itself
is under threat from Western aggression and that Muslims must respond. The
problem spans the Western world, the Indian subcontinent and Afghanistan,
and a number of countries in Africa and elsewhere. Nor do Islamist groups
represent the only terrorist threats: many conflicts have historically featured
the use of terrorist tactics, and continue to do so.

The means available to and used by security agencies to address terrorist
threats have evolved considerably. For example, there is much greater coop-

eration between the agencies of different countries, and recognition of the need to obtain and share actionable intelligence – though this is never going to be as complete or automatic as some might wish. The development of watch lists has made it harder for terrorists to travel freely, and organisations and individuals involved in financing and supporting terrorist groups have come under increased scrutiny and pressure. Terrorist websites and communications networks are being more systematically monitored. However, strategies for dealing with terrorism have also been problematic, presenting many challenges in the detection, arrest, detention, prosecution, imprisonment and release of terrorist suspects. Eight years after the 11 September attacks, Osama bin Laden and other important al-Qaeda leaders are still free. The United States is the object of widespread opprobrium for its treatment of detainees. The Obama administration is finding that its efforts to forge a new approach – viewed as crucial to reversing a slide in America's international standing – are running into some of the intractable difficulties that had beset its predecessor.

The US response: struggle to set a new agenda

Until 2001 the US response to the emergence of al-Qaeda had been to treat it as a problem to be dealt with through intelligence work and law enforcement. In the wake of 11 September that approach was seen as no longer sustainable and the need to deny al-Qaeda the safe base it had established in Afghanistan became the paramount concern. The 11 September attack produced an upsurge of international sympathy, and the military operation to overthrow the Taliban enjoyed a high level of international consent. But that operation, and a discourse on terrorism couched solely in military terminology, created within the Islamic world a widespread perception that Washington was concerned only with pursuing its interests through the application of hard power. And as it became apparent that in so doing the United States had set aside the values it claimed to represent, much of the initial sympathy felt for it in the immediate aftermath of 11 September ebbed away in the face of actions that appeared overly self-interested and characterised by the application of double standards.

Before 11 September, al-Qaeda had been involved in a number of attacks on United States interests, such as the East African embassy bombings in 1998. But the United States had not initially been the primary focus of the individuals and groups which combined to form the organisation. Al-Qaeda is perhaps better understood as an overarching ideological movement rather than as a terrorist organisation per se, even though it has many of the charac-teristics of the latter. The first priority for its constituent organisations, such as Ayman al-Zawahiri's Egyptian Islamic Jihad, was replacing what they perceived as corrupt and unrepresentative regimes in the Arab Middle East with a form of governance that purported to represent a more 'pure' form of Islam as practised during the time of the Prophet. These organisations had their intellectual origins in the Islamism of the Islamic Brotherhood as developed by Sayyid Qutb, an Egyptian Islamist writer who died in 1966, combining a discourse rooted in a particular interpretation of Islamic theol-ogy with a political organisation that owed much to Leninist principles.

Having signally failed to prosecute their agenda of overthrowing so-called 'apostate regimes' which, though domestically unpopular, were able to deal with their opponents, members of these movements went to Afghanistan during the time of the anti-Soviet jihad and subsequently relo-cated there permanently following the establishment in 1996 of the Taliban regime. The formation of al-Qaeda was an attempt to capture and sustain the momentum of the perceived victory over the Soviet Union which, bin Laden divined, would otherwise be dissipated by the pursuit of narrow parochial agendas; and to turn this momentum into a global movement aimed at creat-ing a revolution throughout the Islamic world. Around the same time, the idea was conceived that al-Qaeda's efforts should focus not on the 'apostate' regimes – the Near Enemy – but rather on the United States – the Far Enemy – whose support for these regimes was critical to their ability to remain in power. Removing US influence from the Islamic world thus became a key al-Qaeda objective, evolving into what has come to be known in the Western world as the single narrative – the proposition that Western oppression is the sole explanation for all the ills afflicting Islam.

The main criticisms of the 'global war on terror' approach are well known: that it led to the United States engaging in a military war on the enemy's terms, implicitly accepting the concept of a war of civilisations and according al-Qaeda members unmerited status as combatants rather than criminals. The implied objective – the elimination of terrorism – was unachievable, and the resources devoted to that objective disproportionate. In the minds of many Muslims, it made Islam appear as the real US target. This perception was substantially reinforced by the 2003 US-led invasion of Iraq, an event which proved to have no justification in terms of dealing with al-Qaeda-related terrorism and which acted as a major catalyst for global jihadism.

While it is easy in retrospect to criticise a US approach couched in the rhetoric of war and emphasising a conventional military response, it is important not to lose sight of the fact that in 2001 al-Qaeda did represent a security challenge to the status quo different from anything previously experienced. It was a global insurgency which linked and inspired many different terrorist groups and which required a coordinated, global, security-focused response. In that regard the United States played the central role, with the Central Intelligence Agency (CIA) taking the lead in knitting together a global coalition of intelligence and security services. With their assistance Washington was able to start mapping out the dimensions of the post-Afghanistan al-Qaeda threat and to begin to create the circumstances in which it could be contained. No other nation could have achieved this. Although over time the United Nations did much to create an institutional framework that provided a context for and legitimisation of international counter-terrorism efforts, the UN could never have coordinated the requisite operational response.

> **It is easy to criticise the US approach in retrospect**

US engagement and pressure – amounting to coercion in the case of some states, such as Pakistan – had the effect of persuading many countries to improve security, intelligence, policing and judicial capabilities which had previously been inadequate to deal with such a complex threat. The US approach made it harder for states to turn a blind eye to the presence in their territory of terrorist groups not seen as constituting a direct threat to their own security. One result was that people who were engaged in facilitation and support of terrorism, particularly among diaspora communities, came under much greater pressure. However, the post-11 September climate also enabled states facing opposition from ethno-separatist movements to include these in the widespread proscription of terrorist organisations. Another less desirable effect was to elevate countries with questionable records on human rights to the status of allies of the West, at least in the realm of intelligence.

US-instigated policies introduced after 11 September thus had both positive and negative effects. In no area were the dilemmas more apparent than in the nexus of issues surrounding procedures for the detention and interrogation of terrorist suspects which began in the immediate aftermath of the 2001 invasion of Afghanistan. The invasion gave rise to large numbers of non-Afghan detainees with whom an almost non-existent Afghan judicial and penal system had no means of dealing. They did not fit conveniently into any legal definition, as they were accused of fighting not for a state but for a globally deployed non-state organisation against which combat operations were deemed to be continuing. Hundreds of detainees, ranging from hard-core al-Qaeda operatives to men guilty of nothing more than being in the wrong place at the wrong time, and selected on no consistent criteria, were taken to a detention centre constructed in the US military base at Guantanamo Bay on Cuba's eastern tip.

This was, arguably, an understandable initial response to a difficult logistical and legal challenge. But having established the detention facility, the US government then failed to achieve a quick and durable legal resolution of what had been an ad hoc response to the pressure of events. Many detainees were eventually returned to their countries of origin, notably to Saudi Arabia which introduced a programme designed to de-radicalise detainees and reintegrate them into society. Some, however, remained in a legal and administrative limbo for up to eight years, with efforts to try some of them in military tribunals stalling in the face of legal complexities.

The need to close Guantanamo Bay came to be accepted in the latter part of the Bush administration, which introduced a process of military tribunals as part of an attempt to bring the episode to a close. One of Obama's earliest acts as president was to declare that the camp would be closed within a year. This decision, however, ran into a series of practical difficulties. First was the need for a legal process to deal with those inmates believed to be dangerous. Considerable opposition was voiced to the idea of moving them to face legal proceedings in the United States. Obama was forced to resuscitate the idea of military tribunals; at the time of writing, however, there was no clear indication how these might function differently from the Bush-era format previously abandoned as unworkable. Secondly, a means had to be found to deal with inmates who were judged eligible for release, but who could not be returned to their countries of origin for fear that their human rights would be abused there. Efforts by the US government to persuade other countries to accept some of these detainees were largely unsuccessful, although Bermuda accepted four Uighurs and the Pacific territory of Palau also agreed to accept a further 13. European countries agreed to take a small number.

The Guantanamo Bay issue encapsulated the difficulty faced in setting a new counter-terrorism agenda for the United States. This agenda adopted by Obama has focused on a reaffirmation of American values and an effort to renew relations with the Islamic world. The former was spelled out by a speech given by Obama at the National Archives in May 2009, which he used to defend his plans for closing Guantanamo. He characterised the response of the previous administration to 11 September as comprising 'hasty decisions ... based upon fear rather than foresight' and spoke of America going off course. He said: 'We are indeed at war with al-Qaeda and its affiliates ... but we must [deal with the threat] with an abiding confidence in the rule of law and due process'. The latter has manifested itself both through a renewed commitment to promoting a two-state solution for Palestine, and a more general public-relations campaign aimed at persuading Muslims worldwide of the benign intentions of the United States. In this context Obama made a major speech in Egypt in June 2009, in which he referred to the years of mistrust which had characterised relations between the United States and Islamic states, called for a new beginning and asserted that the United States was not at war with Islam.

> "Congress denied the funding to close Guantanamo"

However, Obama's more open approach fed into a poisonous political atmosphere in which right-wing Republicans – notably including former Vice President Dick Cheney who, it appeared, had championed 'enhanced' interrogation techniques – portrayed Obama as endangering the United States. The question of Guantanamo Bay's closure became embroiled in a fierce political argument as Republicans sought to present Obama's counter-terrorism policies as rendering the United States more vulnerable to attack and hence eroding purported security achievements of the Bush administration. Under Republican pressure, Congress denied the administration the funding it was seeking to close Guantanamo, pending more specific proposals as to how the closure would be achieved. Republican – and some Democratic – politicians raised a series of objections to the proposition that some detainees not deemed to pose a threat might be permitted to settle in the United States.

A complex situation also arose as a result of Obama's decision to halt the use of 'enhanced' interrogation techniques, which had been used on detainees held at secret detention centres run by the CIA in a number of countries. Some of these techniques, particularly waterboarding, in which detainees are subjected to the sensation of drowning, are generally deemed to constitute torture. Obama decided to close the detention facilities. He banned waterboarding and some other interrogation techniques and released a series of memoranda from Bush administration officials setting out the arguments justifying such techniques and listing in minute detail what interrogators were permitted to do. Obama sought to give an assurance that CIA officers who had employed the now-banned techniques would not be subject to sanction provided they had confined themselves to implementing the instructions as set out. But the basis for his assurance was unclear as it went against the principle established in the Nuremberg trials after the Second World War that the fact an accused was following orders is no defence in cases involving human-rights violations. That question, along with the associated issue of whether the Bush-era lawyers who produced the legal arguments legitimating such measures should be subject to sanction, is unlikely to be quickly or easily resolved. It remains to be seen whether Washington's politicians will be able to resist the temptation to scapegoat the CIA, as happened in the 1990s, with serious consequences for the agency's operational effectiveness, over collaboration with regimes committing human-rights abuses in Central America. However, as questions were asked in Washington about who knew what and when, it became apparent that members of Congress were briefed in some detail about the techniques at the time it was decided to implement them.

Recent allegations suggest that much of the waterboarding was carried out in response to pressure from members of the Bush cabinet to establish evidence of connections, which in fact had never existed, between al-Qaeda and Saddam Hussein, the Iraqi leader toppled in the 2003 invasion. According to the Justice Department documents, Khalid Sheikh Mohammed, who was described in the official 9/11 Commission report as the principal architect of the 2001 attacks, was waterboarded 183 times in March 2003, immediately after being arrested in Pakistan and taken into US custody. Abu Zubaydah, another Guantanamo detainee whose role was probably as a facilitator who had important information about senior al-Qaeda figures, was waterboarded 83 times in August 2002.

Among the arguments made against their treatment is that it apparently did not result in the disruption of specific terrorist attacks. While this may be so, information derived at least in part from interrogations of detainees did enable the CIA to map out the nature and scale of al-Qaeda, about which, even by the time of the 2001 attacks, relatively little was known. Counter-terrorism work by intelligence agencies primarily involves patient analysis and weaving together of information to establish links between seemingly unconnected individuals and groups with the aim of building a full picture of a terrorist organisation and its capabilities. From the knowledge the CIA gained from interrogations, it was believed to have been able to develop a range of operational leads. Investigation of these led over time to reduced reliance on information derived from interrogations. However, it is impossible to know to what extent – if at all – the ability to gain information was augmented by torture.

These issues epitomise the tensions involved in balancing strategic and tactical considerations in counter-terrorism campaigns. Policies used with the intent of enhancing national security in the short term may risk causing damaging longer-term consequences – and may in fact be counterproductive. Revelation of what appeared to be institutionalised prisoner abuse in US detention centres in Afghanistan and Iraq, taken together with the detention and interrogation practices described above, undoubtedly caused damage to the international standing of the United States, as well as creating strains in relations with allies. Radical Islamist organisations such as al-Qaeda used revelations of prisoner abuse to mobilise popular sentiment against the United States within the Islamic world.

Obama came to office with no terrorist attacks having taken place on the US mainland since 11 September, with the threat posed by al-Qaeda much better defined, and amidst a tide of opinion that the Bush administration's actions had been counterproductive. It was therefore understandable that he should have decided to try and turn the page. But doing so has proven more difficult than expected. Moreover, it appeared that Obama did not intend to ban some other contentious practices of his predecessor, including 'extraordinary renditions' in which detainees are transferred by the United States from one third-country jurisdiction to another.

The military component: Iraq and Afghanistan

While the US campaign against al-Qaeda is no longer being called a war, it remains a global campaign with a significant military element. Operations in Afghanistan were conducted as part of efforts to combat terrorism because al-Qaeda had based itself there and allied itself with the radical Taliban regime. The risk that terrorist groups could again base themselves in an insecure Afghanistan is still used to justify military deployments there. While the invasion of Iraq could not be justified on grounds of counter-terrorism, it did provoke an upsurge of terrorist activity in Iraq, and attracted the involvement of al-Qaeda – thus justifying the retention of military operations there.

142,000 American troops were deployed in Iraq at mid 2009, and 28,000 in Afghanistan alongside 30,000 non-US NATO forces. However, disengagement from Iraq and, in due course, Afghanistan forms a critical part of the Obama administration's counter-terrorism strategy.

Progress against the organisation generally referred to as al-Qaeda in Mesopotamia (AQM) has been one of the more encouraging features of the US campaign against al-Qaeda. Founded in 2003 by the Jordanian jihadist and former petty criminal Abu Musab al-Zarqawi, AQM had the objectives of expelling the US invaders from the country and creating the beginnings of a global caliphate in Iraq. It engaged in a campaign of widespread suicide bombings and targeted assassinations against, among others, foreign diplomatic envoys and aid workers. It also waged a relentless assault on the Iraqi Shia population to a degree which led al-Qaeda leader Ayman al-Zawahiri to remonstrate – unsuccessfully – with al-Zarqawi on the grounds that this activity was damaging al-Qaeda's image in the wider Islamic world. AQM's brutality and extremism eventually alienated Sunni tribes who had originally seen it as an ally in their insurgency against the United States and the now-dominant Shi'ites. The resultant Anbar Awakening, in which the Sunni tribes rose up and expelled AQM from their midst, coincided with a surge operation led by US General David Petraeus which emphasised the importance of good counter-insurgency practices involving US troops being based among the populations they were there to protect. The Sunni tribes found themselves working in close concert with US forces, and the combination of US firepower and the intelligence provided by the Sunni led to a rapid decline in AQM's fortunes. What was left of the organisation is now largely confined to an enclave in Mosul where it continues to pose a lethal, though much diminished, threat which may now be within the power of the Iraqi security forces to contain. Under an agreement reached by the Bush administration, US forces are due to leave Iraq by the end of 2011 – though it remains to be seen whether the security situation will permit the drawdown to proceed as planned (see Iraq, pp. 244–54).

In Afghanistan, by contrast, a troop 'surge' has been under way in 2009 with the United States sending 21,000 more troops and urging other countries to increase their commitments (though with little success). The aim is simultaneously to improve the level of security and to step up training of Afghanistan's military and police so that they are better able in future to maintain it – thus preparing the way for foreign forces to exit. To facilitate this, the previous American refusal to countenance a political settlement involving the Taliban may be giving way to a more pragmatic approach – though opinion within the US administration still appears divided between those thinking in terms of a political negotiation and those who, like Petraeus, think more in terms of splitting off individuals and groups within the Taliban who are prepared to reach an accommodation with the Afghan government whilst appearing to rule out a wider political negotiation (see Afghanistan, pp. 303–14).

A renewed focus in Washington on the Afghanistan conflict was demonstrated by the almost simultaneous appointments of Petraeus, the former commander in Iraq, to head Central Command, the US regional command covering the Middle East and Gulf region; General Karl Eikenberry, former US commander in Afghanistan, as US ambassador to Kabul; and veteran diplomat Richard Holbrooke as presidential envoy for Afghanistan and Pakistan. Because of the attention given to Iraq, Afghanistan had become the forgotten war, under-resourced and given insufficient top-level focus. As the Bush administration drew to a close and its successor began to formulate policy, there was a recognition of the need to adopt an integrated regional approach which would bring together the military and civilian components of the campaign and would give equal attention to Pakistan – given that the insurgent problems in the two countries were related and that militants flowed freely between them.

> Nation-building had not been on the US military agenda

Over the course of its engagement in Iraq and Afghanistan, the US military's approach to counter-insurgency has undergone a significant transformation. Prior to 11 September the focus had been on implementing a 'transformation' which envisaged US forces fighting technologically sophisticated enemies using relatively small numbers of technically enabled forces. Nation-building, as then Defence Secretary Donald Rumsfeld made clear, was not on the US military agenda. Very few US troops were committed to the fight to overthrow the Taliban in 2001, and the reluctance of US commanders to deploy forces to block the exit of al-Qaeda fighters as they fled to Pakistan meant that the latter lived to fight another day. In 2003 the invasion of Iraq was undertaken with much lower troop levels than had conventionally been seen as necessary for such a task. Once in occupation, US forces were located in heavily fortified bases from which they conducted patrols and raids characterised by immediate 'kinetic' responses to apparent threats. But a military which initially had had no interest in classic counter-insurgency warfare demonstrated over time an ability to learn from its experiences and to evolve techniques more appropriate to actual operational conditions. This was epitomised in the 2007 Iraqi surge operation led by Petraeus, which required US forces to live and fight with their Iraqi colleagues among the populations they were there to protect and to focus on the 'hold' and 'build' strands of a classic counter-insurgency campaign. The appointment of General Stanley McChrystal as US commander in Afghanistan suggests that there too there will be a shift in methodology away from an overly kinetic approach which has led to significant civilian casualties and which has had the effect of alienating local populations, towards an approach more centred on protecting populations, focusing on the human-security dimension and creating space within which economic reconstruction and development can take place.

The Indian subcontinent: the new front line

Following its expulsion from Afghanistan in 2001, the al-Qaeda leadership re-established itself in the Federally Administered Tribal Areas (FATA) of Pakistan, initially in South Waziristan and more recently in the northernmost district of Bajaur. This process was facilitated by the relationships which had been established in the region by some of the 'Afghan Arabs' – the term used to describe fighters from Arab states who had gone to Afghanistan to take part in the anti-Soviet jihad – and which included marriages and business partnerships with the local Pashtun tribes. Initially focused on survival, the leadership of the movement was sufficiently restored to recommence attack planning against Western targets and to build up a substantial operation producing and distributing propaganda videos to television networks and the Internet. At mid 2009, the consensus of opinion within Western intelligence circles was that Osama bin Laden himself was alive – as evidenced by his periodic media broadcasts – and was located somewhere in the tribal areas living under tight security. It was thought that he had little day-to-day control over al-Qaeda's operational activities. The same may be to some degree true of his deputy al-Zawahiri, who has been visible mainly through writings and pronouncements that have sought to link the al-Qaeda agenda to developments in the wider Islamic world. Below al-Zawahiri, al-Qaeda has a hierarchy of leaders predominantly from Egypt and Libya which has managed to sustain and renew itself despite losses caused mainly by CIA missile strikes in Pakistan from unmanned aerial vehicles.

Overall 'core' al-Qaeda numbers are thought to be no more than three or four hundred. As such they do not constitute a guerrilla or terrorist force in their own right but provide ideological guidance, resources, training and tactical advice to groups such as the Afghan Taliban and other extremist groups such as the Tehrik-e-Taliban, a Pashtun tribal organisation based in Pakistan's tribal areas and modelled on the Afghan Taliban. Co-located with al-Qaeda in the FATA are a number of other foreign Muslim extremist groups which share broadly similar agendas. These include the Waziristan-based Islamic Movement of Uzbekistan (IMU), an organisation which though nominally affiliated to al-Qaeda has in practice not subscribed to the latter's global agenda and remains focused on the overthrow of the Karimov government and the establishment of an Islamic state in Uzbekistan; the Islamic Jihad Union, another Uzbek group which is more closely aligned with al-Qaeda and which has sought to exploit links with Turkish diaspora communities in western Europe through propaganda and terrorist training; Uighurs from China's Xinjiang province; and Chechens.

Al-Qaeda has also sought to develop tactical alliances with indigenous Pakistani extremist groups. A case in point is Lashkar-e-Tayiba (LeT), a Kashmiri group which in the past has been used by the Pakistani Inter-Services Intelligence agency (ISI) to apply pressure on India through militants' activities in Indian-held Kashmir. Following an India–Pakistan military confrontation in 2002 which aroused international concern because of the risk of nuclear escalation, Pakistan came under strong pressure from abroad and LeT was sidelined. Many of its militants moved to the tribal areas, where its training camps were used to train foreign jihadists including some from western Europe, some of whom went on to carry out terrorist attacks in their own countries. Over time, LeT has expanded its agenda towards a more global interpretation of jihad explicitly linked to the al-Qaeda agenda. This was shown by its attack on the Indian city of Mumbai in November, in which at least 166 people were killed when a 10-man group travelled by sea from Pakistan and attacked targets including the main railway station, the two main hotels used by Westerners, and a Jewish centre. A focus on India appears to constitute a new dimension in al-Qaeda's campaign as it seeks to exploit whatever developments appear most propitious to its cause. India has suffered sustained violence from Kashmiri groups supported and trained by the ISI since the late 1980s. But as a non-Islamic state which has developed a closer relationship with the United States, it appears to have become an al-Qaeda target in its own right, with evidence of efforts to promote militancy within India's substantial Muslim minority population.

However, it is clear that Pakistan has become the key battleground in al-Qaeda's efforts to establish a base area to replace the one lost in Afghanistan. The decision by then President Pervez Musharraf in 2001 to ally himself to the US 'global war on terror' was a major factor in ensuring some of the CIA's early operational successes, including the capture of al-Qaeda leaders such as Khalid Sheikh Mohammed and Ramzi bin al-Shibh. This in turn led al-Qaeda to engage with Pakistani extremists to undertake multiple assassination attempts against Musharraf, some of which involved members of Pakistan's armed forces.

While there is undisguised hostility between the Pakistani government and al-Qaeda, Pakistan's attitude to the Afghan Taliban is more ambivalent. This reflects a long-standing Pakistani conviction that a Pashtun-dominated government in Kabul represents Pakistan's best option for managing relations with Afghanistan. It also reflects doubts about the willingness of the United States and its NATO allies to stay the course there. Consequently, the Afghan Taliban

> " Pakistan's attitude to the Afghan Taliban is ambivalent "

leadership have remained largely undisturbed in their headquarters in Quetta, capital of the Pakistani province of Baluchistan. Taliban fighters have been able to move freely across the Afghan–Pakistan border, to the increasing frustration of NATO commanders. There have even been suggestions that Pakistani intelligence may have been used to alert Taliban commanders to operations planned against them.

For the global campaign against terrorist groups, the most serious development of recent years has been the 'Talibanisation' of Pakistan's tribal areas as the authority of traditional leaders has been eroded. The Pakistani government has never had direct control of these mountainous areas, which have been governed by tribal leaders applying Pashtun norms. These leaders have gradually been replaced as authority figures in many parts of the tribal areas by extremists such as Baitullah Mehsud, the leader of the Tehrik-e-Taliban Pakistan (TTP). This group, which came into existence in late 2007, has aligned itself with al-Qaeda's global agenda. It is hard to say with confidence what the TTP's main objective is. Membership of this umbrella movement is far from fixed or stable. Originally and probably still predominantly concerned with local tribal issues, it has under Mehsud's leadership expanded its declared objectives to include support for the struggle of the Afghan Taliban, endorsement of the al-Qaeda objective of establishing a global caliphate, demands for the establishment of sharia law in Pakistan, and now apparently the overthrow of the Pakistani state. It has been responsible for training large numbers of young Pashtun men to serve as suicide bombers in Afghanistan and Pakistan and also appears to have been responsible for sending some operatives to Spain to conduct an ultimately unsuccessful terrorist attack. The growing influence of the TTP in the tribal areas has to be seen partly as the result of local issues such as the control of smuggling routes. But the effect has been to create an atmosphere of increasing lawlessness and a challenge to the authority of the Pakistani state.

This challenge has been steadily growing for some time. The 2007 occupation of the Red Mosque in Islamabad was an early and high-profile harbinger of a rising tide of jihadist activity. The TTP claimed responsibility for the 2007 assassination of Benazir Bhutto. Its campaign since then encompassed further high-profile attacks, including those on the Marriott Hotel in Islamabad in 2008, on the Sri Lankan cricket team in Lahore in 2009, and later on the Pearl Continental Hotel in Peshawar. There have been numerous attacks on Pakistani security-force installations and other public places, including mosques. There is concern about the degree to which extremist groups in the Punjab, an area previously little affected by terrorism, have become more active, including recruiting among a substantial underclass of landless peasants with many grievances to be exploited.

Under pressure from Washington to deal with an increasingly worrying situation, the Pakistani military began in 2004 to undertake operations against militant groups in the FATA, a region which had never experienced a permanent Pakistani military presence. These military incursions proved uniformly unsuccessful and led to a series of negotiated settlements whereby the tribes undertook not to let their territory be used as a base from which to attack other states, and to expel 'foreign fighters'. None of these agreements produced the desired effect, and they served only to reinforce the influence of militant groups. Within Pakistan, efforts to subdue the tribal areas by force were unpopular as they were widely seen as Pakistan being compelled to fight America's war. But as long as military action was confined to the FATA, there was a sense that the violence was remote and could be contained. What altered this perception was the takeover of Swat, one of the 'settled areas' of the North-West Frontier Province (NWFP), by Pakistani Taliban groups led by Maulana Fazlullah, nicknamed 'Mullah Radio' because of his local radio broadcasts in which he demanded the imposition of sharia law. Following tentative and inconclusive military operations against these Taliban groups, an agreement was reached in early 2009 permitting the introduction of sharia – which quickly turned into the enforcement, by brutal means, of a Taliban ideology under which women's rights were severely curtailed, all forms of entertainment prohibited, harsh penalties applied and pro-Pakistani officials murdered.

When in April 2009 the TTP, in violation of the Swat agreement, moved into the NWFP district of Buner where they attempted to impose a similar regime, the Pakistani army responded with massive force, seeking to regain control of both Buner and Swat. While this was done partly as a result of pressure from Washington, it also reflected recognition by the military of an existential threat to the state – evidenced by withdrawal of units from the border with India to take part in the operation. And although the operation led to the displacement of as many as 2.5 million people, as well as extensive destruction of property, the army's actions appeared to enjoy a high level of civilian consent, indicating widespread opposition to the brutal TTP regime. The TTP responded with a bombing campaign in major cities and seemed likely to regroup in spite of suffering significant casualties.

It remains unclear whether the Swat campaign will prove to have been a turning point in terms of the Pakistani government's approach to extremism. This is seen as crucial in Washington following the adoption by Obama of a strategy embracing Afghanistan and Pakistan together, and the belief that the problems of Afghanistan cannot be solved without addressing threats based in Pakistan. The Swat campaign was reminiscent of events in the urban areas of Pakistan in 2002–04, when a campaign of terrorism by indigenous extremist groups linked to al-Qaeda also seemed to threaten the survival of the state. This campaign was characterised by numerous bombings in the main urban centres and the assassination of Pakistani officials. However, it did not result in a fundamental reappraisal of the state's policy of embracing extremist groups to gain what it saw as strategic advantages – as it had in assisting the Afghan Taliban and in sponsoring the LeT and other Kashmiri groups. It remains to be seen whether the events in Swat will occasion a more radical re-think of Islamabad's – and in particular the army's – differentiated attitude towards extremist groups.

Pakistani army leaders may believe that events in Afghanistan favour its continued attachment to the Afghan Taliban as US ambitions are scaled back and the odds shorten on an eventual political settlement involving the

Taliban. There is also no sign that Pakistan will comprehensively close down Kashmiri groups such as LeT as long as India's position on Kashmir remains unchanged. It now appears that, as a result of pressure arising out of the 2008 Mumbai attack, ISI's S Division, the entity responsible for dealings with jihadi groups, is not currently funding LeT. But that, paradoxically, means that it is now less able to exercise control over the organisation. If Pakistan's default position remains unchanged, it seems likely that it will continue to be plagued by high levels of extremist violence and that this will create persistent difficulties for counter-insurgency operations in Afghanistan. Western countries will also continue to be affected by terrorism with connections to Pakistan. However, the intensity of Pakistani army operations against the TTP and the popular support these enjoyed suggest that the doomsday scenario of Pakistan becoming a failed state whose nuclear arsenal falls into the hands of extremists is unlikely to become a reality in the foreseeable future.

Al-Qaeda in other regions

There are three other areas where al-Qaeda shows some potential to pose a strategic threat. The first is Somalia, a failed state whose UN-recognised transitional administration controls virtually no territory and exercises no effective functions. Following the withdrawal in early 2009 of an Ethiopian military occupation force, parts of the country have come under the control of al-Shabaab (The Youth), an extremist organisation with some affinity with al-Qaeda which has inter alia been responsible for suicide bombings. There are allegations, denied by the Eritrean government, that armaments are being supplied to Somali jihadist groups by Eritrea, which is embroiled in an unresolved border dispute with Ethiopia. A key concern is the presence in Somalia of foreign fighters, predominantly from Somalian expatriate communities in the United States and western Europe, who have acquired a reputation as some of the most effective and disciplined forces operating there. The fear is that, if Somalia falls under the control of al-Shabaab, it will turn into a regional centre for the export of terrorism. A related concern is the risk of 'blowback' in the event that fighters return to their points of origin imbued with jihadist ideology, combat skills and the cachet that comes with being a veteran jihadi (see Somalia, pp. 275–81).

A related concern is Yemen, a state long characterised by weak governance, poor economic performance and high levels of indigenous violence. There is evidence that following its defeat in Saudi Arabia at the hands of the Interior Ministry, al-Qaeda in the Arabian Peninsula (AQAP) has made

Yemen its main base of operations, mounting attacks there at regular intervals, including some on foreigners. Efforts by the Yemeni government to emulate the Saudi Arabian programme for rehabilitating jihadists are regarded as unsuccessful, resulting in high levels of recidivism. For example, a Yemeni returnee from Guantanamo Bay, Abdullah Ghulam Rasoul, who passed through the Yemeni programme, later assumed command responsibility within AQAP. Given the geographical proximity and close unofficial trading links between Yemen and Somalia, there is concern about links between insurgent groups. A further concern is that some al-Qaeda foot soldiers appear to have migrated from Pakistan to Yemen and Somalia. The numbers involved are, however, still small and it appears unlikely that the bulk of the al-Qaeda leadership will attempt to relocate to either place.

The third area of concern is Algeria, where al-Qaeda in the Islamic Maghreb (AQIM) has undertaken a number of attacks. AQIM began as a resistance movement within Algeria but later forged links with al-Qaeda. An example of its activity was the reported murder in 2009 of a British hostage. AQIM had used him in an attempt to negotiate the release of Abu Qatada, a Jordanian extremist cleric who has been described as al-Qaeda's chief representative in Europe and who has been imprisoned in the United Kingdom pending extradition to Jordan.

Possible futures for al-Qaeda

Since al-Qaeda's attack on the United States and the subsequent US-led invasion of Afghanistan, there has been much debate amongst Western intelligence officers and analysts about al-Qaeda's likely future direction and the degree to which the organisation might be seeking to implement a coherent long-term strategy. In his 2006 book *Al Zarqawi: The Second Generation of al Qaeda*, the Jordanian journalist Fouad Hussein, drawing on interviews with al-Zarqawi, the Jordanian leader of al-Qaeda in Mesopotamia who was killed by US forces in 2006, and Saif al-Adel, a senior al-Qaeda operative and ideologue born in Egypt, posited an improbably precise six-phase al-Qaeda strategy leading to eventual victory within 20 years. Other jihadist thinkers whose ideas have emerged over the past four or five years have been much less categoric and arguably more realistic in their assessment of what might be possible.

For a period following al-Qaeda's expulsion from Afghanistan it began to look as though the movement's future would be characterised by the activities of small disaggregated groups operating locally on their own initiative – the 'system, not organisation' (*nizam, la tanzim*) referred to by jihadist thinker

Mustafa Setmariam Nasar, a Syrian-born al-Qaeda member writing under the name Abu Musab al-Suri in his 2006 Internet publication *A Global Islamic Call to Resistance*. This approach was further developed by al-Qaeda theoretician Sheikh Abu Bakr al-Naji, author of an earlier treatise entitled *The Management of Savagery*, in his most recent publication *Governance of the Wilderness*. In this work al-Naji, whose identity remains a mystery, argues that al-Qaeda should forsake the idea of capturing actual territory and attempt instead to create areas of virtual wilderness through multiple random low-level acts of terrorism rather than concentrating on the large-scale but infrequent mass-casualty attacks which have been al-Qaeda's hallmark to date. Under this approach, the aim should be to create parallel administrations: no-go areas which challenge the authority of states and in due course undermine them, creating a vacuum which al-Qaeda can then fill. The high levels of violence which would necessarily accompany this approach, and the alienation of populations, are seen as an inevitable price to pay.

However, al-Qaeda's own leadership has shown continued attachment to occupying actual territory, as it did in Afghanistan. This is evidenced by al-Qaeda in Mesopotamia's efforts to create base areas designed to serve as building blocks for an eventual caliphate, and by its current preoccupation with overthrowing the government of Pakistan. Al-Qaeda has also kept up efforts to orchestrate attacks on Western states from its base areas on the Afghan–Pakistan border, though at mid 2009 there had not been a successful attack for four years. In spite of this, Western security agencies were continuing to monitor many Islamic extremist groups that were planning attacks, some of which continue to be directed out of Pakistan.

Fragile progress

Since 11 September 2001 the world has become significantly more aware of the threat from terrorism and there has been a concomitant increase in political will to confront it. This has led to a significant increase in counter-terrorism capabilities and intelligence cooperation which has to some degree eroded, though very far from eliminated, the asymmetric advantages enjoyed by terrorist groups. But the progress that has been achieved is fragile, and could be undone by another spectacular attack such as 11 September. Even if the United States manages to re-engineer its image in the Islamic world, failure by Islamic states to offer their populations economic opportunities and social justice will make it easy for organisations such as al-Qaeda to exploit local grievances and seek to co-opt them to a wider, globalist agenda. Meanwhile there is a risk that the campaign against terrorism may weaken. Populations in Western states may weary of the continuing demands of overseas military campaigns which are likely to remain an essential ingredient in dealing with a globalised threat. Some of the measures that form part of counter-terrorist policies will continue to arouse concern about erosion of essential liberties. Balancing the provision of effective security with legitimate political and social aspirations is unlikely to become less difficult.

Europe's Energy Security

European countries are generally well placed in terms of energy security, defined as adequate supply at affordable prices. But they face several energy-related challenges, most notably with regard to Russia's position as their largest supplier of gas. European leaders are belatedly adopting a more collective approach, and are moving to develop policies designed to achieve lower demand and longer-term security of supply. However, they face the prospect of continued reliance on Russia – and a potentially awkward relationship – for the foreseeable future.

Europe's overall energy-supply position is not uncomfortable. European countries have a wide range of supply sources. They are mostly rich enough to afford the sharp price peaks that occur in the oil market and that pull gas prices up with them. They are technically competent to run reliable grid and pipeline systems. Their energy use is diverse in type and mix, ranging from France, which generates 80% of its electricity with nuclear plants, to Poland, which generates 95% of its power by burning coal. And 27 European countries have, in the European Union (EU), a loose federal form of governance that ought to be capable of turning this individual diversity into a source of collective security against problems affecting any one type of energy in any one country.

It is true that the EU is an increasingly heavy importer of hydrocarbons. All EU states but Denmark are net importers of oil, and all but Denmark and the Netherlands are net importers of gas. Before introducing new energy and climate-change policies in 2008, the EU projected its energy-import dependence (including coal) would increase from around 50% to 65% by 2030, with imports of gas rising from 57% of its needs to 84% and imports of oil rising from 82% to 93%.

However, Europe is fortunate that a combination of geography and geology give it relatively easy access to fossil-fuel imports. It has in Norway a reliable long-term source of oil and gas. Norway does not belong to the EU, but as a part of the European Economic Area, it has to obey the open trade and investment provisions of EU energy policy. (The United States would appear to be more secure than Europe because it has two oil-exporting neighbours, Canada and Mexico, that are fellow members of the North American Free Trade Agreement (NAFTA). But NAFTA does not cover energy, allowing Mexico to maintain a total ban on outside investment in its oil sector.)

Like every net oil-consuming region, Europe can draw on the worldwide oil market. No comparable world market for gas exists, but Europe has a ring of regional suppliers within the 3,000–4,000km upper limit at which pipelines can be operated economically. They include Norway, Russia, Azerbaijan, Algeria and Libya. Some 90% of Europe's gas imports are piped in. But coastal suppliers further away, such as Qatar or Nigeria, are able to ship liquefied natural gas (LNG) to Europe.

The Russian gas problem

In spite of being nearly as well positioned for energy supplies as the United States and far better placed than Asia, Europe nevertheless has an energy-security problem that springs largely from its heavy use of Russian gas. Holding a quarter of world gas reserves (a higher ratio than Saudi Arabia's 21% share of world oil reserves), Russia currently supplies 42% of EU gas imports, with 24% coming from Norway, 18% from Algeria and 16% from elsewhere. It is likely to be Europe's mainstay for the foreseeable future.

The commercial relationship is one of mutual dependence. Europe will be Moscow's sole source of gas-export earnings until Russia builds up gas exports to Asia and starts exporting LNG from the Arctic to the United States. This is a relationship fixed in geography (with expensive pipelines) and in time (through long-term contracts which many European companies have with Russia's Gazprom monopoly, running until 2035). But several factors give it a mutual awkwardness:

- *Russia's resource nationalism and its Gazprom monopoly.* Energy nationalism and monopolies are commonplace around the world. But in Gazprom Europe faces the world's biggest integrated monopoly, which controls not only the outlet for all Russia's production but Central Asia's output as well. Europe has tried, but failed, to get Gazprom to agree to a legal framework for freer gas transit and to loosen its control on gas going through its pipes. While in recent years European companies such as Shell and BP have had to cede ground to Gazprom in their upstream operations in Russia, Gazprom has been able to continue to invest in the European downstream, creating or investing in gas-marketing, -trading and -storage companies in addition to the minority stakes it holds in a number of transmission pipelines inside the EU (mainly in Germany and the Baltic states).

- *Mutual distrust between Russia and new EU members.* With their history of forced membership of Soviet alliances, institutions and (in the case of the Baltic states) of the Soviet Union itself, the new EU members bring an anti-Russian animus to discussions in Brussels about how to improve EU–Russian relations. For example, in return for agreeing in 2008 to give the European Commission a mandate to open negotiations for a new EU–Russia partnership accord, Lithuania insisted that Commission negotiators raise the issue of compensation for Soviet deportations from the Baltic states.

- *Repeated disruption of Russian gas transit across Ukraine.* Russia and Ukraine remain bound together by Soviet-era pipelines (which carry 80% of Russian gas exports to Europe) long after political and other economic ties between them have weakened. Moscow and Kiev have been unable to put their energy relationship on a stable commercial basis.

Two disputes between Russia and Ukraine have resulted in temporary interruptions of supplies of Russian gas to European customers. In January 2006 Gazprom and Ukraine were in dispute over gas prices and the terms on which Russia would ship Turkmen gas to Ukraine. Russia cut off its supply of gas for Ukrainian use for three days, Ukraine diverted to its own use some Russian gas destined for European customers, and supplies to some central European states fell briefly as a result.

In January 2009 a similar dispute with more serious consequences developed, when Moscow and Kiev failed to agree on the price Ukraine would pay for Russian gas and the tariff that Russia would pay for the transit of its gas to Europe. Russia again stopped exports to Ukraine. After a week, all Russian gas shipments to and through Ukraine were halted for a further two weeks. The total cut-off caused some short-term suffering in central Europe and the Balkans and long-term damage to Russia's reputation as a supplier and Ukraine's reputation for transit, and prompted remedial action from the EU.

To these disputes directly about energy should be added the August 2008 war between Russia and Georgia over South Ossetia. While this was not an argument about energy, it had implications for the use of Georgia as a transit state for non-Russian energy from the Caspian region to Europe. Georgia is the middle link in the Baku–Tbilisi–Ceyhan (BTC) oil pipeline and the Baku–Tbilisi–Erzerum (BTE) gas pipelines from Azerbaijan to Turkey. These had been seen as alternative conduits to transit through Russia. But the conflict, and the prospect of Russian tanks and jets remaining nearby, diminished their attractiveness. In March 2009 Azerbaijan signed an agreement with Gazprom for the transport of Azeri gas to Russia in a pipeline that until recently had carried Russian gas to Azerbaijan.

Differing degrees of concern

Anxieties about European dependence on Russia for energy, and especially gas, date back almost to the first arrival of Soviet gas in western Europe in the early 1970s. For a long time it was not a great worry for European governments, who by the early 1980s had grown so confident of the supply reliability of the Soviet Union (which had no transit problems with Soviet Ukraine or Soviet Belarus) that they were willing to defy the Reagan administration's attempt to curtail European dependence on Soviet gas. In 1982 Washington sought to prevent European companies selling the Soviet Union gas turbines and compressor equipment for a new European–Siberian gas pipeline by forbidding the re-export of any US-origin technology in the European equipment to the Soviet Union. European governments, led by British Prime Minister Margaret Thatcher, ordered their companies to ignore the US restrictions. This defiance did not, however, stop Washington continuing over the years to express worry about Europe's reliance on Russian gas.

The break-up of the Soviet Union gave the United States a chance to turn this concern into a partial solution, as Washington encouraged the transit of oil and gas from newly independent Azerbaijan across newly independent Georgia. The aim was to challenge Russia's supply monopoly in the region. It promoted the BTC oil pipeline and the BTE gas pipeline bringing Azeri gas to Turkey – and latterly the proposed Nabucco pipeline from Azerbaijan to central Europe. The United States did so not because of the direct economic benefit it could obtain, but rather because of a general concern about Russia using its dominance as an energy supplier to obtain political leverage over America's allies in Europe.

Washington's concern has at times irritated the larger western European countries, which have tended to promote special ties on energy with Moscow. A particular example was the personal cultivation of the Russian–German energy relationship by Gerhard Schröder. Having approved, as German chancellor, an export-credit loan to the Russian–German Nord Stream pipeline project, Schröder became chairman of the joint venture shortly after he left office. But the US approach has been appreciated by the new EU member states from Central and Eastern Europe. Poland in 2006 sought to link energy directly to European security when it requested an 'energy solidarity' commitment from the NATO Alliance. It knew it would get a sympathetic hearing from the United States and from NATO's then Secretary-General Jaap de Hoop Scheffer, who had repeatedly and publicly urged the Alliance to see what it could do to bolster energy security.

NATO stated in a formal declaration at its 2006 summit in Riga, Latviam that energy security was one of its concerns, and at its 2008 summit in Bucharest, Romania, the Alliance provided some precision on how it might help on this issue. However, the idea of anything akin to an Article V commitment for member states to come to the aid of any ally whose energy security was threatened gained little ground. It faced particular opposition from France, which saw any NATO involvement as detracting from the role of the EU, and from Germany, which was nervous about a hostile Russian reaction.

Poland was more successful in 2007 when, with the support of Lithuania, it raised the energy-solidarity idea in EU negotiations on what was to become the Treaty of Lisbon. The treaty, which at mid 2009 was awaiting full ratification to enter into force, included for the first time a specific article on energy that spoke of 'a spirit of solidarity'. It contained language giving the EU the new duty to 'ensure security of energy supply in the Union'. However, there was also an important caveat that the new treaty 'shall not affect a member state's right to determine the conditions for exploiting its energy resources, its choice between different energy sources and the general structure of its energy supply'.

Europe's evolving energy policies

Despite the new treaty language, no collective action on energy security might have been taken had it not been for the August 2008 conflict in Georgia and the January 2009 gas cut-off in Ukraine. The Georgian conflict led to a special EU summit on 1 September at which EU leaders asked the European Commission to come up with new initiatives on 'diversification of energy sources and supply routes'. The clear implication that the diversification was to be away from Russia was reinforced by the summit decision to suspend talks on a new EU–Russia agreement. These talks were aimed at replacing the 1997 EU–Russia Partnership and Cooperation Agreement with a wider political and economic accord that would include more substantial energy provisions. Since Brussels has intrinsically more to gain than Moscow from a new energy agreement, it was not surprising that in autumn 2008 the EU decided to resume the talks with Russia. However, the Georgian conflict had forced EU leaders to realise that they needed to act collectively on energy security, a realisation dramatically reinforced by the January 2009 Ukraine gas crisis.

These immediate pressures to achieve greater energy security coincide with a much longer-term effort by Europe to move to a low-carbon economy. This is driven by concern about climate change, and Europe's desire to be a global leader on the issue. But the EU's climate-change policies will have an impact on energy security because they are, in practice, a huge import-substitution programme, designed to replace fossil fuels that, in the case of oil and gas, come mainly from abroad.

Europe has therefore come to see reduction of demand for hydrocarbons as serving the goal of energy security as well as of climate-change mitigation. This is similar to the drive for energy efficiency adopted by Japan since the 1970s oil shocks, and contrasts with the historic American tendency (though this is changing under President Barack Obama) to focus more on supply-side solutions such as turning more home-grown corn into biofuels to 'replace Arab oil' rather than on demand-side solutions such as increasing the tax on gasoline.

The focus on reduction of demand was an important theme of two Strategic Energy Reviews conducted by the European Commission in 2007 and 2008. A target was set for a 20% improvement in energy efficiency by 2020 – not an absolute cut in use, but a reduction relative to whatever amount Europe would otherwise be consuming on a business-as-usual basis. An EU directive on energy efficiency in buildings was tightened. Three other binding targets for 2020 have been legislated by the Council of Ministers and the European Parliament: an EU-wide 20% reduction in emissions (from 1990 levels), an average 20% renewable-energy share of total energy consumption across the EU, and a 10% minimum biofuel or renewable share of road-transport fuel in each EU member state.

If all the policies to fulfil these targets were to work as planned, and if the oil price were to return to and stay at $100 a barrel, then Europe could, according to the European Commission, actually be importing slightly less gas in 2020 than it does today. This is, however, unlikely, since, while the economic recession reduced energy demand, it also brought the oil price and the price of carbon (on Europe's Emissions Trading Scheme) in 2009 down below the level at which they act as incentives for development of renewable energy and biofuels.

Partial fulfilment of the 2020 goals will, however, enhance Europe's energy security. To achieve them, some European countries will have to address a tension between policies to improve energy security and address climate change. For example, climate-related goals tend to increase the use of gas because it is cleaner than coal, cheaper than nuclear power and the most flexible back-up fuel for intermittent renewable energy such as wind and solar power. Poland has decided to invest in nuclear power, and is cleaning up the use of its large coal output with carbon capture and storage technology, rather than risk increasing its relatively small imports of Russian gas.

A second thrust of the revitalised EU energy policy is to improve the resilience of European energy markets to external shocks. This involves steps to improve connections between national grids and pipelines, and more coherent arrangements for energy stocks and sharing in the event of emergencies, as well as more efficient or cleaner use of indigenous resources such as renewables and coal.

The 1992 Maastricht Treaty gave the EU notional responsibility for filling in the missing links in Europe's cross-border energy infrastructure. But the European Commission's programme for this, known as Trans-European Networks, had neither the money nor the authority to achieve anything. The Commission has used its market-liberalisation powers to try to rid energy networks of discrimination and protectionism; a third package of market-structure reforms was passed into law in spring 2009. However, it has become clear that this will not automatically fill in the missing links, or at least not quickly enough given the possibility of more disruption of Russian gas supplies.

The January 2009 crisis indicated where the gaps were. Bulgaria, Slovakia, Serbia, Macedonia and Moldova lost all their gas supply, while the reduction ranged from one-third to two-thirds of supply in Greece, Austria, the Czech Republic, Slovenia, Hungary, Poland and Romania. Extra gas was brought into central Europe, mainly from Norway and the Netherlands and from storage in Germany; and into Italy from Libya and Algeria. Some countries shared supplies: the Czech Republic with Slovakia, and Hungary with Serbia. The crisis showed the need for more north–south gas links in a system historically designed for east–west flows of gas from Siberia to central Europe. It also underlined the need for modern compressors capable of reversing the normal flow of gas to send it either way. More interconnections are also needed in electricity: the Baltic states' only sizeable outside electricity connection is to the Russian grid, though Estonia has a small link to Finland that is to be strengthened and a major connection is also planned between Lithuania and Sweden. Europe's power grids also need to be extended to offshore wind turbines.

As part of economic stimulus measures to offset the recession, the EU is to spend €4 billion on energy infrastructure in 2009–10, its first serious funding in this area. Of the total, €1.44bn will go to gas pipelines, including Nabucco; €1.05bn to commercial demonstration of clean-coal technology; €910m to electricity-grid connections; and €565m to promoting offshore wind power in the North Sea and Baltic.

In parallel with new money for infrastructure, European governments are stepping up their arrangements for emergency gas supplies. The EU already had legislation requiring a minimum level of oil stocks, and the 19 EU states that also belong to the International Energy Agency (IEA) are obliged to comply with minimum IEA oil-stock levels. But gas storage is more problematic. Even if countries have the right geology for underground storage – not all EU states do – gas is five times more expensive per unit of energy to store than oil (partly because it is less dense a store of energy than oil, and partly because a certain amount of 'cushion gas' has to be held in reserve to maintain the pressure). As a result, governments and the gas industry object to mandatory measures for large-scale, long-term storage.

Thus, EU lawmakers neutered a 2002 proposal on gas security from the European Commission. The resulting 2004 directive failed to set any requirement on governments for emergency gas provision. It defined a 'major supply disruption', which would trigger an EU-wide response, as a loss of 20% of all EU imports for a period of eight weeks – a threshold never likely to be met in peacetime. In the two interruptions of gas through Ukraine, the EU lost 10% of imports for 36 hours in 2006, and 20% of imports for two weeks in 2009. In the wake of the January crisis, the EU plans to rewrite its 2004 directive with a more realistic trigger for Community action.

Reducing dependence on Russia

While measures to lower demand and improve infrastructure and resilience will enhance Europe's energy security overall, the most pressing issue will remain the supplier–customer relationship with Russia – one that clearly has broader strategic dimensions.

European and American attitudes are inevitably coloured by the two disruptions to Russian supplies via Ukraine, with suspicions of political motives bound to recur, as well as fear that Russia will try to use its position to exact concessions from Europe in discussions on unrelated issues. However, the difficulty in such interpretations is that the 2009 crisis seemed to be the result of a mutual miscalculation of each other's positions in a genuine price dispute – and that it cost both Russia and Ukraine dearly in terms of money and reputation. Ukraine claimed that Russia halted supplies, while Russia said that Ukraine blocked them.

The immediate argument was over the price of gas, which is linked (with a lag) to the price of oil. In July 2008 the price of crude oil hit a record high of $147 per barrel, but it had plunged by the end of 2008, just as Russia and Ukraine were negotiating a new agreement. Gazprom demanded a price of $250 per million cubic metres, wanting a high price in anticipation of a drop in the market price. With the same expectation, Ukraine offered only $201 per mcm. Kiev could afford to wait and haggle, because the recession meant that, unusually, it had plenty of gas in storage. For its part, Russia appeared to want to force a showdown with Ukraine, perhaps having grown impatient with the fact that much perceived Russian supply risk was really Ukrainian transit risk. Prime Minister Vladimir Putin called for an international consortium to take over the running of the Ukrainian gas-transit system. Ukraine meanwhile had some cause to fear that Gazprom wanted to take over more than just the running of the system. Kiev suspected that Gazprom really wanted to do in Ukraine what it had done in Belarus – take partial ownership of the transit-pipeline system in payment of gas debts – and was determined to resist Gazprom repeating this in Ukraine.

After the two-week total cut-off of gas, the Russian and Ukrainian gas companies reached a new agreement. This provided for one final year (2009) of preferential terms before Ukraine has to pay the full European-level purchase rate for Russian gas and Russia has to pay Ukraine the full European-level gas-transit rate. No one seemed very confident that the agreement would hold. On conclusion of the agreement, José Manuel Barroso, the European Commission president, said the EU could not allow itself in future to again be placed at the mercy of a Russo-Ukrainian fight. Alexander Medvedev, deputy chief executive of Gazprom, chose to underline his company's determination to be a reliable supplier to Europe, saying 'it is clear that the sooner this diversification of transit routes [away from Ukraine], the better for Europe'. For his part, President Victor Yushchenko of Ukraine said that while his country would abide by the agreement, it was a 'bad deal' for Kiev.

While Europe may not want to increase its dependence on Russia, it has little scope – without breach of contract – to significantly reduce reliance on Russian gas for the next 25 years. Routes bypassing Ukraine have been planned, but would take 3–5 years to build. So Europe will continue to be overshadowed by the Russian–Ukrainian relationship – one that is coloured by history and affected by chronic political infighting within Ukraine that partly reflects differing views about Ukraine's strategic posture vis-à-vis Russia and the West.

> The EU could not allow itself to be placed at the mercy of a Russo-Ukrainian fight

The commercial relationship between Moscow and Kiev cannot be patched up if the two sides remain determined to quarrel, particularly over what needs to be done to improve Ukraine's ageing pipe system. In March 2009 the European Commission hosted a Ukrainian gas-investment conference, the main purpose of which was for Ukraine to sign a declaration promising that it would observe 'transparency and openness' in the financing of such modernisation, and that it would follow EU rules in unbundling its gas-network company and allowing it to operate in an independent commercial way. However, Putin was offended by the lack of any reference in the declaration to Russia as the supplier of gas. While he blamed the EU for this, he delayed planned talks with Ukraine.

If European governments determine that Ukraine was chiefly culpable for the 2009 gas crisis and is unlikely either to smooth relations with Russia or to open up sufficiently to attract foreign investment to improve its gas system, they would incline towards seeking alternative transit routes. Russia's most advanced bypass project, in terms of planning, is the Nord Stream pipeline project, planned to run from near St Petersburg under the Baltic Sea to Germany. It is controversial, raising environmental concerns among littoral countries and political complaints from Poland, which is nervous about Russia bypassing the long-standing gas pipeline running across Belarus and

Poland. But a more likely conduit for Russian gas diverted from Ukraine is the South Stream pipeline planned to run across the northern half of the Black Sea from Russia to the eastern Balkans. Its planning is less advanced than Nord Stream, but Russia already has governmental agreement for South Stream from Bulgaria, Hungary, Serbia and Greece.

The more radical option of diversifying a large part of Europe's gas supplies away from Russia could follow from any determination that Russia has been a troublemaker in Ukraine, and that its growing share of EU imports of gas (and oil, coal and uranium) is a risk to European energy security. The Nabucco project is the only non-Russian gas-pipeline plan that could dilute Russian dominance in central and eastern European gas markets. This could bring gas from the Caspian (Azerbaijan) and, if a trans-Caspian pipeline were built, from Turkmenistan, Kazakhstan and Iran into the Balkans and central Europe. The Nabucco consortium contains the main gas companies of Austria, Hungary, Romania, Bulgaria and Turkey as well as Germany's RWE. But it has been seen so far as more a political project, because it lacks commitment from a major gas producer. The nearest producer to Nabucco is Azerbaijan, which already ships some gas to Turkey, but it is unwilling to commit itself to filling Nabucco, and would not in any case have the resources to do so entirely by itself. As noted earlier, Azerbaijan was in discussion with Gazprom in spring 2009 about selling gas to Russia.

Diversification would put Europe in a stronger bargaining position vis-à-vis Russia, but it could carry risks. If Europe were to launch an aggressive, but ultimately vain, search for alternatives to Russian gas, it could end up worse off by alienating its best long-term source. Gazprom would complain of the lack of security of demand from Europe for its gas, just as OPEC countries complain about European and US development of biofuels sapping demand for their oil. New sources of gas from the Caspian might also prove to be no real alternative if they turned out, because of Russian influence in the region, to be in effect controlled by Moscow.

However, fears that Russia could orchestrate a cartel of suppliers of energy to Europe seem exaggerated. In 2008, Russia did propose a memorandum of understanding to OPEC, under which it would second officials to the OPEC secretariat and pool analysis of the oil market. However, it did not suggest that it should join OPEC, and it would thus not be obliged to comply with its production quotas. Most OPEC members were unimpressed by the Russian proposal. Chakib Khelil, the Algerian oil minister and a past OPEC president, said: 'We sign MOUs with anybody. The only thing that counts is membership.' Moscow has played an active part in the Gas Exporting Countries Forum (GECF), but this body seems unwilling, and almost certainly unable, to regulate the gas market as OPEC does with oil, given the totally different nature of the two markets.

Strategic options

With the likely continuing dominance of Russia as a gas supplier, and a long-term desire to reduce energy demand and carbon emissions, European countries have a set of sensible options. A reasonable strategy would be to rely primarily on the EU to do the maximum internally to reduce demand and to improve gas interconnections and storage, and to pursue a measured policy of diversifying energy routes and sources. This would stop short of panic steps such as forcing the pace of political pipelines like Nabucco – since panic is not justified.

Secondly, they could clarify what NATO can and cannot do. The Alliance's potential role in energy security has been exaggerated by some of its proponents and opponents. Any suggestion that NATO use troops to guard pipelines in non-NATO countries such as Georgia would be inflammatory. But NATO, with an extensive oil-pipeline system of its own and experience in securing critical infrastructure and dealing with civil emergencies, could offer advice to non-NATO countries and could help patrol sea routes that are important for energy supplies. At its 2008 Bucharest Summit, the Alliance said it saw its specific role in energy security as sharng information and intelligence and supporting the protection of critical infrastructure. Restatement of this limited ambition could be useful at a time when the new US administration and NATO are trying to 'reset' their relationship with Russia, to begin it again on a more positive note.

Towards a New Asian Security Architecture

Discussions about a new kind of 'security architecture' in Asia reflect the widespread understanding among regional governments that they have a common interest in designing political structures that would allow an orderly and peaceful strategic future. The conversation, carried on intensively at regional gatherings including the annual IISS Shangri-La Dialogue, and in internal national debates, reflects the intersection of two contemporary regional realities. First, there is growing awareness that changes in the distribution of power among the major state actors in the Asia-Pacific, upon which the region's strategic outlook in large measure depends, may render existing approaches to security outdated and consequently require new institutional structures. Above all, the rise of China and to a lesser extent India, fuelled in both cases by rapid economic growth, is significantly altering the regional power balance. Meanwhile, the United States and Japan face the prospect of a corresponding relative decline in their regional power and influence. There is also the possibility of a united (and perhaps nuclear-armed) Korea once the Kim Jong Il era has ended. Secondly, a wide array of structures for interstate cooperation, possessing either explicit or implicit security roles, has developed in the Asia-Pacific since the 1980s.

Despite these developments, American-led bilateral alliances and security partnerships continue to underwrite the Asia-Pacific regional order. These include the bilateral security relations based on the US–Japan Mutual Security Treaty, similar alliance relations between the United States and South Korea, and the ANZUS alliance which has in effect become a bilateral pact between Washington and Canberra since New Zealand's ban on nuclear-armed ship visits during the 1980s. The United States also has bilateral treaty arrangements with the Philippines and Thailand, and looser but still significant security partnerships or collaboration with Singapore and other Southeast Asian states. While these alliances and partnerships remain for the time being central to the strategic policies of the Asia-Pacific states involved, it is doubtful that they are suited to the demands and challenges of the coming decades, particularly if the United States' relative power in the region and globally does decline. As China becomes a more powerful military actor able to challenge US regional military predominance, small and medium powers may find that security links with America fail to provide the same degree of reassurance that they did in the past.

Asia's changing major-power relations

A regional power transition in Asia is by no means unprecedented. Examples from the last half-century include the withdrawal of European colonial powers in the 1950s and 1960s, and the collapse of the Soviet Union in 1991 bringing the diminution of Moscow's naval presence in the Asia-Pacific. Both the European and Soviet retreats enhanced the United States' regional pre-eminence. In the first case, America's continuing presence, despite the Nixon Doctrine of 1968 which sought to limit US responsibilities in Southeast

Asia, prolonged Western dominance of maritime Asia. In the second case, Washington's enduring role in Asian security obviated fears of a post-Cold War regional power vacuum.

The current transition appears different in that the new regional strategic equation will be determined by changes in the strength of Asia's own major powers. The region's only other similar modern experience, when Imperial Japan dominated much of East Asia in the late 1930s and early 1940s, was painful for those subjugated and ultimately for Japan itself. While a repetition of that catastrophic hegemony seems unlikely, tensions and suspicions between Asian countries persist as a result of the region's historical legacy. Asia's small and medium powers, which could be vulnerable to a large-scale power transition, have become accustomed to the United States playing a balancing role that in effect keeps their stronger neighbours' ambitions in check. It is understandable that these lesser powers are nervous about an impending era in which Chinese and perhaps Indian power might come to the fore, and that they would prefer the long-established US regional security role to endure – even though their public statements do not always indicate this.

The scale of the contemporary power transition has generated significant uncertainty regarding Asia's strategic future. First, the potential of individual major powers is unclear. The long-term extension of the economic growth rates enjoyed by China over the last decade would result in the country becoming a strategic giant with global, let alone regional, consequences that would be hard even for Beijing to predict. But doubts – reinforced by the current global economic crisis – about the validity of extrapolating such trends warn against assuming that China is destined to grow inexorably stronger. A slowing of China's economic growth in the medium to long term would raise the question of whether it could maintain increases in defence spending and the pace of its impressive efforts at transforming the People's Liberation Army.

The sense of uncertainty regarding Asia's strategic future is magnified because the nature of relations between the region's powers is unpredictable as their economic and military strength evolves. The extent to which China, India, Japan and the United States – not to mention a unified Korea – might be able to work together to keep the region secure depends not just on how their national power develops or deteriorates, but also on the domestic politics of each and the evolution of relations among them. The unequal national consequences of the global recession, which seem likely to undermine

America's reputation and Japan's self-confidence while leaving China and India relatively unscathed, are also a complicating factor. In consequence, even if China is to become the leading power in Asia in a generation's time, it is not known how much freedom its leaders will have to use or misuse their growing influence in the Asia-Pacific. Beijing's leaders could find that other powers balance China, but alternatively they might find that they have a relatively free rein in the region. The desire to build a more suitable regional security architecture for Asia is above all an attempt to manage this high degree of strategic uncertainty. In particular, it seeks to minimise challenges to regional order by binding all parties, especially larger ones, into a structure of relations in which rising powers do not unsettle the region's hard-won stability and prosperity. The major powers themselves, as well as the region's smaller states, have good reasons for wanting to maintain a strong regional order in which they can continue to prosper in security.

Asia's existing security architecture

Two main types of security structure already feature in Asia's strategic landscape. The first is the set of American-led bilateral alliances and security partnerships established from the 1950s onwards. These have survived significant strategic changes in the region, including the US defeat in Vietnam, China's adoption of a revised, non-revolutionary foreign policy and its re-engagement with the global economy, and the cessation of the Soviet challenge. Washington's Asian allies and other regional partners value their security links with the United States highly and have come to rely on American strategic reassurance.

The second set of security structures comprises Asia's burgeoning array of multilateral groupings, including the original regional institution, ASEAN. Established in 1967, ASEAN has benefited from sturdy foundations: a common commitment among its core members to keep the organisation alive by maintaining and strengthening the original delicate peace between them through the principles of non-interference and mutual respect for each other's sovereignty. Though there have been signs of the peace between certain ASEAN members fraying on occasion (for example, the border clashes between Thailand and Cambodia in 2008–09), and Myanmar's domestic policies have embarrassed and frustrated other ASEAN members, these norms have been observed more often than they have been neglected. Since the 1990s, ASEAN has been at the centre of a proliferation of regional institutions, including the pan-regional ASEAN Regional Forum (ARF), which focuses on security dialogue, together with other spin-off bodies exercising wider remits, such as ASEAN+3 (the ten Southeast Asian countries with China, Japan and South Korea) and the East Asia Summit (which additionally involves Australia, India and New Zealand). Their overlapping membership has complicated efforts to define clearly the roles of the latter two institutions.

While primarily concerned with economic issues, APEC (the Asia-Pacific Economic Cooperation forum) has also touched on security matters in its deliberations. Meanwhile, the Shanghai Cooperation Organisation involves China, Russia and Central Asian states in security collaboration. Northeast Asia has its own venue for multilateral dialogue in the form of the sporadic Six-Party Talks, focused on the single issue of restraining North Korea's nuclear programme.

When ASEAN was the only prominent structure of its type, and even when APEC was established in the late 1980s as the Cold War was ending, it could still have been said that Asia suffered from a deficit of regional organisations. This is clearly no longer the case. However, it remains unclear whether this expansion of Asia's institutional fabric has lent it greater depth as well as breadth. There is an almost inevitable inefficiency and even a sense sometimes of competition deriving from the existence of so many dialogue forums with overlapping ambits. There have been calls within the region for some of the older institutions such as the APEC and ARF to be dissolved on the basis that they have little more to contribute to regional cooperation. Some critics argue that APEC is now much less useful than it was when it was established in 1989 because of the declining relative economic weight of the United States and other Western states, which were among its most important initial supporters. APEC's efforts earlier this decade to assume a security role – for example, in relation to counter-terrorism – never amounted to much; it has continued to be concerned primarily with trade liberalisation. Meanwhile, despite its efforts to facilitate focused discussions on issues of practical significance to its members such as maritime security, counter-terrorism, disaster relief and peacekeeping, ARF is widely criticised for its persistent failure to move beyond the status of a talking shop concerned mainly with confidence-building and to start managing the region's security. One major drawback of ARF is that its lead participants are foreign ministers; it is only in the context of the IISS Shangri-La Dialogues that defence ministers from across the whole of Asia have the opportunity to confer. However, there are strong supporters as well as critics of existing institutions and no consensus among participant governments on their usefulness or redundancy.

Redesigning the regional architecture

It is clear that the region's security architects do not have a clean slate. Instead, they face a complex array of security institutions, including bilateral security arrangements as well as multilateral groupings. Some of the latter are more useful and valued than others. The challenge is to make sense of the existing range of regional structures, to build connections between some of them while possibly reconsidering the usefulness of others. There are several practical ways of ensuring that the collection of regional security institutions amounts to something greater than the sum of its parts. One vision, which finds some favour in Washington and to some extent in Tokyo, is to build connections between existing bilateral alliances. Such connections are already manifest to a limited extent in the Trilateral Security Dialogue, which involves the United States and its closest regional allies, Australia and Japan. But the attempt in 2007 by Shinzo Abe's short-lived Japanese government to reach out further and create a quadrilateral security format including India backfired. India is not an ally of the United States, despite the US–India agreement on civil nuclear cooperation, and has no intention of becoming one. The quadrilateral idea looked too much like an attempt to contain China, which raised particular concerns for Canberra, given that Australia's economy has prospered from close relations with Beijing. Indeed, the need to maintain simultaneously strong links with China as well as the United States is felt by many small and medium powers in the region. That the involvement of India and fear of offending China were central to the quadrilateral proposal and its demise underlined the growing profile of the two largest Asian powers in the region's decision-making on security.

Meanwhile, little headway has been made towards rationalising Asia's proliferating multilateral forums, all of which to a greater or lesser degree concern themselves with security matters. Each forum has its champions: Japan and the US remain the effective sponsors of APEC, while Beijing favours ASEAN+3. Most regional states would evidently prefer to acquiesce through participation in the present collection of institutions rather than risk self-exclusion from any of them.

Efforts to connect the bilateral alliances with the multilateral groupings seem unlikely to make significant progress. Attempts to emphasise democratic values, shared between the United States and most of its security partners in the Asia-Pacific, only antagonise the non-democracies and illiberal semi-democracies which still constitute many of the region's states. Rather than creating a democratic bloc and a set of 'alliances for good', the unhappy result of a region divided according to regime type would be more likely. The real value of the bilateral alliances remains the security provided by extended deterrence for the Asia-Pacific partners, the benefits of military cooperation for all parties, and a forward US military presence, particularly in Japan and South Korea but also in Australia and Singapore, even if the long-term future of that presence is somewhat uncertain. While there has been a degree of bilateral security networking among US allies and partners (most importantly between Australia and Japan) during the present decade, the heterogeneity of America's Asia-Pacific allies and security partners precludes them from working as a regional collective, with or without Washington, oriented to common goals.

It is also hard to imagine any of the region's existing multilateral forums being transformed into de facto alliances, or even moving significantly in that direction. Such a development would repudiate their original rationale. If Asia-Pacific states are unready to use multilateral forums to take concrete action on major regional security issues, then it seems inconceivable that they could agree through an institution such as ARF to cooperate militarily on a multilateral basis. Even military cooperation intended to combat transnational non-state actors such as pirates and terrorists could easily offend Asian states, most of which take their sovereign rights and duties extremely seriously. This was evident, for example, in the strongly negative reaction from littoral states led by Indonesia and Malaysia in 2003–04 after the United States proposed a Regional Maritime Security Initiative to combat piracy in the Malacca Strait. Similar sensitivities have been apparent in some Asian states' resistance to involvement in the US-led Proliferation Security Initiative.

Nevertheless, the region's diverse security structures do support each other in indirect ways. The US alliance system has undergirded the relative stability and prosperity on which regional institutions have built: Asian states have possessed greater room for considering their common interests in multilateral endeavours against the background of a regional distribution of power in which none of them can hope to achieve hegemony. In turn, the region's multilateral forums, and the norms of inclusiveness and non-aggression they promote, have allowed a number of regional states to build close bilateral defence and security relations with the United States under the cover of a wider commitment to multilateral security cooperation.

Towards an Asia-Pacific Community?

Because the region's existing security architecture is complex and eclectic but by no means broken, there is a strong argument that tinkering with it – let alone attempting to redesign the overall institutional structure – is unnecessary. The performance of the existing architecture may be decidedly suboptimal in terms of its ability to manage if not resolve regional security challenges, and it may be difficult to prove the extent of its contribution to the Asia-Pacific's three decades of peace among major powers and prosperity (notwithstanding temporary setbacks unrelated to security concerns in the late 1990s and since 2008). At least, though, the existing structures are more benign than harmful.

Yet the growing interest, manifest since mid decade in debates at the IISS Shangri-La Dialogue among other venues, in the future shape of the regional security architecture signals unease that existing regional structures are inadequate to meet future challenges as Asia's power transition unfolds. This is the inchoate premise behind the proposal first made in June 2008 by Australian Prime Minister Kevin Rudd to establish an Asia-Pacific Community (APC) by 2020. This, he announced, should be a single organisation which could address the region's security, economic and political challenges. The involvement of China, India, Indonesia, Japan and the United States would be vital to its success. Over the following year, as Australian diplomats took soundings in the region regarding its feasibility, Rudd refined the APC concept. Speaking at the 8th IISS Shangri-La Dialogue in Singapore in May 2009, he emphasised that the APC was not a prescriptive idea, and that Australia would soon convene a 'one and a half track' meeting of regional representatives to flesh out Canberra's thinking on how best to advance the proposal. However, he stressed the necessity for effective management of relations between China, India, Japan and the United States in the context of the rise of the former two powers: there was a need for mechanisms to cope with the likely 'strategic shocks and discontinuities'. Without such a mechanism, he said, there was a danger of potentially dangerous 'strategic drift'. In essence, despite the deference that Rudd has paid in his speeches on the topic to the roles of existing institutions, the APC proposal is essentially for a concert of powers to help manage the incipient regional transition to greater multipolarity.

The mixed, and in some cases frosty, reception which greeted Rudd's proposal in the region indicated the challenges this attempt to begin constructing an overarching regional institution will face. Besides criticising the lack of specific recommendations in the proposal, some governments (principally those in Southeast Asia not listed by the Australian leader as key potential contributors to the Community) made it clear that they had felt overlooked by Canberra's failure to forewarn or consult them. This illustrated an important conundrum: attempts to recognise the hierarchy of states that helps bring order to the region are likely to be contested by the region's small and medium powers, whereas a more inclusive architecture could mistake unanimity for progress and increase the chances of lowest-common-denominator politics of the sort that has dogged efforts to enhance multilateral security cooperation through ASEAN and its associated institutions such as ARF.

Rudd's proposal has raised eyebrows in the region among some who think that the time has passed when Western states can propose major regional security initiatives for Asia, given that an increasing proportion of the power to be managed will be indigenous Asian power. The flurry of Australian and US activity which helped give rise to APEC and ARF in the late 1980s and early 1990s was superseded later in the decade by a distinctly East Asian agenda which resulted from the 1996–97 financial crisis and led to the establishment of ASEAN+3. Moreover, the East Asia Summit is notable for its exclusion, so far at least, of the United States. The APC proposal assumes that Australia, hardly a major regional power, would almost naturally be involved at the centre of the proposed community. There is, in addition, a question of philosophical preference: many Asian states would apparently prefer any new regional architecture to evolve incrementally rather than result from a sweeping initiative. Those major powers with time on their side – China and India – are in no hurry to set the architecture in place now as their influence over its form can only grow in future.

Beyond an Asian architecture

However it evolves, a security architecture based on institutional development cannot on its own ensure the Asia-Pacific region's peace and security. One key development stands out as a factor permitting Asia's enjoyment of a relatively benign security order, in which major-power conflict has been avoided over the last 30 years: the rapprochement between China and the United States in the early 1970s. This was not a question of formal arrangements; it was not based on a new treaty-based alliance or multilateral forum, but on a common understanding between the leaders of two of the region's major powers. The heart of the matter was a mutual interest in restraining bilateral competition. This feature has underscored elements of the regional order which are still apparent. Indeed, US President Barack Obama has inherited a relationship with China which is essentially robust.

As Rudd has noted, an enduring accommodation between the Asia-Pacific's major powers is key to the region's future security order. Asia's states could develop an extensive regional security architecture based on an intricate array of interlocking institutions, but without the necessary accommodation the major powers would be unable to restrain their pursuit of self-interest sufficiently to allow development of a stable regional order. Achieving this underlying consensus would require that the Asia-Pacific's great powers in effect make room for one another. This is much easier said than done. The Obama administration wishes to be more consultative and less adversarial in its foreign policy than was its predecessor, but it still views the United States as the leading power globally, including in Asia. China and Japan have come to at least a temporary accommodation since Chinese Premier Wen Jiabao's visit to Tokyo in April 2007, but the price for a long-term rapprochement may be Japan's de facto recognition of China's pre-eminence. A more powerful India, like a more powerful China, may require smaller Asian states to make compromises. And future relations between China and India could be unstable while these two rising powers work out their own bilateral accommodation.

Rudd's APC proposal has at its core a notion that amounts to a concert of powers based on accommodation among the region's leading geopolitical players. Such a concert will naturally not be welcomed by at least some of the region's small and medium powers, which would find it necessary to moderate their insistence on being consulted at every turn. The attachment of these states to places at each and every multilateral grouping in the region parallels the commitment of some of them to maintaining security links with the United States. Both of these understandable priorities may encourage a continuing focus on developing institutional aspects of the Asia-Pacific's security architecture, the external and visible superstructure of regional cooperation. However, the striking of bargains among the key major powers is likely to provide the real foundations for future regional order.

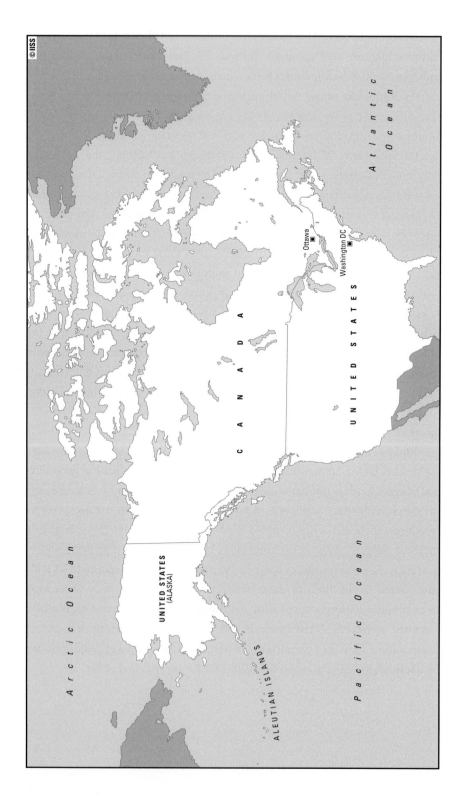

Arctic Ocean

UNITED STATES
(ALASKA)

ALEUTIAN ISLANDS

Pacific Ocean

C A N A D A

Ottawa

Washington DC

U N I T E D   S T A T E S

Atlantic
Ocean

Chapter 3

North America

The United States: The Primacy of Politics

If meant to be a joke, it was pretty serious. In the Roosevelt Room of the White House, US Treasury Secretary Henry Paulson fell to one knee in front of Speaker of the House Nancy Pelosi, and begged her not to let an emergency bailout package for failing banks 'blow up' in Congress. 'I didn't know you were Catholic', Pelosi is reported to have replied. 'It's not me blowing this up, it's the Republicans.' 'I know', said Paulson. 'I know.'

This was on Thursday, 25 September 2008. The previous morning, Democratic presidential candidate Barack Obama had called his Republican rival, Senator John McCain, to suggest that they could calm teetering financial markets by issuing a joint statement in favour of the Bush administration's rescue package. McCain wasn't available to take the call, and when he called back Obama was unavailable. McCain's next move could be seen as heroic or erratic. He announced that because of the financial crisis he was 'suspending' his campaign and returning to Washington to help hammer out a plan for restoring market confidence. He called on Obama to do the same, adding that they should cancel their televised debate scheduled for Friday.

Far from restoring confidence, what ensued was a fiasco that deepened the crisis, further traumatised Wall Street and brought the US treasury secretary to his knees. A bemused Obama said that he saw no sense in suspending campaigns or cancelling debates, but he did agree to join McCain the next day in a White House meeting with President George W. Bush, treasury officials and congressional leaders. That meeting did not go well. The White House and Democrats had thought they were close to a deal, but House Republican leader John Boehner said his caucus would not support spending $700 billion to buy 'toxic' mortgage assets that were paralysing the system. McCain did not commit himself either way. Democrats, in theory, had the votes to pass it on their own, but said they needed bipartisan buy-in for a plan that was itself politically toxic. Bush, as he watched the supposed deal disintegrating, is reported to have told the meeting, 'if money isn't loosened up, this sucker' – presumably, the financial system and economy – 'could go down'.

Four days later, on Monday 29 September, the House of Representatives rejected the package, with 95 left-wing Democrats joining 133 Republicans to send it down. Wall Street reacted in the manner of a witness to a historic calamity: the percentage fall in the Dow Jones Industrial Average was the largest one-day drop since trading had resumed after 11 September 2001. On Wednesday, a revised bill was passed by the Senate, where the votes had always been solid, and on Friday, with the sense that an abdication of economic stewardship would not be forgiven, the House passed the bailout plan by a 92-vote margin.

These 10 days in September made up just one brief episode in the steep, steady and stomach-wrenching unwinding of a stupendously leveraged economy – an unwinding that started in summer 2007 and still continued in mid 2009. It was an episode, however, that captured as well as any the essential truth of this crisis: that while it may have had global social and structural causes – starting with the problematic economic symbiosis between America and China – it could only have a political solution. That is to say, the main hope for escaping a repeat of the Great Depression – and the economic trend lines were ominously similar – was to avoid the political and policy blunders that were committed by the leaders of the major economic powers in the late 1920s and 1930s.

In this light, and perhaps counter-intuitively, Americans were probably fortunate that it was in the midst of a presidential election campaign that their financial system seized up. They turned at that moment to the candidate who for two years had promised in sometimes exhilarating oratory to abandon the political gamesmanship and ideological posturing of recent decades. It was not a renunciation of politics that Barack Obama was offering, however, but something like the opposite: a return to politics as the art of the sensible, transcending partisan categories and seeking consensus on effective solutions to huge problems.

There is no doubt, to be sure, that Obama's ideas about effective solutions entailed a significant leftward reversal of the right-wing course of American politics since 1980. In this sense, Obama was also lucky that the financial crisis occurred in the final weeks of his candidacy. This factor should not be overstated, however. It was not the economic crisis alone that delivered the keys of the White House to Obama. He had led McCain in the polls consistently since April and for most of the weeks before that. McCain had pulled barely ahead for a few days after the Republican nominating convention in the first week of September, but long-term economic anxieties, a deeply unpopular incumbent president, and the natural end of a political cycle were among the factors that made it a promising year for the Democrats.

Still, it was important that, for stewardship of a nation in crisis, voters found Obama's deliberative demeanour more plausible than McCain's heroic impulse. In any event, if the financial crisis did not make Obama president, its economic consequences were very likely to make or break his presidency. Six months earlier, it had been fair to assume that wars in Iraq and Afghanistan would be the defining challenges for a new president. In voters' preoccupation, if not in long-term significance, these wars were now second-order affairs.

> Wars in Iraq and Afghanistan were now second-order affairs

So Obama's victory was partly born of crisis. But it was also occasion for a national celebration that seemed to transcend the fact – incredible enough by itself – that the United States had just elected its first African-American president. The crowds that gathered in cities across the country were, to be sure, teary-eyed and disproportionately black, but there was never a hint in these celebrations that the rest of America did not own in equal measure this constitutional and generational achievement. It was, in this sense, much like the 1960 election of John F. Kennedy, which had established the fact of a transformed America emerging from the struggle and mobilisation of the Second World War. Now, half a century later, a similar claim could at least be ventured: the ideological, racial and social fractures of those post-war decades had produced, not decline, but attractive new strength. There would be plenty of troubles ahead to test this proposition. At the moment, however, for the propagandists among hostile movements and states, this had to be a frustrating development. For alienated friends, it had to be reassuring. For many Americans themselves, to judge by the spontaneous eruptions in city streets, it was simply exhilarating. This was important – before America's image abroad could be improved, its conception of itself had to be restored.

Amazing race

Obama's win, if not exactly a landslide, was resounding. He was the first Democrat since Jimmy Carter in 1976 to win a majority of the popular vote – 53% to McCain's 46% – and Obama's was the largest majority for a Democratic candidate since Lyndon B. Johnson (LBJ) in 1964. By winning the states won by John Kerry in 2004, plus Ohio, Florida, Virginia, North Carolina, Colorado, New Mexico, Nevada, Iowa and Indiana, he relegated McCain's Republicans to what was left of the South, plus thinly populated Great Plains and Rocky Mountain states. The Illinois senator, moreover, was 'blue' as well as black: that is to say, he was the first northern liberal since John F. Kennedy to win the White House.

The latter circumstance seemed to challenge the notion of America as an intrinsically conservative country. That notion may have been a stretch anyway; it relied on the oft-repeated calculation that Republicans had held the presidency in seven of the last ten elections, but glossed over the fact that Al Gore in 2000 won the popular vote. Framed over half a century, Obama's election meant that the Democratic candidate had now taken the most votes in seven of the last 13 presidential elections.

It was true, however, that from the late 1960s Republicans had found a way to keep Democrats and liberals on semi-permanent defensive by tapping into pervasive bewilderment over the civil-rights movement, Vietnam protests, black riots and urban crime. *Sub rosa*, the American Civil War had never ended. The Texan LBJ knew this well enough on the day he signed the 1964 Civil Rights Act – a huge step towards fulfilling the promise of the American Revolution which required all of Johnson's legislative wiles and ruthlessness to enact. When Johnson aide Bill Moyers found him that evening in the Oval Office, subdued and morose, he asked why. 'We have lost the South for a generation', replied the president. In his 'Southern Strategy', Richard Nixon did not hesitate to rub salt on the wound, part of a larger strategy of stoked resentments and cultural division that Nixon bequeathed to the country. 'Cut the Democratic Party and country in half', wrote Nixon aide Pat Buchanan in a 1968 memo to the Republican candidate. 'My view is that we would have far the larger half.' During the 2008 election campaign, historian Rick Perlstein devoted a best-selling book to the thesis that 'Nixonland' was the same polarised country that had made political life so bitter and raw in the Bill Clinton and George W. Bush administrations.

It was Barack Obama's crucial strategic insight that Nixonland might be fading away. This was the theme of the 2004 Democratic National Convention keynote speech that brought Obama to national attention: 'We worship an "awesome God" in the Blue States, and we don't like federal agents poking around in our libraries in the Red States. We coach Little League in the Blue States and yes, we've got some gay friends in the Red States.' The presidential campaign that he started two years later was premised on the same confidence that a liberal political programme could be sold to the American people couched, in the style of Franklin D. Roosevelt (FDR), in a 'first-class temperament' and sunny nationalism.

That McCain, a Vietnam War hero and 22-year senator from Arizona, might be defeated by the end of Nixonland was a somewhat sad irony, for he was a Republican who had become famous for resisting the country's ideological polarisation. As his long-time aide Mark Salter noted, this was a man held for five years and tortured as a prisoner of war in Hanoi who would later come to count Vietnam War protesters among his friends, and who joined the drive for normalised relations with Vietnam. McCain's notable legislative efforts had been those produced in the role of bipartisan entrepreneur: McCain–Feingold, the Bipartisan Campaign Reform Act of 2002; McCain–Kennedy, the failed comprehensive immigration reform bill first introduced in 2005, was an unusual double-act between a border-state senator and the foremost symbol of northeastern liberal values; and, after a long and personal fight, the passage of the McCain amendment to the Detainee Treatment Act of 2005 marked the point at which the Bush administration was forced publicly to commit in writing to the prohibition of cruel, inhuman and degrading treatment of US-held detainees.

But if he recognised and in some sense welcomed the blurring of divisions, McCain was prevented by his precarious position, in a Republican Party that had moved well to his right, from acting on it. His choice of Alaska Governor Sarah Palin as his running mate turned into a political disaster on many levels, but it was perhaps most damaging as a pure symbol of identity politics, of small-town American values set up against urban otherness and supposedly unpatriotic, Eastern 'elites'. 'We believe that the best of America is in the small towns that we get to visit, and in the wonderful little pockets of what I call the real America, being here with all of you hard-working, very patriotic, very pro-America areas of this great nation', said Palin in a typical stump speech.

It was not obvious from the start, however, that the Palin choice would prove a disaster. Announced the day after Obama's speech accepting the Democratic nomination in Denver, the Palin pick was timed to step on the polling 'bounce' that candidates count on coming out of a successful convention. At first the plan worked pretty well. The 44-year-old mother of five – including a just-delivered baby with Down's syndrome – was young, attractive and vaguely exotic in a way that comported nonetheless with the rudiments of American mythology: Alaska being a distant, libertarian-conservative, oil-rich wilderness, the kind of place where a woman governor might well know how to shoot a moose and then make a stew out of it.

This healthy exoticism could be contrasted with Obama's allegedly more sinister version. During the hard-fought primary battle, Senator Hillary Clinton kept winning the big states with large white working-class populations such as Pennsylvania and Ohio. Her campaign pointed to Obama's relatively poorer performance among these so-called 'Reagan Democrats' as evidence that, whatever the Illinois Senator's virtues of intellect and charisma, he was unlikely to be electable against a Republican opponent sure to harp on themes of patriotism and somewhat visceral invocations of 'authentic' American values. The far-right reaches of cyberspace became a fever swamp of speculation that Obama, whose atheist Kenyan father had Muslim relatives, was himself a secret Muslim.

McCain–Palin rallies themselves became agitated affairs, with unsavoury expressions of bigotry and xenophobia from the crowds. McCain stepped in at least twice to admonish his supporters: one for voicing her fear of the 'Arab' Obama; another for emphasising Obama's middle name – Hussein – with vitriolic relish. (Other Republican leaders were less scrupulous than McCain, however, and it was their propagation of the Muslim rumour that was cited by Colin Powell, the former secretary of state in the George W. Bush administration, in his eloquent abandonment of his own party to endorse Obama.)

The McCain–Palin campaign's official attack on Obama focused on three perceived vulnerabilities. First, it sought to turn his star power against him. This strategy emerged most clearly when Obama travelled in July to the Middle East and Europe. The trip culminated in a speech before 200,000 cheering – and American-flag-waving – Germans in Berlin's Tiergarten, and McCain promptly took to the airwaves with a political advertisement comparing the celebrity Obama to Paris Hilton and Britney Spears. The Democrat's campaign aides later admitted that they were sufficiently worried about this line of attack that they decided to cut back on the big campaign rallies where their candidate succeeded in so mesmerising his supporters. These were to be replaced by smaller town-hall type gatherings where Obama could prove his capacity to talk straight and empathise with the troubles of individual Americans. This self-imposed restraint was not sustainable, however, because it conflicted with the imperative to get as many Obama voters as possible to the polls as early as possible in the numerous states that allowed early voting. The way to do that was to get them fired up, best accomplished in large crowds by way of the candidate's spellbinding oratory.

The second line of attack was a traditional effort to exploit Republicans' perceived advantages as the 'stronger' party more willing and able to do what was necessary to protect Americans' national security. This line was strengthened, the Republicans thought, in early August when Mikheil Saakashvili, the American-educated president of the Caucasian republic of Georgia, launched an attack to recover the breakaway territory of South Ossetia, and the Ossetians' Russian ally responded with a massive incursion into Georgian territory. McCain immediately declared that 'we are all Georgians', and posed the crisis as a test of Western resolve in the face of Russian aggression. Obama's response was more measured at first, but he took a progressively harder line against Moscow as the war progressed. This hardening was partly a matter of political nervousness and partly a matter of conviction: many of Obama's aides, including his

> **Obama took a harder line as the war progressed**

vice-presidential running mate Senator Joe Biden, were friends of Georgia in general and Saakashvili in particular, and long-time supporters of the proposition that more-or-less open-ended NATO enlargement would be a stabilising process that would benefit everyone, including Russia itself. Hence the campaign did not provide an opportunity to debate that highly questionable proposition, even as the crisis provided a textbook case study of the dangers for an over-extended superpower in making open-ended strategic commitments to small, and unpredictably reckless, client states.

The third line of attack was mounted in a series of campaign commercials and speeches that combined insinuations about Obama's 'otherness' with more explicit warnings about his supposed 'socialist' radicalism. Because of the racial connotations, McCain declared off-limits any reference to Obama's former pastor, the incendiary Jeremiah Wright. However, much was made of the Illinois senator's incidental association with William Ayers, a self-confessed former underground 'Weatherman', who had gone on to a Chicago career in education. According to Sarah Palin, Obama had been 'palling around with terrorists'; she told a group of campaign donors that Obama 'is not a man who sees America as you see America and as I see America'.

Such allegations constituted Palin's patent contribution to the campaign, and in a different climate they might have worked. The problem for McCain, however, was that after the initial excitement over her selection, Palin herself turned into the wrong kind of story. A series of interviews with CBS News anchor Katie Couric demonstrated disastrously that Palin lacked the knowledge, and probably the temperament, to be president. Since she was serving as understudy to a 72-year-old cancer survivor – McCain would have been the oldest man ever elected president – the prospect of this untested woman suddenly presiding over the most powerful nation on earth was more than theoretical. Actuarial risks aside, the choice reflected on McCain's own judgement and fitness for the presidency. His campaign was hoist with its own petard: a somewhat gimmicky effort to capitalise on the 24-hour news cycle exploded into cycles of embarrassing revelations and bitter recriminations inside a campaign on the road to defeat.

Meltdown

The several months' lag between electing a new president and his swearing into office is a historical anachronism, dating from times when communications were by horse and coach. Since the early twentieth century this lag has proven sometimes problematic, as in 1932 when President Herbert Hoover and President-elect Franklin Roosevelt traded insults while the economy contracted (in fact, the lag was reduced to three months from four by a constitutional amendment introduced two days before Roosevelt's inauguration and ratified in 1933). During the most recent handover, cooperation between the incumbent White House and incoming administration was distinctly better, yet the problem of President Bush's diminished authority at a time of insolvent banks and failing auto companies was manifest. Bush was unable to marshal enough votes in the Senate to pass an auto-industry bailout bill, and was forced to use $17.4bn of money voted to help troubled financial institutions instead; Obama supported the effort to rescue the nearly bankrupt General Motors and Chrysler but declined to take a very visible role. (The car companies survived long enough to be restructured, with a huge federal-government stake, early in Obama's term.) In general Obama demurred from taking a leading role in the credit crisis, repeating his mantra that America only has one president at a time. This prompted the acerbic Barney Frank, a Democratic Congressman from Massachusetts, to complain that Obama was 'overstat[ing] the number of presidents we have at this time'.

There are, roughly speaking, two kinds of recessions. The first, tied to the natural business cycle, can be worsened when central banks decide that it is necessary to squeeze inflationary pressures out of the system through tight monetary policy; the consequent rise in unemployment can be depicted as unpleasant but necessary medicine for the purposes of sustainable, low-inflation growth in the future. The United States has suffered through ten such recessions since the Second World War, sometimes in unfortunate sync with its major European and Japanese trading partners. The second kind of recession is far scarier. When inherently speculative bubbles of asset prices keep expanding on the basis of a pervasive belief that the prices will continue rising, the bursting will almost invariably reveal an economy that was dangerously leveraged on the basis of imagined wealth that has suddenly vanished. What follows is a sharp reverse dynamic, with irrational exuberance replaced by vicious cycles of self-fulfilling pessimism. Households and businesses shift from a mass readiness for borrowing to a mass mentality of saving. The 'paradox of thrift', identified by John Maynard Keynes, is that this new-found propensity to save, rational and even virtuous for individuals, will be disastrous for the economy as a whole when everyone does it. Generally speaking, the more irrational and exaggerated the bubble, the more savage and panic-laden the reversal. In this case, the asset was housing and the bubble was fed by continued high levels of consumer spending in the United States, a savings glut and ensuing capital flows from China, easy mortgage credit as American banks and other lending institutions sought to profit from booming house prices, and practically unregulated financial markets that devised ever more complex instruments to bundle and 'securitise' the mortgage assets. Risk assessments for these securities were based on mathematical models that factored in just about every conceivable data point and price relationship except one: the possibility of a general and sustained fall in house prices.

The March 2008 collapse of Bear Stearns was the first signal failure of an investment bank under the pressure of the credit crisis. In the first week of September, Fannie Mae and Freddie Mac – government-sponsored enterprises that buy up home mortgage loans from primary lenders – were placed under the protection of federal 'conservatorship', entailing quarterly investments of government money. On Monday 15 September Lehman Brothers, a large investment bank which had suffered heavy losses, filed for Chapter

11 bankruptcy. Over a weekend of meetings in Manhattan, it had been made clear that Lehman would not be rescued with federal funds, and with $54bn of mortgage-backed securities on its books, no buyer could be found. In parallel negotiations, Merrill Lynch, in the knowledge that Lehman was close to failing, and similarly exposed to toxic mortgage-backed assets, was sold to Bank of America for $50bn.

The collapse of two of Wall Street's biggest names was a clear signal that the crisis of credit was systemic, and that it had the potential to become catastrophic. Lehman's demise was especially unnerving because it undermined the comfortable assumption that certain investment houses were too big for the Treasury and Federal Reserve to let fail. Paulson, the treasury secretary, drew criticism for what some said was this decisive miscalculation, which heightened banks' fears of lending to one another. Ten major banks did agree to create a joint fund of up to $100bn to cope with the effects of Lehman's demise, but the immediate worry was that American International Group (AIG) was now critically exposed. On the evening of Lehman's collapse, AIG's credit rating was downgraded, and it was forced to post $14.5bn in collateral. This time, the federal government decided that the insurer was indeed too big to fail; the holders of AIG's debt spanned a vast range of financial institutions. On 16 September the government took control of AIG in an $85bn deal that came at the price of its chief executive's resignation.

> Officials thought they were looking at a true financial apocalypse

There was a moment in September when Treasury and Federal Reserve officials thought they were looking at a true financial apocalypse: not just a freezing of credit, but a panicked withdrawal of most funds from the system. This worst case was averted. But credit markets were still dangerously frozen when Obama took office on 20 January 2009.

The crisis therefore took up the lion's share of his attention for the first six months, a time when key administration posts, especially in the Treasury Department, remained unfilled, and the new treasury secretary, former New York Federal Reserve Bank President Timothy Geithner, was criticised for being too close to Wall Street and inspiring insufficient confidence in the country at large. He did succeed, however, in launching some formidable programmes in a remarkably short period.

The 'Geithner plan', announced in March, expanded and repackaged Paulson's bank bailout, establishing a public–private investment programme involving $70–$100bn of new capital from the bailout funds, leveraged to buy up to $1 trillion of toxic assets from banks.

The second prong of the Obama administration's response was a huge stimulus package: $787bn in tax cuts, public infrastructure investment and aid to the states – whose dire fiscal situation and inability to borrow threatened a pro-cyclical contraction in spending at just the time when the opposite was required. Congressional Republicans opposed the package in lockstep, with particular opprobrium for the $300bn in state aid. An $819bn version of the stimulus package passed the House on 28 January without a single Republican vote. By 10 February Senate Democrats had managed to secure the votes of three moderate (then-)Republicans – Senators Arlen Specter of Pennsylvania (who later switched sides to the Democrats) and Olympia Snowe and Susan Collins of Maine, enough to close off a filibuster – by revising an initial $900bn measure down to something closer to the House bill. The administration's stated aim before the beginning of the stimulus battle had been a bipartisan solution to dire national economic need. In the face of Republican intransigence, that goal was modified to passing as large a measure as feasible as quickly as possible, with bipartisan coalitions where available on individual issues. The bill moved quickly through conference, and by 18 February Obama was in a position to sign into law a stimulus package of historic proportions, less than a month after taking office.

Obama, on his first overseas trip as president, travelled to Europe in April, including a stop in London for a meeting of G20 leaders. American strategy was to seek a coordinated fiscal stimulus on a global scale, and the United States found willing partners for this in Britain and China. More generally, however, the trip had a Canute-like effect on the American president's reputation: Obama's powers of persuasion were considerable but not magical. Continental Europeans, led by Germany's Chancellor Angela Merkel and France's President Nicolas Sarkozy, resisted the American's economic arguments for two stated reasons. First, they said that Europe's economies had already enacted considerable fiscal stimulus, including the 'automatic stabiliser' effects of more generous welfare states to continue paying the unemployed (which had the added political–psychological effect of making the crisis feel like less of an emergency than in the United States). Secondly, countries such as Greece and Italy were already heavily indebted to the point of near insolvency, and the euro system as a whole was not willing to risk future inflation even to fight immediate deflation. The restoration of Keynesian thinking and practices in the United States was not quite mirrored in some European countries.

Merkel and Sarkozy wanted Obama to concentrate on what they saw, not without reason, as the core cause of the crisis: inadequate regulation of reckless financial players. For reasons both political and philosophical, no American president would be likely to support the kind of global re-regulation that the Europeans preferred. Moreover, the Americans complained – again, with some justification – that focusing on this issue instead of fiscal demand management was akin to shoring up the foundations of a burning house. In June, however, the Obama administration did propose fairly extensive reforms. First, the Federal Reserve's powers would be expanded, with increased capital and liquidity requirements, to include supervision of all firms deemed large enough to affect the financial system as a whole. This was meant to bring investment banks and 'shadow' financial institutions back under an effective regulatory framework. In addition, the government would be empowered to take over non-bank financial institutions in time of crisis. Secondly, the proposals envision the creation of a Consumer Financial Protection Agency to improve transparency and curb predatory lending practices. Finally, a collection of smaller changes included a requirement that lenders retain a 5% stake in any loan assets that they might sell to third parties.

A liberal restoration?

'You never want a serious crisis to go to waste', said Rahm Emanuel, Obama's appointed chief of staff, a few weeks after the election. He went on to explain: 'things that we had postponed for too long, that were long-term, are now immediate and must be dealt with. This crisis provides the opportunity for us to do things that you could not do before.'

Obama's appeal to a post-partisan spirit of consensus certainly did not mean that his legislative ambitions were ideologically unfamiliar. The new president's February speech to a joint session of Congress offered a vision for America that sounded as radically ambitious as any presidential agenda since Lyndon Johnson's Great Society, if not FDR's New Deal. The great piece of liberal unfinished business was a guarantee of universal access to health care – a right enjoyed by the citizens of every rich democracy except the United States, and one that President Harry Truman had almost managed to enact at more or less the same time that Britain established its National Health Service. The American problem with health care was not just a matter of social equity but also of huge economic costs and inefficiencies. Not only were tens of millions without health insurance – and therefore unable to seek treatment except for the most dire of emergencies – but tens of millions more were afraid to move jobs, or terrified of losing their current job, because it was their only claim to health insurance. Those who had insurance coverage often found, at the worst possible time, that it was inadequate. Much of the American middle class was just one extended health crisis away from bankruptcy. And all of this came at a per-capita share of GDP that could be twice as much as for European states that delivered as good or better health results. Part of the problem was a patchwork insurance system employing hundreds of thousands of administrators to decide who could be covered and what claims could be paid. Part of Obama's proposed solution was a 'public option' – government insurance akin to the already existing Medicare for the aged – intended to compete with and thereby bring down the prices of private insurers.

The difficulty of getting the health reforms through Congress would be rivalled if not exceeded by opposition to the president's plans on energy and climate change. Again, the problem of energy security went back decades – at least to the OPEC embargo and price shocks of the Nixon years. The mind-concentrating crisis, however, came with the prospect of catastrophic 'externalities' from carbon-based energy – the impending significant rise of global mean temperatures. The conjunction with global recession gave the administration a window to include $18.5bn in the economic stimulus package for energy-efficiency measures and renewable-energy development. The more politically problematic part of the president's plan was the proposed establishment of a 'cap-and-trade' mechanism for industrial carbon-dioxide (CO_2) emissions, imposing a national limit on emissions by large entities (utilities, oil companies, industrial producers), providing fixed allowances for entities that emit more than 25,000 tonnes of CO_2 per year, and encouraging the development of a free market in emissions permits.

The bill to enact this scheme was introduced in the House of Representatives by Democrats Henry Waxman, chair of the Energy and Commerce Committee, and Edward Markey, chair of the Energy and Environment subcommittee. It passed the full House on 26 June 2009 by a narrow margin of seven votes. Its fate in the Senate was uncertain.

No one imagined that the Waxman–Markey legislation would, by itself, make a significant dent in, much less solve, the climate crisis. But the theory of its impact was twofold. First, America's first regulation of carbon emissions would send out market signals that there are future profits to be made in clean-energy and energy-efficiency technology. The resultant technological innovation should be further encouraged by – and should directly raise – expectations of more stringent regulations in the future. Secondly, successful international negotiations for a global regime would become possible only once leadership from the United States – by far the world's biggest per-capita emitter – was demonstrated.

Serious action on health care and climate change would constitute truly radical achievements, and there was some logic to the Rahm Emanuel hope that an economic crisis would put everyone in the appropriate frame of mind. The opposite was also plausible, of course: even if Obama could argue that his health-care, energy and education reforms were necessary investments bringing economic growth for the future, they carried large start-up costs for the present. Since the last year of the Clinton administration, the federal government had turned an $800m budget surplus into a projected $1.2tr annual deficit for the years 2009–12. A detailed *New York Times* analysis demonstrated what common sense suggested: most of this massive deficit was the result of Bush administration tax cuts, wars and other spending programmes, plus the sharp fall in tax revenues due to recession. The programmes that were Obama initiatives accounted for just $201bn of the $1.2tr deficit. The swing began years ago.

Whoever's fault the deficit was, however, Obama was now the man in possession, and if his policies were not the cause, they might constitute the absence of a solution. This remained a political challenge to the Obama economic agenda. In a *Wall Street Journal* poll conducted in June, 58% of respondents said that the president and Congress should worry more about keeping the deficit down, even if it meant taking longer for the economy to recover, rather than worrying more about boosting the economy.

In truth, with the country approaching a painful threshold of one-in-ten out of work, Obama's political fortunes were far more likely to rise or fall based on the number of employed or unemployed than on the size of the deficit. Likewise, in the current economic circumstances, jump-starting growth would have a more direct impact on bringing the budget closer to balance than any conceivable spending cuts, and by mid summer 2009 many economists had reached the conclusion that the economy needed more, not less, spending in the form of a second stimulus package. But the administration faced a catch-22 in Congress: uniform Republican opposition to a second stimulus could be assumed, and an important bloc of centrist-to-conservative Democrats was also wary. The Democratic leadership was, in a certain sense, victim of its own success. They had won a large majority of seats in the House and, with the Minnesota State Supreme Court verdict on a contested Senatorial election six months after the polls closed, a crucial 60 out of 100 seats in the upper house. In theory this gave the Democrats the necessary supermajority to cut off procedural filibusters which had been used ever more frequently in recent years to block legislation that had majority support. In practice, however, their encroachment on Republican territory meant a group of new members who were nervous about holding on in more conservative constituencies. The Congressional Democratic Party had become a broad church that was more difficult to organise.

> **Democrats in Congress were more difficult to organise**

The Republicans' opposite problem was far worse, however, because it set up a dynamic of self-marginalisation. The country as a whole was becoming more socially liberal on such issues as gay rights, and more demographically diverse – especially with the growth of a Hispanic population that George W. Bush and John McCain had tried to woo, but which their increasingly nativist party was alienating decisively. Having lost, in both Houses, the leavening presence of moderate Republicanism – a venerable and all-but-extinct tradition in New England, for example – the Republicans were left to defend right-wing bastions in the South and rural West. These were religious and extremely conservative constituencies with no plausible prospect of a successful challenge from the left, but every reason to worry about Republican primary challengers on the right if the incumbent strayed from party orthodoxy. This situation bred an astonishing uniformity of rejectionist views. The party uniformly rejected the administration's Keynesian framework for substituting government demand for the collapse of domestic demand. (The Republicans accepted Keynes' logic in one area only, regarding the stimulating effects of tax cuts.) The party uniformly rejected, as European-style 'socialised medicine', any serious efforts to rationalise costs or extend coverage to the many millions who could not afford health insurance. And Republicans were almost as united in rejecting the overwhelming evidence that climate change could be catastrophic, or the notion that there was something their government might do to combat it.

Torture: the limits of change

For the most part, Republican politicians also rejected the view that America had any reason to apologise for or correct the previous administration's equivocation about torture of terrorist suspects. This was a position that set the United States up for significant future discord. In his inaugural address, President Obama had disavowed his predecessor's policies in unusually sharp language, saying 'we reject as false the choice between our safety and our ideals'. Two days later, Obama signed three executive orders that constituted a comprehensive repudiation of the Bush policies on detention and interrogation. The detention centre at Guantanamo Bay was to be closed within a year; all CIA detention facilities abroad would be closed 'as expeditiously as possible'; and interrogation methods would henceforth be limited to those authorised by Army Field Manual 2-22.3. On 16 April, Obama ordered the release of four memoranda from the Office of Legal Counsel written between 2002 and 2005, which detailed the Bush administration's attempt to construct a legal framework to justify torture. For example, Abu Zubaydah was placed in stress positions, deprived of sleep for days, slammed against an artificial wall, confined in a box containing an unidentified insect (he was afraid of insects), and subjected to 'waterboarding' (simulated drowning). Zubaydah, who entered US custody with a wound sustained during his capture, was waterboarded 83 times. According to one of the released documents, an August 2002 memo by Assistant Attorney General Jay Bybee, the techniques were deemed not to inflict severe physical or mental pain or suffering, and therefore not to violate the prohibition of torture under US law (18 U.S.C. Section 2340A).

In releasing the torture memos, however, Obama knew that he was playing with fire, and he took efforts to contain the recriminations in general, and effects on CIA morale in particular. He stated that CIA operatives who in good faith had followed Justice Department guidance should not be subject to criminal prosecution (though there ensued some confusing back-and-forth about whether the decision on criminal investigation resided solely with the attorney general, Eric Holder). Obama also maintained that a 'truth commission', advocated by some congressional Democrats, would be divisive and counterproductive. Similar thinking contributed to Obama's decision to block the release of 44 photos showing abuse of prisoners in US custody; the administration argued that the risk of the photos fuelling violence against US troops outweighed the demands of transparency.

Other Obama administration decisions tended to support the obvious point that the Bush administration had faced truly difficult dilemmas. In a speech at the National Archives in mid May, Obama declared that military tribunals would continue to be used to try some terrorist suspects, and that the government would continue to hold some individuals 'to keep them from carrying out an act of war' – in essence, maintaining a system of preventive detention.

The Bush administration in its later years had already moved away from its most notorious post-11 September practices. What the Bush administration would not do, however, was to repudiate those practices, so the United States was unable to reap the benefits of restored moral credibility by drawing a line under what might be explained as panicky departures from its own values, traditions and commitment to the rule of law. This was the line that Obama was trying to draw, but he was challenged by an unreconstructed Republican right, with former Vice President Dick Cheney leading the charge. In a speech to the American Enterprise Institute on the same day as Obama's speech at the National Archives, Cheney claimed that the release of the torture memos was 'flatly contrary to the national security interest of the United States', and that to rule out 'enhanced interrogation methods' would be 'recklessness cloaked in righteousness, and would make the American people less safe'.

Cheney's case was trumpeted endlessly by the Fox television news network, which devoted hours to the proposition that 'enhanced interrogation' had foiled terrorist plots and saved American lives. Such broadcasting rarely addressed the on-the-ground testimony from officers and analysts in Iraq, who were convinced that the true stories of torture had fed recruits to the insurgency, and thus very palpably *cost* American lives. The United States was currently run by a party and a president subscribing to the view that torture was both wrong and harmful to national security. It could not be said, however, that there was a bipartisan American consensus against torture.

Foreign policy: changing the narrative

The Obama administration took over US foreign policy as self-declared 'realists'. For Democratic foreign-policy elites in general, this explicit new branding followed naturally from the general repudiation of the Bush administration's neoconservative idealism. During the election campaign Senator Obama had frequently cited the foreign policies of the first Bush administration as a model worthy of emulation, pointing specifically to the axis of realists among the elder Bush's advisers, including Brent Scowcroft, James Baker and Colin Powell.

The word 'realism', of course, can be no more than a slogan and an implicit claim that one's views are realistic and one's opponent's are not. It refers to a specific school and theory of international relations, but that theory transfers only partially and imperfectly to the realm of real politics and strategy. The word's fuzziness is demonstrated by the fact that it can be used to support a greater emphasis on hard military power or a greater emphasis on diplomatic accommodation. Obama's emphasis was the latter, and the approach opened him up to two general allegations: first, that his administration was ready to sacrifice basic values, as when Secretary of State Hillary Clinton travelled to China and subordinated the problem of human rights in favour of necessary strategic cooperation with Beijing; secondly, that his overtures to rivals such as Iran were naive because they were unlikely to be reciprocated.

> One word he never mentioned: terrorism

But Obama in his campaign rhetoric and the first six months of his presidency demonstrated a somewhat different aspect of foreign-policy realism that might best be described as 'psychological realism': an intuitive understanding that the United States was unable to impose its own moral and historical narrative on the rest of the world. Obama asserted the American narrative and was unabashedly proud of it; he was an authentic American nationalist. But he did not imagine that he could make progress with the rest of the world dependent on the world sharing that narrative.

This intuition came through most clearly in Obama's 4 June 2009 speech, delivered in Cairo and addressed to the Muslim communities of the world. Its most striking statement was one word that he never mentioned: terrorism. Obama described terrorism and denounced its evils, but he knew well enough that for many otherwise reachable Muslims, the 'war on terrorism' had become a toxic synonym for a war on Islam. The speech was also striking for the president's obvious determination to speak to his audience like adults. It was time, said Obama, to 'say in public what we say in private' and to 'act on what everyone knows to be true'. The Obama administration had started on that plan by demanding, without loopholes or equivocation or secret codicils, that Israel finally stop its expansion of settlements in the occupied territories.

This administration demand set up a surprisingly early confrontation with Israel's new coalition government under Likud Prime Minister Benjamin Netanyahu. The Israelis claimed that the US administration was reneging on an oral agreement that had been reached with the Bush White House, under which US opposition to settlement construction would allow for the exception of 'natural growth' to existing settlements. Obama officials said they knew nothing of such an unwritten understanding and, in any event, the unending spectacle of new Israeli buildings was terribly corrosive to Palestinian confidence that the Israelis would ever contemplate giving the territories back in a negotiated settlement.

The Israelis seemed genuinely puzzled that the new administration was taking the settlements issue so seriously. On 18 May, during his first visit to Washington after becoming prime minister, Netanyahu pressed his case that the far more urgent problem was dealing with Iran's nuclear programme, which Jerusalem considers an existential threat. Only once that threat was removed could Israel contemplate serious further concessions to the Palestinians for the purpose of a final peace agreement. At a joint press conference after their White House meeting, Obama contradicted his Israeli guest rather sharply: if there was a linkage between the two issues, the president argued, it went in the other direction; progress on the Israel–Palestine front was needed in order to enlist Arab support for a strategy of containing and pressuring Iran.

On the face of it, Obama, the supposed pragmatist, was taking a rather bold gamble by staking so much of his prestige on a settlement of both Israel–Palestine and the Iranian nuclear crisis. In particular, Obama had laid down a huge marker to his Arab audience, that he would be able to press Israel to stop building settlements in the occupied territories. It was not entirely clear how he would accomplish this. Moreover, the last two presidents waited until late in their terms before investing political capital in pursuit of a peace settlement. They calculated, presumably, that the status quo, however uneasy, was preferable to a costly failure to achieve what many observers thought was unachievable anyway. Obama appeared to have made a different calculation: that the status quo was on an incline to catastrophe.

Events, meanwhile, appeared to have wrong-footed the administration's diplomatic strategy for countering Iran's nuclear ambitions. On 20 March, the president had delivered videotaped New Year's greetings to the Iranian people and, conspicuously, to the clerical regime, which he addressed as the 'Islamic Republic of Iran'. This was seen as confirmation that he was not going to contest the legitimacy of a regime with which he hoped to negotiate a settlement of the nuclear issue. The problem for this strategy, however, became obvious a few days after the Cairo speech. It was precisely the regime's legitimacy that millions of Iranians themselves questioned in weeks of stirring, and brutally repressed, street demonstrations after President Mahmoud Ahmadinejad 'won' re-election by a clearly preposterous margin.

In the initial days of protests and repression, the US administration's response was decidedly low key. This posture was attacked by Republicans, including notably John McCain, for positioning the United States on the wrong side of history. The United States was certainly more cautious in its statements than many of its European allies, including France and the UK. But Obama clearly believed, as he stated repeatedly, that while America's ostentatious association with the protestors might make Americans feel better, it could discredit and undermine the protesters themselves, who had taken great care to adorn their rebellion with the symbols and rhetoric of Islamic piety and Iranian nationalism. As compelling as his logic might have been, however, Obama's diffidence was probably unsustainable, and as the repression became more brutal, he spoke out against it more forcefully. The administration still maintained that it was ready for engagement with the Iranian regime. Yet, aside from the moral costs of such engagement, there was real doubt whether the turmoil in Iran left its leaders in any position, or mood, to reciprocate. Netanyahu had returned to Israel from his White House meeting claiming that Obama had conceded an end-of-year deadline for engaging Iran, beyond which the United States would have to try something else. In reality, Obama had offered no deadline, but it was nonetheless true that many administration officials defended the policy of engagement as laying the groundwork, if engagement were to be shown to have failed, for organising a stronger international coalition to impose tougher sanctions.

One aspect of refreshing realism in the Obama administration's approach was the frank acknowledgment that it needed the help of foreign partners to ameliorate its myriad foreign troubles. The problem, of course, was that this was also an implicit acknowledgement of US weakness, and some foreign governments no doubt found this a happy state of affairs. For example, the administration had a theory, based on reasonable empirical assessment, that Iran had its own rational interests in a stable Iraq and an Afghanistan that was not under the sway of the Taliban, one of

Tehran's long-time enemies. Therefore (and this logic made the administration's envoy for Pakistan and Afghanistan, Richard Holbrooke, a strong advocate of engaging Iran), there should be room for an arrangement by which Tehran would help rather than hinder Obama's promised orderly withdrawal from Iraq, and support rather than stymie America's increased military effort in Afghanistan. What no one knew, however, was how the Iranian regime would balance these rational interests against its undoubted desire to see America suffer.

There is a similar problem with Russia. As soon as it came into office, the Obama administration made clear that it wanted a major 'reset' in America's relations with Russia, relations that had deteriorated badly over the course of six years. Whether this reset was possible was an open question: Russia under President and now Prime Minister Vladimir Putin had turned increasingly authoritarian; Moscow had been angered by US plans for missile-defence installations in Poland and the Czech Republic; and the continued expansion of NATO had led to a Russian siege mentality that culminated in the Russia–Georgia war in summer 2008.

> They drew on the moral authority of Ronald Reagan

The US administration accepted, however, that it had to set priorities and make choices. In a letter sent early in his presidency to the new Russian president, Dmitry Medvedev, Obama reportedly suggested that he would be willing to slow down or even scrap the East European missile-defence installations if Moscow was willing and able to deliver Tehran for a deal. Again, it was difficult to know whether Russia really saw it in its interest to help relieve the United States of the highly vexing Iranian problem.

In July Obama travelled to Moscow for a meeting reminiscent of Cold War summitry, signing, together with Medvedev, a framework commitment to negotiate another round of strategic nuclear-arms reductions by the end of 2009. By themselves these cuts would not significantly modify the world's strategic arsenals, but they were important to Moscow insofar as the Russians have some difficulty maintaining their present arsenal. And they were important to Obama for another change of narrative that he tried to effect. During the election campaign, Obama came out in favour of the new movement for nuclear abolition recently championed by a group of American elder statesmen, including Henry Kissinger, George Shultz, William Perry, Sam Nunn and Max Kampelman. They drew on the moral authority of Ronald Reagan, whose vision of a nuclear-free world, shared and apparently discussed seriously at several meetings with Mikhail Gorbachev, was derided at the time as utopian and naive. During his April 2009 trip to Europe, in a speech in Prague, Obama reiterated his support for the movement, adding that it was unlikely to happen in his lifetime. Some critics argue that the vision was not to be taken seriously, and would be seriously destabilising if anyone tried. But Obama's main reason for wanting to establish it as official American policy had to do with the fragility of the Nuclear Non-Proliferation Treaty (NPT). The original NPT was based on a grand bargain under which the recognised nuclear-weapons states promised to work towards eventual dismantlement of their own arsenals. Without this promise, the idea that the rest of the world would allow just five countries to enjoy a nuclear monopoly never made much sense. During the Cold War, the promise could be filed under business for the distant future, but the Cold War ended 20 years ago. In his Prague speech Obama said that the United States had not forgotten its promise.

Pragmatic radicalism

The radicalism of Obama's ambitions was somewhat hidden by the calm of his presentation. Under the slogan 'No Drama Obama', the candidate had presided over a campaign that was remarkably free of the *Sturm und Drang* and generally hysterical contentiousness of such operations.

The president set out to repeat this achievement in the White House. Message discipline across all of the agencies remained strong well into the administration's first summer. When the president-elect had asked his chief Democratic rival, Hillary Clinton, to serve as secretary of state, there was understandable speculation that she would complicate his foreign policy by bringing her own ego and her own agenda to the State Department. By most accounts, however, she has proven a loyal and effective cabinet officer, working well with his national security adviser, retired Marine General James Jones, and avoiding the frictions that have famously beset that inherently difficult institutional relationship.

Perhaps the most striking example of radicalism in conservative clothes was the role of Robert Gates, the Bush administration's second defence secretary who accepted Obama's request that he remain in the post. A quintessential establishment figure, with decades of service in the intelligence and defence communities of both Democratic and Republican presidents going back to Carter, Gates now took upon himself the daunting task of challenging the shibboleths of the military–industrial complex. In an April speech detailing his department's recommendation for the 2010 budget, Gates argued that 'these past few years have revealed underlying flaws in the priorities, cultural preferences, and reward structures of America's defense establishment', and proposed a shifting of resources away from conventional war fighting and towards current priorities. 'This is a reform budget', Gates said, 'reflecting lessons learned in Iraq and Afghanistan … [presenting] one of those rare chances to match virtue to necessity; to critically and ruthlessly separate appetites from real requirements.' The recommendation proposed a $2bn increase in intelligence, surveillance and reconnaissance capabilities, including maintaining a total of 50 unmanned *Predator* drones; a $500m increase for helicopters; $500m more for partnerships with foreign militaries; and a range of equipment to aid mobility and flexibility of US forces. The recommendation called for an increase in purchases of the F-35 fighter, but for production of the expensive F-22 to be ended. Gates also proposed a $1.4bn cut in the missile-defence budget, called for the number of aircraft carriers to be cut from 11 to 10, and said that the $26bn Transformational Satellite (TSAT) programme would be terminated.

> Gates proposed a cut in the missile-defence budget

The radical pragmatism of this approach was to recognise the relevance of the fact that America spends nearly as much on defence as the rest of the world combined. Gates argued that 'every dollar spent … to "run up the score" in a capability where the United States is already dominant [is] a dollar not available to take care of our people … [and] win the wars we are in'. He also emphasised that the proposed reforms would occur in the context of broad spending cuts necessitated by the economic crisis.

Gates was trying to take on the military–industrial habits and interests that President Dwight D. Eisenhower decried when the secretary of defense was a teenager. This must say something about the prospects of success. As a general proposition, the problems this administration faced were dismayingly familiar. War in Afghanistan, a radical and hostile Iran, economic crisis, energy insecurity (and its mutation into climate catastrophe) – these were the same or the direct descendents of crises that destroyed the presidency of Jimmy Carter. The hopes of a changed America, for which Barack Obama was the emblem, were real, but the dangers of failure were real as well.

Canada: Conservatives' Tenuous Hold

Though Canada continued to be led by a Conservative minority government under Prime Minister Stephen Harper, events in autumn 2008 underlined the fragility of his party's hold on power. After meeting with the leaders of the opposition Liberal Party, New Democratic Party (NDP) and Bloc Québécois in early September 2008, Harper determined that there was not sufficient common ground for the Conservative agenda to be passed through the scheduled autumn session of Parliament. He therefore called a federal election for 14 October 2008.

The timing of the election coincided with national polls indicating that the Conservatives were within striking distance of a majority in parliament. The likelihood of a majority was bolstered by the inability of Canada's official opposition party, the Liberal Party led by Stéphane Dion, to connect with Canadian voters. Central to the party's platform was its 'Green Shift' plan that promised to lower greenhouse-gas emissions through the implementation of a carbon tax. Though the Liberals maintained that this would reap both environmental and economic benefits, the plan failed to resonate with voters and proved vulnerable to Conservative attacks that it was simply a tax hike.

In the election, the Conservative Party failed to achieve the majority it was seeking, due partly to its failure to secure seats it expected to win in Quebec. In spite of earlier attempts to curry favour in the province by, for example, recognising Quebeckers as a 'nation' within Canada, the party's chances there were doomed by, among other issues, proposed government cuts to the arts. In total, the Conservatives took 143 ridings (districts) across Canada, a gain of 16 seats, while Liberal Party candidates were elected in 77 ridings, a loss of 18 seats. The Bloc Québécois and NDP won 49 and 37 seats respectively.

The political drama did not cease with the results of the election. In late November, the Conservative Party announced in a fiscal update that it planned to revoke civil servants' right to strike for three years; in addition, it proposed eliminating subsidies given to opposition parties based on the number of votes received in elections. The announcement sparked outrage among the Liberals, NDP and Bloc Québécois, not just because of the strike ban and subsidy cuts but also because the update offered little in the way of economic stimulus to help Canada's ailing economy. In response, Dion sent a formal letter to Governor General Michaëlle Jean on 1 December announcing that Canada's three opposition parties had lost confidence in the Conservative government and intended to form a coalition government to take its place.

Harper responded to the threat by asking the governor general to prorogue Parliament until 26 January 2009 in an effort to avoid a confidence motion scheduled for 8 December 2008, which would likely have resulted in the fall of the Conservative government. The governor general approved the prime minister's request, despite accusations from the opposition that prorogation represented an abuse of executive power without precedent in the history of the Canadian parliament. Cracks in the opposition coalition began to emerge soon after the governor general's decision, reflecting in part a deeply divided Canadian public on the legitimacy of an unelected coalition government.

Succumbing to pressure from within his own party, Dion resigned as leader of the Liberal Party on 8 December 2008. This paved the way for Michael Ignatieff, then deputy leader of the party, to replace him. The move effectively killed the proposed coalition government; Ignatieff and other key members of the Liberal Party had reportedly turned against the idea. Though the prospects of a coalition government subsided, the continuation of minority government in the country meant there was a chance another federal election could be held in the near future if the Liberal Party was able to make significant gains in its approval rating under new its leader.

Economy under stress

The Canadian economy went into recession in the fourth quarter of 2008. In January 2009, the government released its 2009 budget, entitled 'Canada's Economic Action Plan'. The budget offered a stimulus package of nearly C$40 billion through 2009 and 2010, while also fulfilling the country's G20 pledge to join other nations in providing stimulus funds of 2% of GDP to bolster domestic demand. The package aimed to improve access to financing and to strengthen Canada's financial system; stimulate housing construction; offer financial support to Canadians affected by the recession; provide money for infrastructure; and provide financial support to businesses and communities.

Canada's automobile industry, which is closely integrated with that of the United States, was particularly affected by the recession. On 20 December 2008, Prime Minister Harper and Ontario Premier Dalton McGuinty announced that the federal government and government of Ontario would

provide General Motors and Chrysler with up to C$4bn in short-term repay-
able loans to assist the struggling industry. They later took an equity stake
in General Motors as part of a US government rescue.

The Conservatives often pointed out that Canada was one of the last countries to be affected by the global economic downturn, and the government
remained confident that it would be among the first to recover. However, just
weeks after the budget was announced, Parliamentary Budget Officer Kevin
Page informed the House of Commons Finance Committee that the recession would be 'sharper' than reported in the budget. While the 2009 budget
estimated that Canada would incur budget deficits of C$34bn in 2009/10 and
C$30bn in 2010/11, the Office of the Parliamentary Budget Officer's revised
estimates showed Canada incurring a C$38bn deficit in 2009/10 and one of
C$35bn in 2010/11 – and that Canada would lose more than 380,000 jobs in
the first half of 2009.

In the international arena, Canada's primary goals at the G20 summit
in London were to promote anti-protectionist trade measures and reform
global financial markets. The pledges made by G20 leaders not to raise new
trade barriers for a period of 12 months and to strengthen supervision and
regulation of the global financial markets were therefore viewed as victories
for Canada.

The 'Canada First' defence policy

The Canadian government's strategic vision for defence was outlined in its
Canada First Defence Strategy, published in May 2008. The strategy stated
that the Canadian Forces must be an active and able partner in the shared
defence of North America, as well as a key contributor to international security. Central to achieving this strategic vision was allocation of a sufficient
level of funding to the country's armed forces.

To this end, the strategy promised stable funding for the armed forces for
20 years, with defence spending increasing by 2% annually from FY2011/12.
The defence budget would increase from C$18.3bn in FY2008/09 (up from
C$16.9bn in the previous year) to over C$30bn in 2027/28.

Specific goals of the strategy included enhancing the armed forces' ability
to rapidly deploy and sustain missions abroad, as well as modernising defence
infrastructure and core equipment. To achieve this, the strategy called for an
increase in military personnel from current levels of 65,000 regular forces and
26,000 reserves to 70,000 regular forces and 30,000 reserves. In addition, it
planned for the acquisition of 17 C-130J *Hercules* transport aircraft, 16 CH-47-F

Chinook helicopters, 2,300 trucks and up to 100 *Leopard* II tanks. The government also recently acquired four C-17 *Globemaster* strategic-lift aircraft.

On the domestic front, the government envisioned military forces that could respond effectively to a terrorist attack; help provide security and support for major international events held in Canada, such as the 2010 Winter Olympics to be held in Vancouver; and support civilian authorities during a crisis, including natural disasters.

Securing Canada's Arctic region has become an increasingly important security objective of the Canadian government. As Arctic ice continues to melt, the possibility of an ice-free Arctic, which would make the region accessible to shipping vessels, grows. This situation would make Canada's northern sea routes more vulnerable to security and environmental threats. In addition, several Arctic nations, including Russia, the United States, Norway and Denmark, are vying for control over potentially lucrative northern shipping routes and untapped oil and gas resources.

In response, Canada has actively tried to assert its sovereignty in its northern territory. To this end, the government moved ahead with plans to procure up to eight Arctic offshore-patrol vessels to begin operations in 2013; to begin building a deep-water port in Nanisivik in 2010; to construct an Arctic training centre; and to expand the country's Arctic Ranger force from 4,300 to 5,000 by FY2011/12.

In August 2008, Harper announced that Canada would require all ships in Canadian waters to report their presence, and expanded the amount of Arctic Ocean the country planned to patrol to enforce Canadian environmental regulations from 100 to 200nm off shore. The move could lead to political friction between Canada and other Arctic nations, particularly over the right of navigation through the Northwest Passage. While all other Arctic nations claim the Northwest Passage is an international strait that can be used freely by all vessels, Canada contends that it has sole jurisdiction over the waterway.

In January 2009, the United States released an Arctic-policy document that failed to recognise Canada's sovereignty claim in the region and officially declared the Northwest Passage an international strait. The EU's own Arctic-policy document, released just weeks before the United States', also challenged Canada's sovereignty in the Arctic. Given the US and EU policy positions, and Russia's continued aggressive pursuit of Arctic territory, Canada will likely face significant political obstacles in its effort to assert its sovereignty in the region.

Afghanistan and NATO

On the international front, Afghanistan remained the Canadian government's primary focus. Canadian forces have been involved in Afghanistan since 2002 and remained there as part of the UN-authorised, NATO-led International Security Assistance Force. The majority of Canada's 2,800 military personnel deployed in the country at mid 2009 were based in the southern city of Kandahar, one of the most volatile regions in Afghanistan.

Canada's strategic vision to help allied forces counter the insurgency in Afghanistan was rooted in the Canadian government's 'whole of government' approach to stabilising failed and failing states. This approach attempted to integrate Canada's military and civilian resources to further diplomatic, security and development initiatives in conflict-affected areas. In Afghanistan, Canada actively tried to fulfil this vision, contributing more than C$1bn in aid, and sending more than 100 diplomats to complement Canadian forces in the country.

Progress was, however, difficult to sustain. The Canadian government continued to highlight better infrastructure, improved access to health care and education, progress in developing the Afghan army, and improvements made in securing the Afghan–Pakistani border as signs of improving stability in Kandahar. Nonetheless, increasing violence and a strengthening insurgency in the region continued to overshadow modest gains made in stability and governing capacity.

Over the year to mid 2009, Canada's mounting costs both in terms of causalities and resources, combined with NATO's failure to stabilise Afghanistan, made it increasingly difficult for the Conservatives to persuade the Canadian public that the mission in Afghanistan was worthwhile. Opinion polls conducted by the *Toronto Mail* and Angus Reid consistently showed that just over half of respondents believed that Canada should not extend its mission in Afghanistan beyond 2011. The same polling data also revealed that nearly half of respondents felt the Afghan government would be unable to meet its security needs after 2011 in the absence of international assistance. In addition, roughly two-thirds of Canadians believed that Canada was 'shouldering too much of the burden' of NATO's mission in Afghanistan.

Slow progress, high costs and waning domestic support forced the government to maintain its pledge to end Canada's combat mission in Afghanistan in 2011—a timeframe to which Liberal leader Ignatieff was also committed. Harper said, however, that the government might propose maintaining some form of Canadian presence in Afghanistan after 2011 that would focus primarily on reconstruction and development. It was reported that this force might include helicopters, police and army trainers, a Provincial Reconstruction Team and CF-18 fighter aircraft.

The government sought to communicate what could reasonably be expected from the mission in Afghanistan. In interviews in February and March 2009, Harper declared that any expectation that NATO forces could completely defeat the insurgency and establish a modern liberal democracy in Afghanistan was unrealistic. Instead, he defined success in Afghanistan as the establishment of a central government with the capability to maintain its own security. Canada also said in March 2009 that it would consider talks with moderate Taliban insurgents, but only those who had renounced the use of violence. The announcement marked a stark shift in the government's position, as it had previously been unwilling to consider reaching out to any element of the Taliban.

Canada's primary objective for the NATO summit in April 2009 was to emphasise the importance of NATO's mission in Afghanistan. While the United States' revised strategy and commitment to increase resources for NATO's mission in Afghanistan was welcomed by the Canadian government, Canada and the United States failed to persuade key European leaders significantly to boost their contributions to the mission. The Canadian government also used the summit to condemn a proposed law by the Afghan government that would have severely undermined women's rights. Canada's broader position had been underlined at the Munich Security Conference in February 2009, where Defence Minister Peter MacKay stressed the need to reform the Alliance to meet complex security challenges. To succeed in Afghanistan and elsewhere, greater 'unity of effort' was required. The Alliance would have to develop a policy framework that ensured soldiers, diplomats, aid workers and decision-makers undertaking missions in fragile states and elsewhere worked together as a comprehensive, single unit.

Adapting to a new US political landscape

The actions and policies of the United States – Canada's most important trading partner and strategic ally – have always received close scrutiny from its northern neighbour. Canada's Conservative government had to quickly adapt to the ideological differences between itself and new US President Barack Obama on matters of security, the economy and the environment.

On security matters, the Canadian government welcomed Obama's increased focus on Afghanistan and call to renew alliances. On the president's first trip to Canada in February 2009, Obama and Harper agreed to work closely on key international security issues, including Afghanistan, but highlighted their intention to coordinate on security matters in the Americas as well.

On border security, the president maintained many of the security regulations enacted by his predecessor, including a travel regulation that, from June 2009, required anyone entering the United States from Canada to carry a passport or other travel documents recognised by the US government. Many Canadian and US firms had hoped the new administration would ease travel regulations implemented after 11 September 2001 that make cross-border trade more cumbersome.

Also high on the agenda of Obama's first visit to Canada were key environmental and economic issues facing both countries. Given the highly integrated nature of the Canadian and US economies, the economic downturn in the United States had a considerable impact on its northern neighbour. A primary concern both of Canada's private sector and government was that the United States would resort to protectionist policies to address the economic crisis. Obama's statement during the primary elections that he intended to renegotiate the North American Free Trade Agreement (NAFTA) after becoming president was not well received in Canada and led many to question Obama's stance on free trade.

Though he backed away from his proposition to renegotiate NAFTA later in the election campaign, Obama's support of the 'Buy American' clause included in the American Recovery and Reinvestment Act of 2009 renewed concerns that the United States was shifting to protectionist measures to address its economic woes. The clause stated that only American iron, steel and manufactured goods might be used in construction projects funded by the stimulus bill. Once again, however, Obama attempted to quell Canada's (and other nations') concerns. In an interview with the Canadian media in February 2009, he reiterated that the United States intended to fulfil its obligations under World Trade Organisation and NAFTA agreements. He said he was fully aware of the importance of the Canada–US trade relationship and recognised that it was not in the interest of either country to pursue policies that would serve to contract trade between them.

In the area of energy and the environment, Canada had to adjust to the likelihood of a United States much more active on environmental issues than during the George W. Bush administration. Less than a day after Obama's electoral victory, the Canadian government called for a joint US–Canada climate-change pact. During Obama's visit to Canada, the two leaders agreed to establish a senior-level US–Canada Clean Energy Dialogue that could help facilitate such an agreement.

According to Environment Minister Jim Prentice, Canada was likely to seek a common cap-and-trade system with the United States, as well as shared fuel-efficiency and low-carbon-fuel standards. The move was prompted by the Canadian government's desire to protect not only the environment but also the economy. Competitiveness concerns have been raised on both sides of the border with respect to how environmental regulations might affect the cost of exports should either government unilaterally pursue a domestic strategy to address climate change.

Another major issue between Canada and the United States was Obama's campaign pledge to wean the United States off 'dirty oil' in favour of cleaner energy sources. The pledge was viewed in Canada as a potential threat to Alberta's lucrative oil sands, which require a more carbon-intensive refining process than conventional oil but also represent a major source of US oil imports. Since becoming president, however, Obama has been careful not to single out the oil sands for criticism over their large carbon footprint, nor has he expressed any intention to restrict US oil imports from Alberta. Rather, during his first visit to Canada, Obama stressed the need to pursue technologies that would mitigate the carbon footprint of the oil sands and other carbon-intensive sources of energy, such as coal, and that would allow countries to use fossil fuels in a more environmentally sustainable manner.

Looking ahead

Canada's focus looked likely to continue to be fixed on the economy over the next year. The government's fate looked to hinge on whether its policy decisions, particularly its stimulus package, were perceived by the Canadian public as steering the country toward economic recovery. The Conservatives had the added challenge of addressing the crisis as a minority government and would have to contend with a revitalised Liberal Party that had found a more capable leader in Ignatieff. Meanwhile, escalating violence in Afghanistan and NATO's slow progress securing that country looked to contribute to growing unrest regarding Canada's mission there.

© IISS

MEXICO

Havana THE BAHAMAS

Mexico City

CUBA DOMINICAN
REPUBLIC
BELIZE JAMAICA HAITI Santo Domingo
GUATEMALA Belmopan Kingston Port-au-
Guatemala City Tegucigalpa Prince
EL SALVADOR HONDURAS
San Salvador NICARAGUA TRINIDAD &
Managua COSTA RICA TOBAGO
San Jose Panama Caracas
PANAMA City VENEZUELA Georgetown
Paramaribo
Bogotá Cayenne
GUYANA SURINAM FRENCH GUYANA
COLOMBIA

Quito
ECUADOR

PERU BRAZIL

Lima

La Paz Brasília

BOLIVIA

PARAGUAY
Asunción

CHILE

URUGUAY
Santiago Buenos Aires Montevideo

ARGENTINA

Atlantic Ocean

Pacific Ocean

Falkland Islands (UK)

South Georgia (UK)

■ Capital Borders

0 1,000m

0 1,500km

Chapter 4

Latin America

In recent years Venezuelan President Hugo Chávez's radical populism, accented with fiery anti-US rhetoric, has dominated the discourse of Latin America's leftward shift. Over the past year, however, while the region continued down a leftist path, many of its rising leaders sought to emulate Brazilian President Luiz Inácio 'Lula' da Silva's 'third way', characterised by more conciliatory centre-left policies and economic stability, rather than Chávez's more petulant and ideological approach.

Two leftist leaders elected over the past year indicated they would govern as progressive moderates, emphasising reconciliation in their countries while maintaining a focus on poverty alleviation. In Paraguay, the election of a leftist former bishop, Fernando Lugo, ended 61 years of conservative one-party rule, marking the country's first peaceful, democratic transition since independence in 1811. In March 2009 El Salvador became the region's latest country to elect a leftist, with former television journalist Mauricio Funes of the Farabundo Marti Liberation Front (FMLN) narrowly prevailing with 51% of the vote. Marxist guerrillas of the FMLN had fought the US-backed Salvadoran government from 1980 to 1992, when a UN-brokered peace agreement ended the civil war and facilitated the FMLN's transition into a non-violent political party. Funes's election ended 20 years of rule by the right-wing National Republican Alliance (ARENA).

A further example was Chilean President Michelle Bachelet, a socialist elected in 2006 who had been briefly imprisoned by the government of US-backed dictator Augusto Pinochet. She has approached truth and reconciliation with respect to Chile's authoritarian past quietly but decisively. Governing non-ideologically and independently, she enjoyed a 67% approval rating in mid 2009. Bachelet is not eligible for re-election in 2010 under Chile's constitution, and early opinion polls in May 2009 gave centre-right candidate Sebastián Piñera a slight edge over Eduardo Frei Ruiz-Tagle of Bachelet's centre-left Agreement of Parties for Democracy (CPD).

The election of US President Barack Obama opened up opportunities for further cooperation between the United States and Latin American governments. Obama sought to repair relations with southern neighbours disaffected by the perceived complacency and neglect of the Bush admin-istration. By loosening embargo restrictions on Cuba and approaching involvement in Mexico's drug war with a spirit of respect and cooperation, the incoming US president shifted the tone of US–Latin American relations.

Latin America nevertheless faced hard times as a result of the economic crisis originating in the United States. Leftist presidents have raised high expectations among the poor, yet poverty-reduction programmes through-out the region were subject to increasing economic constraints. As resources continue to grow scarcer, pressures will mount for governments to step up efforts to aid those affected by the economic downturn, increasing the likeli-hood of discontent.

Mexico: Drug-war Escalation

Mexican President Felipe Calderón has embarked on the most aggressive counter-drug campaign in Mexican history. After winning a bitterly divisive election in 2006 by less than a percentage point, he launched the anti-narcotics effort in a bid to unite the country and to demonstrate his ability to govern.

Mexico's drug gangs had gained strength after enforcement efforts limited Caribbean trafficking routes in the 1980s and Colombia dismantled the Cali and Medellín cartels in the 1990s. Today 90% of the cocaine in US markets travels through Mexico, contributing to the estimated $14 billion that Mexican drug traffickers reap in annual profits. Calderón deployed 45,000 troops throughout the country, scoring major victories against cartels and disrupting their operations. Mexican troops seized a record 52,000 weapons in the past two years, and in 2008 they confiscated $61 million in illicit proceeds, 20 tonnes of cocaine, and 1,650 tonnes of marijuana. Tens of thousands of traffickers, including several high-level cartel members, have been arrested, causing cartels to splinter into six main groups. US officials reported that Mexican efforts contributed to a decline in both the supply and purity of cocaine in US markets (see Strategic Geography, p. XVIII).

Yet while Calderón's offensive was popular among Mexicans, an unprecedented wave of violence was unleashed as drug gangs battled both the security forces and one another in their quest to control vital trafficking routes and markets. Violence has steadily escalated, with drug-related killings rising from approximately 1,500 in 2006 to 2,700 in 2007 and 6,200 in 2008. Murders have also become progressively more brutal, marked by beheadings and torture. While officials maintained that 90% of those killed were involved in the drug trade, the Mexican public was increasingly affected by the surge in violence. For instance, in September 2008 eight people were killed and 100 injured during a grenade attack on an Independence Day celebration. Targeting of journalists increased, extortion of businesses and schools grew, and kidnappings rose by 8% in 2008. According to government statistics, 65 people are kidnapped on average per month, but independent organisations said most kidnappings go unreported and the real total may approach 500 a month. Polls showed a majority of Mexicans felt the government was losing its war against drug-related violence, and popular discontent over insecurity came to a boiling point after the kidnapped 14-year-old son of a prominent businessman was killed even after his ransom was paid. Marches were held on 30 August 2008 across the country, protesting against the government's inability to protect its populace, with 150,000 people gathering in Mexico City's Zócalo Square. The protest brought out thousands of members of the middle class, which has been particularly affected by the kidnapping epidemic. The arrest of a federal agent involved in the boy's kidnapping highlighted the fact that Mexicans could not rely on the security forces for protection.

Corrupt and unreliable law-enforcement agencies have proven to be one of Calderón's primary stumbling blocks in combating gangs. According to Transparency Mexico, the Mexican arm of the non-governmental organisation (NGO) Transparency International, $2bn is spent on bribes annually, and corrupt officers are frequently on the payroll of cartels. In an effort to stop this, Calderón removed all 284 federal police chiefs in June 2007. A year later, the administration launched *Operation Clean House*, which led to the arrests of 25 high-ranking officials including the former drug czar, Mexico's police liaison to Interpol, and a member of the presidential guard.

Even where police forces are not corrupt, they have often been ineffective. After assessing 56,000 of the country's 375,000 local and state officers, the government announced that over half failed to meet minimum standards. Most Mexicans say they do not report crimes because the police are either involved or inept. In addition to retraining local forces, the Mexican government has been attempting to end impunity through a massive overhaul of its justice system. Yet judicial reforms legislated in June 2008 were to be implemented over the next eight years, providing little short-term relief. Even when criminals have been sentenced, many continued to run their operations from inside prison. This phenomenon led Calderón to extradite a record 95 drug traffickers to the United States in 2008.

> "Hundreds of Mexicans blockaded bridges to the US"

Accustomed to operating with impunity, often in collusion with corrupt officials, drug cartels have visited brutal reprisals on police officers who crack down on organised crime as well as those who work for rival gangs. Approximately 10% of the homicide victims in Mexico are police officers, and other officers are frequently involved. One was arrested, for example, along with four Sinaloa cartel members for the May 2008 assassination of National Police Chief Edgar Millán Gómez. By attacking police forces, cartels have sought to gain control over entire towns. Drug gangs forced the 20-member police force in Villa Ahumada to resign after killing two consecutive police chiefs and other officers. In Ciudad Juárez, cartels delivered on promises to kill an officer every 48 hours until the police chief stepped down.

Faced with such assaults on local and state police forces, Calderón sent in the army to wrest control from drug traffickers and stem the flow of violence. The military, however, was not an adequate long-term solution, as it was ill equipped to perform the policing and intelligence operations necessary to root out drug traffickers. Additionally, the army faced accusations of human-rights abuses, which jumped from 182 in 2006 to 1,230 in 2008, according to the government's National Human Rights Commission. In July 2008 criticism of the security forces' heavy-handed tactics swelled as videos were leaked to the press showing police torturing suspects under the direction of an instructor from a US private security firm. In February 2009, hundreds of Mexicans blockaded bridges to the United States, demanding the army leave their border towns and accusing soldiers of abuses. Officials, however, denounced the protests, insisting that drug gangs had staged them. Although human-rights units have been set up in the army, prosecutors' office and police forces, NGOs argued that the units were ineffective because they lacked investigative powers. Calderón acknowledged that deployment of the army was an imperfect solution, but cast the move as a temporary one that would end when local forces were purged of corruption and the threat from drug traffickers was reduced to a more manageable level. The Mexican army also suffered from desertions, with 18,000 troops abandoning their jobs in 2008. Some drug gangs, such as the Zetas, the paramilitary arm of the Gulf cartel, were formed and recruited from deserters. However, until Mexico was to build an effective national police force, the army appeared to be Calderón's only option.

To assist Mexico in its counter-narcotics efforts, in October 2007 US President George W. Bush launched Plan Mérida, a $1.4bn counter-drug assistance programme for Mexico and Central America. Plan Mérida was originally crafted with Calderón to increase US–Mexican security coop-eration in the spirit of 'shared responsibility'. This spirit of partnership, however, was dampened when the US Congress attempted to place human-rights conditions (including performance evaluations and civil trials for military personnel) on the aid. Legislators in Mexico considered these to be violations of Mexican sovereignty. After a delegation of 11 US lawmakers visited Mexico in June, Congress loosened the restrictions and approved $400m for training and equipment. While the first disbursement of $197m was announced in December 2008, with another $99m following the next month, the Calderón administration complained of slow delivery of aid. By April 2009, only two projects were under way with a mere $7m spent. Furthermore, it remained unclear what kind of impact *Plan Mérida* assistance would have, given its relatively small size compared to the $6.5bn Calderón had dedicated to the drug war since taking office.

Meanwhile, spillover from Mexico's battle against the cartels drew increased public attention in the United States. Although violence in the United States has not been as graphic or widespread, border states have been plagued by drug-related home invasions, kidnappings and killings. Phoenix, Arizona suffered over 360 kidnappings in 2008. Some 755 people connected with the Sinaloa cartel have been arrested in the United States. The US Justice Department's 2009 National Drug Threat Assessment reported that Mexican drug gangs had a presence in at least 230 US cities, controlled the majority of the US drug market, and were increasingly working with US-based gangs.

The report declared Mexican drug-trafficking organisations the 'greatest organized crime threat to the United States'.

Facing mounting domestic concern, the Obama administration dedicated high-level attention to Mexico's drug war. On a visit in March 2009, Secretary of State Hillary Clinton, in a marked change in tone for the US government, took responsibility for US failures in the war on drugs, acknowledging that US drug demand and weapons trafficking had fuelled violence in Mexico. She urged closer cooperation. Seeking a tone of partnership, Clinton smoothed over Mexican outrage concerning recent assessments by US intelligence officials that Mexico was in danger of becoming a failed state. In April US Homeland Security Secretary Janet Napolitano and Attorney General Eric Holder met Mexican officials to outline joint strategies to tackle border issues of drug smuggling, gun running and immigration. Firearms bought in the United States, including assault rifles that are illegal south of the border, accounted for 95% of drug-related deaths in Mexico. Obama set in motion a multi-agency border plan to reduce drugs and violence in border states and limit the outflow of money and weapons to Mexico. American cooperative overtures and a willingness to address the issue of demand suggested a significant departure from the drug policy of past administrations.

While cartel-related violence pushed north of the border, fallout from the United States' financial crisis drifted south. The Mexican economy, which depended on the US to buy 80% of exports, was particularly vulnerable to the fall in American demand. GDP growth sank to 1.5% for 2008, and the economy was expected to contract in 2009. Declining oil prices diminished government revenue, a third of which came from oil sales. Remittances, Mexico's second-largest source of income after oil, fell 3.6% in 2008 and were expected to decline further as fewer Mexicans ventured north for employment in an increasingly tight US job market. Domestic unemployment was also rising, and the Central Bank estimated 340,000 jobs would be lost in 2009. Seeking to limit the impact of the US economic crisis, Calderón introduced a range of measures to stimulate the economy, boosting spending programmes, infrastructure investment and tax breaks and providing welfare benefits and temporary work to the unemployed.

Economic woes, in combination with rising violence, reduced Calderón's approval ratings from around 60% to the mid 50s. There was concern that the economic downturn could feed drug violence as unemployed young men joined drug gangs. As the July 2009 midterm elections approached, the faltering economy seemed likely to dim prospects for Calderón's National Action Party (PAN). PAN was ranked second in polls behind the Institutional Revolutionary Party (PRI), which had governed Mexico for 71 years until ousted by PAN in 2000. While the PAN allied itself with the PRI in Congress to push through some of Calderón's reforms, cooperation may decrease ahead of the 2011 presidential campaign. The Democratic Revolution Party (PRD), whose candidate Andrés Manuel López Obrador narrowly lost to Calderón in 2006, remained divided between those wishing to work with the administration and a faction insisting that López Obrador was the legitimate president. The PRD showed itself capable of disrupting Calderón's agenda. When the president attempted to push an energy reform bill through Congress in 2008, López Obrador staged street protests and PRD legislators in the lower house barricaded the podium while their counterparts in the Senate went on hunger strikes. The PRD forced Congress to debate the bill for months, and what eventually passed was a much-diluted version of Calderón's original proposal.

The long-term success of the Calderón administration, however, depended on whether it could turn the tide of drug violence in Mexico. Officials in both Mexico and the United States maintained that rising violence was a symptom of the success the country had had in disrupting trafficking and sharpening competition among gangs for remaining routes and markets. Nevertheless, as Colombia's success against the Medellín and Cali cartels has shown, neutralising large-scale gangs can cause trafficking operations to fragment rather than disappear. Furthermore, success in Mexico could shift the burden elsewhere. Caribbean countries have already been asking to be included in *Plan Mérida*, and Central American countries have been pressing Washington to expand drug-related assistance.

Colombia: FARC Down but not Out

Elected by a war-weary populace attracted to his hardline stance against Colombia's leftist guerrillas, Alvaro Uribe launched the largest military offensive in the country's history against the Revolutionary Armed Forces of Colombia (FARC). Uribe drove the rebels out of Colombia's cities, forcing them to retreat to strongholds in the country's southern jungles. Homicides dropped by over 40% and kidnappings by over 80%, making the president spectacularly popular. Uribe's efforts against FARC continued to bear fruit, as the guerrillas suffered a series of setbacks in 2008.

In March 2008, FARC lost three of its seven-member secretariat when a Colombian military raid into Ecuador killed second-in-command Raúl Reyes, Iván Ríos was killed by his bodyguard, and 78-year-old FARC leader Manuel Marulanda died of a heart attack. Plagued by deaths, captures and an unprecedented 3,000 desertions in 2008, the number of FARC personnel dropped from a reported high of 20,000 to 8,000. There was also evidence of a breakdown in communications between 'fronts' or cells, with eight fronts disappearing altogether. Furthermore, intelligence from deserters and captured computer files gave the government valuable insights into the group's operations and strategy.

> **The dramatic rescue boosted Uribe's popularity**

On 2 July 2008 FARC suffered an embarrassing setback when the Colombian military's *Operation Checkmate* tricked guerrillas into handing over 15 high-level hostages, including former presidential candidate Ingrid Betancourt and three US military contractors. The guerrillas thus lost their most valuable source of leverage in their quest to secure an agreement for a demilitarised zone from which to negotiate exchanging political hostages for 500 FARC fighters. The dramatic rescue boosted Uribe's approval rating from 76% to 85%. On 20 July, millions throughout Colombia marched in Independence Day protests demanding that FARC release the estimated 700 remaining hostages. In October former Congressman Oscar Lizcano escaped, further weakening FARC's exchange prospects.

The guerrillas' new leader, Alfonso Cano, reconfigured the group's strategy with 'Plan Rebirth'. In a January 2009 communiqué, Cano said that 'in 2009 we must force ourselves to retake the initiative, in the political as well as the military fields'. The following month FARC unilaterally released six more high-level hostages, signalling a dramatic shift away from holding hostages for exchange. The move was undoubtedly designed to improve FARC's political capital with Colombians and the international community. Additionally, it seemed likely that the capacity of the guerrillas to hold long-term prisoners – who impede rapid manoeuvre – had diminished as the territory they control had shrunk. Avoiding direct military confrontations, the FARC stepped up urban bombing and extortion rackets, demonstrating that though weakened the group retained an ability to inflict damage. Thus, while some in the Uribe administration hailed the end of FARC, it appeared that ultimately the government would have to force the guerrillas into negotiations if peace was to be secured.

Uribe's remarkable security successes were tarnished by scandals. In October 2008, he fired three generals and 22 officers after revelations that the military had killed young, often unemployed, men and passed their bodies off as dead guerrillas. The 'false-positives' scandal outraged Colombians. The United Nations warned that extra-judicial killings in Colombia were 'widespread', and the Attorney General's Office was continuing to investigate 1,171 deaths. In addition, the so-called 'para-politics' scandal linked Uribe allies to Colombia's right-wing pro-state paramilitaries. In 2006, a laptop seized from a paramilitary commander shed light on government–paramilitary collusion, and the scandal continued to grow, implicating a quarter of the legislature by August 2008. The paramilitary umbrella organisation, United Self-Defense Forces of Colombia (AUC), began to demobilise in 2006 under an agreement with the government that granted leniency in exchange for confessions. Some 3,200 paramilitary leaders had confessed as of May 2009, and many testimonies were instrumental in leading to investigations of legislators. Human-rights organisations protested Uribe's extradition of cooperative AUC commanders to the United States to face drug-trafficking charges, saying extradition curtails investigations.

In addition, the Administrative Department of Security (DAS), which answers directly to the president, was involved in a wiretapping scandal in which the agency spied on dozens of public officials, including Supreme Court justices and the defence minister. While Uribe denied knowledge of the operations, purged DAS officials and removed the agency's wiretapping authority, the scandal nonetheless damaged the credibility of Colombian security services.

Concerns over Colombia's human-rights record influenced its relationship with the United States. Approval of a US–Colombian free trade agreement (FTA) was held up in the US Congress in large part due to concern over killings of union leaders. US President George W. Bush had strong ties with Uribe, who was one of the key US allies in a region increasingly dominated by leftist presidents seeking to distance themselves from Washington. Bush gave the FTA strong support. President Obama, however, opposed the FTA as a senator and was less dependent on Colombia for regional backing.

Although Plan Colombia, the US anti-drug aid programme, had provided $6bn in counter-narcotics funding since 2000, $72m in funds had been frozen since 2007 due to human-rights conditions. Overall funding fell over the past two years and the US Congress reduced the proportion of military spending in favour of social and economic programmes. The programme improved security but failed to stem coca production. According to the UN, coca cultivation in Colombia increased 27% in 2008. Successful eradication efforts in some areas increased cultivation elsewhere, creating a surge of violence and internal refugees in places such as Nariño province. In February 2008, 17 indigenous Awa people in Nariño were tortured and killed by FARC, who accused them of being army informants. This episode drew international attention to the plight of indigenous peoples in Colombia, who have been acutely affected by the conflict. Colombia has the second-highest number of internally displaced persons, surpassed only by Sudan.

Security gains remained reversible, as FARC continued to launch attacks and demobilised paramilitaries regrouped into armed gangs. While US funding was likely to remain substantial, the Obama administration indicated that financial constraints would require reductions. Colombia's ability to make up any shortfall was limited by falling government revenues. GDP growth slumped from 7.5% in 2007 to 2.5% in 2008 as export revenues and foreign investment declined, and in December the government announced a $1.3bn budget cut for 2009. The economic downturn caused several pyramid schemes to collapse in November 2008, leading tens of thousands of angry investors – around 3m people lost a total of about $270m – to riot in 13 Colombian cities, leaving two dead. Uribe was forced to declare a state of social emergency and the country's top financial regulator resigned.

Anger over the pyramid scam, government scandals and Colombia's slowing economy together served to dent the president's approval ratings and diminished his prospects for securing a third term. Though Uribe's popularity still stood at a remarkably high 70%, support for a third Uribe term declined from 74% in July 2008 to 54% by the end of the year. In 2006, Colombians amended the constitution to allow him to serve a second consecutive term, and another constitutional amendment would be necessary for Uribe to run in 2010. By May 2009 the president had not indicated whether he would seek re-election, but his supporters collected the 5m signatures necessary to petition Congress to hold a referendum on the matter. If allowed to run, Uribe would almost certainly secure another term. But if he were barred from re-election or decided to stand down, a centre-right candidate would likely win as the opposition remained divided and without a clear frontrunner. Agriculture Minister Andrés Felipe Arias resigned to launch a presidential campaign, and Defence Minister Juan Manuel Santos also resigned in May 2009. But both men said they would not run if Uribe sought re-election. Santos would be expected to receive Uribe's backing due to the successful security policies he has overseen.

Venezuela: A Decade of the Bolivarian Revolution

For Venezuelans, 2009 marked ten years of Hugo Chávez and his populist Bolivarian Revolution. Having won a referendum to remove limits on the number of terms he could serve, the provocative president indicated his desire to stay on for another ten years to consolidate his transformation of Venezuelan society. A former colonel whose failed 1992 coup attempt against the country's traditional elites brought him to national prominence, Chávez won office on pledges to replace discredited clientelist institutions with a 'popular democracy' in which the president was directly accountable to the people.

Chávez 'refounded' Venezuela with a new constitution in 1999, the first in a long series of reforms consolidating power in the executive. His revolutionary social agenda, however, was hampered by dwindling oil revenues, which forced him to implement the orthodox stabilisation measures he had campaigned against. Between 2000 and 2002, the president's popularity fell from 70% to 30%, with his remaining support coming from Venezuela's poorest sectors. This core of support helped Chávez to weather a coup attempt in April 2002, national strikes in 2002–03, and a recall referendum in 2004. As the price of oil rebounded, the president's popularity rose due to distributionary social spending. Capitalising on the opposition's failed efforts to oust him, Chávez purged the government, the military and the state-run oil company of suspected disloyal elements and consolidated control over all three branches of government as well as institutions such as the National Electoral Council (CNE) and the attorney general's office. In December 2006, Chávez was re-elected with 62% of the vote, vowing to consolidate his Bolivarian Revolution by implementing 'twenty-first-century socialism'.

A year later, however, Chávez suffered his first defeat at the ballot box when Venezuelans narrowly voted down a package of constitutional amendments that included declaring Venezuela a socialist state, indefinite presidential re-election, and extending executive power over the Central Bank, universities and local government. While Chávez quickly accepted defeat, he pressed forward with his agenda, instituting several reforms in piecemeal fashion. In August 2008, for instance, Chávez implemented by decree 26 laws including measures increasing state control over agriculture, commerce and industry. These decrees also gave Chávez power to appoint regional authorities separate from locally elected officials and established a new military branch, the National Bolivarian Militia, charged with assisting communal councils formed of the president's supporters.

Emboldened by their success in the December 2007 referendum, opposition parties sought to make gains in state and municipal governments in the November 2008 regional elections. Their efforts were strengthened by rising discontent over the economy, crime, corruption and inefficient delivery of services. At the heart of Chávez's Bolivarian Revolution was the politicised distribution of oil revenues. As oil prices soared, Chávez's social spending improved health care and education, and reduced poverty rates from 43.9% in 1998 to 28.5% in 2008. Yet Venezuela suffered from spiralling crime, energy blackouts, shortages of basic goods, and the region's highest inflation rate (30.9% in 2008). These problems, all of which disproportionately affect the poor, eroded Chávez's support among his base. The opposition, however, was up against a powerful state-run election machine. Chávez stepped up his confrontational rhetoric, threatening to send in tanks and withhold funds from states that elected opposition governors. Additionally, 272 candidates, including many key opposition candidates, were barred from running based on suspicion of corruption. While Chávez's allies won the majority of contests, the opposition scored key victories, including five of 22 gubernatorial races and control over Venezuela's two largest cities, Caracas and Maracaibo. Chávez's defeat in traditional strongholds such as Caracas and Petare, one of Latin America's largest slums, indicated that the president's populist agenda had lost some of its currency with his base.

A week after the regional elections, Chávez called for a referendum to lift limits on the number of terms that all elected officials were allowed to serve. The timing of the move was critical, as the opposition's resources were exhausted from the November campaigns while the government unleashed all the resources of the state to promote the 'yes' vote. Public employees campaigned for the president and state-run media broadcast his agenda. Violence marred the campaign as pro-Chávez groups attacked private media offices, tear-gassed the Vatican mission which gave sanctuary to an opposition student leader, and launched a grenade attack on opposition headquarters. While Chávez criticised the violence, he also fuelled it with his rhetoric, warning that without him there would be war. Chávez won the referendum with 55% of the vote, allowing him to run for re-election in 2012. The president announced he would launch the 'third phase' of his Bolivarian Revolution, saying he may need another 10 years in power.

In the aftermath of his referendum victory, Chávez used the National Assembly, dominated by his allies after the opposition boycotted the 2004 elections, to implement what he called a 'new geometry of power'. In March 2009, the legislature transferred control of ports, airports and highways to the federal government, depriving local governments of tariff revenues. Chávez promptly sent the military to seize control of these facilities in the three states that had opposition governors. The following month the legislature created a new district of Caracas, to be governed by an official appointed by the president, thus limiting the purview of new opposition mayor Antonio Ledezma. Ledezma, who was barred by grassroots Chávez supporters – known as *chavistas* – from entering his office building, and was stripped of control over public services. Chávez also planned to shift local governing operations to communal councils, circumventing local governments opposing him. He also backed bills to increase media control, create government-controlled workers' councils to supplant unions, restrict human-rights organisations' funding from abroad, and create a new commission to replace the Supreme Court as the highest judicial body. Chávez meanwhile sought to cripple the opposition by targeting its leaders with corruption allegations. He forced Manuel Rosales, mayor of Maracaibo, into hiding by prompting prosecutors to call for his arrest, and had former Defence Minister Raúl Baduel arrested in April.

> Chávez criticised the violence, but also fuelled it

Chávez stepped up intervention in the economy, seizing facilities of food producers he accused of hoarding and violating price controls. However, declining oil revenues seemed likely to endanger his agenda. The sharp fall in oil prices since their July 2008 peak was constraining government spending. Oil made up 94% of Venezuelan exports and funded half the federal budget. In 2008 GDP growth slowed to 4.8% from 8.4% the year before. In March 2009 the government cut planned spending by 6.7% and sought to offset Venezuela's first fiscal deficit since 2003 through tax hikes and debt sales. These measures, however, were unlikely to close the $10bn deficit. Chávez insisted that Venezuela would weather the downturn, backed by

$100bn in reserves, and promised to maintain social spending. He was loath to cut the distributionary policies on which his popularity depended and to implement the orthodox measures that nearly led to his toppling at the start of his presidency. He made overtures to private enterprise, inviting investment in Venezuela's oil industry, but the attitude of companies would not have been helped by Chávez's past nationalisations, property seizures and denunciations of foreign companies.

Dwindling oil revenues threatened to decrease Chávez's international prominence. He used subsidies and funding to governments and sub-national groups across the region to cast himself as the anti-imperialist counterbalance to the United States. In 2007, Venezuela pledged more than $8.8bn in foreign financing and discounted oil sales. Chávez provided Cuba with 100,000 barrels of oil a day, had pledged $214m to Bolivia since 2006, and had financed over $2bn in oil sales to 18 Caribbean countries since 2005. As economic conditions worsened, however, domestic outcry over distribution of the country's resources abroad seemed likely to escalate.

While Chávez used oil wealth to curry favour with leftist governments in Latin America, he adopted a combative stance toward the United States and its allies and strengthened relations with countries such as China, Iran and Russia. In 2008 Venezuela and Russia signed a series of energy and arms accords and even held joint military exercises in the Caribbean. US–Venezuelan relations had been difficult since the Bush administration failed to denounce the leaders of a 2002 coup attempt. Chávez frequently accused the US of trying to oust him, partly to garner domestic support. In 2008, relations with the US were further marred by diplomatic disputes over Venezuela's increasing role as a conduit for Colombian cocaine. Chávez had suspended US drug surveillance flights in 1999, and in August 2005 ended cooperation with the US Drug Enforcement Administration, accusing it of espionage. US officials estimated that Colombian cocaine travelling through Venezuela quadrupled since 2004. Allegations of collusion with Colombia's drug-trafficking guerrillas increased in March 2008 when a Colombian cross-border raid into Ecuador uncovered documents linking FARC to the Venezuelan and Ecuadorian governments. While Chávez denounced the documents as fabrications designed to encourage his overthrow, in June 2008 he retreated from earlier calls for FARC to be recognised as a legitimate resistance movement, and urged the rebels to lay down their arms.

Though Chávez restored relations with Colombia in July 2008, he kept up his hostility toward US counter-drug efforts. He rejected US requests for cooperation and, in August 2008, denounced a visit by US drugs czar John P. Walters. The following month, Chávez expelled US Ambassador Patrick Duddy in solidarity with Bolivian President Evo Morales, who ejected the US ambassador to Bolivia, alleging that he supported the opposition. A day later tensions escalated as the US expelled the Venezuelan ambassador and the US Treasury Department announced sanctions against two Venezuelan intelligence directors and a former government minister for aiding FARC. The following week the US decertified both Bolivia and Venezuela for having 'failed demonstrably' in their counter-drug efforts.

For all his combative rhetoric, Chávez remained pragmatic in important ways. He refrained from cutting off oil supply to the United States, Venezuela's top customer. The mending of relations with Colombia was in no small measure influenced by the $6bn in annual trade between the two nations. Chávez said he would like better relations with the United States under Obama – but nevertheless called the US president 'ignorant' for criticising his regional influence and accused him of interfering with the 15 February referendum. Rejecting a State Department report which cited skyrocketing Venezuelan drug trafficking, Chávez warned, 'don't mess with me, Mr Obama'. But he warmly greeted the US president at the Summit of the Americas in April 2009, and announced that he would restore diplomatic relations. US–Venezuelan relations were likely to remain difficult, however, as domestic economic pressures increased. Heightened discontent among Venezuelans was likely to make Chávez inclined to maintain a combative stance both at home and abroad.

Bolivia: 'Refounding' a Polarised Nation

Bolivian president Evo Morales, much like his Venezuelan and Ecuadorian counterparts, set out to make a clean break with his country's exclusionary and inequitable past by 'refounding' Bolivia via constitutional referendum. Morales's 'peaceful revolution' sought to emphasise self-governance for Bolivia's 36 indigenous ethnic groups and to reject centuries of foreign exploitation of natural resources at their expense, while keeping them within the country's democratic structures. A leader of Bolivia's coca growers' union, Morales became the region's first indigenous president in 2006 after rising to prominence through his participation in massive social mobilisations that toppled two presidents in 20 months. His campaign promised greater socio-economic equality, political inclusion for indigenous peoples, departure from unpopular neo-liberal economic policies, and rejection of US-backed coca-eradication schemes. Despite holding South America's second-largest natural gas reserves, Bolivia remained its poorest country with over 60% living in poverty and 38% in extreme poverty.

In 2006 Morales deployed troops to seize gas fields, forcing companies to give the government a majority stake. He extended state control over the mining, oil and telecommunication sectors. Nationalisations, along with soaring oil and gas prices, swelled government coffers, funding popular social programmes. Morales's resource nationalism, however, inflamed Bolivia's long-standing divides. The eastern lowland provinces of Santa Cruz, Beni, Pando and Tarija form a resource-rich, crescent-shaped region known as the Media Luna. These lighter-skinned states of Bolivia's traditional elite, fiercely opposing Morales's redistribution of revenues to the indigenous western highlands, launched a campaign for greater autonomy and sought to block constitutional reform.

> Resource nationalism inflamed Bolivia's long-standing divides

Lacking a two-thirds majority, the president's Movement Toward Socialism (MAS) party failed to prevent the opposition from stalling progress in the Constituent Assembly, elected in July 2006 to draft a new charter. In the face of an opposition boycott, MAS deputies approved a draft constitution in late 2007, claiming they only required the votes of two-thirds of those present. Outraged, Media Luna governors unilaterally declared autonomy and scheduled referendums to confirm their pronouncements. Though the referendums were ruled illegal by courts, the first proceeded on 8 May 2008 in Santa Cruz, and was passed with 85.4% support – though with 37.9% abstention. Autonomy measures were then passed in Beni, Pando and Tarija, again with around 80% approval and high abstention.

Seeking to bolster support for his reform efforts, Morales – with two years of his term still to run – decided to hold a referendum on whether voters wished to 'recall' the president, vice-president and governors. Tensions grew ahead of the 10 August vote as opposition groups occupied government offices and airports and clashed with police. Morales secured 67% of the vote, winning the highest proportion of votes of any president since Bolivia's return to democracy in 1982. While two opposition governors and one Morales ally were recalled, the referendum failed to shift the power balance, as the Media Luna governors were also confirmed in their posts.

While Morales's victory strengthened his mandate, it stoked the fires of dissent. Mobs ransacked, occupied or burned down 50 government offices, seized regional airports, erected some 35 roadblocks, and clashed with police and government supporters in the streets. An attack on a natural-gas pipeline temporarily halved Bolivia's exports to Brazil. On 11 September 2008 the murder of up to 30 peasants on a roadside in Pando shocked the country. Morales declared a 90-day state of siege in Pando and arrested its governor on genocide charges, accusing him of orchestrating Brazilian and Peruvian hit men to carry out the attack. The massacre ended the deadlock between government and opposition, as the latter's popular legitimacy diminished and both sides sought to prevent further bloodshed. On 15 September the Union of South American Nations (UNASUR) held its first emergency meeting, expressing support for the Morales government, condemning the violence and urging negotiations to reach a 'lasting solution'.

As tens of thousands of Bolivians embarked upon a 200km march to the capital in support of the draft constitution, the government and opposition sat down to review 100 of the constitution's 411 articles, compromising on issues of autonomy, land reform and natural resources. Opposition governors agreed to reign in supporters and Morales pledged to return a portion of hydrocarbon revenues that he had diverted to pensions for the elderly, and to seek only one more term in office. The president's previous position had been that election under the new constitution would constitute a first term, entitling him to run again in 2014. Based on the compromises reached, Congress ratified the new draft.

On 25 January 2009, 61% of Bolivians approved the charter, which enshrined indigenous rights, granted greater government control over natural resources, and established some rights to regional autonomy. Voters were also asked whether landholdings should be limited to 5,000 or 10,000 hectares, and 70% cast ballots in favour of a 5,000-hectare cap. Morales said approval of the new constitution ended 'internal and external colonialism'. However, more radical indigenous leaders such as Felipe Quispe insisted it did not go far enough and called for complete independence for indigenous groups, while the majority in the Media Luna provinces, meanwhile, voted against the constitution. In April 2009, Morales resorted to a five-day hunger strike to pressure the Senate into approving the bill necessary to hold new elections.

Ahead of the December 2009 presidential elections, Morales looked to face increased protests from supporters frustrated with the slow pace of reform and feeling the effects of the global economic crisis. Morales's numerous social programmes had yet to make a serious dent in poverty levels, and falling commodity prices would constrain government finances. Perceptions of fraud or mismanagement might also disrupt the president's campaign. In January 2009 the administration was rocked by a corruption scandal involving Santos Ramirez, a close friend of Morales and head of the state-run oil company Yacimientos Petrolíferos Fiscales Bolivianos (YPFB). Morales fired several YPFB executives and imprisoned Ramirez, accusing the US Central Intelligence Agency of infiltrating the oil firm.

Morales could face stiff competition from other indigenous candidates. The mayor of Potosí, Rene Joaquino, announced his candidacy and former Vice-President Victor Hugo Cárdenas may run. The home of Cárdenas, an indigenous Aymara, was attacked in March 2008 by indigenous neighbours who beat and evicted his wife and son, angry over Cárdenas's opposition to Morales. Politically motivated violence also looked likely to rise during the run-up to the elections. In April 2009, police killed three men in a firefight in Santa Cruz while attempting to arrest a group – including Bolivians as well as foreign mercenaries – allegedly plotting the president's assassination. Authorities subsequently uncovered a cache of weapons and explosives along with a hit list, oddly composed of both government allies and opponents such as Santa Cruz Governor Reubén Costas.

> The new constitution enshrined coca as an important part of Bolivian culture

The president's electoral prospects were good, as he retained a 60% approval rating and enjoyed support from the majority of Bolivia's indigenous population as well as from the powerful coca growers' union. The new constitution enshrined coca as an important part of Bolivian heritage and culture, and Morales has eschewed the US-backed forced eradication policies that led to deadly clashes. Instead, he has opted for negotiated eradication policies, nearly doubling the amount of land on which coca can be legally grown and cracking down on cocaine production rather than coca producers. While coca production rose by 5% in 2007, cocaine seizures more than doubled, from 14 tonnes in 2006 to 29 in 2008. Morales's 'Coca, yes, cocaine, no' policy has heightened tensions with the United States. But support from Venezuela, which has pledged $214m since 2006, and investment commitments from countries such as Iran, France and Russia have enabled Morales to distance himself from Washington.

Although the United States has provided approximately $130m annually in counter-drug and development assistance to Bolivia, bilateral relations markedly deteriorated in 2008. In February, Morales expelled an American official for alleged espionage, and threatened to eject US Ambassador Philip Goldberg as well. In June, the United States granted asylum to a former defence minister implicated in the 2003 killing of 56 street protesters, and Morales praised outraged Bolivians who marched on the embassy and threatened to burn it down unless Goldberg was removed. Later that month Morales extolled coca growers when they expelled US Agency for International Development personnel from their territory. Relations collapsed further on 10 September 2008, at the height of anti-government protests, when Morales finally expelled Goldberg, accusing him of conspiring with the opposition. The following week Washington announced it would decertify Bolivian counter-drug efforts. Ten days later President Bush suspended Bolivia's trade preferences under the Andean Trade Promotion and Drug Eradication Act, placing $250m in annual revenue and 20–30,000 jobs at risk in Bolivia. In November, Morales ejected US Drug Enforcement Administration agents, saying its programmes were a guise for fomenting rebellion. US officials denied American complicity in plots to oust the president, claiming that Morales was merely making such accusations to distract the Bolivian electorate from problems at home. While this might not always have been his motivation, it appeared to be the case in March 2009 when, in response to the YPFB corruption scandal, Morales expelled yet another US diplomat for alleged involvement with CIA infiltration of the company.

Morales's best chance of avoiding the fate of his two predecessors appeared to lie in addressing domestic discontent. Due to the deep polarisation of Bolivian society, he was compelled both to reach out to his opponents and to address the needs of his base. After centuries of exclusion and poverty, Morales's supporters are understandably impatient for reform. Yet political battles with the opposition, including the numerous referendums of the past year, have diverted critical resources and attention from forging lasting solutions to the country's socio-economic problems. Unless the president is able to free himself from the current political deadlock, he risks encouraging protests from both the far left and the far right and increasing the likelihood that discontent will spill over into violent protest.

Ecuador's New Constitution

Ecuadorian President Rafael Correa was re-elected in April 2009, winning 52% of the first vote to be held following constitutional reforms that he had overseen. When first elected November 2006, he had become the country's eighth president in 11 years. Mass protests had toppled three presidents in nine years in a country desperately lacking institutional mechanisms to channel popular discontent. Pledging to recover political and economic power from discredited elites, Correa set out to 're-establish' the Ecuadorian government through a new constitution. His nationalist, populist platform appealed to the politically and economically marginalised majority.

Underlining widespread disillusionment with the political system, in April 2007 82% of Ecuadorians voted to convene a Constituent Assembly to draft a new constitution. At Correa's behest, the Constituent Assembly dissolved the legislature in November 2007 and assumed its duties. While the move allowed him to press forward with populist policies, it held up progress on the constitution as the assembly became bogged down in legislative matters. A draft constitution was finally approved in July 2008.

The new charter sought to end stalemates between the legislature and executive by increasing presidential power and allowing the executive to dissolve Congress once per term provided the president resigned and called general elections. The president was allowed consecutive four-year terms, giving Correa the opportunity to serve two terms under the new system and potentially hold power until 2017. Government control of the economy was expanded, with the Central Bank placed under the presidency and executive powers of expropriation strengthened. As part of an effort to build democratic channels for popular participation, citizens' councils were created to oversee branches of government. Universal rights to health care, pensions and education were established and the government was given power to redistribute unproductive lands. In a gesture to Ecuador's indigenous peoples, who constitute 35% of the population, the constitution declared the country to be 'plurinational' and 'intercultural' and required prior consultation with indigenous communities concerning large-scale mining operations on their lands.

The new draft constitution drew the ire of business communities opposed to increased government intervention. Meanwhile, opposition groups in Guayaquil, who had staged massive pro-autonomy protests in January 2008, objected to the increased centralisation of power. Additionally, Ecuador's largest indigenous group, Confederación de Nacionalidades Indígenas del Ecuador (CONAIE), was dissatisfied that only prior consultation rather than prior approval was required for launching mining operations on indigenous lands. CONAIE broke with Correa in May 2008 over this issue, and in June the president of the Constituent Assembly, Alberto Acosta, resigned in part to support CONAIE.

Nevertheless, the new constitution was approved on 28 September 2008 with 62% of the vote. Correa hailed his fourth-straight victory at the polls, vowing to consolidate his 'citizens' revolution'. Support for the new constitution in part reflected Ecuadorians' need for a clean break with the past, but Correa's success also stemmed from the popularity of his nationalist, populist economic policies. Rejecting the 'long dark night of neo-liberalism', in 2007 the president ejected International Monetary Fund (IMF) and World Bank officials. In December 2008, and again in March 2009, Correa announced that Ecuador would default on portions of the country's $10bn debt that he considered illegitimate, citing a presidential commission that determined malfeasance had occurred in 40% of debt contracts.

Correa has also extended control over Ecuador's natural resources. In October 2007, he steeply raised taxes on windfall oil profits, prompting companies to renegotiate contracts that gave the government greater control over and profit from oil production. Ecuador is Latin America's fifth-largest oil producer, and oil makes up 60% of its exports and funds 40% of the government budget. In 2008, oil revenues increased 222%, fuelling economic growth and a large rise in government spending. Correa has doubled Ecuador's spending since 2006, and in 2008 51.6% of his budget went to the social sector, financing social programmes and subsidies for low-income families and small businesses. Poverty dropped from 40% to 32% under Correa, boosting his approval rating to over 70%. Seeking greater revenue from the mining industry as well, in April 2008 Correa suspended 80% of mining operations until a new law could be drafted. Despite protests from indigenous and environmental groups, the new mining law was approved in January 2009, entitling the state to the majority of profits from any project. Correa has also used his nationalist economic stance to rally support for his reform agenda. For example, in September 2008 he sent troops to seize a Brazilian construction company days before the constitutional referendum. Expelling the company's managers, Correa threatened to default on a $243m loan from the Brazilian Central Bank, causing Brazil to recall its ambassador. While

Correa pragmatically resumed loan payments to Brazil in January 2009, restoring relations, the move boosted his populist credentials ahead of the vote.

The president's nationalist stance in the international arena has also augmented his popularity. About 80% of Ecuadorians approved of Correa's hardline suspension of bilateral diplomatic relations in response to Colombia's March 2008 cross-border raid on a FARC camp in Ecuador, increasing support for the president and his constitutional reform at a time when Ecuadorians were disenchanted with the Constituent Assembly's sluggish pace. The popularity of his position helped Correa to purge senior officials from Ecuador's powerful military after learning that intelligence officials had operated in conjunction with the Colombians. Correa also replaced his defence minister with his personal secretary, Javier Ponce, an outspoken critic of the military. The move reversed Correa's previously accommodating relationship with the armed forces, which had been instrumental in removing past presidents. While Correa stepped up operations along the border to counter the FARC presence, by mid 2009 Ecuador had yet to restore diplomatic relations with Colombia.

Correa also accused the CIA of assisting the Colombians and infiltrating Ecuadorian security forces, and renewed his pledge to end US use of Ecuador's Manta air force base. The US has run counter-drug operations from Manta since 2000, and approximately 100 drug-surveillance flights leave the base monthly. Ecuador's new constitution prohibited foreign military bases, and Correa ordered the US to vacate Manta when its lease expires in November 2009. In February 2009 Correa expelled the US Immigration and Customs Enforcement attaché and the US Embassy's first secretary, on the grounds that they had threatened to suspend aid unless the US was given veto power over appointments to special police units.

While Correa's stance toward foreign governments and companies was popular, his long-term success depended on Ecuador's new constitution, upon which he staked his political career. Yet the new charter, Ecuador's twentieth since independence in 1830 and third in 30 years, was unlikely to solve critical problems. Declining oil revenues, remittances and foreign reserves looked to decrease Correa's ability to cushion Ecuador from the global economic crisis and sustain social spending. At the same time, the new constitution mandated expanding social programmes, which the president will be hard pressed to fund. Furthermore, Ecuador's recent defaults limit its ability to borrow money to weather the downturn. Foreign investment declined due to Correa's contract renegotiations, making Ecuador even more dependent on oil during a time of declining revenues. Foreign investment looked to fall further, as the new constitution banned international arbitration. While the economy began to slow in the last quarter of 2008, inflation, which in 2008 doubled to 8.8%, continued to erode incomes. Correa's popularity remained high enough to see him through the 26 April 2009 presidential elections, but support could diminish as economic woes rise. Furthermore, it was still unclear whether the country's new charter created adequate democratic channels for popular discontent. The Correa administration, then, remained at risk of facing the kind of massive street protests that destabilised past governments.

Peru: Domestic Backlash

It was a mixed year for Peruvian President Alan García. Success was to be seen in trade and economic growth. García signed free-trade agreements with the United States, Canada and Singapore, and negotiated deals with China and South Korea. He was also courting Brazilian investment in energy, mining and manufacturing, heralding Peru's role in connecting Brazil to markets in Asia and the United States. A $1.3bn highway across the Amazon, to be completed in 2011, will link São Paulo with Lima and other Peruvian ports, allowing Brazil tariff-free access to markets. Lima hosted the Asia-Pacific Economic Cooperation (APEC) forum in November, reflecting García's enthusiasm for expanding Peru's economic relationships throughout the Pacific.

Peru's economy outperformed most of those in Latin America in 2008, with GDP growth of 9.8%. Following the trend of the past seven years, it outpaced the rest of the region due to high global mineral prices and growing output from oil and natural-gas ventures. The subsequent worldwide economic downturn hit Peru with less intensity than elsewhere. At the end of 2008, sharp declines in commodity prices and lower capital inflows reduced GDP growth. García, however, believed that private investment – both domestic and foreign – was the best way to pull Peru out of poverty. The government continued to give land concessions for oil and gas exploration, mining, logging and biofuel crops, despite the recent fall in demand for commodities. Economists predicted that measures including a $3bn stimulus package would keep Peru's growth at a steady 3.1%, which would exceed that of most neighbours. However, the benefits of economic growth had not reached the majority of the population. The poverty rate remained near 40%, and living standards continued to fall as inflation and the cost of food soared in 2008. While Lima and the northern coast enjoyed strong commercial activity, Peruvians in the southern Andes, where poverty exceeds 70%, have struggled to move beyond subsistence farming.

A major blow to the García administration came in October 2008, when he asked his entire cabinet to resign after a bribery scandal. Records and tapes showed that members of his centre-left Alianza Popular Revolucionaria Americana (APRA) party took bribes for awarding oil-exploration contracts to private companies. Among those tendering their resignations were the prime minister, energy minister and head of Petroperú, the state oil company. García eventually reinstated most of his previous cabinet. As a result of the scandal, his approval ratings plummeted to 19%, and as of May 2009 had rebounded only modestly, to 34%. García, still trying to atone for the corruption and ineptitude of his first term (1985–90), faced a fuming opposition which had a congressional majority.

> "Peruvians increasingly took their demands to the streets"

García's new cabinet appointees seemed unlikely to produce large policy shifts. He appointed a few moderate leftists, including Prime Minister Yehude Simon, a former radical leftist who had spent much of the 1990s in jail for links to a guerrilla group until a political epiphany led him into moderate politics as a regional governor. Simon's familiarity with the left and reputation as a negotiator might help quell protests that continued to flare throughout the country. Still, García faced increasing criticism from Peru's poor. His social programmes to redistribute gains from economic growth had been plagued by bureaucratic inefficiency. While the government pledged to reduce poverty to 30% by 2011, the spike in food prices and persistent under-employment strengthened the call for better social programmes, especially in the southern Andes.

Peruvians increasingly took their demands to the streets. Oil and gas exploration and mining continued to incite conflicts over tax revenues, land ownership, indigenous rights and environmental degradation. In June 2008, protesters in the southern province of Moquegua blockaded a mine for one week and took 60 riot police hostage in a dispute over tax revenues from a local copper mine. In July 2008, trade unions in the southern Andes launched a general strike, blocking roads and the railway to Machu Picchu. Government oil- and gas-exploration concessions upset landowners and environmental advocates, who asserted that the government had illegally re-designated and appropriated land. While most protests remained local and disconnected, they were a symptom of Peru's persistent economic inequality and inability to channel demands effectively through political parties.

García blamed protests on leftist agitators such as Ollanta Humala, his opponent in the 2006 presidential election, and claimed leftist groups were being funded by Venezuelan President Hugo Chávez. These worries are not unfounded. Chávez, who loudly supported Humala's campaign, has extended a hand to poor Peruvians. While local governments fumbled to aid areas damaged by the magnitude 8.0 earthquake in Pisco in August 2007, Chávez constructed 100 homes in the neighbouring town of Chincha. His influence was also felt in the southern region of Puno, on the border with Bolivia. Puno's regional governor, Hernán Fuentes, embraced the socialist nationalism touted by Chávez and Evo Morales, attempting to legalise the production of coca and setting up several Casas de ALBA (Venezuelan outreach centres offering free medical care) in the Puno area. Peru's Congress was investigating whether Chávez was directly funding political activities of these facilities.

In April 2009, former President Alberto Fujimori became the first democratically elected Latin American head of state to be convicted by his own country of human-rights abuses. Fujimori was tried for violations during Peru's bloody civil war, incited by the Shining Path guerrilla insurgency in 1980. Judges found Fujimori complicit in the activities of a death squad known as the Colina group, which killed 15 civilians at a barbecue in Lima in 1991 and kidnapped and murdered ten people from a teacher-training college in 1992. The court also convicted him over the kidnapping of two political opponents by intelligence agents. Fujimori appealed his 25-year prison sentence. His daughter Keiko Fujimori, a prominent lawmaker and contender for the 2011 presidential election, vowed to pardon her father if elected.

García's newest challenge was the resurgence of the Shining Path, which had all but disappeared after its leadership was dismantled under Fujimori. An operation to eliminate the remnants proved more complex than expected. Officials estimated that the group now comprised about 600 guerrillas, split into rival groups in the coca-growing regions of Huallaga and in the Ene and Apurímac river valleys. Since García sent in troops in August 2008, rebels have killed at least 30 people, mostly soldiers and police, in a series of ambushes. In 2008, Shining Path stole dynamite from a mine owned by a US company and detonated the explosives on a Peruvian military convoy. Two brothers, Victor Quispe Palomino, alias José, and Jorge Quispe Palomino, known as Raúl, were believed to head the group, which had purportedly replaced a leftist ideological fight with drug trafficking, through which it funded its comeback. As the Shining Path uses its riches to fund social projects and make friends in remote mountain villages, the government may find it difficult to win the support of local populations.

Peru's armed response was controversial with human-rights groups, which accused the army of killing innocent civilians. Opposition leader Ollanta Humala criticised García's strategy as excessive, arguing that because the Shining Path was no longer trying to overthrow the state, the situation should be handled by the police and not the military. García meanwhile boosted military spending to counter shortages in troops, food, weapons and intelligence-gathering.

As Peru wavered between a neo-liberal administration and a growing leftist backlash, the 2011 presidential election seemed likely to be noteworthy. Keiko Fujimori retained a strong left-leaning base, while Humala enjoyed the support of poor Andean regions. Simon seemed to provide a more centrist alternative while also having sentimental appeal for some leftists. In running for a second term, García may have difficulty convincing the poor that he has improved their situation.

Brazil: Lula's Leadership

Brazilian President Luiz Inácio 'Lula' da Silva successfully increased his country's prominence on the world stage, taking a leadership role in Latin America and beyond. Lula reached out to his neighbours in times of political crisis, playing a central role in the UN peacekeeping mission in Haiti, helping to calm tensions after Colombia's cross-border raid into Ecuador, and sending mediators to Bolivia in September 2008. While forging a leftist alternative to radical populism in Latin America, Lula protected Brazil's interests in nearby countries, withdrawing its diplomats from Ecuador after stalled loan payments, resisting calls from Paraguay to renegotiate contracts, and insisting Bolivia maintain its contractual obligations with respect to gas delivery. Meanwhile, he maintained links with radical governments, strengthened ties with Cuba and offered to help mend relations between Hugo Chávez and the United States.

Lula was in the forefront of moves for regional integration, pressing for greater economic cooperation through Mercosur and UNASUR, as well as promoting creation of a South American defence council. In December 2008, he hosted an unprecedented summit in which all 33 countries from Latin America and the Caribbean met without the United States or European countries. The summit showcased Brazil's leadership in regional cooperation while displaying Latin America's desire for greater independence from the United States and Europe.

In a broader international context, Lula played an important role as the G20 met twice to deal with the financial and economic crisis. He pressed for developing countries to have a bigger say in a reformed international financial system. In contrast to its status in previous economic crises, Brazil's economy was relatively stable due to government involvement in the banking sector, strict lending restrictions, low debt and $200bn in reserves. As the US and European economies faltered, Brazil found itself well placed to call on developed nations to 'take responsibility' for the economic crisis. Reminding them of the harsh structural adjustment measures imposed on Latin America during previous crises, which contributed to a rise in anti-US sentiment, Lula insisted that international financial institutions had to be reformed to ensure that fallout from crises in wealthy nations did not unfairly damage the world's poor.

Lula has remained very popular despite a series of scandals. In 2005 the president's chief of staff resigned after a vote-buying scandal and the following year Brazil suffered its worst corruption scandals in a dozen years, leading to indictments of 40 officials. In June 2008, Presidential Chief of Staff Dilma Rousseff was accused of trying to bury a probe into violations of foreign airline ownership laws. The latest blemish on the administration arose in November 2008, when evidence surfaced of illegal wiretaps targeting Lula, Rousseff, the president of the Supreme Court, and a prominent opposition senator. Opposition lawmakers launched an investigation, with some calling for Lula's impeachment, and the president suspended the intelligence director. The fact that the president and his allies were among those tapped cast doubt on accusations that he was involved, but the incident reflected poorly on his efforts to eradicate corruption. The police were meanwhile accused of kidnapping and torturing journalists, heading paramilitary militias in the slums of Rio de Janeiro and São Paulo, and committing human-rights abuses, including extra-judicial killings.

The president has managed to survive scandals in large part because of Brazil's strong economy. During the first three quarters of 2008, Brazil enjoyed its fastest growth since the mid 1990s, as high commodity prices and credit expansion boosted GDP. Lula insisted 'Bush's crisis' wouldn't affect Brazil, but in the fourth quarter the economy slowed. In November and December 2008, the country lost nearly 700,000 jobs, leading the government to unveil a series of stimulus packages and issue reassurances that investment in infrastructure and social programmes would continue. While Brazil was stable compared with its neighbours due to its ability to fund counter-cyclical policies, the economic downturn may have damaged the electoral prospects of Lula's Workers Party (Partido dos Trabalhadores or PT). The declining economy reduced the government's approval level, which fell from 72.5% in January 2009 to 62.4% in March, with Lula's ratings slipping from a record high of 84% to 76.2%.

In October 2008 municipal elections, the PT and its allies won nearly two-thirds of mayoral races, which looked to help rally supporters ahead of the October 2010 presidential election. Chief of Staff Rousseff, a former Marxist guerrilla who was captured and tortured by the military dictatorship in the 1970s, is Lula's chosen successor. Her success will largely depend upon whether the Accelerated Growth Programme, which she oversees and which finances infrastructure and energy investments, insulates Brazilians from the economic downturn. Lula also announced a $15.2bn housing plan, which Rousseff was to implement, designed to build 500,000 low-income homes and create as many as 1.5m jobs. Rousseff, however, will face strong opposition from the centrist Brazilian Social Democratic Party (PSDB). Two PSDB candidates announced their intention to run: Minas Gerais Governor Aécio Neves, and São Paulo Governor José Serra, who lost to Lula in 2002. Of these contenders, Serra was the stronger candidate and March opinion polls showed Serra garnering 45.7% of the vote and Rousseff only 16.3%. Despite Lula's efforts to boost her prospects with social spending, the economic downturn meant that the PT would have to fight hard to hold on to the presidency.

Argentina: The Kirchners' Decline

Argentine President Cristina Fernández de Kirchner was elected in October 2007 in large part because of the populist policies implemented by her predecessor and husband, Nestor Kirchner. Yet these very policies created economic imbalances that in 2009 plagued her presidency. Kirchner's success in guiding Argentina out of the crisis following its 2001 economic collapse made the Peronist president widely popular. During his presidency (2003–07), strong demand for Argentine exports and high levels of government spending fuelled economic growth of over 8% a year, cutting unemployment and poverty levels roughly in half.

Kirchner's expansionary policies, however, contributed to soaring inflation of 20–25%. By manipulating inflation data to report a rate of only 8%, Kirchner saved his country millions in debt payments on loans linked to Argentina's consumer price index, yet he damaged his administration's credibility and enraged many Argentinians. Kirchner's support among his poor and middle-class base faded as food prices climbed, price freezes caused energy shortages, crime soared, and a series of corruption scandals tainted his administration. Although he retained approval ratings of over 50%, Kirchner decided to stand down in the October 2007 presidential elections to allow his wife to run. The move was seen as an attempt to circumvent Argentina's cap of two consecutive presidential terms by alternating power between Kirchner and Fernández. Helped by a fragmented opposition and a $4.4bn pre-election spending spree by her husband, Fernández won an impressive first-round victory with 54% of the vote.

Kirchner had often forsaken building congressional alliances or accommodating his opposition, choosing instead to rule by decree. Argentines hoped Fernández would continue her husband's popular economic policies while adopting a more conciliatory stance. Upon taking office, however, Fernández maintained her husband's governing approach, many of his ministers, and nearly all of his policies. Kirchner, meanwhile, assumed leadership of their Justicialist Party (PJ). He remained a vocal proponent of government policies, often appearing to be the 'shadow' president, eroding Fernández's legitimacy.

Continuing Kirchner's autocratic habits, in March 2008 Fernández sought to finance government spending by decreeing a tax hike on agricultural exports. The move unleashed a protracted battle with Argentina's farmers as they intermittently staged strikes and protests and erected roadblocks.

In May 2008 the country witnessed its largest anti-government protest since Argentina's return to democracy in 1983 when 235,000 pot-banging protesters gathered outside Buenos Aires. For four months the demonstration raged as Fernández refused to back down, accusing the farmers of being wealthy coup-plotters blocking redistribution to the poor. Increasingly, however, this hardline stance failed to resonate with her poor and middle-class base, as food shortages contributed to already soaring inflation. Support within the PJ began to fade as officials, legislators and governors favoured an accommodation to end the crisis. As her popularity plummeted from 56% to 20%, in June 2008 Fernández looked to Congress for validation, asking the legislature to ratify the tax. Despite Peronist majorities in both houses, the Senate reached a 36–36 deadlock, and Vice-President Julio Cobos cast the tie-breaking vote against the measure. The move was a shocking defeat for the president, who subsequently fired six of Cobos's allies and sidelined the vice-president. On 18 July Fernández rescinded her decree.

While her approval ratings eventually rebounded to around 30%, Fernández's troubles did not end with the tax dispute. The global financial crisis hit Argentina in the third quarter, and sinking prices and demand for agricultural exports came as Argentina began to suffer its worst drought in 50 years. Farmers resumed protests in December 2008, and again the following January and March, demanding further export tax reductions. The government resisted, however, as the downturn was likely to cost it $4.3bn in agricultural tax revenues in 2009. Poverty levels were rising, and inflation was estimated at 20–25% despite the government's manipulation of the figures. Additionally, $28bn of debt was scheduled to mature over the following three years, and there was a $10bn financing gap for 2009. With limited access to credit due to previous defaults, Fernández announced in October 2008 the nationalisation of Argentina's pension system, which had the effect of transferring $29bn to the federal government. While the move was popular, critics denounced it as a reckless attempt to fund the country's debt payments. Stocks and bonds fell sharply. Attempting to restore Argentina's credibility with international lenders, in September 2008 Fernández announced she would repay the Paris Club group of official creditors and would open talks on restructuring defaulted debts with lenders who had rejected renegotiation terms in 2005. Facing increased financial constraints, Fernández steadily decreased subsidies and attempted to curtail overall spending. At the same time, however, she announced a $3.8bn stimulus package as well as $21bn in public works designed to create 700,000 jobs. Fernández was set to face mounting pressure to step up government spending as her low-income support base suffers the effects of recession.

The Peronists faced a resurgent opposition, strengthened by Fernández's low popularity and capitalising on farmers' dissatisfaction as well as concerns of corruption and spiralling crime. Important alliances were formed. Gerardo Morales from the Radical Civic Union (UCR) and Elisa Carrió of the Civic Coalition (CC) joined forces to unite support for opposition candidates. Buenos Aires Mayor Mauricio Macri formed an alliance with two Peronist defectors, Felipe Solá, previously a governor and an agricultural minister, and businessman Francisco de Narváez. Midterm elections in June 2009 were expected to be viewed as a referendum on Fernández's presidency. Her stewardship of the economy and efforts to accommodate farmers during the drought would be central to her party's prospects for success. Pressures to maintain populist spending, however, were likely to exacerbate economic problems, dimming the long-term outlook for her administration.

Cuba's Shifting Relationships

1 January 2009 was an important day in Cuba. Fifty years earlier, Fidel Castro's 26th of July Movement overthrew the dictatorship of General Fulgencio Batista, beginning the Cuban Revolution's long and tumultuous reign. The anniversary celebration made clear the many changes that have taken place in Cuba since Castro's victory.

The biggest change had been Fidel Castro's February 2008 resignation from the presidency, a post he held for over four decades. In the years leading up to his departure, the Cuban government moved to improve the country's unstable economy and craft a succession plan to maintain the Communist Party's political dominance. The administration launched a number of reforms to shore up the socialist state. In 2002 Castro had secured a constitutional amendment that declared the socialist system 'irrevocable' and immediately incarcerated 75 pro-democracy dissidents. He followed this move with reforms consolidating Cuba's banking system, outlawing the US dollar and nationalising half the country's fledgling private sector. The message was unequivocal: the Cuban Revolution would persist, with or without Fidel Castro at the helm. Since his resignation, however, Cuba has

taken halting steps toward economic liberalisation under the leadership of
Raúl Castro, Fidel's quieter younger brother.

The first softening came in the form of consumer goods: mobile telephones, computers and microwaves became available for purchase. Later,
Raúl Castro authorised private auto-rental companies, permitted Cubans
to visit tourist hotels, and considered privatising the country's extensive
national taxi service. Computer use spread considerably after the 2008
reforms and occasionally posed challenges to the regime. In February 2009,
a group of students videotaped a heated argument with National Assembly
President Ricardo Alarcón over travel restrictions and the glaring lack of civil
rights on the island. The video spread over the Internet, damaging Alarcón's
credibility and giving publicity to Cuba's pro-democracy advocates.

A land-reform bill in July 2008 granted private farmers the right to lease
up to 99 acres of empty public lands from the government. The move was a
response to rising food and oil prices. In 2007, Cuba had imported $1.5bn in
food, mostly from US producers authorised under a special exemption from
the long-standing US trade embargo. That figure increased to nearly $2.5bn in
2008. Cuba's economy, heavily dependent on imports, was expected to slow
further in 2009 after growth slipped to 4.3% in 2008 from 6.5% the previous
year. The devastation wrought by Hurricanes Gustav and Ike in September
2008 did not help, with 500,000 people displaced or affected. Over 30% of
Cuba's crops and half a million chickens – a core component of Cuba's agricultural sector – were destroyed. Better news, however, was the national oil
company Cubapetroleo's identification of over 20bn barrels of oil reserves
in offshore fields. The discovery placed Cuba in the top 20 oil-producing
nations, almost equal to the United States. Cuba currently produces 60,000
barrels of oil daily but relies on Venezuela for an additional 93,000, which it
receives at heavily discounted prices in exchange for sending thousands of
Cuban doctors to work in Venezuela.

The relationship with Venezuela was a critical aspect of the new administration's foreign policy. Sharing ill feelings towards the United States, the
two countries continued to develop trade relationships in the agricultural,
education and medical sectors. Venezuela supplied a great deal of assistance in the form of oil and food. It donated over $150m for construction of a
petrochemical plant in Cienfuegos on Cuba's southern coast, and planned to
build a liquefied-natural-gas plant in the next three years. Falling oil prices
at the end of 2008, however, added uncertainty to the relationship. Chávez
became more restrained in handing out foreign aid. As a result, Raúl Castro

sought to deepen ties with other regional and global partners, encouraging Brazil to play a larger role in Cuba's economic development. In October and November 2008, Cuba hosted Brazilian investors hoping to capitalise on Cuban sugar markets for ethanol production.

The Castro administration also courted Dmitry Medvedev during the Russian president's December 2008 tour of Latin America. They discussed opportunities for Russian companies to explore oil deposits off the Cuban coast, in addition to planning joint projects in pharmaceuticals, tourism and education. The Latin American tour was a bold move for Russia. Many analysts considered it to be retaliatory Russian muscle-flexing in a region that has historically been the United States' exclusive sphere of influence. Medvedev's pursuit of a relationship with Cuba may have been a response to US support for Georgia and Ukraine. Raúl Castro returned Medvedev's favour in January 2009, signing a commitment in Moscow to a strategic partnership. Russia pledged 25,000 tonnes of grain and $20m in development assistance. The meetings signalled that Cuba and Russia were committed to rebuilding a relationship that had crumbled after the Cold War. However, military matters – once a crucial component of their relations – were conspicuously absent from the discussions.

> Cuba continued to build ties with China

Cuba continued to build ties with China, which was also seeking to expand its strategic influence in Latin America. President Hu Jintao visited Havana in November 2008. Among the agreements reached were a commitment to revitalise Cuba's ports and to boost Chinese purchases of Cuban nickel and sugar. Sino-Cuban trade generated $2.7bn in 2008, making China the island's largest trading partner after Venezuela.

The most significant question for Cuba's international relations concerned the United States. The early months of 2009 showed signs of what might become a gradual thaw in US–Cuban relations. On 13 April, President Obama announced modest changes in US policy toward the island. The administration lifted all restrictions on family visits, travel expenditures and remittances for Cuban Americans, making good on campaign promises to Cuban Americans in 2008. Obama explained: 'Cuban American connections to family in Cuba are not only a basic right in humanitarian terms, but also our best tool for helping to foster the beginnings of grassroots democracy on the island'. There was also a hint of the beginnings of a trade relationship, curtailed since the 1960s by American sanctions, which were tightened under the Bush administration. Obama authorised US communications providers to work with the Cuban government to lay fibre-optic infrastructure for communications between the US and Cuba. The targeted media included radio, satellite media and broadband communications. The new Cuba policy also authorised the transfer of humanitarian supplies, restricted under the Bush administration.

Small though they were, the modifications represented the most significant shift in US policy toward Cuba in decades. They were a drastic departure from the hardline policies of the Bush administration aimed at isolating the island to precipitate regime change. Though the United States' goals for Cuba – democratisation, human-rights recognition and economic liberalisation – remained the same, the Obama administration's approach seemed driven more by the notion that US media exposure and social influence from Cuban-American expatriates – so-called 'soft power' – would be more effective agents of change in Cuba's uncertain political environment. The policy changes, in part, reflected a generational shift within Cuban immigrant communities. Exiles increasingly wanted the United States to engage the government in Havana, arguing that the cold-shoulder approach of the past had failed. The Cuban American National Foundation (CANF), arguably the most influential advocate of the United States' uncompromising policy toward Cuba, was reconsidering its ideological position. It submitted a proposal to the Obama administration that would 'chart a new direction for US–Cuba policy'. Any real policy transformation, however, would depend on the US Congress, which has tended to resist dramatic policy changes regarding Cuba. In April 2009 US lawmakers met Cuban Foreign Minister Bruno Rodriguez in Havana to discuss options for improving the relationship.

Cuba's political situation was changing. In March 2009, Raúl Castro sacked Felipe Pérez Roque, Fidel's provocative foreign minister, and Carlos Lage, architect of the economic-austerity policies of the early 2000s. The decision represented one of the first major political departures the younger Castro had made from his brother. Yet, substantive political change – especially progress toward democracy – was expected to be slow. By mid 2009 Raúl Castro had shown no inclination to be more tolerant of public dissent and formal opposition to the Communist Party. Fidel Castro, though not seen in public since 2006, remained an influential figure, writing weekly editorials discussing the new administration's decisions. If the first year of his 'retirement' was any indication, as long as Fidel still had a piece in Cuba's political game, change would come slowly.

Nicaragua: Ortega's Move toward Autocracy

Former revolutionary Daniel Ortega won the 2006 presidential election with a scant 38% of the vote and laboured to unite Nicaragua's fractured political parties behind his Sandinista agenda. Ortega has recently moved toward authoritarianism, exemplified by the November 2008 municipal elections in Managua, which resulted in violent demonstrations after opposition leaders accused Ortega of rigging the vote to favour the Sandinista party. Eduardo Montealegre, member of the Constitutional Liberal Party (PLC), insisted that he had legitimately won the mayoral race, while the Sandinista-led electoral council claimed victory for Sandinista candidate Alexis Argüello. The council ordered a recount, but barred international observers and reconfirmed Argüello's victory. In response, Washington condemned the elections and suspended $175m in aid.

2009 marked the 30th anniversary of the Sandinista Revolution, which installed a leftist government, led by Ortega, and sparked the controversial Contra War, in which rebel groups were funded in part by US arms sales to Iran. Sensing that Ortega's recent authoritarian, perhaps corrupt, tendencies might indicate a return to Cold War habits, many prominent Sandinistas left the party and began to criticise Ortega. Former Sandinista Edmundo Jarquín, who competed against Ortega for the presidency in 2006 as part of the Sandinista Renovation Movement, was conspicuously left off the ballot in recent municipal elections. When revolutionary icon and poet Ernesto Cardenal spoke out against Ortega in summer 2008, the Nicaraguan courts – increasingly under the president's control – reopened an old slander case against him and froze his bank accounts. Ortega also alienated the departing mayor of Managua, Dionisio Marenco, once one of the president's closest advisers, and launched investigations against international NGOs. Opponents feared Ortega's next step might be to call for a constitutional reform allowing him to run for re-election, mimicking his self-described Venezuelan mentor, Hugo Chávez. Ortega's approval ratings, however, hovered below 25%.

Ortega had difficulty building his government's legitimacy in a country where over half are impoverished. Nicaragua applied for a $300m loan from the Inter-American Development Bank to help it withstand the global economic crisis. Ortega also sought economic support from anti-US governments abroad. Nicaragua received loans, oil and generators from Venezuela, and joined Chávez's regional trade group, the Bolivarian Alternative for the

Americas (ALBA). Falling oil prices, however, meant that Ortega could no longer depend upon Chávez to keep Nicaragua's government afloat.

Decreasing remittances, capital flight and an unsustainable national budget led Ortega to seek aid from Russia. In December 2008, a fleet of three Russian warships visited Nicaragua's Caribbean coast and brought donated computers. At mid 2009, Nicaragua was the only country outside Russia that had recognised the independence of South Ossetia and Abkhazia. Ortega also reached out to Iranian President Mahmoud Ahmadinejad and Libyan leader Muammar Gadhafi. Ortega even granted Thailand's fugitive former Prime Minister Thaksin Shinawatra a diplomatic passport in order to increase investment in Nicaragua. Ortega stepped up his anti-US rhetoric, accusing the United States of financing his opponents and demanding Washington pay reparations for its role in the Contra War of the 1980s. At the Summit of the Americas in April 2009, he delivered a 50-minute tongue-lashing against US belligerence in Latin America. He cited his country's own history, as well as a laundry list of other American policies deemed objectionable throughout Latin America, including the embargo against Cuba. Ortega then turned his attention to Obama, declaring him 'the head of an empire imprisoned by rules he can't change'.

Nicaragua has, however, been surprisingly cooperative with the US-led drug war. In 2008 Nicaragua seized $370m worth of drugs and repeatedly asked the United States to ramp up counter-drug assistance. Yet as Ortega revived the rhetoric and alliances of the Cold War, he effectively limited his list of wider benefactors to those opposing the United States. In so doing, he risked losing the flow of US and European investment and aid to Nicaragua, which remained strong into 2009, as well as the support of the National Assembly. Ortega's impoverished nation may soon grow impatient with a bankrupt and increasingly repressive government.

Haiti: Steps toward Stability

Haiti's political storm has calmed dramatically since the Brazilian-led UN Stabilisation Mission (MINUSTAH) arrived in 2004. The mission was launched in the midst of violent rebellions and political chaos three months after former president Jean-Bertrand Aristide was forced from the country. Since then, MINUSTAH has fulfilled its mandate to quell the violence and help resuscitate the collapsed government. Security has improved, particularly in the past year, following the success of a MINUSTAH campaign against gang violence in Haiti's *favelas* (impoverished, crime-ridden slums). UN forces killed top gang leaders in street fights and arrested over 700 suspected gang members. Despite receiving heavy criticism for violence against civilians and several notable human-rights violations, the offensive is credited with improving conditions on the island. Kidnappings dropped by 70% in 2008, and state police reported only 487 homicides last year, about 5.6 per 100,000 people, substantially below the Caribbean average of 30 per 100,000.

President René Préval, elected in February 2006, has remained in power for three years, a rare achievement for a Haitian politician. He entered with a strong mandate from Haiti's poor majority and was able to pacify the opposition, securing a rapprochement with the country's elite. Préval emphasised the need for national unity to struggle against the many external shocks continuing to plague the country. In 2008, the shock was the global food crisis. In Haiti, food prices rose 40% in 12 months, against a core inflation rate of 8.5%. The food crisis provoked political instability as violent demonstrations and riots rocked the Préval administration in April. The government's hands were tied by a large external debt and a barely operable state budget. The situation, however, stabilised in 2009, owing largely to generous international food aid.

Haiti's economy overall remained relatively dependent on international aid. A large number of farmers (Haiti's principal producers) sold their land to survive the food crisis, and many more consumed their seed stores. The agricultural sector's recovery has been slow and painful. Moreover, unemployment hovered around 80% in 2008, up from between 50% and 70% in 2007, although Haiti's expansive informal sector and high unemployment rates complicated the numbers. Approximately 76% of Haiti's population earned under $2 per day and 55% under $1 per day. Real GDP growth in 2008 was a bare 2.3%, and inflation an estimated 15.8%.

The death of more than 100 children in the collapse of a school outside Port-au-Prince in November 2008 helped renew international concern for the struggling country. The United States, which pulled all but a small advisory team from MINUSTAH in 2004, gave $24m in development assistance in 2008. Trade concessions granted by the Bush administration also accorded textile exporters duty-free access to US markets for the next decade. The Bush administration also provided a relief package of $300m after hurricanes killed more than 800 people, displaced an estimated 1m and caused up to $1bn in damage. Congress, at President Obama's suggestion, made a further pledge of $302m for Haiti's economic development in 2009. US Secretary of State Hillary Clinton visited Haiti in April to meet with Préval. She announced that the Obama administration would reconsider its policy of interdicting and deporting Haitian immigrants arriving in the United States illegally. Currently, more than 30,000 Haitians are scheduled for deportation, which could upset the delicate economic and political balance Haiti has achieved in the past five years.

In what was perhaps the clearest sign of Haiti's increasing stability this year, the Caribbean Community (CARICOM) extended an invitation to join the CARICOM Single Market and Economy (CSME) by summer 2009. Subsequently, the Haitian parliament passed legislation to facilitate free trade within the CSME and launched nationwide public-education programmes to explain CSME functions. In another positive turn, the World Bank authorised $240m in development assistance over three years. The Haitian government also made significant progress under a three-year Poverty Reduction and Growth Facility arranged by the IMF in 2006. Préval applied for the programme's final disbursement, plus $26.5m to allay the effects of the food crisis and hurricane damage over the summer. Haiti also received a bonus from the IMF's Heavily Indebted Poor Countries Fund to cover interest obligations on its external debt.

Sustaining stability in the face of persistent insecurity remained Haiti's most acute problem. At the end of 2008, MINUSTAH's mandate was renewed for the fifth consecutive year. Though the force certainly helped to resolve gang violence in Haiti's largest cities, there was scant evidence the country was ready to go it alone. The UN said in October 2008 that it would not depart until Haiti was able to develop a functional – and politically neutral – national security force. Steps have been made in that direction. Haiti met its goal, established in 2004, of forming a 14,000-officer police force, and negotiated a training arrangement with the Canadian government. Until the country can offer further proof of stability, however, the international presence there is likely to stay.

Towards Pragmatic Re-engagement

During the past decade, in much of Latin America, Hugo Chávez has inspired rejection of the United States' traditionally hegemonic position in the region, and populist resistance to right-wing regimes' economic and political marginalisation especially of indigenous groups. But many, if not most, Latin American countries continue to value their strategic relationships with the United States, and to need its economic cooperation and, in the case of countries like Colombia, Mexico and Peru, its security assistance. These realities have brought to the fore the risks of Chávez-esque combativeness towards Washington, prompted moderation and highlighted the desirability of a 'third way' that yields a greater degree of independence from the United States, on one hand, and a beneficial and fundamentally non-antagonistic bilateral relationship, on the other.

The most promising model for such a dispensation that has emerged is not Venezuela under Chávez but Brazil under Lula. A heavy dependency on shrinking oil revenues has limited Chávez's ability both to reward his domestic supporters for their support for an ideologically flimsy Bolivarian Revolution and to export that revolution to other countries through foreign assistance. Brazil, by contrast, has a bigger, more diversified and more influential economy, and, in Lula and any likely successor, a more pragmatic and approachable leader.

The United States under Obama, for its part, is sensitive to the view held by many that the country 'lost' Latin America during the Bush years. The Obama team is more inclined to concede that it is merely an indispensable power rather than a hegemon as a matter of right, and thus more likely to meet halfway conscientious centre-left leaders – like Lula and Chilean President Bachelet – who are leery of retrogressing to US political dominance and the neo-liberal 'Washington consensus' for economic reform advocated by the IMF and the World Bank. The United States' pressing strategic preoccupations elsewhere and the political and economic limitations imposed by the global recession may hinder its re-engagement with Latin America. But it is probable that pragmatism will prevail in both Washington and most Latin American capitals, and that pressure will grow on outliers like Bolivia, Ecuador, Nicaragua and eventually even Cuba to temper resolutely anti-American policies, moving the hemisphere towards greater cohesion.

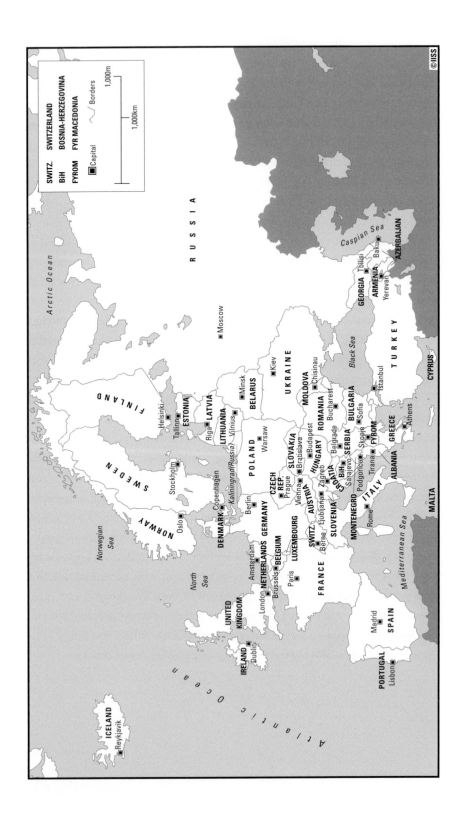

© IISS

SWITZ.	SWITZERLAND
BiH	BOSNIA-HERZEGOVINA
FYROM	FYR MACEDONIA

■ Capital   ⌇ Borders

1,000km

1,000m

Arctic Ocean

RUSSIA

Caspian Sea

GEORGIA
Tbilisi
ARMENIA
Yerevan
Baku
AZERBAIJAN

Moscow

UKRAINE

TURKEY

Black Sea

CYPRUS

FINLAND

Helsinki

ESTONIA
Tallinn
LATVIA
Riga
LITHUANIA
Vilnius

Minsk

BELARUS

Kiev

MOLDOVA
Chisinau

ROMANIA
Bucharest

BULGARIA
Sofia

Istanbul

GREECE
Athens

SWEDEN

Stockholm

Kaliningrad/Russia

POLAND
Warsaw

SLOVAKIA
Bratislava

HUNGARY
Budapest

SERBIA
Belgrade

FYROM
Skopje

ALBANIA
Tirana

Copenhagen

Berlin

CZECH
REP.
Prague

Vienna

AUSTRIA

SLOVENIA
Ljubljana

CROATIA
Zagreb

BiH
Sarajevo

MONTENEGRO
Podgorica

NORWAY

Oslo

DENMARK

GERMANY

SWITZ.
Bern

ITALY
Rome

Norwegian
Sea

North
Sea

Amsterdam

NETHERLANDS
BELGIUM
Brussels
LUXEMBOURG

London

Paris

FRANCE

Mediterranean Sea

MALTA

UNITED
KINGDOM

IRELAND
Dublin

SPAIN
Madrid

PORTUGAL
Lisbon

ICELAND
Reykjavik

Atlantic Ocean

Chapter 5

Europe

The economic downturn dominated the year to mid 2009 in Europe. Even though 27 European countries are members of the European Union, and 16 of them have a single currency, the financial crisis produced a far from unified response. Each took different, sometimes competitive measures to deal with the market dislocations of autumn 2008. While Britain and the United States took basically the same fire-fighting approach, French and German leaders depicted the crisis as a failure of American laissez-faire capitalism. They resisted pressure to introduce large fiscal stimulus into their economies. Meanwhile, some central and east European countries were hit particularly badly and required emergency assistance.

As NATO marked its 60th anniversary and the EU the 10th anniversary of the St Malo agreement on defence cooperation that catalysed development of its own defence capacity, both organisations began to review their strategic priorities. France played an important role in both organisations as holder of the EU rotating presidency in the second half of 2008, which saw French President Nicolas Sarkozy mediate an end to hostilities between Georgia and Russia in August on behalf of the EU. He also tried to refocus the debate within the EU on the generation of better capabilities for crisis management, and in April 2009 achieved his goal of reintegrating France fully into NATO's military command structure.

In the area of military capabilities – often seen as Europe's weak spot in its participation in crisis-management efforts – strategic and tactical mobility emerged as a clear focus, with European governments particularly vexed by the lack of helicopters available for international missions. Within the EU, the European Defence Agency (EDA) quietly put in place a set of strategies designed to facilitate coordinated action by governments in strengthening defence capabilities.

Developments in European Defence

NATO at 60: reviewing its priorities

NATO leaders gathered on 3–4 April 2009 for a summit in Strasbourg, France and Kehl, Germany. With the 60th anniversary summit squeezed between a G20 summit in London and EU–US meetings, heads of state and government had to tackle a crowded agenda involving laying the ground work for a new strategic concept; addressing the challenge of balancing immediate operational needs with the more long-term transformation agenda; debating the future of NATO–Russia relations; agreeing on a new secretary general; and welcoming the reintegration of France into the Alliance's military structures.

NATO leaders adopted a Declaration on Alliance Security drafted by outgoing Secretary General Jaap de Hoop Scheffer. Mindful of member governments' insistence that the declaration should not pre-empt the new strategic concept document expected for 2010, his concise paper reassured members that Article 5 collective defence commitments were not in competition with non-Article 5 missions and asserted the need for unity of purpose and a willingness to share operational risks and responsibilities. By achieving this, the document said, Alliance members 'will improve our ability to meet the security challenges we face that impact directly on Alliance territory, emerge at strategic distance or closer to home'. The declaration also served as a tasking document to begin work on the new strategic concept to be approved at a summit in 2010.

There remained disagreement as to how far the strategic concept under development should differ from the one, drawn up in 1999, it is to replace. Some governments, like Germany, argued for an evolutionary approach, insisting that a core purpose of the new strategy was to forge a renewed consensus about NATO's fundamental role and mission, in particular in light of the significant enlargement NATO had undergone since 1999. Others took the view that the international environment had changed tremendously since 1999, and suggested that a more radical rethink was in order.

The August 2008 war between Georgia and Russia sharpened the debate about whether NATO was striking the right balance between collective defence and crisis-response operations such as the mission in Afghanistan. The US administration of President George W. Bush had for several years argued strongly in favour of Georgia's membership of NATO, but European governments had been more cautious. For newer NATO members who still felt themselves to some extent in Moscow's shadow, the war caused new concerns.

The Summit Declaration asserted that NATO's Article 5 commitment remained the most important task and that the transformation agenda, which was largely designed to increase the usability of forces, would strengthen the ability of Allies to conduct both territorial defence and crisis-response operations outside Allied territory. Hence, the argument that both types of operations essentially require similar capabilities in the current security environment, which had run into some opposition during NATO ministerial meetings in autumn 2008, found its way into the declaration.

The responsibility for striking a balance acceptable to all NATO members will fall upon an appointed group of personalities, working with the new secretary general, Anders Fogh Rasmussen, who stepped down in April as the long-serving prime minister of Denmark to take up the position in August 2009.

The Strasbourg/Kehl Summit Declaration confirmed that further enlargement of NATO was seen as a less urgent matter than in the past. Albania and Croatia were welcomed as new members but Macedonia could not be admitted as a dispute with Greece about the country's name remained unresolved. Following the war in Georgia, leaders deferred the issue of membership for Georgia and Ukraine by confirming their readiness in principle to admit them but stipulating that both countries would have to tackle a significant reform agenda first, and that doing so successfully would require political stability. Hence, NATO validated the view that any enlargement should be in the Alliance's interest and was not an end in itself.

The war between Russia and Georgia was also a severe setback for NATO–Russia relations. The summit declaration said 'our relations with Russia depend on trust and the fulfilment of commitments. Since our last Summit [in 2008 in Bucharest], dialogue and cooperation with Russia have suffered from profound disagreements.' In the wake of the summer war, NATO suspended normal cooperation through the NATO–Russia Council (NRC) and Moscow responded by freezing military exchanges. One lesson from the conflict was that cooperation between NATO and Russia had done very little in terms of gradually influencing mutual perceptions and interests. The NRC had created a network of meetings and exchanges, but without any real influence on the participants. Eastern European allies were quick to point to this strategic failure. Nonetheless, in light of the offer of the incoming administration of US President Barack Obama to 'reset' US–Russian relations, NATO foreign ministers decided on 5 March 2009 to resume formal NRC meetings. A first meeting at ambassadorial level was held on 27 May 2009 and the atmosphere was reported as constructive and focused on enabling a swift return to ministerial meetings. Success in this effort will be determined by whether it leads to the definition of a pragmatic agenda for cooperation on issues like Afghanistan, arms control, and countering terrorism and narcotics trafficking.

Insurgents, pirates and militias: meeting the operational demand

European countries, through a variety of organisational frameworks, continued to be actively involved in dealing with security problems in Afghanistan, the Balkans and Africa, although Britain pulled out of Iraq after six years of deployment there.

At the April summit, NATO leaders sought to rally the Alliance's efforts to bring stability to Afghanistan. Asserting that there was a direct link between the security of Afghanistan and the security of NATO allies, they called on allies to renew their efforts to provide training, mentoring and funding for the Afghan National Army and police. By April 2009, the strength of the NATO-led International Security Assistance Force (ISAF) mission had grown to just over 58,000 troops. America's early-2009 announcement that it would deploy an additional 21,000 troops increased pressure on European allies to raise the level of their commitments. The Obama administration indicated that it was focused not solely on troops, but also on civilian and financial means. The need for heightened security during the Afghan elections scheduled for August 2009 was a priority. European allies promised some 5,000 additional troops plus police trainers with the UK contributing up to 1,000, Germany some 600 and Italy about 500. Some of these were to be deployed specifically in the context of the elections and would thus not be long-term reinforcements (see Afghanistan, pp. 303–14).

A significant increase in piracy off the Horn of Africa prompted increasing involvement of European navies in efforts to combat this phenomenon. According to US Navy statistics, there were some 115 piracy events including 27 successful attacks during the first five months of 2009 compared to 122 events and 42 successful attacks in the whole of 2008. The EU launched its first naval mission, and NATO undertook two missions.

NATO, at the UN's request, provided escorts to UN World Food Programme vessels from October to December 2008 with *Operation Allied Provider*. The operation was conducted by redirecting ships from NATO's

Standing Maritime Group (NSMG) 2, which had been scheduled to conduct port visits in the Gulf. In March 2009 NATO launched *Operation Allied Protector*, a maritime mission to counter piracy and armed robbery off the Horn of Africa, involving vessels from NATO's Standing Maritime Group 1. In June the operation was extended, with vessels from NSMG 2 replacing those from NSMG 1.

The EU began its activities on 19 September 2008 when it set up a military coordination cell, EUNAVCO, in the secretariat of the Council to organise a response to deal with piracy and protect maritime trade. EUNAVCO was to mobilise EU member states and organise escort slots. Its duties were taken over by *Operation Atalanta*, which was launched in December 2008. *Atalanta*, the first EU naval operation, was given a one-year mandate, with operational headquarters at Northwood, UK. As of June 2009, *Atalanta* was composed of vessels and maritime-patrol aircraft from France (four vessels), Germany (three vessels and one patrol aircraft), Greece (one vessel), Spain (two vessels and one patrol aircraft), and Sweden (three vessels).

Other nations deployed ships to the area, and in January 2009, the United States launched a counter-piracy task force, Combined Task Force-151 (CTF-151). Originally commanded and staffed by the US Navy, CTF-151 evolved into a multinational task force and, at the time of writing, was commanded by the Turkish navy (see Somalia, pp. 275–81).

The EU was meanwhile engaged in three missions that, particularly when the naval mission and its continuing commitment in Bosnia were taken into account, demonstrated the widening range of its – albeit still modest – capacity to mobilise capabilities for challenging missions to deal with the world's hotspots.

The EU carried out its planned one-year mission in Chad and the Central African Republic, called EUFOR CHAD/RCA. Its responsibility was handed to the UN mission MINURCAT in March 2009. Some 14 EU member states contributed forces in the field, with others involved in support duties in theatre and at the operations headquarters. EUFOR carried out some 3,000 short-range and some 440 long-range patrols. EU leaders estimated that it enabled some 10,000 displaced persons to return to their villages due to an improved security situation. Furthermore, cooperation with the UN appeared to have matured compared to earlier such attempts in the Democratic Republic of the Congo. EUFOR helped to get MINURCAT established by providing escorts for convoys and securing sites. In contrast to previous practice when contingents from EU member states left the theatre after EU operational duties were completed, some 2,000 troops who served under EUFOR transitioned into the UN force to provide continuity and improve capability. However, the punishing and logistically challenging terrain in the area of operations once more laid bare force-generation problems and, in particular, Europe's lack of support helicopters. Operational demands could only be met with the help of Russian helicopters and crews.

On 1 October 2008, the EU launched a civilian monitoring mission, EUMM Georgia, following the EU-mediated end of hostilities between Georgia and Russia. Within two weeks of the decision, the EU deployed some 200 unarmed monitors from 22 member states. Their one-year task was to monitor implementation of the ceasefire agreement, in particular the withdrawal of Russian forces to the positions held prior to the outbreak of hostilities. EUMM also monitored the deployment of Georgian police and observed whether all parties were complying with human-rights obligations (see Russia, pp. 195–212).

In Kosovo, the delayed civilian EU rule-of-law mission EULEX finally reached full operational capability on 6 April 2009 after deployment accelerated from November 2008 on. By April 2009, EULEX consisted of some 1,710 international staff plus some 825 local staff. Its main objectives were to assist and support the authorities in Kosovo, which declared independence from Serbia in February 2008, in the areas of police, judiciary and customs (see Balkans, pp. 175–82).

Elsewhere, the improvement of the security situation in Iraq led the EU in November 2008 for the first time to contemplate pilot activities on Iraqi territory. So far, training activities for senior Iraqi police officers, prosecutors, judges and prison governors have been carried out exclusively outside Iraq. In Afghanistan, the EU reinforced its activities in support of the Afghan National Police, doubling to 400 the personnel in its police mission EUPOL Afghanistan. The EU also began preparatory work for a possible transition of its *Operation Althea* in Bosnia, currently with 2,200 troops, into a capacity-building and training mission. However, EU leaders said such a move would depend on political circumstances on the ground.

Filling capability gaps

In spite of the expansion of missions involving European forces, European armed services still suffered from significant shortfalls in capabilities, most notably in the fields of strategic and tactical lift, force protection and the technologies involved in intelligence, surveillance, target acquisition and reconnaissance. In the year to mid 2009, the field of strategic and tactical lift received the most visible attention.

On 10 November 2008 a declaration of intent to establish a European Air Transport Fleet was signed by 12 EU member states (Belgium, Czech Republic, Germany, Greece, France, Italy, Luxembourg, the Netherlands, Portugal, Romania, Slovakia and Spain). The goal was the pooling of services and aircraft such as C-130 *Hercules* and the planned A-400M European airlifter. From between 2014 and 2017, member states were to make aircraft available; purchase, provide and exchange flying hours; and pool support functions; all with the aim of increasing availability, generating economies of scale, and making more effective use of assets. Belgium, Germany, France and Luxembourg signed a separate declaration of intent to set up a multi-national unit for the A-400M – though the Airbus-managed project to build the aircraft encountered further delays. On the same day, Belgium, France, Germany, Greece, Italy, the Netherlands, Portugal, Spain and the UK signed a Declaration of Intent to enable the generation of a combined European maritime-strike capability with the European Carrier Group Interoperability Initiative, which aimed to increase interoperability among European navies and associated air groups so that participating countries would find it easier to contribute assets into a composite carrier strike group in support of EU and NATO commitments.

A separate airlift effort was under way within NATO. Ten members (Bulgaria, Estonia, Hungary, Lithuania, the Netherlands, Norway, Poland, Romania, Slovenia and the United States), as well as Finland and Sweden, signed a Strategic Airlift Capability agreement on 1 October 2008. This activated the NATO Airlift Management Organisation, which will acquire three C-17 aircraft, to be flown and maintained by international crews. The C-17s, due for delivery in 2009, were to be based in Hungary and could be employed on NATO, EU and UN operations.

Tactical helicopter transport capability has consistently ranked as one of the most pressing force-generation problems for NATO and the EU. According to EDA figures, only 6–7% of helicopters in the inventories of European armed forces were deployed on crisis-management operations. Thus, the problem was one of availability. Both aircraft and crews were often unable to fly in demanding operational environments such as deserts and mountainous areas. The EDA was to focus on the problem with a three-pronged initiative. For crews, the short-term ambition was to establish a Helicopter Tactics Training Programme to be launched in 2010. In the medium term, the agency aimed to focus on upgrade programmes for heli-copters and in particular the Mi range of Soviet-era models in the inventories of most central- and eastern-European forces. For the long term, the EDA sought to lead the development of a Future Transport Helicopter able to lift up to 13 tonnes with a range of 1,000km.

The EDA's involvement in the helicopter project built on a series of capa-bility-focused initiatives in which it had been involved since its foundation as part of the EU in 2004. During 2008, it put in place a set of strategies designed to identify which capabilities and technologies were needed, and what kind of cooperation and industrial collaboration should be sought. Among the areas to receive a particular focus were to be research and technology, harmonisation of equipment requirements, and collaborative procurement – always a troublesome area in the past. These complemented its 2007 initiative to foster a European Defence Technological and Industrial Base (EDTIB), a Capability Development Plan (CDP) endorsed by EU defence ministers in July 2008, and an effort to streamline operational logistics. The CDP provided member states with information to facilitate decision-making as they consider national choices, and aimed to stimulate cooperation and to facilitate the launch of new joint programmes.

Future directions

In December 2007, the Council of the European Union had tasked Javier Solana, the EU foreign-policy chief, to prepare a report on the implementa-tion of the EU's European Security Strategy (ESS), the creation of which he had overseen in 2003. The original document, forged in the aftermath of the divisions within Europe over the Iraq War, was limited but nevertheless rep-resented a step forward in forging a common approach among EU members to global threats. Solana's task was often misinterpreted as a revision or even re-drafting of the ESS, but this was not the purpose of his report, published in December 2008. The paper called for increased efforts along the lines iden-tified in 2003, and concluded that Europe 'must do more to shape events'. It did not, however, provide a framework precisely to define ambitions or how to achieve them.

In December 2008, the EU Council also adopted a Declaration on Strengthening Capabilities reflecting the desire of the French EU presidency to reinvigorate this topic. The declaration was noteworthy in that it set out in relatively clear terms what the EU's level of ambition would be for civilian and military crisis-management missions (for details, see France, pp. 155–63).

The EU is often seen as having a unique advantage in crisis-management operations because it can mobilise civilian as well as military capabilities. The French-sponsored paper targeted progress on civilian capabilities as a priority alongside a call for EU member states to embrace innovative methods of capability development such as pooling, role and task specialisation and cost sharing.

Overall, amid the pressure of operational challenges in Afghanistan and new demands for engagement in Africa, Europe made quiet progress over the year to mid 2009 towards much-needed improvements in capabilities, and laid the groundwork for important longer-term strategic changes.

France: A Year of Paradoxes

President Nicolas Sarkozy celebrated his second year in office on 6 May 2009. Astonishingly, opinion polls suggested that, although his approval rating was only 35%, he would nevertheless be re-elected with a large majority if the election were to take place in 2009 rather than the due date of 2012 because the socialist opposition, in almost total disarray, had an approval rating of only around 25%. This was only the first paradox in a presidency which had been replete with surprises. A second was that the 'reforming president' who promised to transform France 'from top to bottom' had yet to chalk up a single major reform on the order of Valéry Giscard d'Estaing's legalisation of abortion, François Mitterrand's abolition of the death penalty or Jacques Chirac's phasing out of conscription. It was true that Sarkozy had reintegrated France into NATO's military command structure, but this was merely the last step of a process undertaken by all three of his most recent predecessors.

Sarkozy was nicknamed the 'bling bling' president because of his energy, dynamism and omnipresence, not to mention his flamboyant lifestyle. But his attempts to tackle every issue at the same time led to a sense of generalised blockage, where none of the great campaign promises had really borne fruit. A further paradox was a sense that, although he had made his mark in foreign and security affairs, he had often done so by promoting policies, above all Atlanticism and market-liberalism, about which the French public (and arguably even Sarkozy himself) continued to be ambivalent.

Four major international and security-policy issues dominated the year to mid 2009: the Russo-Georgian War; the French presidency of the EU;

the global financial meltdown; and France's re-integration into NATO's command structures. In all of these policy areas, Sarkozy achieved a measure of genuine success, despite his detractors' scepticism.

War in the Caucasus

When the Russo-Georgian War broke out on 7 August 2008, Sarkozy, like most other world leaders, was in Beijing enjoying the Olympics. However, as president of the European Union for the second half of 2008 under the EU's rotation system, he returned immediately to Paris, and within five days was on his way to Moscow and then Tbilisi to broker a peace agreement. Sarkozy visited the two capitals at an opportune moment. Georgian President Mikheil Saakashvili was more than ready to engage in damage limitation through an international honest broker who could persuade the Russians to accept a peace agreement. Moscow saw that it had probably achieved all the gains it could hope for in Georgia. The six-point ceasefire plan Sarkozy negotiated with Russian President Dmitry Medvedev was in fact a largely cosmetic re-arrangement of the situation on the ground: cessation of hostilities; free access to humanitarian aid; withdrawal of Georgian armed forces to their normal bases; withdrawal of most Russian forces to notional pre-7 August positions (this proved to mean whatever Russia decided); and international discussions on future security arrangements for Abkhazia and South Ossetia. This latter point was rejected by Saakashvili, who, unable to secure a reference to the 'territorial integrity of Georgia', eventually settled for as yet ill-defined arrangements covering 'the future internationalisation of security measures in the region'. Russian troops continued to operate for several weeks in and around the separatist enclaves, including areas inside Georgia proper, incurring the increasing anger and frustration of the international community. On 8 September Sarkozy again travelled to Moscow, accompanied by Solana and European Commission President José Manuel Barroso, and persuaded Medvedev to withdraw all Russian troops from Georgian territory and accept the dispatch of 200 EU peace monitors.

At the time, the EU was the only actor capable of brokering a peace deal, and both Russia and Georgia were ready to sign one. Had the EU presidency been in other hands, peace-brokering might have been more difficult. Sarkozy, as president of France as well as the EU, enjoyed credibility and legitimacy in both Moscow and Tbilisi. He succeeded, through energy, leadership qualities and luck, in maximising the opportunity, and emerged from the crisis with enhanced stature both inside and outside France.

The EU presidency: boosting ESDP

The Georgian crisis, coming on top of the Irish rejection on 13 June 2008 of the Lisbon Treaty and alongside the growing financial crisis, was a major distraction from the agenda which had been set in Paris for France's six-month European Union presidency (July–December 2008). One of the top priorities was to give a significant boost to the European Security and Defence Policy (ESDP). There were two main objectives: to deliver (yet another) kick-start to the process of European capacity-building, and to pave the way for France's return to NATO in spring 2009. But as global financial markets approached meltdown and as some European nations faced bankruptcy, the time was hardly ideal to persuade EU member states to pony up significant additional resources for ESDP. The bar was nevertheless set relatively high at the 7 July launch of the capacity-building process when French Foreign Minister Bernard Kouchner announced that, over the coming decade, the EU should generate the capacity to engage, *simultaneously*, in a broad spectrum of overseas operations: two significant stabilisation-and-reconstruction operations, each involving 10,000 troops over two years; two rapid-reaction operations using battlegroup formations; one major emergency-evacuation operation; one maritime or air surveillance-and-interdiction operation; one civil–military humanitarian mission lasting three months; and about ten civilian nation-building missions of variable duration.

The French presidency devoted considerable energy to the delivery, by the European Council meeting in December 2008, of a package of agreements on new military and civilian capacity. Several EU defence ministers' meetings and several high-level expert seminars were organised, leading to adoption of a 'Declaration on Strengthening Capacities' by the December Council. While many of these agreements were in the form of 'letters of intent', progress was made towards identifying specific member states' involvement in specific capacity-generating projects:

Improvements in operational force projection: modernisation of helicopters and a EDA-driven helicopter crew training programme; blueprint for a future transport helicopter; establishment of a European strategic air transport fleet (12 countries) involving a multinational unit of A400M aircraft and early establishment of a European airlift command; a European Carrier Group Interoperability Initiative (nine countries) involving an aircraft carrier, carrier air groups and escort vessels; development of a concept for the projection of an airbase for a European force.

Strengthening information-gathering and space-based intelligence: provision of *COSMO-Skymed* (Italy) and *Helios*-2 (France) satellite images to the European Union Satellite Centre and a letter of intent to that effect for the *SAR-Lupe* satellite (Germany); preparation of the new generation of observation satellites such as the Multiple Space-Based Imaging System programme (Germany, Belgium, France, Greece and Italy); audit of military requirements in space surveillance.

Increased force-protection assets: launch of a new EDA-driven programme of maritime mine clearance, with 11 countries participating; EDA-launched future surveillance unmanned aerial vehicle project (seven countries); networking of maritime surveillance systems; development of an EU special-operations concept, including cooperation between special forces; plans for the mobilisation of military assets for emergency evacuation of European nationals.

Strengthening interoperability: exchanges of young officers modelled on the *Erasmus* scheme; improved functioning of the European Security and Defence College; creation of European teams of experts to deliver security-sector reform.

Several new developments in the defence industrial sector were also announced, including support for the EDA's strategy for a 'robust and competitive European defence technological and industrial base (EDTIB)', leading to 'the emergence of world-class trans-national European groups, backed up by a network of EU-wide [small and medium-sized enterprises (SMEs)]' organised around key technologies. While recognising that this process must be industry led, the declaration insisted that member states would facilitate its progression, particularly through the 'preservation of key industrial capabilities in Europe, so as to lessen our dependence for key defence technologies on non-EU suppliers'. The Council also proved supportive of the European Commission's so-called 'defence package', promoting intra-Community transfers of defence-related products and the coordination of fully transparent procedures for public defence and security contracts, especially with regard to SMEs. Particular attention was paid to research and technology (R&T), where Europe lags behind the United States. The EDA announced a European defence R&T strategy on 10 November 2008, including a target of 2% of defence spending to be earmarked for R&T; a multinational fund into which states could pay to help finance cooperation between private and public stakeholders in defence R&T; enhanced cooperation between the European Commission and the EDA as well as a new relationship between the EDA and the six-nation Organisation for Joint

Armament Cooperation, in which the latter would take on board some of the executive functions of the former, allowing the EDA to focus more closely on R&T. The role of the EDA was upgraded, its personnel were increased to 110, and its budget was raised to €30 million (the first time an EDA budget increase raised no objections from any member state).

Implementation of this considerable package would depend heavily on inputs from forthcoming Swedish (July–December 2009) and Spanish (January–June 2010) presidencies. The French decision to flag re-entry into NATO lowered Central and Eastern European resistance to ESDP, reinforced by clear signals that Washington officially approved of enhanced, autonomous European capacity. Poland staked out a claim on four of the projects, including the future European transport helicopter; Romania and Slovenia were involved in two projects each and Estonia, Slovakia and Hungary one each. The Czech Republic remained hostage to the euroscepticism of President Vaclav Klaus, while Lithuania and Latvia struggled to find roles. Otherwise, all member states were participating in one or several of these developments, with the exceptions of Ireland and Austria, both of which were unable for domestic political reasons to play a part.

> Threats facing the EU had become more complex

There were two reasons for cautious optimism. The first was that the methodology of capacity generation was now widely accepted. All member states, including the large ones, accepted the necessity of rationalisation, pooling, sharing and specialisation. Paradoxically, the financial crisis helped drive this home. Specific commitments were written into the declaration to this effect. If the Lisbon Treaty were to survive the second Irish referendum in October 2009, the introduction of 'permanent structured cooperation' should give these processes a boost. Secondly, there was growing recognition in EU capitals of the need to shift from a purely reactive ESDP to a more strategic vision. Although a year-long review of the 2003 ESS produced no major breakthroughs, the Council report on the implementation of the ESS, 'Providing Security in a Changing World', also made public at the December 2008 summit, did recognise that, over the preceding five years, the threats facing the EU had become 'increasingly complex', that 'we must be ready to shape events [by] becoming more strategic in our thinking', and that this would involve being 'more effective and visible around the world'. The EU had both a normative responsibility to contribute more to twenty-first-century crisis management and nation-building and the empirical ability to assume a growing share of that global burden. The Obama administration had made it clear that what it expected of the EU was the generation of usable capacity. That was likely to be the real price of partnership in a revitalised transatlantic relationship. Under the French presidency, the EU launched three important new missions: the Georgia peace-monitoring mission, its first naval operation to counter piracy off Somalia, and the Kosovo rule-of-law mission. The French presidency thus achieved real progress in this area.

France and the global financial meltdown

Sarkozy's handling of the global financial crisis was yet another paradox. It was partly as a result of Sarkozy's prompting that international leaders agreed to hold an initial meeting of the G20 in Washington in November 2008 and to renew that encounter in London in April 2009. France argued that the UN was too inefficient a body to handle the global meltdown, and the G8 too unrepresentative. The G20 became the preferred forum for coordination of the international economy. In London, Sarkozy succeeded in projecting himself as an apostle of traditional French state interventionism and an advocate of robust international regulation of the very market forces which, as a presidential candidate, he had energetically promoted. During his 2007 election campaign, he had given the impression – much applauded by the business community and denounced by the left – that he intended fully to embrace market liberalism, which in France is often referred to in scathing terms as the 'Anglo-Saxon model' of capitalism. But while his opponent Ségolène Royal spoke of protecting the French people from globalisation, Sarkozy formulated the rather ambivalent notion of protecting them within globalisation – in other words, a combination of economic liberalism and political interventionism. He insisted that his vision of Europe was categorically not one in which the EU became 'a Trojan horse for a globalisation reduced to the circulation of capital and goods' and he unambiguously denounced the off-shoring and outsourcing of jobs.

There is little doubt that Sarkozy had initially intended to wage all-out war on state-protected restrictive practices and on the stranglehold of special-interest groups. His first battle, against the special pension privileges of the powerful railway workers, ended in victory. He argued that French republican egalitarianism demanded that railway workers retire, like everyone else, after 40 years of employment (rather than at age 50 for train conductors). His discourse resonated with the public, and the striking *cheminots* were left high and dry. However, subsequent campaigns against taxi drivers, fishermen and automotive-industry workers, coinciding with the onset of the financial crisis, saw the French president back off in the face of mass protests in the streets. He then made a complete U-turn and began launching rhetorical attacks against the European single market, against the unfair advantages of the low-wage economies in Central and Eastern Europe (even threatening to prevent the sale in France of Peugeot cars made in the Czech Republic) and eventually in favour of ever-greater protectionism. His opportunistic return to traditional Colbertist values proved to be both significant and effective once the economic crisis really began to hit.

In October 2008, he announced a €360 billion rescue package for French banks and in February 2009 announced a further €26bn package to protect the construction and automobile sectors, as well as tax credits for the poorest families. France thus avoided the near bank failures which plagued the UK, the hesitation and drift which hobbled the German response, and the collapse of entire economic sectors which afflicted Spain. On 12 October, as president of the EU, Sarkozy convened an emergency meeting of the 15 heads of state and government of the eurozone, together with the president of the European Central Bank, to urge upon all European countries the injection of liquidity into the financial system, state guarantees for inter-bank loans and state recapitalisation of banks in difficulty. The supreme irony came in May 2009 when the *Economist* newspaper, for which any hint of Colbertism is anathema, fulsomely praised France and its president for having succeeded better than any other major economy in weathering the financial storm. This traditional mouthpiece of the 'Anglo-Saxon model' noted that, in France, gross domestic product was set to shrink in 2009 by the lowest figure (3%) of any of the major capitalist economies; that the state deficit, as well as household debt, was half that of the United States; that no bank had failed; that the gap between the highest and the lowest income brackets was far smaller than in either Britain or the United States; and that, among many other top-performing French industries, Air France (unlike its main competitor British Airways) was in excellent shape. Sarkozy proclaimed, in March 2009, that 'so far, we haven't put a foot wrong'. He succeeded in presenting his own U-turn as an example of enlightened statesmanship.

Return to NATO

France's much-heralded return to NATO's integrated command structures was formally announced at the Alliance's 60th anniversary summit in

Strasbourg/Kehl on 4 April 2009. There were two very obvious reasons for the move: it made perfect military sense in the present; and it made good political sense for the future.

The military reason had to do with the opportunity costs of staying out. In the 1991 Gulf War, Mitterrand became the first post-1945 French leader to send French troops into battle under American command. The military lessons drawn from the Gulf conflict all pointed in the same direction: France's absence from NATO's integrated structures presented the great-est obstacle to her performing militarily according to her own perception of 'rank'. Once the French armed forces began to find themselves involved in conventional operations, it became obvious that their exclusion from the integrated command structures was a liability. French troops were under fire and, in the Balkans, increasingly under NATO command. Mitterrand re-joined NATO's Military Committee in 1993, and his successor Chirac then moved France's new Alliance policy to a higher level. On 14 June 1995, the newly elected president spent more than an hour in a tête-à-tête with US President Bill Clinton and persuaded him to use NATO bombers against the Bosnian Serbs. Under Chirac, France rejoined every NATO committee but two.

> The step taken by Sarkozy was logical and inevitable

Chirac had tried to return fully to the fold in 1996–97. His bid for full reintegration on two conditions (deep structural reform of the Alliance; and a major European/French command – AFSOUTH in Naples) was rejected by Clinton. This had major implications for Paris during the Kosovo War of 1999. Although France was the second-largest force contributor during that war, the French ambassador to NATO could not attend the key strategic meetings of the Defence Planning Committee and had to drive over to the US ambassador's residence to learn what had been decided in his absence. For the Afghan campaign, in 2002, Chirac deployed a quarter of France's navy. After all this, the step taken by Sarkozy was logical and inevitable. The rewards were appreciable: France will provide the commander of NATO's Allied Command Transformation, based in Norfolk, Virginia, and also that of NATO's Regional Command in Lisbon.

France faced three huge challenges regarding NATO from the day the Berlin Wall fell: how to reconcile its semi-detached status within the Alliance with growing participation in the military missions of the post-Cold War world; how to ensure that its voice carried its full weight in the ongoing debates about where the Alliance was heading; and how to square the growing pressure for an autonomous ESDP with Alliance transformation.

During the internal French debates over NATO reintegration in spring 2009, these political questions generated real heat. The Socialist opposition charged that Sarkozy's policy amounted to re-alignment with the United States, and that France had abandoned her distinctive Gaullist position on the international stage. They argued, disingenuously, that if France had been a full member of NATO in 2003, it would have been obliged to join the war in Iraq and that with reintegration it would in future be under greater obligation to participate in NATO missions. The issues broke down into two separate clusters: questions about France's independence; and those about her future influence.

There was no good reason to assume that NATO re-integration would have any effect on France's diplomatic independence. It could even be argued that it might increase the impact of that independence. Had France, in 2003, been a member of the integrated command structure of NATO, its opposition to the Iraq war might well have been more influential with third countries (particularly in Central and Eastern Europe). France's outsider status allowed critics to castigate its approach to Iraq as further evidence of stereotypical anti-Americanism. But questions about France's future influence over key NATO policy issues were more difficult to answer with any certainty. Although Sarkozy tied up a number of loose military ends, he was taking a political gamble on the future. France intended to be fully involved in the political challenge of deciding the post-Afghanistan fate of the Alliance. But on a number of key issues, France (and Sarkozy) appeared to be at odds with emerging US policy on Afghanistan/Pakistan, relations with Russia, missile defence and on NATO's core mission as well as its future strategic concept and further enlargement.

One of Sarkozy's explicit objectives in rejoining the Alliance command structure was to remove an obstacle to the development of the EU's defence and security capabilities: the attitude of the new member states from the former Soviet bloc, which saw a French-led ESDP drive as undermining NATO. With France fully back inside the Alliance, the Central and Eastern Europeans could no longer argue that there was a contradiction between ESDP and NATO. Yet, as Sarkozy never tired of saying, ESDP was, for France, an 'absolute priority', while NATO's future remained to be defined. With France now back inside the tent the conversation was likely to become lively.

Germany: Vulnerabilities in an Election Year

The year to mid 2009 was dominated in Germany by the economic downturn and by the looming general election, scheduled for 27 September. However, as the economy went into steep decline and unemployment rose sharply following the global financial crisis of autumn 2008, the relative standing of the parties in opinion polls changed little.

The centre-right Christian Democratic Union/Christian Socialist Union (CDU/CSU) grouping led by Chancellor Angela Merkel polled between 34% and 37.5% nationally in April and May 2009, while its partner in the grand coalition, the Social Democratic Party (SPD), had failed to recover from its low point in the polls and continued to register support at 24.5% and 27%. A cluster of second-tier parties in terms of public support – the Free Democratic Party (FDP), the Greens, and the Left Party – all polled between 8% and 16%. It was thus unclear whether the grand coalition would continue after the September 2009 election, or whether the CDU/CSU and FDP would together muster enough votes to form a centre-right coalition. Although the possibility of a coalition government consisting of either CDU/CSU and Greens or a three-party coalition of CDU/CSU, FDP and Greens was sometimes floated in the media and by individual politicians, these scenarios remained very unlikely.

By April 2009, unemployment had risen by 171,000 to 3,585,000, or 8.6%, up from 8.1% a year earlier. The recession was beginning to have a direct effect on the German labour market. The Merkel government, although it took measures along with other countries to shore up the banking system in the financial crisis of autumn 2008, was reluctant to engage in expensive economic stimulus activities; the Chancellor argued she would not participate in a 'pointless race' to bail out the economy. There was no sign that Germany would abandon its traditional model of export dependence, even though exports fell sharply amid the worldwide fall in demand for goods. Exports were down almost 29% and imports by 23% on the previous year in April 2009, the worst month yet. However, with the German economy projected to contract faster than those of other European countries, the government's position had to be adjusted against the backdrop of the general election. In February 2009, the German parliament approved some €50 billion in public investment and tax breaks over two years, the largest stimulus package in German post-war history. Together with earlier measures, this amounted to some 1.2% of gross domestic product, but this was still a modest figure in comparison to other Western countries.

The 2009 defence budget was set at €31.2bn, an increase of some €1.7bn over the previous year. Since about €1bn of this increase covered increases in pay, Germany was expected to continue to struggle to fund investment priorities already identified. However, the Ministry of Defence was to receive some €500m of the 2009 stimulus package, with half to be spent on infrastructure such as renovation and construction of barracks, and the other to buy armoured patrol vehicles, armoured reconnaissance vehicles and underwater mine detection drones.

Terror concerns on the rise

Release of a string of German-language jihadist videos raised concerns that Germany might find itself a target of international terrorists in the run-up to the election. Widely reported in the German media, these videos were the first to threaten Germany specifically and to feature German citizens.

For example, a 21-year-old member of the Islamic Jihad Union (IJU), Erich Breininger, threatened Germany in a video entitled 'A Call from Hindu Kush' in October 2008. On 10 January 2009, an individual calling himself Abu Adam from Germany, an alleged member of the Islamic Movement of Uzbekistan (IMU), called on German 'brothers' to join jihad in a video entitled 'Good Message from Afghanistan'. In March 2009, two brothers of Moroccan origin, Mounir and Yassim C. (aged 27 and 24), believed to be affiliated with the IMU, called for suicide attacks in Germany.

A video released by al-Qaeda's media arm As-Sahab on 16 January 2009, featuring Bekkay Harrach, a German citizen of Moroccan origin, entitled 'A Bailout Plan for Germany' received the most public attention. Harrach had become a German citizen in 1997, and was married to a German. He had been under surveillance since 2001 and was believed to have lived in the Afghanistan–Pakistan border region since 2007. The security services believed he had access to senior al-Qaeda leaders and was trained by Abu Ubaida al-Masri, an al-Qaeda planning chief killed in early 2008 and allegedly linked to the 7 July 2005 London bombings and the foiled 2006 liquid bomb plot which aimed to bring down transatlantic airliners. Harrach was said to live in Waziristan and was allegedly involved in planning attacks against local and international security forces in the area. In the video, he sought to influence German voters and warned of attacks unless German troops were pulled out of Afghanistan. Further videos emerging in June

2009 provided evidence of a direct link between al-Qaeda and the IJU; they showed IJU leaders together with Abu Jahja al-Libi, a prominent religious figure in al-Qaeda's leadership circle.

German officials said the videos represented a qualitative change in that the propaganda was being directly aimed at Germany. August Hanning, former head of the German intelligence service BND and now a senior official in the Ministry of the Interior, said that 'the Islamists apparently want to influence Germany's election'. Jörg Zierke, head of the Federal Criminal Policy Office, remarked that 'we have observed meaningful parallels to the situation in Spain' before the Madrid train attacks of 2004. An official in the German domestic intelligence agency, the Office for the Protection of the Constitution, estimated that the number of Muslims in Germany ready to engage in violence ran to three digits. Between 50 and 100 Islamists based in Germany were thought to have completed training in terror camps in Afghanistan or Pakistan, with at least a dozen believed to be undergoing such training as of early 2009. Even though, as Minister of the Interior Wolfgang Schäuble pointed out, Germany had been on the target list of jihadist terrorists for some time, the increase in directly targeted messages highlighted the vulnerability of Germany as a result of its engagement in Afghanistan. German security services said German companies or citizens in North Africa would be the most likely targets, as intelligence provided by the United States suggested the organisation al-Qaeda in the Islamic Maghreb had been tasked by the al-Qaeda leadership in Afghanistan and Pakistan to carry out attacks. However, it was unclear whether the terror network could work effectively beyond North Africa.

Afghanistan: growing trouble in the north

In October 2008 the Bundestag approved an increase in the ceiling for the number of troops that the government could deploy to Afghanistan. An overwhelming majority of 442 to 96 (with 32 abstentions) voted for the increase from 3,500 to 4,500 with a 14-month mandate, extending the mission beyond the September 2009 election. At a NATO meeting in February 2009, Defence Minister Franz Josef Jung said Germany would increase its deployment by some 600 troops, of whom 200 would be for increased security for the Afghan elections scheduled for August. The remainder would reinforce Germany's quick-reaction force, and improve force protection and training capabilities. The increase would bring Germany close to the new ceiling. A NATO decision on 12 June 2009 to deploy up to four AWACS aircraft to Afghanistan looked likely to force another increase in the German deployment ceiling before the current mandate ran out because a significant number of personnel involved were German. The government was thus discussing plans to ask parliament to authorise up to 300 extra troops in conjunction with the AWACS deployment. The matter appeared likely to come before the Bundestag in July 2009 and the deployment could be authorised in the form of a parliamentary mandate separate from the overall ISAF mandate, in the same way the deployment of *Tornado* reconnaissance jets to Afghanistan was initially authorised. In May 2009, during a visit to Germany by Afghan President Hamid Karzai, Merkel promised additional German efforts for police training. German leaders, however, continued to resist calls by several allies to lift restrictions on where troops could be deployed; the German contingent was to remain in the north of Afghanistan.

> German forces were set to become a key target for the Taliban

Meanwhile, the security situation in the north, particularly in Kunduz province, was deteriorating and attacks on German personnel were becoming more sophisticated. During a surprise visit by Foreign Minister Frank-Walter Steinmeier in April 2009, two attacks killed one German soldier and injured nine. Unlike the hit-and-run or suicide-bomb tactics encountered in the past, the attacks were well-planned ambushes. General Wolfgang Schneiderhan, the armed forces chief, argued that they demonstrated a new quality of threat.

According to NATO's ISAF command, German forces were set to become a key target for a Taliban offensive. US reinforcements in the south and east of Afghanistan were displacing insurgents, whose leaders were said to have decided that Germany's fragile domestic consensus on the deployment, particularly in the context of the upcoming election, made Germany a weak link in the coalition. Local commanders in the north were thought to have begun to cooperate closely with al-Qaeda and to accept direction from insurgent leaders in Peshawar and Quetta in Pakistan.

These events suggested that, even though northern Afghanistan was still a much less hostile environment than other regions of the country, the German narrative that its forces were essentially engaged in reconstruction tasks was becoming harder to maintain. By mid May 2009, 32 German soldiers had been killed in Afghanistan. SPD member of parliament Hans-Ulrich Klose, deputy chairman of the foreign-affairs committee, scolded colleagues for being 'afraid to tell the people [in Germany] that we sent soldiers to Afghanistan to fight there'.

Piracy fuels armed force debate

The issue of piracy triggered further discussion about whether the German basic law (the constitution) would need to be adapted to better reflect the demands of international deployments. With the world's largest container fleet and third-largest merchant fleet, Germany was particularly vulnerable to piracy. As the German navy participated in European Union and NATO anti-piracy missions off the coast of Somalia, there was debate over whether it was legally allowed to pursue and arrest alleged pirates.

The problem received renewed attention in spring 2009 after an aborted attempt to storm a German merchant ship, the *Hansa Stavanger*, which had been hijacked off Somalia in early April. A large part of GSG-9, a German anti-terrorism police unit trained for hostage rescue, was moved to Africa to conduct the operation, but by the time it had deployed more pirates had boarded the *Hansa Stavanger*. GSG-9 conducted a dry run of the planned operation on an American navy vessel which, according to GSG-9 head Olaf Lindner, produced excellent results. Lindner argued that, despite the new facts on the ground, the risks of a rescue operation were acceptable. However, his political masters cancelled the operation at the last minute, citing unacceptable risks to the lives of hostages and GSG-9 personnel. The vessel was still held by pirates at mid 2009.

The political debate which followed reflected a long-running dispute between the parties in the coalition government. According to the coalition agreement, the use of the armed forces in assistance missions to civilian authorities was to be discussed. But the issue was left mostly untouched by the 2006 defence and security White Paper because the CDU/CSU advocated broader changes than the SPD was willing to entertain. The CDU/CSU, which held the chancellery, ministry of defence and ministry of the interior, argued that under the basic law the Bundeswehr was not allowed to become involved in fighting crime, and that the pursuit and arrest of pirates was a police matter. Since the German coast guard did not have the capability to act internationally, the CDU/CSU argued for a change to the basic law to allow the navy to take on this task. The SPD, which held the foreign ministry, maintained that the involvement of the navy would be covered either by the basic law's *in extremis* clause, which allowed the armed forces to play a role in disaster relief or other emergencies, or by international mandates that provided backing to operations. On this argument, it was already legal for the navy to act under current provisions and a change to the basic law would be unnecessary. The SPD's unwillingness to compromise was driven by suspicion that its coalition partner would use the piracy issue to remove limitations on the domestic use of the armed forces. Merkel, Jung and Schäuble were all on the record as being in favour of a change to the basic law, but leading SPD politicians insisted there would be no change before the election.

While the debate about the role of Germany's armed forces lumbered on unresolved, events in the year to June 2009 underlined the complex linkages between the security situation in Germany and in distant theatres such as Afghanistan, as well as the challenge leaders faced in communicating those links effectively to the electorate. It seemed that terrorists and insurgents in Afghanistan had concluded that the 2009 election provided an opportunity to exploit such tensions. Senior government leaders insisted they were committed to operations in Afghanistan, but the fragile domestic consensus on defence and security questions remained a vulnerability.

United Kingdom: Political Drift

In a gloomy year for the United Kingdom, the economy contracted sharply, unemployment and public debt soared, and the government was forced to rescue two of the top four banks by taking significant equity stakes. Although its successful crisis-response measures to restore the stability of financial markets were copied in other countries, they did little for the domestic standing of Gordon Brown, the prime minister. He clung grimly to power. But opinion polls indicated that the Labour party's majority in parliament would be lost in elections due by June 2010.

Under Tony Blair, Labour had ended 18 years in opposition and handsomely won elections in 1997, 2001 and 2005 – the last in spite of British participation in the highly unpopular Iraq War. For ten years, Brown schemed to succeed Blair, and he did so when Blair stepped down in 2007 and the party chose him as its leader. However, his first year in office from June 2007 saw him struggling to articulate a purpose for his premiership as his party became increasingly concerned about his leadership abilities. During his second year, his awkwardness in office was even more in evidence, and he was still unable to give voice to a compelling message. He was highly vulnerable to events – and then the financial crisis broke in September 2008.

Stemming financial mayhem

By the time the world's financial markets seized up, Britain had already experienced the effects of excessive property lending. Northern Rock, a mortgage lender, had obtained emergency support from the Bank of England in September 2007 because the drying up of credit on the wholesale money markets prevented it from funding its loan book. It was taken into state ownership five months later. Some other specialist mortgage-lending banks, which had lent aggressively during the property-market boom, were also in difficulties as real-estate prices fell, loan-default rates rose and they encountered funding problems in the markets. As in many other countries, the problems that had been building up in credit markets came to a head in September 2008 when Lehman Brothers, the US investment bank, went bankrupt, leaving counterparties to its transactions exposed to billions of dollars of losses. London's status as a hub of the world's financial markets, with hundreds of foreign banks represented and very large daily trading volumes in all markets, made it especially vulnerable to the effects of the crisis.

The government quickly engineered the takeover of HBOS, a bank formed through the merger of property lender Halifax with the Bank of Scotland, by Lloyds Bank. But as the crisis escalated, share prices of all banks fell sharply. For the first time in the postwar period, British savers began to be concerned about the safety of their bank accounts. The result was a £500 billion government rescue package for British banks announced on 8 October, including plans to inject £50bn to shore up banks' equity. The principal purpose was to restore banks' confidence in each other so that normal daily business could resume and the extraordinarily high rates they were charging each other for money could fall. Because the measures seemed simultaneously to tackle all points of banks' weaknesses – providing more capital to protect against losses, offering loan guarantees for interbank lending, and increasing short-term loans available from the Bank of England – they halted the panic. The government put its weight behind the banking system, making it clear that banks would not be allowed to fail and that deposits were safe. The package was immediately taken as a model for other countries. The United States and many European countries quickly copied it – and their central banks had already coordinated on interest-rate cuts and moves to assist banks' liquidity.

As the measures were put into effect, the weakest large banks received substantial injections of equity funding. Royal Bank of Scotland, which owned National Westminster Bank and had expanded aggressively through acquisitions, was woefully exposed, and the government took a 70% controlling stake. After several transactions, it owned a 43% stake in Lloyds. While this occurred in a palpable emergency, it was still an extraordinary turnabout for the government. Although the Labour party had nationalised large parts of British business during its heavily socialist past, it had over the past 12 years carried on the process of privatisation begun in the 1980s by Margaret Thatcher. However, the state holdings seemed unlikely to be long term and concerns about a cultural shift towards state-directed banking were further mitigated by the fact that two other main banks, Barclays and HSBC, remained free of government ownership. There was widespread public anger, but a good part of it was directed at the excesses of bankers who were seen as having paid themselves enormous bonuses while putting the country at risk through imprudent lending and trading. In March 2009 the Edinburgh home of the former Royal Bank of Scotland chief, who left with a generous pension when the government took over, was vandalised.

All in all, the handling of the autumn financial mayhem improved Britain's international standing and that of Brown himself. As the financial crunch became a global economic crisis, Brown's international position was further enhanced in April 2009 when he hosted the G20 summit in London – a meeting preceded by months of preparation in which Brown and his ministers and officials travelled extensively. While new measures agreed did not match the extravagant claims of the final communiqué, the summit was widely judged to be a success and a useful step forward towards new forms of global governance.

The UK military after Iraq

Britain's 19-year involvement in military operations in Iraq came to an end in June 2009 as its troops and aircraft pulled out of the south of the country. Britain had contributed significantly to the US-led coalition force that expelled Iraqi forces from Kuwait in 1991, to the air patrols and other operations that followed, to the March 2003 US-led invasion of Iraq, and to the subsequent occupation of the country. There was considerable debate about whether the last part of this sequence, the six years of stabilisation operations in the south, had been a successful venture for the British military. This, in turn, had cast a shadow over a capability in post-conflict reconstruction that had been seen as one of the UK forces' particular strengths. For many Britons, the discussion was clouded by the general belief that the invasion had been a mistake and had been undertaken by the American and British governments on false grounds. However, Iraq in 2009 was a far more stable and less dangerous country than it had been at the height of insurgent violence in 2006, and the coalition military presence had clearly played a role in this improvement.

As the last troops pulled out, Brown announced an inquiry into the Iraq War, which had been called for by many, including relatives of some of the 179 military personnel who had died in Iraq since the 2003 invasion. The inquiry was to be led by a retired civil servant with a small team of eminent ex-officials and historians – but no one with military experience. It was immediately attacked because it was to be held behind closed doors on grounds of national security. Even military officers opposed this, and the government quickly backtracked and said that evidence sessions would be held in public to the greatest extent possible. While the inquiry report, due in 2010, will provide fodder for long-running political arguments, an honest debate was clearly needed about the role, doctrine and capabilities of UK forces in light of the Iraq mission. This, in turn, would hold lessons for a full-scale defence review expected to be carried out following the general election, whichever party won.

The last defence review in 1998, seen as a model process, had set a structure for UK forces based on the expected requirement to take part in a wide range of operations abroad. However, the number, duration and nature of the operations in which Britain participated put both the military and their budget under severe strain. A new review was urgently required to help match future capabilities to national ambitions. The need to ensure adequate capabilities was highlighted by the British presence in Afghanistan, where 8,000 British troops were engaged daily in combat operations against Taliban insurgents in the southern province of Helmand.

Security threats also continued to be evident at home, with a series of arrests under anti-terrorist laws and trials of terrorist suspects. Jonathan Evans, head of Britain's domestic intelligence service (known as MI5), said in January 2009 that 86 convictions in trials of terrorists over the previous two years had had a 'chilling effect' on networks of al-Qaeda sympathisers. Many people who had been involved in attacks in the UK had a link to Pakistan, and al-Qaeda's leaders there wished to mount further attacks using British citizens. Some 2,000 people in Britain were under surveillance, but they were 'keeping their heads down', having learned lessons from trials in which intelligence methods were disclosed. Meanwhile, MI5 was concerned about dissident Irish republicans who had not forsworn the struggle for Irish unity in spite of the peace agreement. On 7 March 2009, two British soldiers were shot dead outside their base in Northern Ireland, hours before they were due to depart for Afghanistan. They were the first British troops to be killed in a terrorist attack there since 1997.

Political malaise

As in other countries, the near-collapse of the banking system brought in its wake a sharp economic recession which had political repercussions. The Organisation for Economic Cooperation and Development projected in June 2009 that the UK economy would contract by 4.3% during the year. Unemployment rose by nearly two percentage points over the year to stand at 7.2% in April 2009. But the biggest cause for alarm was the level of government borrowing. Because of liabilities taken on to deal with the financial crisis, public-sector net debt ballooned to 54.7% of GDP at end of May 2009, compared with 43.6% a year before. The UK Treasury forecast that public-sector net borrowing would almost double in the 2009/10 financial year to £175bn, and would remain at elevated levels for some years. This was caused by a combination of increases in welfare spending reflecting the downturn, and the fall in tax revenues also associated with the recession, including taxes on previously profitable financial services. Even seasoned economists were staggered by the borrowing projections, and warned that official forecasts of future reductions in borrowing needs were predicated on unrealistic forecasts about the pace of economic recovery.

Viewed from its own perspective, the government of Gordon Brown was well qualified to deal with these problems. Brown could boast of his ten years' experience as finance minister (not to mention his previous single-minded and long preparation for that job). The financial and economic crisis, he argued repeatedly, was a global phenomenon that originated in the United States. The success of the October 2008 bank rescue package bolstered his case that he was the man to lead Britain through it.

However, these arguments did not wash at all as a domestic political drama played out in parallel with the financial and economic traumas. Rather than as saviour, Brown was seen as bearing a large share of responsibility for the UK's particular mess. Yes, the crisis had begun abroad, but wasn't Britain's debt already dangerously high because of rapidly rising spending by Brown in his later years at the Treasury – a period in which he had dictated the finances with barely a reference to other departmental ministers? Yes, bankers had behaved badly, but were they not allowed to get out of control because of a poor system of financial regulation introduced by Brown himself? And hadn't Brown promised an end to 'boom-and-bust'? On top of these accusations, there was his brooding personality, his obsessive, dour work ethic, his inability to express a purpose for his government.... Small wonder, therefore, that concerns mounted within his party of a looming electoral disaster. Twice in nine months, in October 2008 and June 2009, he was forced to shuffle his cabinet in efforts to re-launch his government and impose his authority upon it. A clear sign of his desperate position was his decision to bring into government Peter Mandelson, a bitter party rival who had twice had to resign from Blair's cabinet because of personal errors, and who then spent four years as European Trade Commissioner in Brussels. In an extraordinary turnabout, Mandelson rapidly became a powerful government figure, on whom Brown depended.

> "A temporary bounce was soon reversed"

The first reshuffle, combined with the bank rescue five days later, did give Brown a temporary bounce in opinion polls. But as the recession deepened, this was soon reversed. The prime minister's continuing failure to assert himself was seen painfully by the time of the June reshuffle. By then, some cabinet members were manoeuvring to unseat him. At the same time, others found themselves in untenable positions as the *Daily Telegraph* newspaper revealed tawdry details of the expenses claims of all 646 members of the House of Commons, the lower house. The amounts of money involved were small by the standards of, for example, the United States. MPs – whose annual salary was £65,000 (about $100,000) – were allowed to claim up to £23,000 a year to help cover the costs of a 'second home', which might be in London or in their constituency. However, the items for which MPs had claimed within these allowances, as well as the way in which many had switched their designated 'second homes' for financial benefit, did not make good reading. The revelations did no favours to any party, but appeared to accelerate Labour's downward slide. Clamour for a leadership change became loud. But Labour leaders are hard to depose:

the signatures of 70 MPs are required to trigger a leadership election. In the crucial week, a series of resignations among government ministers – some of whom publicly urged Brown to go – failed to find sufficient backing either from other senior ministers or rank-and-file MPs. Helped by the absence of a clear candidate to replace him, Brown refused to go. Mandelson's support was crucial, and he became de facto deputy prime minister.

The year's entire sequence of events left politicians in low esteem among the British public. Only with a general election could come a government that might have the authority to pursue fresh policy directions, whether at home or abroad. The Labour party had, in effect, decided that it was a better bet to retain Brown and thus delay an election until 2010 than to pick a new leader who, as the second successive unelected prime minister, would be expected to call an election within months. While the party might not win the election, the delay might produce a less disastrous result. However, whenever it might be held, the likely outcome was uncertain, in spite of the Conservatives' lead in the polls. The Conservative party under David Cameron continued, as it had for 12 years, to be reticent about its likely future policies, now using the recession and poor government finances as its cover. The political situation remained volatile, the public mood poor and policies in limbo.

Sluggishness in the Balkans

2008–09 presented a mixed picture in the western Balkans. All the western Balkan economies have been hit hard by the world financial crisis, with Serbia alone requiring a $3 billion loan from the International Monetary Fund (IMF). At the same time, there were positive developments across the region, though they were often invisible. One of the most promising signs was rapid development of routine meetings and contacts between the region's officials, from central bankers to policemen to ministers, which in previous years had been scarce. In key regional forums, and despite occasional spats and walk-outs, even Serbian and Kosovar representatives sat together, though the latter insisted that Kosovo be referred to as Kosovo/1244 (citing the now practically defunct UN resolution on Kosovo dating from 1999 that fell short of according it independence) rather than the Republic of Kosovo.

In terms of hard security, Albania and Croatia joined NATO on 1 April 2009. Macedonia was left out after Greece effectively vetoed an invitation for it to join at NATO's Bucharest summit in April 2008. In Bosnia, EU-led peacekeeping troops were drawn down from their previous figure of some 6,000 to 2,016 by July 2009, but a plan to reduce that number further to a symbolic 200 by the end of the year was put on hold. NATO announced that it planned to reduce the number of troops it had in Kosovo from 13,289 in June 2009 to 10,000 by January 2010 and then to 2,500 over the next 12–24 months due to 'the improving security situation'. The European Union Rule of Law Mission in Kosovo, EULEX, designed to reinforce the fledgling state's law-enforcement capacity, increased its personnel to 1,600 internationals and 900 local staff.

The principal disappointment of the year was the stalled integration of Bosnia-Herzegovina, Serbia, Croatia and Macedonia into the EU. The persistent struggle within the former country between Bosniak (Bosnian Muslim) and Serbian leaders reinforced the country's political stagnation and meant that no progress could be made along its EU accession path. Croatia, the closest among the Balkan states to joining the EU, was drawn into an intensifying border quarrel with EU member Slovenia, which blocked its progress. Macedonia's EU path remained impeded by Greece over the 18-year dispute about the country's name. Serbia's EU progress was halted by the Netherlands, which demanded the arrest and extradition to the International Criminal Tribunal for the former Yugoslavia (ICTY) in The Hague of Ratko Mladic, the former Bosnian Serb military commander indicted for, among other alleged crimes, the murder of some 8,000 Bosniak men and boys in the town of Srebrenica in July 1995.

Nationalist fatigue in Serbia

In Serbia, the formation of a new government in July 2008 brought to power a coalition dominated by the pro-European Democratic Party (DS) of President Boris Tadic. To consolidate power, however, Tadic needed to lure the Socialist Party of Serbia, formerly led by the late Slobodan Milosevic, whom Tadic's predecessor as leader of the DS had tried to oust in 2000, from the opposition nationalist group.

Notwithstanding the irony, the new Serbian government came to power with confidence and optimism. Indeed, almost immediately the police arrested Radovan Karadzic, the former Bosnian Serb leader wanted, like Mladic, for war crimes. He was sent to The Hague on 29 July 2008. This left only Mladic and Goran Hadzic, a former Croatian Serb leader, as tribunal indictees at large.

The Karadzic story was a colourful one. Far from hiding in caves or Serbian Orthodox monasteries as had been widely believed, Karadzic had spent several years living in Belgrade under the assumed identity of one Dragan David Dabic, and had begun to carve out a reputation for himself as a noted alternative health guru who sold treatments for impotence. Once arrested, Karadzic shaved off his bushy beard and top knot and reverted to his former self. In The Hague, he argued vigorously that he had been given immunity from arrest by Richard Holbrooke, the US diplomat who brokered the end of the Bosnian war in 1995, in exchange for stepping down from power. Holbrooke, now the US special envoy to Afghanistan and Pakistan, denied this vigorously. The fact that Karadzic was arrested just as the Serbian intelligence service came under the control of the DS suggested that it had known all along where he was and that Vojislav Kostunica, the outgoing prime minister who openly loathed the ICTY, had protected Karadzic.

> **Serbia's political landscape was redrawn**

Upon Karadzic's arrest, nationalists in Serbia, particularly the powerful Serbian Radical Party (SRS) – once led by Vojislav Seselj, who has been held at The Hague for trial since 2003 – promised a 'long, hot autumn'. But instead of mobilising support against the government, the SRS suddenly imploded. Encouraged by Tadic and fed up with executing prison-cell diktats from Seselj, whose politics remained firmly anchored in the war years, SRS party leader Tamislav Nikolic founded a new party and took much of the old one with him. His idea was to move away from warmongering Greater Serbian nationalists mired in the past towards a more moderate nationalist European Christian Democrat position. Serbia's three municipal elections in May 2009 confirmed what opinion polls had shown throughout the winter and spring: that Serbia was indeed ready for his more moderate style of politics. Thus, Serbia's political landscape was redrawn with the emergence of a serious new opposition force that might entertain a coalition with the DS in the future.

In the realm of foreign affairs, Serbia had two main objectives. One was to prevent further recognitions of Kosovo, which declared independence from Serbia on 18 February 2008; the second was to accelerate EU integration. These policies quickly proved contradictory. The EU wanted to deploy EULEX throughout Kosovo, not just in Albanian areas, but Belgrade opposed its presence in the Serbian-controlled north and in Serbian enclaves. Although five EU countries (Greece, Cyprus, Spain, Slovakia and Romania) have not recognised Kosovo, all had endorsed the wide deployment of EULEX. Thus, Serbian opposition was a major hurdle to better relations with the EU. In November 2008, the Serbian authorities, the UN and the EU reached a compromise whereby EULEX could deploy in Serbian areas provided it remained officially neutral on Kosovo's sovereign status. By summer 2009, however, EULEX had only a token presence in the north, and the fact that it had, for example, 16 advisers working in the Kosovo Ministry of Interior cast doubt on its supposed neutrality.

On the ground, Kosovo was mostly quiet. Two notable exceptions were local Serbian protests about what EULEX was supposed to be doing at the border between the north and Serbia, and, in spring 2009, over the rebuilding of houses for the return of Albanians close to the Serbian part of the divided northern town of Mitrovica. The latter prompted EULEX – filling a void in capacity caused when about 150 Serb police officers quit over the declaration of Kosovo's independence – to use teargas against the Serb protesters. In July 2009, however, most of the Serb policemen returned to their duties.

Serbia's Kosovo policy centred on the International Court of Justice (ICJ) in The Hague. Belgrade's strategy was to ask the ICJ to give an advisory opinion as to whether Kosovo's declaration of independence had been legal or not. The hope was that, despite pressure from the United States and others in favour of recognition, having the issue pending in an internationally respected tribunal would deter further recognitions and that, if the Serbian view prevailed, Kosovo would be forced to come back to the negotiating table. The policy was partially successful: while recognitions did not stop, they did slow to a trickle. By July 2009, 60 countries had recognised Kosovo, and it had joined the World Bank and IMF but not the UN. Many of the more recent recognitions came from small states such as the Maldives, but more important states – in particular, Saudi Arabia – weighed in as well. Perhaps most significantly, Montenegro and Macedonia also recognised Kosovar independence, leaving Bosnia as the only holdout on the issue within the region of the former Yugoslavia.

The unstated perverseness of Serbia's Kosovo policy rested on the fact that its architects actually did not want Kosovo back. They understood that it was unrealistic and undesirable for Kosovo, with its hostile ethnic Albanian majority, to be reintegrated into Serbia. In reality, therefore, the policy appeared to be intended to pave the way for partition or, if the ICJ handed down a judgment broadly favourable to Serbia, even an exchange of territory involving the Serbian north and the Albanian-inhabited Presevo valley in southern Serbia.

By summer 2009 it had become clear that Serbia's Kosovo and EU policies were largely backfiring. The government that had come to power in 2008 had assumed that by now it would either have the status of candidate for EU membership or would be well on the way to getting it. Just before the election of 2008 the EU had, as part of an agreement to help Tadic in the poll, accorded Serbia a Stabilisation and Association Agreement (SAA), widely regarded as the first step on the road to membership. At the same time, its implementation was frozen on the insistence of the Dutch, who demanded the arrest and extradition of Mladic first. Even so, Serbia began to implement the SAA unilaterally in the hope that the Dutch would lift their veto and free Serbia to apply for candidacy. Croatia and Macedonia are already candidates, while Montenegro applied in December 2008 and Albania in April 2009.

The long Bosnian hangover

While Serbia's relationship with Kosovo has remained the most prominent political issue in the Balkans, the perennial question of Bosnia also persists. The 1995 Dayton peace settlement gave formal sanction to the division of the country into two sub-sovereign entities: Serbian-dominated Republika Srpska and the Bosniak-Croat Federation. To help implement the arrangement, the international community created the Office of the High Representative (OHR), who was given the so-called Bonn Powers enabling him to intervene legally in Bosnian politics and to dismiss any elected leader whom he deemed to be acting against Dayton. Before 2006, with the prodding of the OHR, Bosnia had made considerable strides in becoming a more normalised state, as administrative functions were increasingly being assumed by the central state in Sarajevo. However, after the Americans failed to persuade Bosniak leader Haris Silajdzic to vote for the 'April Package' of modest constitutional changes in 2006, the country had been caught in a cycle of recrimination and deadlock. The main actors have been Silajdzic, who demanded the abolition of the Republika Srpska, which he condemned as a 'genocidal creation', and its powerful prime minister, Milorad Dodik, who responded that he did not regard Bosnia as his country and threatened a referendum on secession.

From July 2007 to March 2009, the High Representative was Miroslav Lajcak, a Czech with considerable Balkan experience. He came to office determined to rectify the situation but found that he was not sufficiently backed by the international community and accepted the post of Czech foreign minister. He commented that he did not want to be 'the rider on a dead horse', which he was quick to explain did not mean Bosnia as a country but rather the OHR. Lajcak was succeeded by Valentin Inzko, an Austrian. Many European leaders, led by Swedish Foreign Minister Carl Bildt, the first high representative, wanted to shut the office down. They argued that Bosnians needed to stand on their own two feet. The high representative is 'double-hatted', meaning he is also the EU's special representative (EUSR). Most EU governments agreed with Bildt that, at the very least, the OHR should close and that Europe's influence should be exercised through the EUSR. The United Kingdom temporised on the issue while the United States openly expressed extreme scepticism that the divided EU was capable of doing what was necessary in Bosnia. Russia sided with the EU, but suggested an institutional link between the EUSR and the UN Security Council. The EU, however, had no wish to give Russia and China a say in what an EU official should do, and ignored the proposal.

With no consensus on how to proceed, no decision was taken by the Steering Board of the multinational Peace Implementation Council for the Dayton Accords on the fate of the OHR when it met in Sarajevo on 29–30 June 2009, but the question was due to be revisited in November. Bosnian politics remained deadlocked and the Bosniak-Croat Federation virtually bankrupt as its weak government was unable to resist ever-increasing though dubious demands from war veterans' groups for pensions and benefits that it could not afford to pay.

Yet it was not all gloom in Bosnia. In March 2009, a deal was struck resolving the outstanding constitutional status of Brcko, a northern river port town with an autonomous status which does not belong to either entity. Dodik, Bosniak leader Sulejman Tihic and Bosnian Croat leader Dragan Covic also instituted a series of meetings under the banner of the Prud Group aimed at finding a more coherent way forward. On 19 May, US Vice President Joseph Biden visited Sarajevo. In an emotional speech to parliament, he implored Bosnian leaders to end their quarrels and nationalist rhetoric and come together for the good of their people. 'Your only real path to a secure and prosperous future is to join Europe as Bosnia and Herzegovina', he said. 'Right now, you're off that path.'

The speech was received, as it was meant to be, not as hectoring but as an admonition from a sincere friend of Bosnia who was deeply concerned about the current political stagnation in the country. From Bosnia, Biden went to Belgrade for the highest-level visit by an American official there since President Jimmy Carter's in 1980, and then he went to Kosovo. These stops appeared to signal a renewed interest in the Balkans by the United States, though whether such interest would endure remained to be seen.

Aggravations in Croatia

The last year ended a series of good ones for Croatia, when no news had amounted to good news. Slovenia blocked Croatia's EU accession over a dispute about where their border should be drawn in Piran Bay. On 23 October 2008, Ivo Pukanic (editor and publisher of *Nacional*, one of Croatia's most influential weekly papers) and a colleague were murdered in a car bombing in central Zagreb. Hrvoje Petrac, Croatia's most notorious crime boss, was imprisoned for kidnapping the son of General Vladimir Zagorec, who had been extradited from Austria on 2 October to face charges for stealing gems used as collateral in an arms deal during the Croatian war. Four days after being returned to Croatia, his lawyer's 26-year-old daughter, Ivana Hodak, was shot in the head and killed outside her home. For the previous two months, she had been dating Petrac's lawyer.

These sordid high-profile murders shocked Croats and drew attention to the fact that all was not well in Croatia. In general terms, Croatia has been less violent and corrupt than nearby countries like Bulgaria or Serbia, but this was little consolation. According to Croatian journalist Ines Sabalic, 'we pretended, even to ourselves, that we were always better than everyone else in the Balkans. Now this makes us seem as if we were only richer and had more sun.' On 30 June, Croatian Prime Minister Ivo Sanader resigned without notice. While Sanader's reasons for quitting were vague, leading to a torrent of gossip, lurid speculation and anger, his remark that 'the project of European integration ha[s] no chance if the principle of blackmailing is accepted as a principle of acting within the EU' suggested that frustration over his failure to advance Croatia's accession had something substantial to do with it. Sanader's resignation also came just as Croatia began to feel the full impact the world financial crisis. On the day he quit, the Croatian Central Bureau of Statistics reported that the country's GDP had contracted by 6.7% since the first quarter of 2008, that domestic demand had dropped by 10%, and that imports had fallen by 20.9% and exports by 14.2%.

The bigger picture

The single most important issue for ordinary people in the Balkans remained that of visas. To travel anywhere outside the region, all citizens of the western Balkans, except Croats, need a burdensome array of documents to secure visas. The problem for Serbia, to take an especially intractable example, turned on the issue of Kosovo. As it officially considered Kosovo an integral part of Serbia, it could not deny Kosovar Albanians passports. But the EU did not want to accord visa-free travel to Serbia only to open the door for large numbers of Kosovar Albanians to receive new biometric Serbian passports enabling them to travel to the Schengen area and stay and work there illegally. Thus, the EU required Serbia to find administrative ways of preventing large numbers of people from obtaining the new passports. In July 2009, however, the European Commission announced that Serbs, Macedonians and Montenegrins would likely be allowed visa-free travel to the European Schengen area by the beginning of 2010, though Bosnia and Albania were not ready. Kosovo was not even assessed.

Difficult though the visa issue was in terms of relations between the western Balkans and the EU, it was widely understood in European foreign ministries that it was important for ordinary people to be rewarded for work by their pro-European governments: if they were not, they might elect candidates who were unfriendly to Europe and their own neighbours. This argument carried little weight with some interior ministers, who saw the visa barrier as a way to keep undesirables, criminals and illegal migrants out of the EU space. But, especially in light Sanader's resignation, the dominant consideration appeared to be that visa restrictions would make the task of integrating the Balkan states into the EU all the harder.

European integration is the most influential factor in the politics of the western Balkans, and the promise of progress on that front has been Balkan leaders' principal source of political capital. As the Balkan states' parochial disputes, residue of conflict and economic recession, as well as EU member states' reluctance to ratify the Lisbon Treaty and rising wariness about enlargement, slow down the process, political positions centred on the rewards of EU accession will lose some traction. Yet the abandonment of integration for the Balkans is practically infeasible. With political dysfunction rising in the Balkans, it may fall to the EU to refuel the appeal of EU integration among the Balkans' electorates.

Turkey: Continuing Domestic Wrangles

On 30 July 2008, Turkey's Constitutional Court found the ruling Justice and Development Party (AKP) guilty of trying to undermine the principle of secularism embedded in the country's constitution, but narrowly voted against closing the party down, opting instead to impose a fine. The ruling put an end to months of uncertainty that had overshadowed Turkish politics and had effectively made it impossible for the AKP to implement policy. There were hopes that a verdict which satisfied neither the AKP nor its hardline secularist opponents might finally persuade both of the need for compromise and create an opportunity to heal the deepening divisions in Turkish society.

But it soon became clear that the Constitutional Court decision had merely increased mutual suspicions. For the secularists, satisfaction at a verdict that was interpreted as validating their claims that the AKP had a radical Islamist agenda was tempered by frustration that the punishment was not harsher. Within the AKP, the decision was regarded as an undemocratic assault on the national will and proof that there was still a difference between being in office and being in power.

Through late 2008 and into early 2009, the AKP focused almost exclusively on trying to tighten its grip on the administrative apparatus by securing a resounding victory in the nationwide local elections scheduled for 29 March 2009. There were also signs that AKP sympathisers in the bureaucracy were increasingly prepared to abuse their powers to try to intimidate – and even imprison – the party's critics and opponents.

Courthouse calculations

The case against the AKP had been triggered by its attempt to amend the Turkish Constitution to lift the ban which prevents female students who wear the Islamic headscarf from attending university. Even though its leaders began their careers in hardline Islamist parties, the AKP has always insisted that it is committed to the principle of secularism enshrined in the Turkish constitution by the founder of the modern republic, Mustafa Kemal Ataturk (1881–1938). But it has never made any secret of its opposition to the way in which secularism has traditionally been interpreted, particularly the headscarf ban. Hardline secularists regard lifting the ban as merely the first step in what they believe are the AKP's long-term plans to Islamicise first Turkish society and eventually the Turkish state.

The Turkish military has long seen itself as the ultimate guardian of Ataturk's ideological legacy, known as Kemalism. Until 2007, it was able to rely on the support of President Ahmet Necdet Sezer (a committed Kemalist) and secularists in the upper echelons of both the judiciary and the Higher Education Council (YOK), which oversees tertiary education and is responsible for the enforcement of the headscarf ban. So, after it first came to power in November 2002, the AKP proceeded cautiously. It avoided controversial policies and stifled its protests when Sezer used his presidential veto to block the appointment of hundreds of AKP sympathisers to key positions in the country's highly politicised bureaucracy.

The turning point came in spring 2007, when parliament was to elect a new president to succeed Sezer, due to retire after completing his seven-year term. On 27 April 2007, Chief of Staff General Yasar Buyukanit implicitly threatened to stage a coup if the AKP pushed ahead with its plans to appoint Foreign Minister Abdullah Gul to the presidency. The AKP responded by seeking a fresh public mandate. In the early general election of 22 July 2007, the AKP was returned to power in a landslide, increasing its share of the vote to 46.6% from 34.3% in November 2002, and taking 341 seats in Turkey's 550-member unicameral parliament. Stunned and humiliated, the military remained silent as Gul was appointed president in August 2007. Nor did it react as Gul approved the lists of bureaucratic appointments presented to him by the AKP. On 10 December 2007, Gul appointed Yusuf Ziya Ozcan, a relatively unknown sociology professor, as head of YOK. Ozcan was not only close to the AKP leadership but a fierce opponent of the headscarf ban. On 9 February 2008, the AKP pushed a series of constitutional amendments through parliament to try to lift the ban. The main secularist opposition party, the Republican People's Party (CHP), immediately applied to the Constitutional Court for the amendments to be annulled. On 14 March 2008, the chief public prosecutor, Abdurrahman Yalcinkaya, went one step further and applied to the Constitutional Court for the AKP to be outlawed, arguing that its attempt to lift the headscarf ban was part of a concerted campaign to eradicate secularism.

With the military marginalised after its clumsy attempt to prevent Gul from becoming president, and with both the presidency and YOK now controlled by AKP supporters, many hardline secularists regarded the upper echelons of the judicial system as their last line of defence. Under Turkish law, the 11 members of the Constitutional Court are appointed by the president and, barring disability, usually remain in their posts until they reach the retirement age of 65. Seven of the 11 had been appointed by Sezer and only one of the other four was regarded as being potentially sympathetic to the AKP. However, even those who were opposed to the AKP were aware of the implications of outlawing a party which had recently won the support of nearly half the electorate; not least the danger that it would simply re-form itself under another name and win an even larger share of the popular vote.

On 5 June 2008, the Constitutional Court annulled the AKP's constitutional amendments. On 31 July, the court voted by 10–1 to uphold Yalcinkaya's application that the AKP had been attempting to eradicate secularism. However, only six members of the court voted that the AKP should be outlawed, one short of the seven required under Turkish law. Instead, the AKP was handed a $20 million fine. In announcing the decision, Constitutional Court President Hasan Kilic warned the AKP that it would definitely be outlawed if it attempted to reintroduce the initiatives which had prompted Yalcinkaya to apply for its closure.

There was little the AKP could do. None of the members of the court were due to step down until 2010, when three would reach retirement age. Even if Gul replaced them with AKP sympathisers, the next-oldest member of the court was not due to retire until 2013. As a result, the Constitutional Court would still have an anti-AKP majority until well after 2011, the deadline for the next general election.

From secularism to sleaze

The CHP opposition party had based its opposition to the AKP on what it claimed were its plans to erode secularism. In August 2008, with the closure case over, the CHP abruptly shifted the focus of its attacks and began to distribute documents to the media which allegedly contained evidence of corruption involving leading members of the AKP.

The AKP had always tried to use its members' reputation for piety as proof that they were more honest than their political rivals. In reality, in common with its predecessors, allegations of corruption had dogged the AKP ever since it first took office and had increased the longer the party stayed in power. But it was only when the CHP began putting documents in the public domain that the AKP was forced to take notice.

On 2 September Saban Disli, the AKP deputy chair and a long-time associate of Prime Minister Recep Tayyip Erdogan, tendered his resignation after the CHP produced documents allegedly showing he had accepted a $1m bribe to change the zoning classification on a plot of land to enable it to be used for development. Worse was to follow.

On 17 September a court in Frankfurt, Germany, convicted three Turkish-born executives at the German-registered Islamic charity Deniz Feneri e.V of fraud. All pleaded guilty. The court found that, of the €41.4m in donations collected by the charity in the period 2002–07, at least €16.9m had been illegally diverted to other business interests in Germany and Turkey, almost all of them owned by figures associated with the AKP, including several close associates of Erdogan.

The news of the trial in Germany was broken by newspapers belonging to Dogan Yayin Holding, the largest media organisation in Turkey, which quoted German officials as claiming that the Turkish Justice Ministry had failed either to cooperate with the German investigation or to attempt to trace the money that had been channelled to Turkey. Erdogan reacted furiously, publicly calling on AKP supporters to boycott newspapers owned by Dogan Yayin, but no attempt was made to launch an investigation into the German court's allegations.

Over the months that followed, companies belonging to the Dogan Group, owner of Dogan Yayin, received an unprecedented number of visits from Ministry of Finance tax inspectors. On 19 February 2009, the Dogan Group received a notification to pay 826m lira (approximately $525m) in unpaid taxes and fines. Over 93% of the amount related to the sale of a 25% stake in Dogan Yayin to Alex Springer of Germany for €375m. In November 2006, the two parties had signed a memorandum of understanding (MoU) detailing the terms of the sale, which was to take place in January 2007. The transaction and transfer of the payment were duly realised in January 2007, when Dogan Yayin registered the sale and paid the appropriate tax of 30m lira (approximately $19m). This amount was not disputed by the Ministry of Finance. However, it declared that the MoU was the deed of sale. The Turkish tax year is the same as the calendar year, so the ministry claimed that, by paying the tax in 2007 rather than 2006, Dogan Yayin had engaged in a carriage of receipts and was guilty of fraud. Dogan Yayin had no right of appeal. All it could do was to apply to the courts for the annulment of the fine, a process which, even if successful, could take several years. Both the Ministry of Finance's interpretation of the status of the MoU and the size of the fine were without precedent.

On 20 April 2009, the Turkish Energy Ministry banned fuel retailer Petrol Ofisi, owned by the Dogan Group and OMV of Austria, from supplying state-owned companies. It alleged that the fuel supplied by Petrol Ofisi to a state-owned power plant had contained a higher than permitted level of sulphur. The charge was denied by Petrol Ofisi. On 21 April 2009, the ban was extended to exclude all Dogan Group companies from bidding for state contracts.

Ergenekon: a conspiracy too far?

Suspicions that AKP sympathisers in the bureaucracy were being selective in their pursuit of alleged criminal activity were reinforced by what became known as the Ergenekon investigation. On 12 June 2007, the Turkish police discovered 27 grenades in a house in one of the shantytowns that surround Istanbul. As the investigation continued, pro-AKP public prosecutors began to claim that they had uncovered an ultranationalist Kemalist terrorist group called Ergenekon dedicated to destabilising the AKP government through acts of violence. The investigation gathered pace through 2008 and into 2009 as a series of simultaneous police raids on multiple targets resulted in hundreds of suspected Ergenekon members being taken into custody. By May 2009, over 200 suspects had been detained, of whom 142 had been formally charged. Two separate indictments, totalling 4,427 pages, accused them of being 'members of an armed terrorist organisation'.

The detainees ranged from a handful of known members of the Turkish underworld to journalists, academics, trade unionists, retired members of the military, one of Turkey's leading actresses, a transsexual concert organiser, members of a charity which provided scholarships for young girls whose parents could not afford to send them to school, and the wife of one of the Constitutional Court judges who had voted for the AKP's closure. The two indictments claimed that Ergenekon had not only carried out terrorist attacks in its own right but had been controlling almost every militant group active in Turkey, ranging from the Kurdistan Workers' Party (PKK) to the Marxist Revolutionary People's Liberation Party Front (DHKP-C) and the Turkish Hizbullah. Yet neither indictment offered any convincing proof that the Ergenekon organisation even existed. Indeed, the only characteristic shared by the accused appeared to be that all were committed secularists.

Meanwhile, transcripts of private telephone conversations involving the government's critics appeared in pro-AKP newspapers and on pro-AKP websites. AKP officials dismissed suggestions that party sympathisers in the police were responsible, arguing that wiretapping equipment was freely available on the black market. But they made no attempt to explain why it was only the party's opponents who appeared to be having their telephones tapped.

The AKP's first electoral setback

Given the prevalence of conspiracy theories in Turkey, it is possible that the Ergenekon investigators sincerely believed they had uncovered a vast, clandestine terrorist organisation. But it is less easy to explain the massive growth in state aid in the form of food, coal and even refrigerators and washing machines distributed to poorer people during the first months of 2009, particularly as it was concentrated in areas in which the AKP hoped to do well in the 29 March local elections.

The sudden increase in state largesse coincided with Turkey opening negotiations with the IMF over a new Standby Agreement. Throughout 2008, the AKP had ignored repeated warnings from the Turkish business community that the pace of economic growth had begun to slow and that unemployment was set to rise. In late October 2008, as much of the world was still reeling from the first shock of the global financial crisis, Erdogan assured the Turkish public that the crisis had already bypassed Turkey and that the country's gross national product would grow by 4% in both 2008 and 2009. However, by the beginning of 2009, he had accepted that a Standby Agreement which included an IMF-monitored economic programme would reassure an international financial community which had become very wary of investing in emerging markets. However, on 27 January 2009, after 18 days of negotiations in Ankara, an IMF delegation left Turkey without an agreement. The main stumbling block was Erdogan's refusal to countenance any curbs on government spending in the run-up to the local elections.

The local election campaign was fought almost entirely on national issues. But, when the results came in, it soon became clear that the electorate was concerned about rising unemployment and the prospect of an economic recession. In the country as a whole, the AKP secured only 38.4% of the vote, down not only on its 46.6% share in the July 2007 general election but also on the 41.7% it had won in the previous local elections in March 2004. Although it finished comfortably ahead of the CHP on 23.1% and the ultranationalist Nationalist Action Party (MHP) on 16.0%, the AKP vote declined in many of the areas where it had distributed the greatest volume of state aid. This was particularly true in the predominantly Kurdish southeast, where the AKP had been expecting to make substantial gains at the expense of the pro-Kurdish Democratic Society Party (DTP). In fact, the DTP increased its vote across the region. In Diyarbakir, the largest city in the southeast, the DTP's candidate for mayor took 65.4% of the vote and the AKP candidate 31.6% .

Kurdish issue: an intractable stalemate?

The strong showing of the DTP in the local elections came as a shock not only to the AKP but also to the Turkish military, which had been hoping that the AKP would emerge as the dominant party in southeast Turkey (though not the rest of the country), mainly because the DTP was regarded by most of both its supporters and opponents as being very close to the outlawed PKK, which has been waging an often bitter violent campaign for greater Kurdish rights since 1984.

The PKK was no longer as strong militarily as it had been in the early 1990s, when it effectively controlled large swathes of southeast Turkey after dark. Unable to confront the Turkish military on the battlefield, in recent years the PKK had been pursuing a two-front strategy in what appeared to be a campaign of psychological attrition designed to force the Turkish state to enter into peace negotiations (something which remains anathema to Ankara). In southeast Turkey, the PKK had concentrated primarily on laying mines, long-range harassing fire and occasional ambushes; while simultaneously pursuing an urban bombing campaign in the west. But a strong base of public support, as well as the rugged mountain terrain in southeast Turkey and northern Iraq, where the PKK had its main bases and training camps, made it impossible for Turkey to eradicate the organisation.

Starting in late spring 2008, as the melting winter snow freed up the mountain passes, the PKK once again began to exact a steady death toll, mostly through mine attacks against the Turkish military. Improved intelligence enabled the security forces to reduce the number of PKK bombings in western Turkey. However, there were also signs that, probably as the result of frustration at Ankara's continued refusal to enter into negotiations, the PKK was becoming more ruthless. On 27 July 2008, two improvised explosive devices were detonated within the space of ten minutes on a crowded street in the working-class neighbourhood of Gungoren in Istanbul, killing 17 civilians and injuring 155. Unlike previous PKK bombings, there were no political or economic targets in the vicinity of the explosions, which appeared to have been designed merely to kill as many civilians as possible. On 3 October 2008, in what seemed to have been a calculated display of strength before the winter snows brought the campaigning season to a close, the PKK staged a mass attack on a Turkish military outpost in Aktutun, on the border with Iraq. A total of 17 soldiers were killed and 23 wounded. On 8 October 2008, the PKK demonstrated its ability to strike in urban areas when it ambushed a bus carrying police personnel in the centre of Diyarbakir. Six people were killed and 21 wounded.

The success of the DTP in the local elections suggested that Kurdish nationalism was likely to be at least as difficult to eradicate as the PKK. In addition to distributing state aid, in January 2009, the AKP launched a Kurdish-language channel on state-owned television, something which would have been unthinkable as recently as five years earlier. Yet, in an indication of how Kurdish aspirations were continuing to grow at a faster pace than the Turkish state's willingness to make concessions, most Kurds dismissed the move as electorally motivated tokenism. Increasingly, the demand was for the lifting of the continuing restrictions on privately owned Kurdish-language television and radio channels and for allowing Kurdish not only to be taught in schools but to be used as a language of instruction.

By mid 2009, it was unclear whether the AKP was prepared to make more concessions to Kurdish rights. What was clear was that Turkey's accession to the EU, which the AKP had used as a shield against Turkish nationalist criticism when it lifted some of the restrictions on the expression of Kurdish identity in 2003–04, was no longer a political priority.

The EU: hopes receding

After it initiated official accession negotiations with the EU in October 2005, the government made little attempt to introduce the numerous reforms that needed to be implemented if Turkey was ever to become a full member. Hopes that the AKP would use its landslide victory in the July 2007 general election to launch a reform programme proved misplaced, and had to be suspended completely while the AKP was facing the possibility of closure by the Constitutional Court. In autumn 2008, with the closure case behind it, the AKP preferred to concentrate on the local elections rather than the EU. On 9 January 2009, Erdogan appointed Egemen Bagis as Turkey's new chief negotiator for the EU process, replacing Ali Babacan, who had been combining the position with his responsibilities as foreign minister. It was an indication of Erdogan's increasingly introspective leadership style that Bagis was better known for being a member of the small circle of the prime minister's advisers than for his knowledge of EU affairs. In March 2009, Bagis was privately insistent that the AKP would introduce a package of EU reforms immediately after the local elections. By mid June 2009 the package had yet to materialise.

Nor, by mid June, had Turkey implemented a July 2005 commitment to open its ports and airports to ships and planes from the Greek-Cypriot administered Republic of Cyprus, which it was obliged to do under the terms of its 1996 Customs Union agreement with the EU. Ankara had no diplomatic relations with the Republic of Cyprus, which joined the EU in May 2004. Turkey remained the only member of the international community to recognise the Turkish Republic of Northern Cyprus, which administers the northern third of the divided island. In December 2006, the EU suspended negotiations on eight of the chapters of Turkey's accession process pending Ankara's implementation of its commitment to open the ports and airports, giving Turkey three years to comply. Initially, Turkey had intended merely to delay opening the ports pending what it hoped would be a rapid resolution of the Cyprus problem. On 3 September 2008, Greek and Turkish Cypriot leaders finally resumed UN-sponsored negotiations to reunify the island. But, by mid June 2009, no substantive progress had been made and hopes of an imminent settlement were beginning to fade. The EU was due to review the situation at the EU summit in December 2009. Ankara's continued intransigence seemed likely to result in an increase in calls from opponents of Turkish membership inside the EU for the accession process itself to be suspended, particularly if the AKP continued to delay introducing a reform programme. Although a complete suspension of the accession process appeared unlikely, there was a danger that Turkish membership could in effect be put off indefinitely.

From West to East?

Even if Turkish politics in the year to mid 2009 were dominated by introspection and the lack of progress in the country's ties with the EU, there were nevertheless signs of movement in Turkey's relations with Armenia and the Middle East.

On 6 September 2008, Gul became the first Turkish head of state to visit Armenia when he travelled to Yerevan to attend a World Cup football qualifying match between the two countries. The relationship between Ankara and Yerevan had long been overshadowed by claims – denied by Ankara – that ethnic Armenians in Anatolia were subjected to a genocide during the final years of the Ottoman Empire. In 1993, Turkey closed the land border between the two countries in protest at Yerevan's support for the ethnic Armenians in the breakaway Nagorno-Karabakh region of Azerbaijan.

Although Gul's visit did not result in any immediate breakthrough, it did at least demonstrate the two countries' willingness to resolve their differences through dialogue. Hopes of a rapprochement received a further boost after the visit to Turkey by US President Barack Obama on 5–7 April 2009. On 22 April 2009, under pressure from the United States, Turkey and Armenia announced that they had drawn up a roadmap to improve bilateral relations. The document avoided any commitments on Nagorno-Karabakh or the genocide. When the roadmap was announced, Azerbaijan angrily announced that its traditionally close ties with Turkey would be severely damaged if Turkey normalised relations with Armenia before a resolution of the Nagorno-Karabakh dispute. Erdogan was forced to issue a statement assuring Azerbaijan that the settlement of the dispute was a precondition for normalisation of Turkey's relations with Armenia.

Ankara's cautious attempts at rapprochement with Yerevan were in marked contrast to Erdogan's reaction to Israel's assault on Gaza in late 2008. Since it first came to power in 2002, the AKP had pursued a policy of increased engagement with the Middle East in an attempt to establish Turkey as a major regional power. In May 2008 it emerged that Turkey had been brokering indirect peace negotiations between Syria and Israel since February 2007. On 22 December 2008, when Israeli Prime Minister Ehud Olmert visited Ankara, Turkish officials were privately predicting that Israel and Syria would soon be ready to hold direct talks.

On 27 December 2008, however, Israeli forces launched what would become a three-week military offensive against Gaza. Erdogan was furious, not only at the high level of Palestinian civilian casualties but because he believed he had been assured by Olmert five days earlier that Israel had no plans to launch such an operation. Over the weeks that followed, Erdogan repeatedly and bitterly condemned Israel in a series of speeches and public statements, while the AKP launched fund-raising campaigns to send humanitarian aid to the Palestinians. Erdogan's anti-Israeli rhetoric culminated in an extraordinary attack on Israeli President Shimon Peres during a debate at the World Economic Forum summit in Davos, Switzerland, on 29 January 2009. 'You know very well how to kill people', he shouted at Peres before storming out of the room after the panel moderator attempted to cut short his tirade. He returned to Turkey to a hero's welcome.

The solitude of power

Erdogan's emotional outburst in Davos reflected the recent increasing personalisation of Turkish government policy. The appointment of Gul to the presidency in August 2007 removed the only other member of the government who had been prepared to contradict Erdogan at cabinet meetings.

Erdogan's reluctance to delegate authority meant that in June 2009 he not only dominated decision-making in the AKP but wielded more political power than any other individual in recent Turkish history.

After the party's disappointing performance in the March 2009 local elections, Erdogan commissioned a study to discover why it had lost popular support. The results suggested that voters had been disillusioned by the AKP's failure to stamp out corruption or take measures to ameliorate the economic downturn, and believed that party leadership had lost contact with the people. On 1 May, Erdogan announced a comprehensive cabinet reshuffle, dismissing eight ministers and bringing three of his closest advisers into the cabinet for the first time. Erdogan's foreign-policy adviser Ahmet Davutoglu, an academic with no seat in parliament who had been the architect of Turkey's policy of engagement with the Middle East, was appointed foreign minister.

There was no evidence that Erdogan ordered either the Ergenkon investigation or the fine imposed on Dogan Yayin. Indeed, the available evidence suggested that both were initiatives by AKP sympathisers in the bureaucracy. However, the increasing concentration of political power in Erdogan's hands was weakening institutional control over the actions of individual government officials. Moreover, the trend towards making any policy initiative dependent on Erdogan's active involvement also appeared to be slowing the process of government – an unfortunate development given that the economy was heading into a deep recession and faced a confrontation with the EU in late 2009.

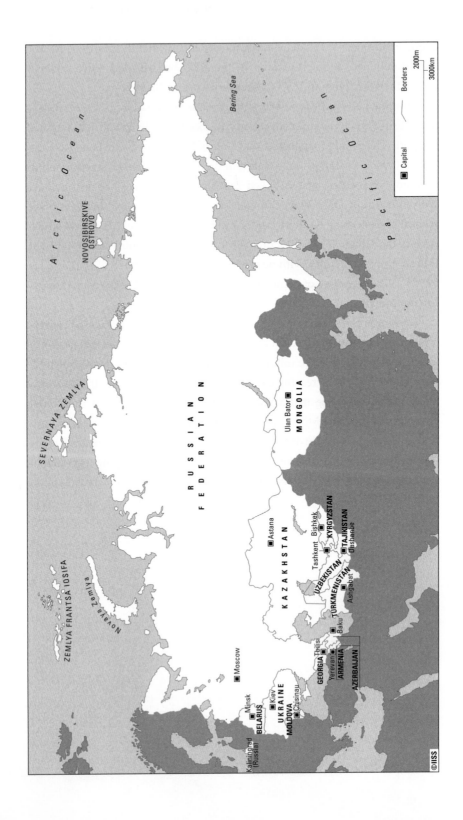

Chapter 6

Russia

Russia faced many challenges in the year to mid 2009. After a decade of uninterrupted economic growth, it was severely affected by the world financial crisis and the decline in global energy prices. The first half of 2009 saw an extraordinary double-digit contraction in GDP and the return of a large budget deficit. Meanwhile, the August 2008 war in Georgia delivered a major blow to relations between Russia and the West, stalling Russia–NATO cooperation and alarming some of Russia's neighbours. Moreover, a dispute between Russia and Ukraine over natural-gas prices, which resulted in an interruption of supplies to many European countries in January 2009, prompted Europe to pay more attention to ensuring future energy security.

As President Dmitry Medvedev marked, in March 2009, the first anniversary of his election to the presidency, the Russian political elite continued to view his predecessor, Prime Minister Vladimir Putin, as the real political leader and strategic decision-maker. Medvedev, Putin's chosen successor, remained loyal to his predecessor, although some differences emerged in their outlook on both domestic and foreign-policy issues.

The sudden decline in the economy exposed a number of vulnerabilities. Partly because of Putin's reluctance to embrace economic reforms, Russia had remained highly dependent on revenues from gas and oil, and control of the economy was heavily centralised. The crisis enhanced the position of economic reformers within the government, although they faced strong opposition from those who favoured authoritarian control – and the latter seemed to be strengthened as the state bailed out prominent businessmen who ran into financial problems. Over time, however, the economic troubles seemed likely to throw into question the sustainability of the implicit social contract under which the Russian population – including a nascent middle class hit particularly badly by the crisis – sacrificed political freedoms in exchange for the state's promise to deliver an ever-improving quality of life for its citizens. Protests resulting from the crisis were isolated, but the political outlook for 2012, when Medvedev's presidential term expires, began to look uncertain.

A period of strain in US–Russian relations was not helped by the crisis in Georgia, which saw US Navy ships enter the Black Sea to deliver aid to Georgian ports, and the US Air Force fly in aid – though Georgian hopes for more extensive American intervention were frustrated. Moscow had long viewed with alarm the expansion of NATO into a region it saw as its own sphere of influence, and was particularly concerned at George W. Bush's strong support for NATO membership for Georgia and Ukraine. American plans to locate missile interceptors and missile-defence radars in eastern Europe added to Russian fears of encirclement. Hence, despite weeks of mutual provocation (including exchanges of fire between Georgian and South Ossetian forces, as well as almost simultaneous US–Georgian and Russian military exercises), Georgia's 7 August move on the South Ossetian capital of Tskhinvali, during which Russian peacekeepers came under attack, was treated in the Russian media as the equivalent of the 11 September 2001 attacks on the United States. After a brief period of combat, Moscow ignored repeated Western calls to pull its intervening troops out of Georgia. Russia paid a high diplomatic price for its hasty recognition of Abkhazia and South Ossetia as independent states following the intervention. Only Nicaragua followed Moscow's lead, leaving it isolated.

Tensions over the August war resulted in a temporary suspension of relations with NATO and a delay in negotiations over a strategic treaty with the EU. A window of opportunity, however, was opened by the change of US administration. Newly elected President Barack Obama showed a personal commitment to improving relations with Russia, and his vice president, Joe Biden, said at the Munich Security Conference in February 2009 that Washington wished to 'press the reset button' on US–Russian relations. Following a brief meeting between Obama and Medvedev in April 2009 at the G20 London summit, the two countries began intense negotiations to upgrade relations, and particularly on renewing the Strategic Arms Reduction Treaty (START) which was to expire in December 2009. Obama's visit to Moscow on 6–7 July produced progress on arms control and US military transit through Russia to Afghanistan, but not on US missile defence in eastern Europe or NATO enlargement. Questions remained as to Russia's willingness – and Medvedev's ability – to achieve a major breakthrough with the United States. Important figures in Russia continued to mistrust the United States and saw no value in seeking strategic rapprochement.

Russia, meanwhile, sought to expand its room for manoeuvre in both West and East. It hosted summits of the Shanghai Cooperation Organisation (SCO) and the BRIC (Brazil, Russia, India and China) group of emerging economic powers. Medvedev travelled to Latin America, Africa and the Middle East and offered loans to several Central Asian countries. Overall, despite the shift in Russia's economic fortunes, there was little change in the assertive and ambitious tenor of its foreign policy, seeking to drive tough bargains with the West and to assert its influence in post-Soviet Eurasia.

Reversal of fortunes

The impact of the global financial crisis was severe, and took the country's leadership by surprise. In March 2008, when Medvedev was elected president, Russia's remarkable economic revival was both the foundation of Putin's legacy and a guarantee of his continued political power. In the eight years of Putin's presidency, Russia enjoyed robust growth of around 7% annually, accumulated very large foreign-exchange reserves and ran large budget surpluses. Foreign investment grew sharply; the rouble became a stable currency, steadily appreciating against the dollar; and the population enjoyed a remarkable rise in living standards. Russia's economic growth fuelled its foreign-policy ambitions and assertiveness.

By May 2009, however, Russia's economic fortunes – like those of many other emerging economies – had turned upside down. Following the fall in oil prices and amid global recession, the Russian economy contracted by 10.2% over the first five months of 2009. Although the government spent heavily to prop up the rouble, the currency declined by 35% against the dollar between July 2008 and April 2009. The Russian stock market at one point had lost over 75% of its value, but later recovered slightly; in May 2009 it stood at around half its May 2008 value. In the year to May 2009 industrial production declined by over 17%, and the Ministry of Economy estimated that in January–April 39% of all industrial enterprises were making losses.

Like other emerging markets, Russia experienced a major outflow of foreign capital, which started in August 2008 during the war with Georgia and continued at least to mid 2009. In 2008 net capital outflow was estimated at around $130 billion, although it had slowed considerably by mid 2009.

In the first quarter of 2009 foreign investment was down over 30%. Foreign trade contracted sharply, with May 2009 exports down 45% year-on-year and imports down 44.6%. Russia had a budget deficit for the first time in many years, expected to exceed 7% of GDP in 2009. For the time being Russia could cover this deficit from its reserves and the returns on its investments. However, if the economy continued to contract and oil prices remained at around $60 per barrel, reserves could become severely depleted. The economy remained overwhelmingly dependent on the export of oil, gas and other commodities, the prices of all of which were well below their 2008 peaks.

The government was slow to react. For months Putin and Medvedev argued that it was not Russia's crisis, and that Russia would remain an island of stability amidst a Western, and particularly American, economic collapse. But as the effects began to reverberate through the Russian economy – the decline in oil prices, the outflow of foreign capital, the fall in the Russian stock market and growing pressure on major Russian private companies to pay off large foreign debts – the leadership shifted from denial to anger, portraying the crisis as a deliberate tool used by the United States to halt Russia's rise. Eventually reality sank in, and Medvedev was compelled to admit that the crisis had specific Russian characteristics and was partly a result of Moscow's own policies.

> The leadership shifted from denial to anger

The delay meant that only emergency measures could be taken, including bailing out industrial oligarchs who faced default, increasing financial support for state-owned enterprises and spending a large part of the country's reserves to slow down the depreciation of the rouble. No major economic stimulus funds were allocated until the economy was in deep recession.

In January 2009 the first signs emerged of friction between Medvedev and Putin, who as prime minister was primarily responsible for dealing with the crisis. Medvedev criticised government policies on several occasions as too slow and ineffective. He dismissed some officials and governors and stepped up an anti-corruption campaign. Putin, however, remained firmly in charge as head of the United Russia Party, which dominated the parliament, and through the support of a loyal political and business elite and regional leaders, as well as popular backing.

The financial crisis increased the influence of the technocrats (often referred to as liberals in contrast to the authoritarian *siloviki*, officials who came from the security services). Technocrats such as Finance Minister Alexei Kudrin and First Deputy Prime Minister Igor Shuvalov were outspoken, warning that conditions would remain difficult and that a rapid recovery in oil and gas prices should not be expected. They argued that Russia should use this window of opportunity to restructure the economy away from its dependence on commodities. They were sceptical about the value of propping up the rouble, and argued against putting more funds into state-owned conglomerates.

By mid 2009 Russia had developed a more sophisticated policy response, which included funds to support the banking system, high-tech companies and investment in infrastructure; cuts in oil-export duties and corporate and personal taxes; and provision of greater social support, including unemployment benefits, pensions and re-training. The unemployment rate reached 10% in March and the World Bank forecast that it would reach 13% in 2009, the highest level since Putin became president in 2000. Many people, moreover, were subject to salary cuts or shorter work weeks, and the volume of overdue wages increased sharply. Towns built during the Soviet era around a single major industrial plant were particularly badly hit: labour mobility remained very limited, partly because of Russia's vast distances and varied climate. The World Bank predicted that 17% of the population would be below the poverty level in 2009, an increase of 4.8 percentage points from 2008.

Although the Russian political elite expressed concern about the possibility of social unrest, the political impact of the crisis was muted. There were a number of protests, but these did not escalate into sustained action against the government. Police in Vladivostok used force to suppress demonstrations against the introduction of import duty on foreign cars. But when large enterprises halted work in Pikalevo, southeast of St Petersburg, and people blocked the major east–west highway, Putin paid a visit and insisted on television that Oleg Deripaska, once one of Russia's richest tycoons, should restart production and pay arrears. Deripaska, who was only holding on to his assets thanks to a state bailout, had no choice but to comply.

Although protests were not widespread, public attitudes were changing. Opinion polls showed that fewer people were confident that the country was 'on the right track'. An authoritative poll conducted by Levada-Center in May 2009 showed that 29% of respondents were confident that the government would be able to improve the situation in the near future, down from 37% a year before. The same poll showed a decline in Medvedev's approval rating from 63% to 58% in the first five months of 2009. In addition, 81% believed he was simply continuing Putin's policies, and only 2% thought he was implementing new policies.

These attitudes seemed to accurately reflect the balance of political power between Putin and Medvedev. It appeared that Medvedev had decided not use the opportunity presented by the economic crisis to launch a bid for real power by relying on members of the Russian middle class dislocated by Putin's emergency measures. With a weak domestic power base, Medvedev focused primarily on foreign policy, where his ability to promote change was hampered by geopolitical uncertainties generated by the crisis and by the lengthy transition between the George W. Bush and Obama administrations. While Medvedev occasionally criticised Putin's decisions and pushed for political changes, he did not offer a significantly different strategy. On those occasions when Medvedev and technocrats in the government sought to advance their agenda – for example, on Russian accession to the World Trade Organisation (WTO) – Putin was able to effectively and directly assert his power and in most cases to prevail. His decision to put forward a common bid for WTO membership with Kazakhstan and Belarus, members of the Eurasian customs union, which only existed on paper, was unlikely to be accepted and was likely only to delay Russian entry, which was backed by the Obama administration and the EU.

By mid 2009 a moderate increase in oil prices, which stood at over $65 per barrel in June 2009, relieved pressure for reforms and provided resources that could be used to quell public discontent. It therefore appeared unlikely that the financial crisis would serve as a springboard for political and economic change. Meanwhile, Medvedev's willingness and ability to challenge Putin and to construct an independent power base remained in doubt.

The August war

In August 2008, Russian and Georgian forces fought a five-day war. Moscow justified its deployment of troops as a response to an attack by Georgia on its breakaway region of South Ossetia. Although the actual fighting was limited and Russia easily defeated the Georgian forces, the conflict sent shock waves through Europe and post-Soviet Eurasia. Russia's show of force in Georgia, the first open and properly organised use of its military against a neighbouring state in the post-Soviet period, sent a signal not only to the West (which had failed to reach consensus at the Bucharest NATO summit in April 2008 regarding NATO membership for Georgia), but also to other neighbours seeking to join NATO and the EU. Russia demonstrated its resolve to defend its interests in Eurasia. Medvedev's signature on 26 August of a decree recognising South Ossetia and Abkhazia, the other break-away region, as independent states was a further show of defiance against Western criticism.

The war's origins went back to the end of the Soviet Union and the emergence of an independent Republic of Georgia dominated by ethnic Georgians and involved in conflicts with two ethnic minorities, Ossetians and Abkhazians. Both previously had their own autonomous regions within Soviet Georgia, and sought greater autonomy and eventually independence from the newly established republic. Conflict in South Ossetia took place in 1991–92, and in Abkhazia from 1992 to 1993. In both cases Georgia initiated military activity and Russia provided support – both organised and in the form of volunteers from the North Caucasus – to the breakaway territories. These conflicts remained unresolved, and South Ossetia and Abkhazia both functioned as self-proclaimed and de facto independent states outside Georgia's control. Georgian President Mikheil Saakashvili came to power in 2004 vowing to re-establish the republic's territorial integrity. After his unilateral offers of autonomy to Abkhazians and South Ossetians failed to win their support, Saakashvili began to prepare for a military solution, while at the same time pursuing closer ties with the United States, which supported NATO membership for Georgia. Bush supported Georgia as a success story for his democracy-promotion agenda. However, a number of European states grew concerned over Saakashvili's increasing recklessness, and Germany and France blocked the US push to advance Georgia's membership process at the April 2008 NATO summit in Bucharest.

Russia viewed Georgian support for 'colour revolutions' in Eurasia and its striving for NATO membership as a direct security threat, and had imposed economic sanctions on Georgia. Moscow had already issued Russian passports to the majority of residents of Abkhazia and South Ossetia, anticipating that it would only be a matter of time before Saakashvili decided to use force rather than accepting that both regions were lost.

After several weeks of escalating violence in and around Abkhazia and South Ossetia, which some suspected Russia of provoking, Georgian troops moved into South Ossetia on 7 August and began a massive and indiscriminate bombardment of its capital Tskhinvali. Russia reacted swiftly, as its troops were already in position on the other side of the Caucasus following large-scale military exercises just a few days prior to the Georgian attack. Russia moved its tanks and troops into South Ossetia on 8 August, and defeated the Georgian troops, which withdrew on 10 August. Simultaneously, Russian troops moved into Abkhazia, and later took positions beyond Abkhazia and South Ossetia in Georgia proper, where they established a large security zone, and bombed and damaged Georgian military installations across the country. The Russian advance stopped some 50km short of the Georgian capital Tbilisi.

The war formally ended on 12 August when President Nicolas Sarkozy of France, which held the rotating EU presidency, mediated a ceasefire on the basis of a six-point plan which called on both sides to stop hostilities, move troops to pre-7 August positions and allow access for humanitarian organisations to the areas with affected populations or internally displaced persons. Russia defied mounting Western criticism that Russia's use of force, involving taking up positions well inside Georgia proper, was disproportionate. After agreeing to an EU monitoring mission, Russia took two months to withdraw from Georgia proper, meeting a 10 October deadline. However, Russian troops stayed in both Abkhazia and South Ossetia, where they established military bases on the basis of treaties agreed after Russia recognised the two territories as independent states. Russia also vowed to guard their borders with Georgia and pledged substantial funds to support economic reconstruction.

> Mutual trust remained a problem

Thus Russia won the war, but paid a high political and diplomatic price; its relations with the United States and Europe hit their lowest point since the end of the Cold War. Russia–NATO and Russia–EU relations were briefly suspended and countries that had once been part of the Soviet Union openly demonstrated they would not back Moscow on issues where their interests were at stake, no matter how much pressure was applied. The war occurred against the backdrop of the mounting international credit crisis, and investors started to pull money out of the Russian market, heightening the impact of the global crisis on the Russian economy.

A year after the conflict, however, the strategic cost seemed to have diminished. Russia had established a political and military presence in Abkhazia and South Ossetia which it had no intention of surrendering. Relations with the EU and NATO were re-established, although mutual trust remained a problem. Russia–US relations improved following the election of Obama, who abandoned, for the time being, the promotion of NATO membership for Georgia and Ukraine. Russia's relations with other former Soviet states, which had refused to recognise the separatist regions, were normalised as Moscow used chequebook diplomacy to bail out its neighbours during the financial crisis. However, Russia's recognition of Abkhazia and South Ossetia remained a source of friction with the United States and Europe.

For Georgia the price of its August gamble in South Ossetia was much higher. It effectively lost any chance to integrate Abkhazia and South Ossetia into Georgia on its own terms; or even to hope for a settlement short of full integration. It failed in its goal of internationalising the issue. Russia established bases in Abkhazia and South Ossetia and blocked the extension of UN and OSCE missions in these territories. Moreover, domestic political instability in Georgia increased as Saakashvili's political opposition called for his resignation and persistently staged protest rallies. Once it became clear that Georgia had started the war, even if under provocation, Saakashvili lost support and credibility in the West. Georgian–Russian relations were broken, with Moscow insisting that normalisation was not possible without a change of government in Tbilisi.

Other reputations were battered by the August conflict. The Bush administration was viewed as bearing some responsibility through its strong support for Saakashvili, its failure to restrain his belligerence and its strategic mistake of putting a Membership Action Plan for Georgia on the agenda of the Bucharest Summit without ensuring that the idea enjoyed the full support of NATO allies. The OSCE, which was responsible for promoting the Georgia–South Ossetia peace process and had a monitoring mission deployed in South Ossetia, failed to prevent and contain the conflict due to disagreements among its members – which include both Georgia and Russia. Russia later blocked the extension of the OSCE mandate establishing separate missions to Georgia and South Ossetia, which closed on 30 June 2009.

The UN Observer Mission in Georgia, deployed for over 16 years and operating on both sides of the administrative border line in Abkhazia and Georgia proper, met a similar fate when Russia vetoed a UN Security Council resolution proposed by the United States and Britain to extend the mission. Moscow demanded that separate missions be established in Georgia and Abkhazia and that there be no explicit reference to Georgia's territorial integrity. The mission was thus effectively closed down on 16 June 2009 and was to be fully withdrawn within three months. The UN had been operating in the Gali region of Abkhazia, home to thousands of ethnic Georgians who returned to live in Abkhazia over a decade ago and whose security was potentially at risk as Abkhazian forces and Russian border guards moved in without external monitoring. The UN mission had also played an important role in facilitating communication between Georgia and Abkhazia, with regular helicopter flights which could bring in international officials and experts. With the mission's closure and Georgia's refusal to allow foreign diplomats and humanitarian organisations to enter Abkhazia, travel into the Abkhazian capital Sukhumi became extremely difficult. Moreover, UN reports on the Georgia–Abkhazia conflict, regularly issued on the basis of monitors' reports, had provided impartial and accurate information on developments for both sides in the conflict, as well as for the international community. These independent assessments were no longer available.

> The EU played an important role in ending the war

The EU, through France, played an important role in ending the August war. Under the terms of the ceasefire brokered by Sarkozy, the EU deployed a 200-strong unarmed civilian EU Monitoring Mission (EUMM) to Georgia. Its main tasks included monitoring and analysing the situation, including compliance with the six-point agreement; monitoring and analysing the return of internally displaced persons and refugees; and contributing to the reduction of tensions through liaison, facilitation of contacts between parties and other confidence-building measures.

Since the EU did not recognise the independence of Abkhazia and South Ossetia, and treated them as part of Georgia, the monitoring mission made several attempts to negotiate permission to operate in Abkhazia and in South Ossetia. Russia was reluctant to accept the EUMM's mandate in the breakaway republics, and both refused it permission to enter. The EUMM thus operated only on the Georgian side of the boundary. Moscow's interpretation of the agreement brokered by Sarkozy was that the EU now guaranteed that Georgia would not start another war. Russia and South Ossetia regularly claimed that Georgian troops were being concentrated on the border with South Ossetia, although the EUMM found no evidence substantiating these claims. Unless renewed, the EUMM mandate was to expire in September 2009, and there were differences within the Union regarding the mission. Some believed that it should continue as a symbol of the EU's growing role in the region, even if it was only able to operate on one side of the border. Others argued that the EU mission had been deployed in conjunction with the long-standing OSCE and UN missions and, as the latter were closing down, the EUMM could not be left to operate alone. Moreover, the EUMM's mandate did not provide for long-term deployment. Even if the EUMM mandate were extended beyond September 2009, there would be a smaller chance that it would be extended again in 2010.

The EU was also involved in facilitating an informal dialogue in Geneva between the parties to the conflict and international actors. The EU's special representative for the crisis in Georgia, French diplomat Pierre Morel, led the discussions, along with co-chairs representing the UN and OSCE. Although there were initial difficulties in resolving status questions surrounding potential participants, several rounds of meetings took place and a 'status-neutral' format was established. However, with the exception of an informal agreement on a (yet to be implemented) incident-prevention mechanism, as of mid 2009 the talks had not produced any practical results. The future of the Geneva discussions was also in question after the OSCE and UN mandates in Georgia ended. Russia expressed reservations about turning them into permanent negotiations.

The prospects for the two breakaway territories were also uncertain. South Ossetia had been less keen to pursue real independence than to be integrated with the Russian Republic of North Ossetia, where the majority of Ossetians live. But Abkhazia had always sought independence from both Georgia and Russia. Although the majority of Abkhazians welcomed the presence of Russian troops and felt secure for the first time in 16 years, the end of the UN mission was a major blow to those who feared being swallowed by Russia, especially in light of the 2014 Winter Olympics in Sochi, a few kilometres from the border. Russia announced that it intended to pursue Olympic construction and infrastructure projects in Abkhazia and that it planned to open a naval base at Ochamchire in Abkhazia for part of its Black Sea fleet currently based at Sevastopol, Ukraine. Russia planned to keep around 1,700 troops in Abkhazia and to deploy border guards on the Abkhazia–Georgia border.

Resetting US–Russian relations
Given the legacy of mistrust during the Bush administration, Russian officials did not rush to embrace the wish expressed by new US Vice President Joe Biden at the Munich Security Conference in February 2009 to 'press the reset button' in relations with Russia. But at the G20 summit in London in April 2009, Medvedev and Obama agreed to negotiate substantial cuts in

strategic nuclear weapons and to reflect these in a successor to START. They also pledged to cooperate on issues from Afghanistan to non-proliferation and the Middle East peace process. And Washington and Moscow cooperated on preparing a UN resolution condemning North Korea's May 2009 nuclear test.

On 6–7 July Obama travelled to Moscow for what was a major test of the ability of the United States and Russia to translate good intentions into practical agreements and compromises. Although the visit did not produce any breakthroughs and reflected continuing reservations on both sides, important agreements were reached. Moscow agreed to allow US military supplies for Afghanistan to transit its territory, with up to 4,500 flights per year, saving the US government $133m annually and enabling it to rely less on transit through Pakistan. Moscow had already signed similar accords with Germany, France and most recently Spain. Russia also agreed to cooperate with the United States on training the Afghan army and police and to participate in economic-development efforts in Afghanistan. In return, the United States agreed to step up cooperation on fighting poppy cultivation and drug trafficking from Afghanistan, a major problem for Russia.

The United States and Russia agreed to establish a bilateral commission co-chaired by Obama and Medvedev but coordinated by US Secretary of State Hillary Clinton and Russian Foreign Minister Sergei Lavrov. The commission consisted of 13 working groups covering topics as varied as security, education, business and civil society. The idea was to establish a strong inter-agency network to support US–Russian relations.

Despite such progress, the area where the summit promised most produced disappointing results. The two sides failed to agree ambitious new cuts in strategic nuclear weapons, settling on a target range for a START replacement agreement of 1,500–1,675 warheads on each side by 2017, only a minor advance on the Moscow Agreement signed by Bush and Putin calling for 1,700 by 2012. The range for delivery systems remained quite large at 500–1,100. Lavrov said a significant reduction of delivery systems would be a Russian priority, but Washington was less keen because it was considering converting some of the systems to conventional payloads. For Russia a direct link between reduction of offensive weapons and missile defences was a priority, but the United States made no commitment to abandon its plans for missile defences in Europe. The differences reflected the scale of challenges faced by negotiators on both sides as they try to produce a new START agreement before the end of the year.

The tone of the summit was perhaps its most striking feature. Obama refrained from criticising Russia's domestic political system and only briefly raised US–Russian differences on Georgia. However, much more time and concrete steps looked to be needed to rebuild trust and a new spirit of partnership.

Military reform

Although Russian forces prevailed easily in Georgia, technological and other weaknesses were shown up by the modernised Georgian military. Deficiencies were exposed in command and control, equipment, training and recruitment. Russia was fighting with old weapons, with conscripts and with limited flexibility and mobility. On 2 October 2008, plans were announced for a major restructuring, reduction and modernisation of the armed forces. Changes included a move from the division to the brigade as the main operational unit, a large reduction in the number of officers, speeding up recruitment of professional (contract) soldiers, revamping the entire system of military education and training, introduction of professional non-commissioned officers, and undertaking large-scale modernisation and re-equipment of the armed forces.

The reform plans ran into fierce resistance. Many military officers believed that such fundamental changes to an already fragile system, which had suffered years of neglect, could fatally damage the institution. Secondly, powerful political and security figures argued that the new armed forces would be unable to fight a large-scale war with NATO, which they continued to see as the main threat to Russia. Bolstering this view, a new National Security Strategy approved by Medvedev in May 2009 clearly stated that Russia anticipated growing tensions between major powers over access to energy resources in regions such as the Arctic and Central Asia. It focused on threats posed by the movement of NATO infrastructure closer to Russia's borders and NATO's orientation towards global threats; pointed out that US–Russian relations still played a key role for the international system as a whole; and reaffirmed Russia's commitment to maintaining strategic nuclear parity with the United States. Among key military threats, the document identified 'policies of some developed states directed at establishing military superiority, first of all in strategic nuclear weapons, precision, informational and other high-tech weapons, strategic conventional weapons, and unilateral steps for deploying missile defence'.

When the plans were unveiled, the Russian leadership was still hoping the global financial crisis would not impact Russia. A significant increase in funding for reorganisation and modernisation was promised. But in the first half of 2009 the budget deficit prompted cuts in defence spending, and the defence industry was badly hit as reduced access to credit disrupted the practice of partial pre-payment for domestic orders. In 2009 the Sukhoi aerospace firm declared it was running at a loss. A number of defence plants were on the brink of closure.

Russia's foreign-policy ambitions, however, required greater use of the military. Partly in response to US military cooperation with Georgia and Ukraine, in 2008–09 the Russian navy made friendly calls on Cuba and Venezuela. Russia sent ships to fight piracy in the Gulf of Aden and the army staged large-scale military exercises in the Caucasus (including Abkhazia and South Ossetia) and with the SCO in Central Asia. Russia also pushed its allies in the Collective Security Treaty Organisation (CSTO) to establish a new operational reaction force. Envisioned as a standing force to deal with threats in Central Asia and other parts of Eurasia, this would rely heavily on the Russian military. Previous CSTO initiatives to set up joint forces had failed, and the capacity of the organisation to implement it with just a handful of disparate states with drastically different military capabilities was in question. Belarus and Uzbekistan did not join the initiative.

The past year provided reminders that long-standing threats to Russian security remained extant. On 16 April 2009 Medvedev issued a decree officially ending the counter-terrorist operation in Chechnya, marking the end of a ten-year conflict that cost tens of thousands of lives. Russia was expected to begin withdrawing its 25,000 troops, all limitations on travel to Chechnya were to be removed, and Grozny airport was set to open for international flights. The end of the Second Chechen War in 2000, with Chechnya still firmly under Russian sovereignty, had helped Putin rise to and consolidate power. But as Medvedev ended the subsequent counter-terrorism effort, there were growing concerns over security and stability in the North Caucasus as a whole. In the first half of 2009 over 300 violent incidents took place across the North Caucasus. Their targets were mostly government and law-enforcement officials. In May the interior minister of Dagestan was shot dead, and on 22 June the president of Ingushetia, Yunus-Bek Yevkurov, was critically wounded in a suicide-bomb attack.

Russia and Ukraine

Further damage to Russia–Western relations in 2008–09 was caused by the January 2009 dispute between Russia and Ukraine which led to the interruption of natural-gas supplies to many of Russia's EU customers. The EU depends on Russia for just over a quarter of the gas it consumes – some 130bn cubic metres out of 501.4bn in 2007. Just over three-quarters of this gas is transported via pipeline through Ukraine, another 20% through Belarus and the remainder direct to Finland. Some smaller central and southeast European countries are entirely or overwhelmingly dependent on Russian gas supplied via Ukraine. European gas consumption is projected to grow and to rely increasingly on imports, which will amount to 84% of the total by 2030, according to the European Commission. The dispute brought into question Russia's reliability as a supplier and Ukraine's as a transit route.

While an earlier disruption of gas supplies in 2006 took many by surprise, there was plenty of warning leading up to the events of January 2009. In February 2008, Russia's state-controlled energy giant Gazprom announced it was owed more than $1.5bn in unpaid bills by its Ukrainian counterpart, Naftohaz Ukrainy. In March, Turkmenistan, the major gas supplier to Ukraine via Russia, announced it wanted to raise its export prices significantly from the start of 2009, to levels that Ukraine could not afford.

Thanks to its historical ties to Russia during the Soviet era, Ukraine had paid below-market prices for its gas for years. In October 2008, Putin and Ukrainian Prime Minister Yulia Tymoshenko signed a memorandum envisioning the gradual increase of gas prices from $179 per thousand cubic metres (tcm) to European 'market prices' by 2011. They also agreed that Gazprom and Naftohaz should trade directly, rather than via RosUkrEnergo, a Swiss-registered joint venture between Gazprom and two Ukrainian businessmen. In November, other outstanding amounts owed by Naftohaz to Gazprom surfaced, coupled with fines for late payment. Ukrainian President Victor Yushchenko – long locked in a destabilising power struggle with his former ally Tymoshenko – made reassuring noises but took no practical steps to support the Putin–Tymoshenko memorandum.

When price negotiations for 2009 began in November, Gazprom initially offered to sell gas at $250 per tcm. Ukraine responded with a counter-bid of $201, so long as the transit fees that Russia paid for moving its gas across Ukraine – also well below the market rate for historical reasons – were increased from $1.70 to $2 per tcm per 100 kilometres. On 30 December, as tensions escalated, Gazprom CEO Alexei Miller withdrew the rejected

$250 offer and announced that Gazprom would deliver gas to Ukraine from January at what he said was the European market rate of $418 per tcm. Naftohaz CEO Oleh Dubyna countered with an offer of $235, together with a $1.80 per 100km transit fee.

On 31 December, eleventh-hour talks failed to produce agreement, even after Naftohaz said it had paid its arrears for supplies delivered in November and December. On 1 January 2009, Gazprom cut all gas supplies destined for Ukrainian use, but said it was pumping additional volumes to ensure gas reached its European customers. Naftohaz claimed it had several months' gas in storage and that European gas in transit via Ukrainian ter-ritory continued to flow normally. The crisis began to have a real impact on Europe on 7 January, when Russia halted all supplies, alleging that Ukraine was stealing gas intended for other customers. Ukraine denied this, saying Russia was not sending enough 'technical gas' to drive the compressors pumping gas towards Europe and to keep the pipes sufficiently pressurised. By 8 January, industrial plants were being forced to slow or stop production, particularly in southeast Europe.

> The EU felt bound to take action

At this point, the EU felt bound to take action. By 11 January, with both Russian and Ukrainian agreement, teams of EU monitors were deployed at gas-transit sites in both countries. On 16 January, the EU stepped up politi-cal pressure: German Chancellor Angela Merkel met Putin and warned that Russia was losing credibility as a gas supplier, while European Commission President José Manuel Barroso warned of 'significant financial, economic and political consequences' for both countries if they did not resolve the dispute. Finally, on 19 January, the Russian and Ukrainian prime ministers signed an agreement under which Ukraine would pay 80% of the 'market price' – the exact figure was not disclosed – for gas imports in 2009, before rising to the full fee in 2010. In exchange, Naftohaz would hold its transit fee for Gazprom unchanged at $1.70. On 20 January, Russia resumed gas flows.

The gas dispute showed a need for the EU to concentrate on diversifica-tion and to help improve the capacity of Ukraine's pipeline system. In May 2009 the Czech presidency of the EU hosted an energy summit in Prague that brought together leaders from Azerbaijan, Egypt, Georgia, Iraq, Kazakhstan, Turkey, Turkmenistan and Uzbekistan to discuss the Southern Corridor, the planned energy-supply route from the Caspian. Its most important component was to be the Nabucco gas pipeline, envisioned as a means to lessen dependency on Russian gas by bringing Caspian and Iraqi gas to Europe via Turkey. However, the major potential supplier, Turkmenistan, did not sign the summit declaration, and there were still issues regarding the charges Turkey could collect for transit of gas across its territory. Frustrated with slow progress on Nabucco and insufficient support from the EU, Azerbaijani President Ilkham Aliev announced in Moscow in June that some Azeri gas previously reserved for Nabucco would be sold to Gazprom, although the volume of 0.5bcm constitutes only a fraction of Azeri gas production. At the same time, Turkmenistan signed a 30-year deal with China to supply gas via a pipeline scheduled for completion in December 2009, further reducing the prospects for trans-Caspian gas supplies to Europe. The best hope for the Nabucco consortium was northern Iraq. Without supplies from Turkmenistan, however, the pipeline would still provide only a small percentage of Europe's needs and would not dent Gazprom's dominance of the EU gas market.

The EU's efforts to help modernise Ukraine's pipeline system were equally tentative. In March 2009 Ukraine signed an agreement with the EU on modernising its gas-transportation system at an estimated cost of $3.4bn. The Russian delegation, including Energy Minister Sergei Shmatko, walked out of the meeting in protest at the exclusion from the deal of Russia, the main supplier of gas through Ukraine. Putin criticised it on the same grounds. Ukrainian leaders, including Yushchenko, backtracked and invited Russia to join the project. Moscow was, however, unlikely to participate in an initiative which did not offer the prospect of acquiring some degree of control or ownership of the Ukrainian pipelines, which Kiev insisted would remain in the hands of the state.

Ukraine's economic woes – the collapse in global demand, especially for steel, forced it to agree a rescue loan package with the International Monetary Fund – made it difficult to meet the terms of the January agreement with Gazprom, whereby payment for gas would be made on a monthly basis. Gazprom warned that it would not continue to supply Ukraine if payment was not received. Tensions between Russia and Ukraine were likely to heighten further as January presidential elections approached, in which Yushchenko was expected to lose to one of his long-standing political rivals – Tymoshenko or Victor Yanukovich, head of the formerly pro-Russian Party of Regions.

Reality check

The global economic crisis provided Russia with a serious reality check on its domestic, regional and global ambitions, which had grown during years of economic growth driven by oil and gas revenues. The Russian political system showed itself poorly adapted to dealing with the crisis. Internationally the strategic impact for Russia of its August 2008 war with Georgia was muted by the economic crisis and the change of US administration. However, relations with NATO and the EU looked to remain difficult for Moscow. Obama's initiative to reset US–Russian relations could open a window to strengthening cooperation on arms control, non-proliferation and Afghanistan. However, as the July summit demonstrated, the two sides still had a long way to go to rebuild the trust damaged by the legacy of the Bush era. Russia's own growing security challenges in the North Caucasus, difficulties in implementing defence modernisation and reform and limited resources for foreign-policy adventures could limit Moscow's appetite to continue with unilateral assertiveness and might lead it to seek a new accommodation with the United States and Europe.

Strategic Geography 2009

Legend

——————— subject country international boundaries

——————— other international boundaries

················ province or state boundaries

`ANBAR` province or state

■ capital cities

● state or province capital cities

● cities/ towns/ villages

GLOBAL ISSUES: Global recession

The world economy is undergoing its most severe recession since the Second World War. Real GDP has dropped in 2009, with advanced economies contracting sharply and leading developing economies experiencing an abrupt slowdown. Massive fiscal stimulus packages have resulted in record budget deficits. Ten emerging nations have had to rely on loans from the International Monetary Fund (IMF) to avert a collapse of their banking systems and currencies.

World leaders have vowed to act decisively to avoid a repeat of the Great Depression of the 1930s. Yet despite this, the overall picture remains gloomy, as these figures from the world's leading economies demonstrate.

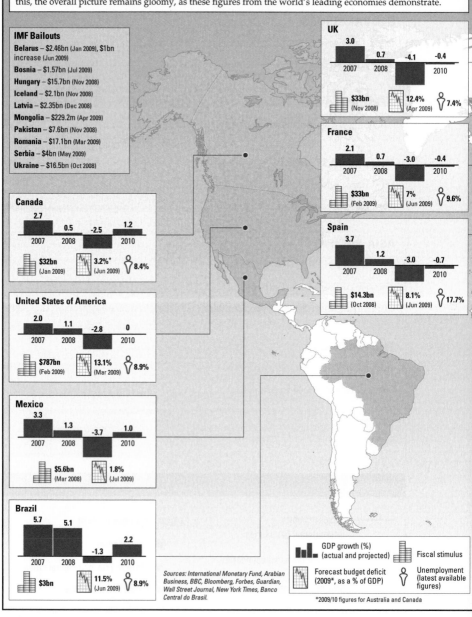

IMF Bailouts

Belarus – $2.46bn (Jan 2009), $1bn increase (Jun 2009)
Bosnia – $1.57bn (Jul 2009)
Hungary – $15.7bn (Nov 2008)
Iceland – $2.1bn (Nov 2008)
Latvia – $2.35bn (Dec 2008)
Mongolia – $229.2m (Apr 2009)
Pakistan – $7.6bn (Nov 2008)
Romania – $17.1bn (Mar 2009)
Serbia – $4bn (May 2009)
Ukraine – $16.5bn (Oct 2008)

UK
3.0 | 0.7 | -4.1 | -0.4
2007 | 2008 | | 2010
$33bn (Nov 2008) | 12.4% (Apr 2009) | 7.4%

France
2.1 | 0.7 | -3.0 | -0.4
2007 | 2008 | | 2010
$33bn (Feb 2009) | 7% (Jun 2009) | 9.6%

Spain
3.7 | 1.2 | -3.0 | -0.7
2007 | 2008 | | 2010
$14.3bn (Oct 2008) | 8.1% (Jun 2009) | 17.7%

Canada
2.7 | 0.5 | -2.5 | 1.2
2007 | 2008 | | 2010
$32bn (Jan 2009) | 3.2%* (Jun 2009) | 8.4%

United States of America
2.0 | 1.1 | -2.8 | 0
2007 | 2008 | | 2010
$787bn (Feb 2009) | 13.1% (Mar 2009) | 8.9%

Mexico
3.3 | 1.3 | -3.7 | 1.0
2007 | 2008 | | 2010
$5.6bn (Mar 2008) | 1.8% (Jul 2009)

Brazil
5.7 | 5.1 | -1.3 | 2.2
2007 | 2008 | | 2010
$3bn | 11.5% (Jun 2009) | 8.9%

Sources: International Monetary Fund, Arabian Business, BBC, Bloomberg, Forbes, Guardian, Wall Street Journal, New York Times, Banco Central do Brasil.

GDP growth (%) (actual and projected)
Fiscal stimulus
Forecast budget deficit (2009*, as a % of GDP)
Unemployment (latest available figures)

*2009/10 figures for Australia and Canada

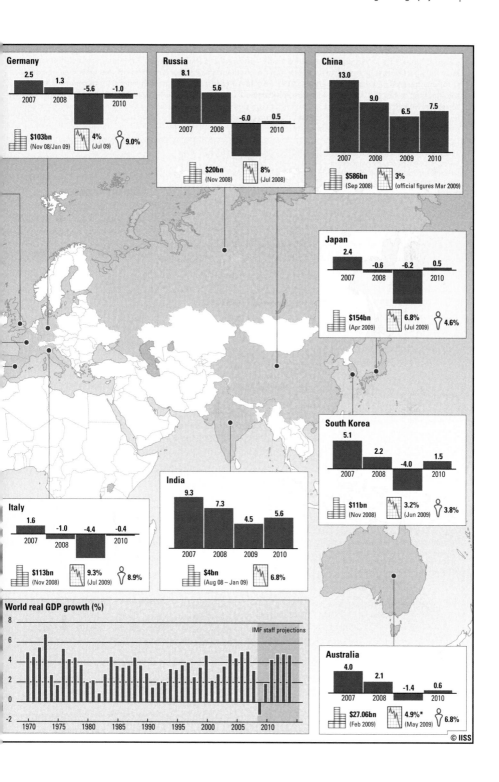

Germany
2.5 | 1.3 | -5.6 | -1.0
2007 | 2008 | | 2010

$103bn (Nov 08/Jan 09) | 4% (Jul 09) | 9.0%

Russia
8.1 | 5.6 | -6.0 | 0.5
2007 | 2008 | | 2010

$20bn (Nov 2008) | 8% (Jul 2008)

China
13.0 | 9.0 | 6.5 | 7.5
2007 | 2008 | 2009 | 2010

$586bn (Sep 2008) | 3% (official figures Mar 2009)

Japan
2.4 | -0.6 | -6.2 | 0.5
2007 | 2008 | | 2010

$154bn (Apr 2009) | 6.8% (Jul 2009) | 4.6%

South Korea
5.1 | 2.2 | -4.0 | 1.5
2007 | 2008 | | 2010

$11bn (Nov 2008) | 3.2% (Jun 2009) | 3.8%

Italy
1.6 | -1.0 | -4.4 | -0.4
2007 | 2008 | | 2010

$113bn (Nov 2008) | 9.3% (Jul 2009) | 8.9%

India
9.3 | 7.3 | 4.5 | 5.6
2007 | 2008 | 2009 | 2010

$4bn (Aug 08 – Jan 09) | 6.8%

World real GDP growth (%)

8
6
4
2
0
-2
1970 | 1975 | 1980 | 1985 | 1990 | 1995 | 2000 | 2005 | 2010

IMF staff projections

Australia
4.0 | 2.1 | -1.4 | 0.6
2007 | 2008 | | 2010

$27.06bn (Feb 2009) | 4.9%* (May 2009) | 6.8%

© IISS

GLOBAL ISSUES: Slump in container trade

Cargo shipping has found itself in troubled waters during the global recession. First there was a decline in the bulk transport of raw commodities such as iron ore, coal and grains. A sharp drop-off was then seen in container shipping, transporting consumer goods. After decades of uninterrupted growth, container trade has shrunk for the first time in history, shipping fees have plummeted and container ships joined the idle 'ghost fleets' anchored off-shore. Even though the decline in consumer confidence and world trade in consumer goods may have been levelling off in the second quarter of 2009, container throughput in the first three months of the year at selected major ports illustrated a bleak economic picture.

All volumes are expressed in TEUs, or twenty-foot equivalent units, representing the cargo capacity of a standard container 20ft long and 8ft wide.

GERMANY – HAMBURG

	Q1 08	Q1 09	
TEUs	2.42m	1.86m	-23.1%

NETHERLANDS – ROTTERDAM

	Q1 08	Q1 09	
TEUs	2.68m	2.25m	-16.0%

US – LOS ANGELES

	Q1 08	Q1 09	
TEUs	1.84m	1.52m	-17.4%

US – NEW YORK / NEW JERSEY

	Q1 08	Q1 09	
TEUs	987,950	820,000	-17.0%

US – LONG BEACH

	Q1 08	Q1 09	
TEUs	1.54m	1.09m	-29.5%

BELGIUM – ANTWERP

	Q1 08	Q1 09	
TEUs	2.07m	1.74m	-15.9%

As of 30 March 2009, laid-up ships totalled 11.3% by capacity of the total global fleet of cellular container ships (ships carrying only containers and no other cargo). In April, however, Paris-based consultant AXS-Alphaliner reported only 1.31m TEUs of idle capacity, as some very large-capacity vessels returned. Conversely, with new ships still entering service, Alphaliner suggested an oversupply of 3m TEUs may appear by 2010 if the economy remained sluggish.

World fleet TEU capacity
12.56m

11.3%
Idle TEU capacity
1.42m

Source: AXS-Alphaliner

ARGENTINA – BUENOS AIRES

	Q1 08	Q1 09	
TEUs	284,935	198,600	-30.3%

Sources: AXS-Alphaliner, Drewry, Informa/Lloyds List, European Liners Affairs Association, Eye for Transport, Journal of Commerce, PIERS (Port Import Export Reporting Service), Port of Buenos Aires, Port of Hamburg Marketing, Port of Long Beach, Port of Los Angeles, Port of St Petersburg, Saudi Ports Authority.

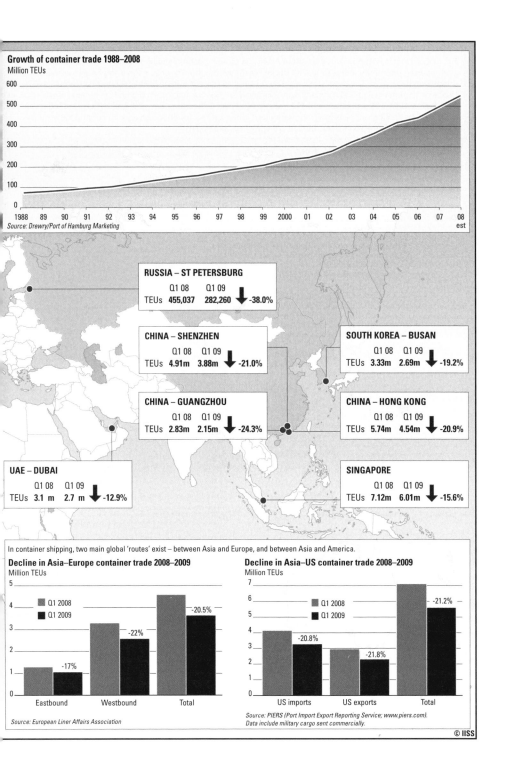

Growth of container trade 1988–2008
Million TEUs

Source: Drewry/Port of Hamburg Marketing

RUSSIA – ST PETERSBURG

	Q1 08	Q1 09	
TEUs	455,037	282,260	↓ -38.0%

CHINA – SHENZHEN

	Q1 08	Q1 09	
TEUs	4.91m	3.88m	↓ -21.0%

SOUTH KOREA – BUSAN

	Q1 08	Q1 09	
TEUs	3.33m	2.69m	↓ -19.2%

CHINA – GUANGZHOU

	Q1 08	Q1 09	
TEUs	2.83m	2.15m	↓ -24.3%

CHINA – HONG KONG

	Q1 08	Q1 09	
TEUs	5.74m	4.54m	↓ -20.9%

UAE – DUBAI

	Q1 08	Q1 09	
TEUs	3.1 m	2.7 m	↓ -12.9%

SINGAPORE

	Q1 08	Q1 09	
TEUs	7.12m	6.01m	↓ -15.6%

In container shipping, two main global 'routes' exist – between Asia and Europe, and between Asia and America.

Decline in Asia–Europe container trade 2008–2009
Million TEUs

- Q1 2008
- Q1 2009

Eastbound -17%
Westbound -22%
Total -20.5%

Source: European Liner Affairs Association

Decline in Asia–US container trade 2008–2009
Million TEUs

- Q1 2008
- Q1 2009

US imports -20.8%
US exports -21.8%
Total -21.2%

Source: PIERS (Port Import Export Reporting Service; www.piers.com).
Data include military cargo sent commercially.

© IISS

AFRICA: Anti-piracy operations off Somalia

The marked increase in piracy in the Gulf of Aden and off the coast of Somalia since 2008 has galvanised the international community into action, with dozens of ships from more than 20 nations deployed to protect shipping in the region. The pirates' success rate dropped in the first half of 2009, down to 22% from 38% in 2008. However, the International Maritime Bureau said more ships were attacked in the first six months of 2009 than in the whole of 2008: 133 compared with 111. Patrolling a huge, 2.85 million km² area and with no unified command of the various taskforces (see below), ships involved in the anti-piracy effort can only ameliorate, rather than solve, a problem whose roots lie in Somalia's lawlessness and poverty.

Taskforces involved in anti-piracy operations

Robust rules of engagement remain to be defined for the wide variety of naval ships on anti-piracy duties in the region. Cooperation on the tactical level seems to be on an ad hoc basis and effective coordination is lacking on a strategic level.

CTF 150

Transferred to the Horn of Africa after September 2001 in support of *Operation Enduring Freedom*, the multinational Combined Task Force 150 responded to the growing threat of piracy by establishing the Maritime Security Patrol Area (MSPA) in August 2008. Led by the Danish ship HDMS *Absalon* until April 2009 and then under French command, it was involved in preventing attacks and apprehending pirates.

CTF 151

In January 2009, the United States Fifth Fleet headquarters in Bahrain announced this Combined Task Force to combat piracy off the Somali coast. Particularly active in the Gulf of Aden, some of its ships have sailed as far south as the Seychelles. Originally US led, at mid 2009 it was commanded by a Turkish Rear Admiral with approximately the following composition:

- 4 US
- 1 Turkey
- 1 UK
- 1 S. Korea
- 1 Singapore
- 1 1 Australia

EU NAVFOR's *Operation Atalanta*

Operation Atalanta, the European Union's anti-piracy mission, was launched in December 2008 and reached full strength in February 2009. In support of UN Security Council Resolutions 1814 (2008), 1816 (2008), 1838 (2008) and 1846 (2008), it helps to protect WFP (World Food Programme) vessels delivering food aid and other vulnerable vessels, as well as deterring and preventing piracy. In mid 2009, it comprised the following:

- 4 1 France
- 3 Sweden
- 2 1 Spain
- 2 1 Germany
- 1 Greece
- 1 Italy
- 1 Norway

NATO's *Operation Allied Protector*

In March 2009, the North Atlantic Council agreed that NATO would again contribute to anti-piracy efforts off the Horn of Africa. Standing NATO Maritime Group 1 (SNMG1), below, was due to be replaced by SNMG2 in the latter half of 2009, as NATO decided to maintain a presence in the region for the time being.

- 2 Germany
- 1 US
- 1 Spain
- 1 Portugal
- 1 Netherlands
- 1 Canada

Vessels under national command

Several other nations have also deployed ships. Crucially, in what is seen as a step towards greater global engagement, these include China.

- 3 China
- 3 Russia
- 2 Japan
- 2 Iran
- 2 Saudi Arabia
- 1 UK
- 1 India
- 1 Malaysia

Somali exclusive economic zone
Somali territorial waters
Yemeni territorial waters
'Anchorage sites' often used by pirates for hijacked vessels
Aden
Bab el-Mandab
DJIBOUTI
Berber
ETHIOPIA
BAKOOL
GEDO
BAY
SHABEELLAH HOOSE
JUBBADA DHEXE
KENYA
JUBBADA HOOSE

Sources: IISS; IMO; IMB; AFP; AP; Reuters.

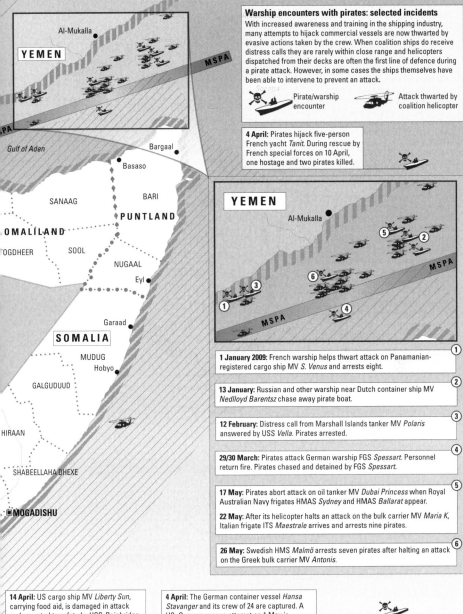

Warship encounters with pirates: selected incidents

With increased awareness and training in the shipping industry, many attempts to hijack commercial vessels are now thwarted by evasive actions taken by the crew. When coalition ships do receive distress calls they are rarely within close range and helicopters dispatched from their decks are often the first line of defence during a pirate attack. However, in some cases the ships themselves have been able to intervene to prevent an attack.

Pirate/warship encounter

Attack thwarted by coalition helicopter

4 April: Pirates hijack five-person French yacht *Tanit*. During rescue by French special forces on 10 April, one hostage and two pirates killed.

YEMEN

Al-Mukalla

MSPA

MSPA

1 January 2009: French warship helps thwart attack on Panamanian-registered cargo ship MV *S. Venus* and arrests eight.

13 January: Russian and other warship near Dutch container ship MV *Nedlloyd Barentsz* chase away pirate boat.

12 February: Distress call from Marshall Islands tanker MV *Polaris* answered by USS *Vella*. Pirates arrested.

29/30 March: Pirates attack German warship FGS *Spessart*. Personnel return fire. Pirates chased and detained by FGS *Spessart*.

17 May: Pirates abort attack on oil tanker MV *Dubai Princess* when Royal Australian Navy frigates HMAS *Sydney* and HMAS *Ballarat* appear.

22 May: After its helicopter halts an attack on the bulk carrier MV *Maria K*, Italian frigate ITS *Maestrale* arrives and arrests nine pirates.

26 May: Swedish HMS *Malmö* arrests seven pirates after halting an attack on the Greek bulk carrier MV *Antonis*.

Al-Mukalla

YEMEN

Gulf of Aden

Bargaal

Basaso

SANAAG

BARI

PUNTLAND

OMALILAND

OGDHEER

SOOL

NUGAAL

Eyl

Garaad

SOMALIA

MUDUG

Hobyo

GALGUDUUD

HIRAAN

SHABEELLAHA DHEXE

MOGADISHU

14 April: US cargo ship MV *Liberty Sun*, carrying food aid, is damaged in attack and escorted to safety by USS *Bainbridge*. A French warship later arrests the pirates.

4 April: The German container vessel *Hansa Stavanger* and its crew of 24 are captured. A US–German rescue attempt on 1 May is aborted. The ship and its crew are still hostage in July 2009.

8 April: Danish-owned MV *Maersk Alabama* and its 21 American crew captured. At least one US ship on anti-piracy duties participates in a successful rescue operation on 12 April.

25 April: Italian cruise ship MSC *Melody* repels attack when fired on by pirates, but is then escorted through the Gulf of Aden by Spain's PF *Marques de la Ensenada* while other ships arrest the pirates.

© IISS

MIDDLE EAST/GULF: West Bank settlements

The US administration of President Barack Obama has signalled that it wants movement towards peace in the Middle East, and a separate Palestinian state is central to its proposed solution. But Israeli settlements in the Palestinian territories continue to be a major obstacle to any Israeli–Palestinian deal. Despite Israel's unilateral withdrawal from Gaza in 2005, some 120 settlements remain in the West Bank, which Israel has occupied since the 1967 Arab–Israeli war. More than 100 other 'outposts' – new neighbourhoods in existing settlements – have been built since Israel pledged in 1996 to stop building new settlements. Many analysts worry that the facts on the ground already make it impossible to establish a viable Palestinian state, particularly as many settlers are opposed to a two-state solution. Others predict densely populated settlements near the border being ceded to Israel, leaving other settlers to live in any new Arab state. Israeli Prime Minister Benjamin Netanyahu resisted international calls to halt settlements.

10 miles
16 km

Jenin

WEST BANK

Tulkarm

Nablus

Qalqilya

Ramallah

Jericho

ISRAEL

East Jerusalem

Bethlehem

Hebron

Dead Sea

JORDAN

Population statistics

The international community regards all settlements in the West Bank as illegal under international law. Israel generally disagrees, although many newer 'outposts' are illegal even under its law. Under the US-backed 'road map' for peace, Israel is committed to dismantling all those established after February 2001, but critics claim it has taken little real action.

2.42 million - Palestinians in the West Bank (excluding East Jerusalem)

289,600 - Number of settlers in the West Bank

About 3,000 - Number of settlers in illegal outposts

4.5% - rate of growth of settler population in 2008

1.5% - overall population growth in Israel in 2008

253,395 - Palestinians in East Jerusalem

193,700 - Israelis in East Jerusalem

Sources: Palestinian Central Bureau of Statistics, Special Report on the 61th Anniversary of the Nakba (May 2009); Israeli Central Bureau of Statistics (December 2008); Peace Now (July 2008); Jerusalem Institute for Israeli studies, Statistical Yearbook 2007/8.

Israeli settlements
Settlement municipal areas
Land cultivated by settlers
▲ Outposts
Arab-controlled areas
– – – 1949 Armistice Green Line
—— Separation barrier
•••••• Barrier under construction/planned
ooooo Road barrier

New building in West Bank settlements 1989–2008

5000
4000
3000
2000
1000
0
1989   95   00   05   08

© IISS

MIDDLE EAST/GULF: Iran's disputed election

Were the June 2009 Iranian presidential elections rigged? Even the country's highest constitutional authority, the Guardian Council, has admitted there were some – insignificant, in its opinion – voting irregularities. However, there will almost certainly never be a definitive answer to the question. This has left the opposition, led by reformist candidate Mir Hossein Mousavi, disputing the outcome and analysts drawing conclusions from the Iranian Ministry of Interior's official results. The incumbent president, Mahmoud Ahmadinejad, won in all 30 of Iran's provinces, but questions have been posed in many regions, including the examples below.

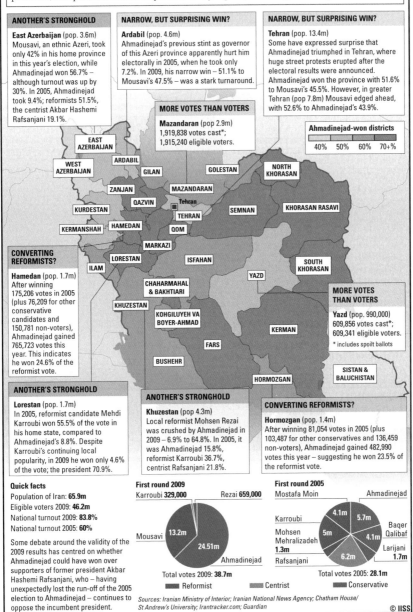

ANOTHER'S STRONGHOLD

East Azerbaijan (pop. 3.6m)
Mousavi, an ethnic Azeri, took only 42% in his home province in this year's election, while Ahmadinejad won 56.7% – although turnout was up by 30%. In 2005, Ahmadinejad took 9.4%; reformists 51.5%, the centrist Akbar Hashemi Rafsanjani 19.1%.

NARROW, BUT SURPRISING WIN?

Ardabil (pop. 4.6m)
Ahmadinejad's previous stint as governor of this Azeri province apparently hurt him electorally in 2005, when he took only 7.2%. In 2009, his narrow win – 51.1% to Mousavi's 47.5% – was a stark turnaround.

NARROW, BUT SURPRISING WIN?

Tehran (pop. 13.4m)
Some have expressed surprise that Ahmadinejad triumphed in Tehran, where huge street protests erupted after the electoral results were announced. Ahmadinejad won the province with 51.6% to Mousavi's 45.5%. However, in greater Tehran (pop 7.8m) Mousavi edged ahead, with 52.6% to Ahmadinejad's 43.9%.

MORE VOTES THAN VOTERS

Mazandaran (pop 2.9m)
1,919,838 votes cast*;
1,915,240 eligible voters.

Ahmadinejad-won districts

40% 50% 60% 70+%

CONVERTING REFORMISTS?

Hamedan (pop. 1.7m)
After winning 175,206 votes in 2005 (plus 76,209 for other conservative candidates and 150,781 non-voters), Ahmadinejad gained 765,723 votes this year. This indicates he won 24.6% of the reformist vote.

MORE VOTES THAN VOTERS

Yazd (pop. 990,000)
609,856 votes cast*;
609,341 eligible voters.
* includes spoilt ballots

ANOTHER'S STRONGHOLD

Lorestan (pop. 1.7m)
In 2005, reformist candidate Mehdi Karroubi won 55.5% of the vote in his home state, compared to Ahmadinejad's 8.8%. Despite Karroubi's continuing local popularity, in 2009 he won only 4.6% of the vote; the president 70.9%.

ANOTHER'S STRONGHOLD

Khuzestan (pop 4.3m)
Local reformist Mohsen Rezai was crushed by Ahmadinejad in 2009 – 6.9% to 64.8%. In 2005, it was Ahmadinejad 15.8%, reformist Karroubi 36.7%, centrist Rafsanjani 21.8%.

CONVERTING REFORMISTS?

Hormozgan (pop. 1.4m)
After winning 81,054 votes in 2005 (plus 103,487 for other conservatives and 136,459 non-voters), Ahmadinejad gained 482,990 votes this year – suggesting he won 23.5% of the reformist vote.

Quick facts

Population of Iran: **65.9m**
Eligible voters 2009: **46.2m**
National turnout 2009: **83.8%**
National turnout 2005: **60%**

Some debate around the validity of the 2009 results has centred on whether Ahmadinejad could have won over supporters of former president Akbar Hashemi Rafsanjani, who – having unexpectedly lost the run-off of the 2005 election to Ahmadinejad – continues to oppose the incumbent president.

First round 2009

Karroubi 329,000   Rezai 659,000

Mousavi 13.2m
24.51m
Ahmadinejad

Total votes 2009: **38.7m**

First round 2005

Mostafa Moin   Ahmadinejad
Karroubi 4.1m / 5.7m
Mohsen Mehralizadeh 1.3m   5m / 4.1m   Baqer Qalibaf
6.2m   Larijani 1.7m
Rafsanjani

Total votes 2005: **28.1m**

▬ Reformist   ▬ Centrist   ▬ Conservative

Sources: Iranian Ministry of Interior; Iranian National News Agency; Chatham House/ St Andrew's University; Irantracker.com; Guardian

© IISS

ASIA-PACIFIC: Afghanistan: military supply routes

The difficulties of transporting military supplies into Afghanistan were highlighted in early 2009 when Kyrgyzstan threatened to close down its Manas air base, which the US had been using as a key refuelling point for its aircraft, as well as an important transit point for troops and non-lethal military supplies into Afghanistan. With US and NATO convoys increasingly being attacked by Taliban militants on the main Pakistani routes, the allies are looking for alternatives. This means courting former Soviet republics and negotiating a deal with Russia. Some 'outlier' options have included routes via Iran and Kuwait.

With the deployment in early 2009 by President Barack Obama of an extra 17,000 US troops to join the 60,000 foreign troops already stationed in Afghanistan, the pressure on a limited number of supply routes into the country will be felt ever more acutely.

DISCONTINUED ROUTE
Karshi-Khanabad, Uzbekistan
Logistically, Uzbekistan provides an excellent gateway, especially as Karshi-Khanabad, or K2, has access to one of the few rail links into Afghanistan. But it is politically awkward dealing with Uzbekistan's authoritarian regime. The Americans were asked to leave K2 in 2005, after criticising the Uzbek government's bloody suppression of unrest in Andijan. Recently, however, President Islam Karimov has again offered the use of Uzbek facilities.

NEW & POTENTIAL ROUTES
Navoi, Uzbekistan
Despite concerns about Uzbekistan's human-rights record, an expansion of Termez or a return to Karshi-Khanabad (K2) have been discussed. In May, President Karimov announced that the cargo airport in Navoi was already being used to ship supplies to coalition forces in Afghanistan, but did not give details. South Korea is overseeing a major renovation to turn the Uzbek airport into a commercial freight hub. The airport should eventually be able to handle 300 tonnes of cargo daily, the Uzbek press reports.

EXISTING ROUTE
Termez, Uzbekistan
Since 2002, Germany's ISAF contingent has used the Termez air base as a transit point into Afghanistan. Although it housed 100,000 Soviet troops in the 1980s, Termez has been a minor ISAF hub; in its first five years, the German military shuttled around 175,000 troops and 15,500 tonnes of freight through here. US troops attached to ISAF have been allowed to use Termez on a limited basis since early 2008. The Soviet-built bridge over the Amu Darya River provides a land route into Afghanistan, and there is now talk of giving US troops wider access to Termez.

NEW ROUTE
Russia, Northern Distribution Network (NDN)
In March 2009, US Transportation Command announced its first non-lethal consignment by rail through Russia, Kazakhstan and Uzbekistan, and that 'significant progress' had been made on plans to transport 100 containers daily. All goods would be first shipped to the port of Riga. However, some concerns exist about Russia's control over some of the 5,000km land route, which would also be one of the longest military-supply routes in history.

Sources: IISS, ISAF/NATO, Latvian US Embassy, Luftwaffe, Global Security, International Relations and Security Network (ISN), BBC World Service, Christian Science Monitor, Eurasianet, Guardian, Reuters, Wired.

EXISTING ROUTE

Manas, Kyrgyzstan

Every month, 15,000 troops and 5,000 tonnes of supplies pass through Manas. Established in 2001, it is the only US base in Central Asia following the 2005 withdrawal from Uzbekistan. In late 2008, Kyrgyzstan complained about the low annual rent (initially $2 million, increased in 2006 to $17.5m with another $100m in funding). In February 2009, after accepting a $2.15bn Russian loan, Kyrgyz President Kurmanbek Bakiyev gave the US notice to leave. But after negotiations in which the US agreed to pay $180m, in June 2009 the Kyrgyz parliament endorsed a deal to keep it open.

EXISTING AND POTENTIAL ROUTES

Kulyab/Dushanbe, Tajikistan

Kulyab had been used since 2001 by the US-led coalition. A large military airfield used by the Soviets in the 1980s, it is still used by the Russian military in support of 201 Motor Rifle Division. Under new plans, Western supplies would be flown into either Dushanbe or Kulyab. They would then be trucked south via a new US-funded bridge over the Panj River. Tajikistan has also reportedly agreed to allow US supplies along its railways, so may form part of the Northern Distribution Network [below left] in future. However, some analysts have expressed worries about Tajikistan's infrastructure and instability.

EXISTING ROUTE

Khyber Pass, Pakistan

About 75% of non-lethal US and NATO military supplies to Afghanistan are shipped to Karachi, then trucked via the Khyber Pass (1,500km) or Chaman Crossing (see below). There is no official breakdown of the volumes travelling each route, but all sources agree that the Khyber Pass is the principal road corridor used. In February 2009, Taliban militants blew up a bridge outside Peshawar forcing the temporary closure of this famous mountain route. This has not been the only interruption. Vehicles have been frequently ambushed, destroyed or hijacked, and drivers killed. In March 2009, the head of US Transportation Command, General Duncan McNabb, said 140 containers go through the Khyber Pass daily.

EXISTING ROUTE

Chaman Crossing, Pakistan

This 825km route through Baluchistan has also been disrupted, most notably when local tribesmen blocked the Quetta–Chaman highway in January 2009, to protest the killing of one of their own by Pakistani anti-narcotics forces. Pakistani customs officers have told Reuters news agency that Chaman handles about a third as many containers as traverse the Khyber Pass.

KAZAKHSTAN

Almaty

Manas

Bishkek

KYRGYZSTAN

UZBEKISTAN

Navoi

Qarshi-Khanabad (K2)

Dushanbe

Kulyab

TAJIKISTAN

Friendship Bridge

Termez

Kunduz

Balkh

Bagram

Jalalabad

Peshawar

Islamabad

AFGHANISTAN

Kabul

Khyber Pass

INDIA

Kandahar

PAKISTAN

Chaman Crossing

Quetta

Key to map

═══	Major roads
✈	Airport
⌣	Road crossing

© IISS

ASIA-PACIFIC: The rise of Pakistan's Taliban

Pakistan has long been accused of doing too little to combat a growing Islamist insurgency. Local Taliban groups and al-Qaeda affiliates have taken hold in the volatile Federally Administered Tribal Areas (FATA) bordering Afghanistan and have expanded into North-West Frontier Province (NWFP). Questions have been asked about the close relationship between Taliban insurgents and elements in the government's Inter-Services Intelligence (ISI) directorate, although former president General Pervez Musharraf denied any such links.

Under increasing pressure from the United States, however, the Pakistani government decided to tackle the problem directly this year. A brief attempt to placate militants – allowing sharia law in a large part of NWFP – collapsed in May, and Islamabad announced a full-scale military operation to regain the territory. The release of a shocking video exposing Taliban cruelty, a Taliban assault on the Sri Lankan cricket team in Lahore and other terror attacks shifted public opinion behind the government for the time being.

Timeline of recent events

January 2009: Militants are reported to control almost all of Swat, where they have banned education for girls, among other restrictions.

15 February: Tehrik-e-Nifaz-e-Shariat-e-Mohammadi (TNSM) militants and NWFP government agree to Islamic sharia law in Malakand division.

21 February: The local Tehrik-e-Taliban (TTP) declares an indefinite ceasefire in Swat, after the sharia agreement.

1 March: After a six-month campaign, the Pakistan Army declares victory over militants in Bajaur and Mohmand.

3 March: 400 kilometres from NWFP, in Lahore, Taliban commandos attack the Sri Lankan cricket team.

3 April: A video of a teenage girl being flogged by extremists in Swat is broadcast nationally, sparking widespread condemnation.

13 April: Pakistani President Asif Ali Zardari signs a regulation imposing sharia law in Malakand division.

22 April: Taliban fighters move into parts of Buner, setting up checkpoints and patrolling streets.

23 April: Taliban members enter Shangla.

26 April: The Pakistan Army begins the 15,000-strong *Operation Toar Tander-I* (Black Thunderstorm) to retake Buner, Lower Dir, Swat and Shangla from the Taliban. Frontier Corps start operations in Lower Dir.

28 April: Military operations are launched in Buner.

4 May: Taliban enter the main town of Mingora, violating the deal in Swat.

5 May: The army begins a pushback in Swat.

7 May: PM Yousaf Raza Gilani formally announces a full-scale military operation against militants in Malakand division. Civilians begin to flee.

23–30 May: Security forces enter and regain control of Mingora.

4 June: The army claims to have arrested TNSM leader Sufi Mohammed, but the TNSM disputes this.

12 June: At least ten soldiers and 39 Taliban militants are killed in battles for Chuprial and Kabal in Swat. The army claims 1,430 militants killed in operations so far; 126 soldiers have also been killed.

14 June: The army declares the success of *Operation Toar Tander-I*, but continues to tackle areas of resistance.

19 June: After attempts in 2004, 2005 and 2008, Islamabad launches a new offensive in South Waziristan against TTP leader Baitullah Mehsud and his estimated 5,000 militants.

6 July: President Zardari vows to successfully defeat radical Muslim groups.

7–8 July: Remotely piloted US drones, now a common weapon in the fight against militants in Afghanistan and Pakistan, kill 20 militants in South Waziristan.

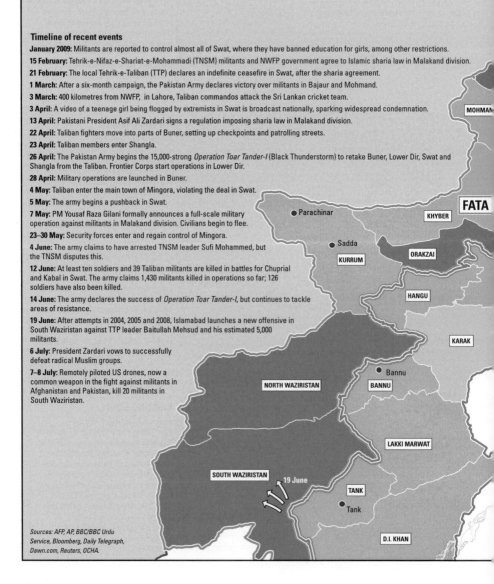

Sources: AFP, AP, BBC/BBC Urdu Service, Bloomberg, Daily Telegraph, Dawn.com, Reuters, OCHA.

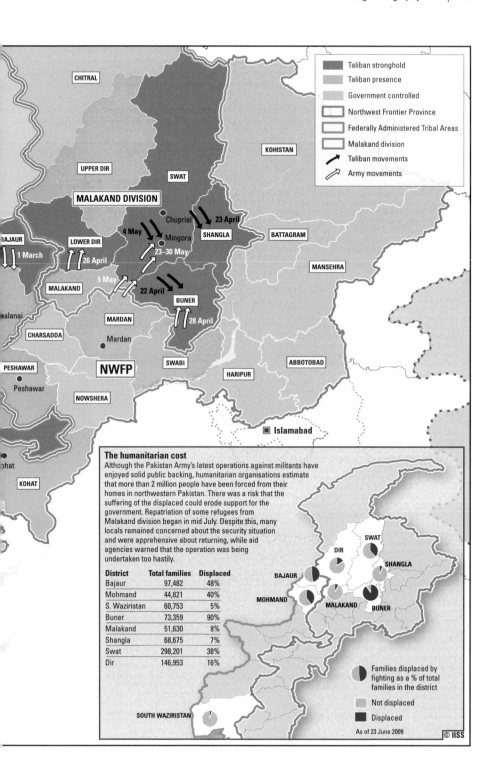

Taliban stronghold
Taliban presence
Government controlled
Northwest Frontier Province
Federally Administered Tribal Areas
Malakand division
Taliban movements
Army movements

CHITRAL

KOHISTAN

UPPER DIR

SWAT

MALAKAND DIVISION

Chuprial   23 April

4 May   Mingora   SHANGLA   BATTAGRAM

BAJAUR

1 March   LOWER DIR

26 April   23–30 May

MANSEHRA

5 May   22 April

MALAKAND   BUNER

alanai   28 April

MARDAN

CHARSADDA   Mardan

PESHAWAR   SWABI   ABBOTOBAD

NWFP   HARIPUR

Peshawar

NOWSHERA

ohat   Islamabad

KOHAT

The humanitarian cost
Although the Pakistan Army's latest operations against militants have
enjoyed solid public backing, humanitarian organisations estimate
that more than 2 million people have been forced from their
homes in northwestern Pakistan. There was a risk that the
suffering of the displaced could erode support for the
government. Repatriation of some refugees from
Malakand division began in mid July. Despite this, many
locals remained concerned about the security situation
and were apprehensive about returning, while aid
agencies warned that the operation was being
undertaken too hastily.

District	Total families	Displaced
Bajaur	97,482	48%
Mohmand	44,821	40%
S. Waziristan	60,753	5%
Buner	73,359	90%
Malakand	51,630	8%
Shangla	68,675	7%
Swat	298,201	38%
Dir	146,953	16%

SWAT

DIR   SHANGLA

BAJAUR

MOHMAND   MALAKAND   BUNER

Families displaced by
fighting as a % of total
families in the district

Not displaced

Displaced

SOUTH WAZIRISTAN

As of 23 June 2009

© IISS

ASIA-PACIFIC: Confrontation in the Korean peninsula

North Korea's nuclear and missile programme has mainly been seen as an effort to gain concessions from the outside world. In 2009, however, it has raised the stakes, firing a long-range missile, conducting a second nuclear test, recommencing plutonium reprocessing, acknowledging a uranium-enrichment programme and threatening a 'merciless offensive'.

With leader Kim Jong Il in poor health and trying to maintain his family's grip on power, the Democratic People's Republic of Korea (DPRK) responded defiantly to international condemnation and new sanctions agreed by the UN Security Council on 12 June 2009.

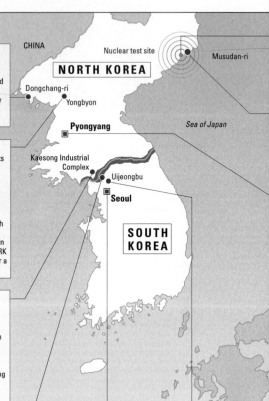

DONGCHANG-RI
In June, Japanese intelligence warned that the DPRK had moved a long-range missile to this new west-coast launch site – closer to the Yongbyon nuclear facility – and appeared to be preparing a new test firing. Analysts speculated that North Korea might fire a missile from here at Hawaii in early July; US President Obama and Defense Secretary Robert Gates both said that necessary precautions were in place.

YONGBYON
On 14 April 2009, North Korea abandoned earlier agreements to shut down the 5MWe experimental reactor at the Yongbyon Nuclear Scientific Research Centre and cease plutonium reprocessing. Resuming activity at Yongbyon, North Korea also expelled international inspectors and quit the Six-Party Talks (between it, South Korea, China, the US, Russia and Japan) on its nuclear programme. The reactor went critical in 1985, was closed in 1994 under the US–North Korea Agreed Framework and was restarted in 2003, producing plutonium that added to the stockpile later used in the country's first nuclear test in 2006. In June 2008, the DPRK demolished the 20m-tall cooling tower at the complex under a Six-Party Talks agreement.

KAESONG INDUSTRIAL COMPLEX
Recent North Korean demands could threaten this joint industrial complex's economic attractiveness or even viability. Since Kaesong opened in 2004, South Korean factory owners (currently just over 100) have benefited from access to a cheap, educated and Korean-speaking labour force of about 40,000. The complex boosted trade between the Koreas to more than $1.8bn, but as South Korea scaled back aid to the North last year, the North retaliated by halting trains to Kaesong and expelling some South Korean managers. In June 2009, it was insisting on a monthly pay rise for North Korean employees from $75 to $300, a $500m rent payment and more. Tensions also exist over a South Korean manager arrested in March and not seen since.

Demilitarised Zone (DMZ)
On 27 May 2009, the DPRK renounced the armistice that ended the Korean War in 1953, further heightening tensions. Since 1953, the two Koreas have been divided about the 38th parallel, separated by a 250km-long, 4km-wide buffer zone, called the Demilitarised Zone. The US estimates that up to 70–75% of North Korean military units are stationed within 100km of the DMZ, although the quality of their kit is poor. Twenty-one of 22 regular South Korean divisions remain in the region, with state-of-the-art equipment. Applying the same percentages to South Korean military figures leads to these estimates of forces near the border:

North Korea	South Korea
800,000 troops,	330,000–440,000 troops
13,600 artillery systems	5,400 artillery systems
3,900 tanks	2,300 tanks

Sources: IISS, US Department of Defense, South Korean Defence Ministry, South Korea Ministry of Unification, AFP, AP, BBC, Wall Street Journal.

SEOUL
Less than 50km from the border, the South Korean capital (pop 10.4m) is within easy reach of a North Korean military strike. In addition to about 18,000 artillery pieces, the DPRK is estimated to have at least five to seven battalions of *Scud*-type *Hwasong*-5/-6 missiles with ranges of 300–500km. Any first military strike against Pyongyang would incur mass casualties in retaliatory attacks. South Korea had a defence modernisation programme in place before the current crisis, including an upgrade of its F-16 fighter aircraft to be able to drop Joint Direct Attack Munition smart bombs. Its F-15K planes already have a precision-strike capability.

UIJEONGBU
As a deterrent against the North, the United States keeps troops – numbering 24,655 at the end of 2008 – with headquarters at Camp Red Cloud near Uijeongbu. On 28 May 2009, the South Korean–US combined forces command increased their alert level from 2 to 3, the highest since 2006, when the North conducted its first nuclear test.

NUCLEAR TEST SITE
On 25 May, North Korea conducted its second underground nuclear test. The seismic data, registering the explosion at 4.5–5 on the Richter scale, suggests a device of about 4 kilotonnes – the size the DPRK promised its first nuclear test in October 2006 would be, but ten times greater than that device actually delivered. As 4kt is still relatively small, many analysts believe the device probably failed to detonate properly. But this could have been a higher-tech device designed for a small yield to fit a missile warhead. The use of tritium, which North Korea probably can produce, would allow a smaller critical mass of plutonium.

Trajectory of rocket

MUSUDAN-RI
North Korea stepped up the pressure this year, when it launched a long-range missile over Japan on 5 April. The third stage of the *Unha*-2 missile failed to ignite, but the missile still flew 3,200km, showing significant progress towards an intercontinental range. North Korea said the Unha-2 (a variant of its *Taepo-dong*-2 technology) was launched to put a communications satellite into orbit. However, since its last long-range test of a *Taepo-dong*-2 in July 2006 failed after 40 seconds, this was doubtless a missile test to prove its capabilities. On 4 July, US Independence Day, North Korea fired seven *Scud*-type ballistic missiles from its east coast, which flew 400km before crashing into the Sea of Japan.

PYONGYANG
The North Korean capital (pop. 3.4m) is heavily defended, with estimates of at least 150 anti-aircraft artillery sites and four surface-to-air missile positions. However, most of this is thought to be outdated for modern warfare.

Tokyo

JAPAN

The greatest fear is that North Korea could miniaturise nuclear warheads to mount on missiles and then deliver such a weapon. Few analysts believe they can currently achieve this, although Japan believes they could do so 'in a relatively short period of time'. Crucially, the DPRK has yet to test re-entry vehicles to survive the extreme stresses of atmospheric re-entry. If improved, its *Taepo-dong*-2 could, in theory, hit cities in the US.

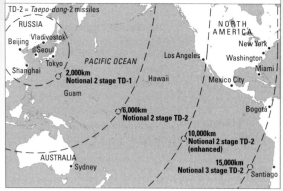

TD-2 = *Taepo-dong*-2 missiles

The two Koreas: a quick comparison
	South Korea	North Korea
Population	48.4m	23.5m (2008 figs)
GNI per capita	US$20,045	US$1,152 (2007 figs)
Troops (total)	655,000	1.1m (2008 figs)

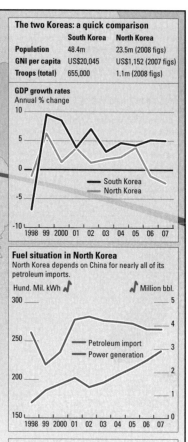

Fuel situation in North Korea
North Korea depends on China for nearly all of its petroleum imports.

The food situation in North Korea
In March 2009, North Korea rejected food aid from the US, its largest donor. The UN's World Food Progamme (WFP) has said that the country's citizens now face a 'crisis'. With demand long outstripping production (see chart) the DPRK has relied on food aid from China, South Korea and aid agencies. According to the WFP representative in Pyongyang, 'a very large part of the population has been undernourished for 15 or 20 years'.

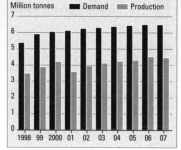

© IISS

THE AMERICAS: America's decaying infrastructure

Is the US a superpower in decline? An examination of its ageing national infrastructure might indicate so. In 2009, the American Society of Civil Engineers (ASCE) issued a 'report card' showing the lack of necessary investment. As well as dams and levees at risk of collapse and decades-old power-generation systems, the US particularly suffers from weaknesses in transport facilities.

Decaying and congested roads

Alaskan Way Viaduct, Seattle, WA
Up to 110,000 vehicles continue to travel on this traffic artery daily, although an earthquake in 2001 sunk some of its supports and weakened it. A tunnel replacement was proposed in early 2009.

Circle Interchange, Chicago, IL
Roughly 300,000 vehicles a day converge here from three expressways and one parkway, causing an estimated 25 million hours' delay here each year.

* AASHTO (American Association of State Highway and Transportation Officials) figures

States graded** according to the percentage of major roads in poor or mediocre condition

Grade A (0–10%) Grade B (11–19%) Grade C (20–29%) Grade D (30–59%) Grade F (>59%)

More than 3 million Americans drive at least 50 miles each way to work daily – on increasingly deteriorated and congested roads. The poor state of the nation's roads contributes to the 14,000 lives lost annually in accidents and costs motorists $67 billion per year in repairs and operating costs. The ASCE estimates $930bn is needed over five years to bring roads and bridges up to standard.

D the overall grade engineers give US infrastructure

$2.2tr how much investment they calculate is needed to maintain US infrastructure over five years

$93.4bn spending allocated for infrastructure in the federal stimulus plan

The 2009 ASCE report card

Aviation D	Public Parks and Recreation C-
Bridges C	
Dams D	Rail C-
Drinking Water D-	Roads D-
Energy D+	Schools D
Hazardous Waste D	Solid Waste C+
Inland Waterways D-	Transit D
Levees D-	Wastewater D-

Sources: American Society of Civil Engineers; www.infrastructurereportcard.org; Popular Mechanics; New York Times; Speaker of the House, House Ways and Means Committee, Senate Finance Committee; US Department of Transportation, Federal Railroad Administration, AASHTO.

** Grades for individual states have been calculated by the IISS using percentage data from, and a grading scale similar to that employed by, the ASCE. However, the ASCE has not issued grades for individual states, either generally or on roads and bridges.

Strategic Geography 2009 | XVII

Problem bridges

Dover Bridge, ID
The money needed to fix this north Idaho bridge has finally been allocated in the federal stimulus package. Discovered with some of its deck hanging by its steel reinforcing in 2006, it scored just 2 out of 100 in a National Bridge Inventory.

Minneapolis I-35 bridge, MN
Now rebuilt, this bridge provided a wake-up call on America's poor infrastructure when it collapsed in August 2007, killing 13 and wounding nearly 100.

Brooklyn Bridge, NY
America's oldest and most iconic suspension bridge isn't in danger of collapse, but some of its approaches have rusting steel and it has been labelled 'structurally deficient'.

States graded* by the percentage of bridges that are structurally deficient or functionally obsolete

■ Grade A (0–10%)   ■ Grade B (11–19%)   ■ Grade C (20–29%)   ■ Grade D (30–59%)   ■ Grade F (>59%)

In December 2008, the ASCE found that of the 600,905 bridges in the US, 26.9% were structurally deficient or functionally obsolete. The problem was growing faster in heavily trafficked urban areas. Usually designed to last 50 years, the average American bridge is now 43 years old.

Part of the solution? US plan for high-speed rail

Citing the damage that clogged highways and overburdened airports do to the US economy, President Barack Obama allocated $8 billion for high-speed rail in his $789bn financial stimulus package. With an extra $1bn a year annually to be spent over another five years, the money is intended to help bring America's below-par rail network into the 21st century. Ten potential routes, each 150–950km long, have been identified.

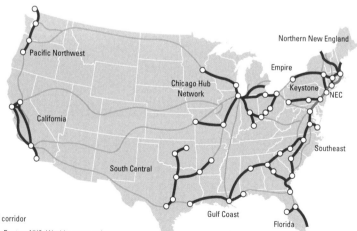

■ Designated high-speed rail corridor

■ Northeast corridor (existing Boston–NYC–Washington route).

— Other passenger rail routes

© IISS

THE AMERICAS: Drug-cartel violence in Mexico

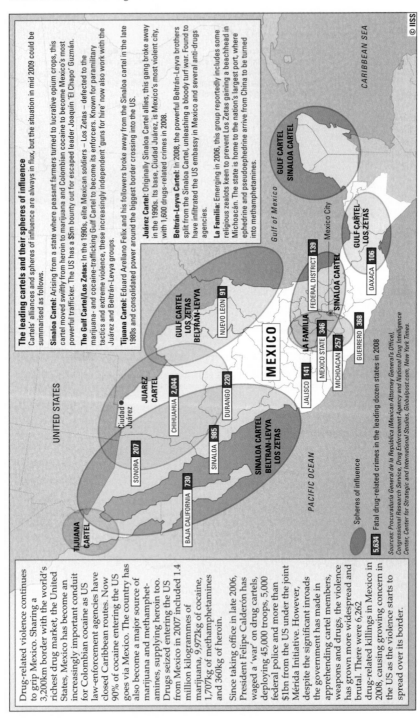

Drug-related violence continues to grip Mexico. Sharing a 3,200km border with the world's richest drug market, the United States, Mexico has become an increasingly important conduit for Colombian cocaine as US law-enforcement agencies have closed Caribbean routes. Now 90% of cocaine entering the US goes via Mexico. The country has also become a major source of marijuana and methamphetamines, supplying heroin too. Drugs seized entering the US from Mexico in 2007 included 1.4 million kilogrammes of marijuana, 9,972kg of cocaine, 1,707kg of methamphetamines and 360kg of heroin.

Since taking office in late 2006, President Felipe Calderón has waged a 'war' on drug cartels, deploying 45,000 troops, 5,000 federal police and more than $1bn from the US under the joint Mérida Initiative. However, despite the significant inroads the government has made in apprehending cartel members, weapons and drugs, the violence has grown more widespread and brutal. There were 6,262 drug-related killings in Mexico in 2008, causing growing concern in the US as the violence starts to spread over its border.

The leading cartels and their spheres of influence

Cartels' alliances and spheres of influence are always in flux, but the situation in mid 2009 could be summarised as follows.

Sinaloa Cartel: Arising from a state where peasant farmers turned to lucrative opium crops, this cartel moved swiftly from heroin to marijuana and Colombian cocaine to become Mexico's most powerful trafficker. The US has a $5m bounty out for escaped leader Joaquín 'El Chapo' Guzmán.

The Gulf Cartel/Los Zetas: In the 1990s, elite Mexican soldiers – Los Zetas – defected to the marijuana- and cocaine-trafficking Gulf Cartel to become its enforcers. Known for paramilitary tactics and extreme violence, these increasingly independent 'guns for hire' now also work with the Juárez and Beltrán-Leyva groups.

Tijuana Cartel: Eduard Arellano Felix and his followers broke away from the Sinaloa cartel in the late 1980s and consolidated power around the biggest border crossing into the US.

Juárez Cartel: Originally Sinaloa Cartel allies, this gang broke away in the 1990s. Its base, Ciudad Juárez, is Mexico's most violent city, with 1,600 drugs-related crimes in 2008.

Beltrán-Leyva Cartel: In 2008, the powerful Beltrán-Leyva brothers split from the Sinaloa Cartel, unleashing a bloody turf war. Found to have infiltrated the US embassy in Mexico and several anti-drugs agencies.

La Familia: Emerging in 2006, this group reportedly includes some religious zealots keen to prevent Los Zetas gaining a beachhead in Michoacán. The state is home to the nation's largest port, where ephedrine and pseudoephedrine arrive from China to be turned into methamphetamines.

UNITED STATES

MEXICO

PACIFIC OCEAN

Gulf of Mexico

CARIBBEAN SEA

Mexico City

Ciudad Juárez

TIJUANA CARTEL

JUAREZ CARTEL

SINALOA CARTEL BELTRÁN-LEYVA LOS ZETAS

GULF CARTEL LOS ZETAS BELTRÁN-LEYVA

LA FAMILIA

SINALOA CARTEL

GULF CARTEL LOS ZETAS

GULF CARTEL SINALOA CARTEL

SONORA 207
BAJA CALIFORNIA 730
CHIHUAHUA 2,044
SINALOA 985
DURANGO 220
NUEVO LEON 91
JALISCO 141
MEXICO STATE 346
MICHOACAN 257
FEDERAL DISTRICT 139
GUERRERO 368
OAXACA 106

Spheres of influence

5,634 Fatal drug-related crimes in the leading dozen states in 2008

Sources: *Procuraduría General de la República (Mexican Attorney General's Office), Congressional Research Service, Drug Enforcement Agency and National Drug Intelligence Center, Center for Strategic and International Studies, Globalpost.com, New York Times.*

© IISS

Chapter 7

Middle East / Gulf

The election of Barack Obama as American president signalled the application of new energy to the many challenges of the Middle East region. Obama sought to set a new tone in relations between the United States and the Muslim world. However, his arrival coincided with the advent of a right-wing Israeli government that did not favour compromise with the Palestinians, who themselves remained badly divided. Israel's effort to divert Washington's attention towards Tehran and away from itself did not succeed. But Obama's desire to engage Iran in dialogue was in abeyance as President Mahmoud Ahmadinejad's disputed election victory heralded a new period of domestic political uncertainty.

Iran: Election Sparks Protests, Nuclear Programme Advances

Notwithstanding the potential for military conflict over Iran's nuclear programme, the most serious challenge to the Islamic Republic since the 1979 revolution came from the domestic reaction to the announcement that President Mahmoud Ahmadinejad had won re-election by a wide margin on 12 June 2009. Protesters perceived this outcome as a massive fraud.

As many as two million people took to the streets to protest against Ahmadinejad's declared 2–1 margin of victory over reformist challenger Mir Hossein Mousavi. The protests were met with government violence, mostly meted out by the Basij militia, that left at least 20 dead according to the official count and largely stilled the demonstrations after two weeks.

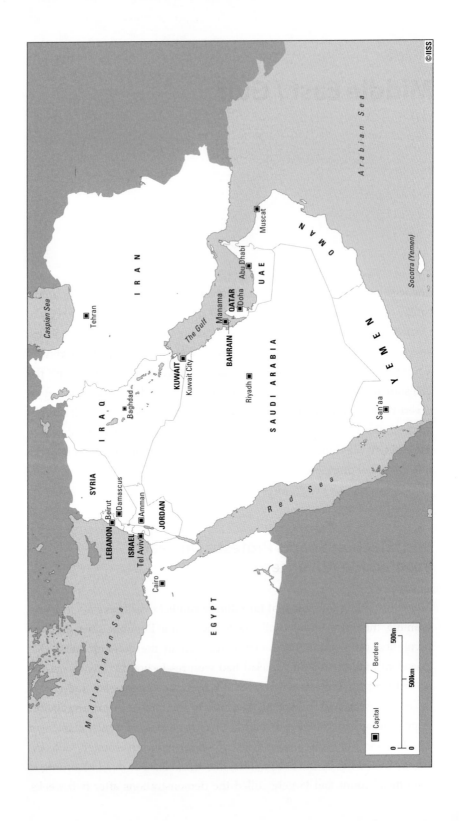

Some foreign journalists were expelled, and mobile phones and many Internet services were disrupted. The arrest of hundreds of reform-inclined journalists, political activists and former government officials deprived the protests of leadership. Mousavi used his website to label the government illegitimate, a charge backed in early July by the most important group of religious leaders in Iran. The moral authority of Supreme Leader Ayatollah Sayyid Ali Khamenei was undermined by his hasty decision to side with Ahmadinejad. Unprecedented divisions thus appeared within the political elite and clergy and the government lost legitimacy both at home and abroad.

The apparent vote rigging made any reconciliation between Iran and the United States all the more difficult. Meanwhile the chronic Iranian nuclear crisis entered a more dangerous stage in the past year. Tehran demonstrated beyond doubt that it had mastered the uranium-enrichment process, and by early 2009 Iran had produced sufficient low-enriched uranium (LEU), if further enriched, for a nuclear weapon. While the major powers and most of Iran's neighbours continued to demand that it suspend its enrichment programme, they had failed to stop Iran before it achieved the theoretical capability to produce the bomb. Newly elected US President Barack Obama thus spoke not of preventing the capability but of stopping Iran from acquiring nuclear weapons. His offer to engage Tehran without preconditions set a new context for Iran–US relations. However, Khamenei's hardline stance and distrust of the United States boded ill for Obama's timetable of waiting until the end of 2009 for results from his outreach strategy before turning to new sanctions. Meanwhile, a new Israeli government, led by conservative Prime Minister Benjamin Netanyahu, threatened to take unilateral action to stop Iran's nuclear programme if diplomacy did not manage to do so within a short time.

Election controversy

In the run-up to the June elections, moderates initially pinned their hopes on former President Mohammad Khatami, who wavered for months and finally withdrew from consideration on 16 March, saying he did not want to split the reformist camp. Former Prime Minister Mousavi was judged to have a better chance of winning on grounds that he would be more acceptable to the Revolutionary Guard and other hardliners. There was concern that Khatami would not be allowed to win in any case, and some conservative newspapers even indicated he might be assassinated.

When campaigning started on 21 April, the field had been narrowed down to four candidates: Ahmadinejad; Mousavi; former head of the Revolutionary Guard Mohsen Rezai, who was in the race as a spoiler aiming to draw conservative votes away from the president; and former speaker of the parliament Mehdi Karroubi, the only cleric among the four. A total of 471 others who had registered to run were disqualified by the Guardian Council for allegedly failing to meet the constitutional requirements. Other potential challengers, including popular Tehran mayor Muhammad Qalibaf, were persuaded not to run.

An unprecedented series of television debates between each pairing of candidates and a carnival-like explosion of popular interest in the final two weeks of the campaign gave reformists hope of enlisting support from the 40% of the electorate who sat out the 2005 presidential election. Mousavi, 67, lacked charisma. He was not considered a moderate when he was prime minister in 1981–89, but he was generally to the left on economic issues and a relative liberal on social issues. He was also seen as an effective manager for having overseen a well-run rationing system during the Iran–Iraq War, and as a rebel for having battled with Khamenei at that time. He withdrew from politics in 1989 after losing that battle. In 2009, after two decades of devoting himself to art and architecture, he said he had returned to the political fray as a matter of 'obligation', to try to overcome divisions in the establishment because he considered himself acceptable to both reformists and conservatives (who go by the name 'principlists').

As it turned out, Mousavi's appeal to reformists proved to be decidedly unpopular with the principlists who were in power. Watching his rallies grow in size and fervour and capitalise on the campaign's signature green hue (not coincidentally, the colour of Islam), the leadership may have begun to fear the prospects of a colour revolution akin to the soft-power revolutions that had swept out authoritarian governments elsewhere in Eurasia.

A 3 June debate between the two front-runners turned into a sharp exchange of personal accusations. Mousavi accused Ahmadinejad of moving Iran towards dictatorship and said his foreign policy suffered from 'adventurism, illusionism, exhibitionism, extremism and superficiality'. Ahmadinejad linked Mousavi with the previous government and said it had gotten nothing from temporarily suspending uranium enrichment. Ahmadinejad pulled out an intelligence file on his opponent's wife, Zahra Rahnavard, and accused her of bypassing the entrance-exam process to get into a PhD programme. Rahnavard, a former university chancellor who campaigned with her husband and even held hands with him in public, was popular with many women, but the attacks apparently resonated with conservatives. The unbridled enthusiasm of Mousavi's supporters, including some young women who danced without headscarves in public rallies, may also have worked against him among religious-minded voters. Ahmadinejad also apparently won favour through his accusations of corruption against former President Ayatollah Ali Akbar Hashemi Rafsanjani, who had thrown his weight behind Mousavi.

Two hours after the polls closed, the Interior Ministry announced that Ahmadinejad had won with 63% of the vote, compared with 34% for Mousavi, 2% for Rezai and less than 1% for Karroubi. The 84% voter turnout was the highest in the 30-year history of the Islamic Republic. The government proclaimed that the election was also the cleanest ever, a claim many disputed. Citing various irregularities, Mousavi declared the announced results a 'dangerous charade'. Although polls in Iran are unreliable, opinion surveys a week before the election had shown Mousavi ahead by 10–20 points. Many found it hard to believe that, contrary to every other Iranian election, the large turnout would work in the conservatives' favour

> Mousavi declared the results a 'dangerous charade'

and that Ahmadinejad, who was widely disliked among youthful urbanites who abstained in the 2005 election, would win 8m more votes than in that election. Among other statistical anomalies, the lack of regional and ethnic variations in Ahmadinejad's vote percentage also struck many as suspicious, including his large margins in Mousavi's home Azerbaijan province and Karroubi's Luristan home base.

To some analysts, it was only the margin of victory that was surprising. No incumbent had ever lost in Iran's previous presidential elections and Ahmadinejad had all the advantages of incumbency. His hardline allies had won all the parliamentary and local elections for the past four years and wielded all the levers of power. The principlists controlled all the state institutions, including the executive, legislature and judiciary branches, the military, the intelligence agencies, the Revolutionary Guard and the paramilitary Basij volunteers. Iranian television and other state-run media gave Ahmadinejad flattering and disproportionate coverage. Perhaps most importantly, Ahmadinejad had the obvious, albeit inexplicit, support of the supreme leader. In mid May Khamenei defended Ahmadinejad against 'untrue' criticism of his economic policies, and he urged voters to 'elect those who live in a simple, modest way', which is precisely Ahmadinejad's self-projected image. A few days later Khamenei urged the nation not to elect a president who could adopt a pro-West stance.

An information clampdown beginning on election evening shut down text messaging nationwide, the Tehran mobile-phone network and many pro-Mousavi websites, temporarily leaving Twitter, a social-networking website on which users post and view short messages, as the main medium for information on the ensuing protests. The worst civil unrest in Iran in 30 years took place as rioting protesters called the announced results a coup. Over 600 supporters were arrested and Mousavi temporarily placed under informal house arrest. He was labelled a US agent by one prominent Ahmadinejad ally. Khamenei, in a ferocious 19 June sermon, accused the 'treacherous' United Kingdom of fomenting the protests. Seeking to revive resentment of historical British interventions and alarmed at the domestic popularity of the new BBC Persian service, the Iranian authorities detained nine of the British Embassy's Iranian staff for varying periods and forced several political prisoners to confess to foreign-inspired conspiracy. A new phase had begun in the troubled tenure of the Islamic Republic.

The protesters sought not to overthrow the regime, but simply to have their votes counted by means of a re-vote. Infusing their movement with symbolism from the 1979 revolution, they nightly shouted '*Allah-hu akbar*' (God is great) from the rooftops. Yet the effect of the election and its aftermath was to seriously wound the regime, which may have strengthened its grip on power for the short term yet lost its legitimacy and moral authority in the process. In hastily blessing the election results and condemning the protesters as enemies of the state, Khamenei undermined his own authority. Protests that started over the confined issue of election fraud evolved into a challenge to the ideological core of the Islamic Republic: the concept of *velayat i-faqih*, or 'rule by jurisprudence' (sometimes interpreted as 'Islamic republicanism' in the West). Some commentators said the brutality of the crackdown highlighted what had been a growing trend under Ahmadinejad of a state guided not by revolutionary clerics but by the Revolutionary Guard.

Economic issues

The poor state of the Iranian economy was a main election issue, as the nation faced the double whammy of a global recession and falling oil prices, as well as increasing international financial pressure over the nuclear issue.

Failure to meet his past election promises to manage the economy was seen as Ahmadinejad's Achilles heel. In particular, his subsidy policies and heavy public spending significantly fuelled inflation, which hit 30% in 2008. According to Iran's central bank, approximately 14 million of Iran's 70m citizens lived below the poverty line and unemployment was at 10% (although it was in fact probably higher). A substantial cushion of foreign reserves helped the government bridge deficits caused by the sharp drop in oil prices, but many Iranian citizens asked why revenues were not more wisely spent during the fat years. Inadequate investment in maintenance and new technologies had seen oil production declining by about 5% a year.

Disputes over economic policy flared throughout the year. In October, government plans to introduce a 3% value-added tax were shelved after several days of protests from traders. In November, 60 prominent economists published a letter arguing that Ahmadinejad's foreign and domestic policies were causing economic ruin directly and through the loss of trade and investment opportunities as a result of sanctions. To combat inflation, the government at the end of 2008 announced plans to cancel $90 billion worth of subsidies on essential goods but to make up for the blow to the lower-income classes by providing cash handouts. Iran's Parliament Research Centre predicted that this could see the inflation rate rising to 50% after the election. In September 2008, Ahmadinejad had dismissed Central Bank Governor Tahmasb Mazaheri because of his opposition to this plan.

Yet, in the end, without any vote-rigging, Ahmadinejad's subsidies and income-redistribution policies might have been the basis for a narrow victory. Mobilising his support in rural areas and the urban poor, he had spent the past four years criss-crossing the country, promising economic development and to fight bureaucratic corruption. Notwithstanding the impact on inflation, he had increased income equality. Ahmadinejad combined this economic populism with a personal embodiment of political purity and religious piety that proved appealing to many.

Nuclear programme: break-out capacity

Foreign-policy issues also garnered an unusual amount of electoral attention. Despite sustained criticism, from fellow conservatives among others, of Ahmadinejad's undiplomatic management of foreign policy including his repeated questioning of the Holocaust, his staunch defiance of the West over the nuclear issue appealed to nationalistic impulses. Rejecting five UN Security Council resolutions mandating suspension, Iran continued to develop its uranium-enrichment and plutonium-production capabilities. By the end of January 2009, Iran's Natanz enrichment plant had produced 1,010kg of gasified uranium enriched to the 3.5% U_{235} level needed for most nuclear-power-plant fuel. If further enriched to 90% or more, this would be sufficient, in principle, to provide the fissile material for one nuclear weapon. The report by the International Atomic Energy Agency (IAEA) of this stockpile, and of an undercounting by Iran of its enriched-uranium production, led to alarmist reports in the press, not all of which added the caveat that further enrichment could not be done without tipping off the agency, which regularly inspects the plant.

On 5 June 2009, the IAEA reported that Iran's LEU stockpile had grown to 1,339kg, or by approximately 2.75kg per day since January. By the end of May, the underground enrichment plant at Natanz was operating 4,920 first-generation centrifuges and had 2,132 more centrifuges installed and operating under vacuum, for a total of about 7,000. Installation work was continuing for an additional 8,000 centrifuges, which would bring the total to 15,000 at some unspecified future date.

Iran appeared to have overcome many of the technical problems it had previously experienced in the operation of centrifuge cascades. With 7,000 centrifuges operating, Iran may be able to produce the LEU feed material for two weapons' worth of fissile material by the end of 2009. At an above-ground pilot plant at Natanz, Iran was also experimenting with three versions of later-model centrifuges, which might be up to 2.5 times as efficient in producing enriched uranium. Meanwhile, it continued work on a 40MWe research reactor at Arak which would be capable of producing weapons-grade plutonium, although a reprocessing facility would also be needed to separate the usable plutonium from the rest of the reactor spent fuel. The Arak reactor was scheduled to be completed in 2011.

Not all of Iran's nuclear facilities presented a proliferation challenge. In February, the nation's first nuclear power plant at Bushehr underwent pre-commissioning. Under construction by Russia since 1995, the facility was scheduled to start operation by the end of 2009, although 2010 is more likely. The power plant has a clear civil-energy purpose and is not a proliferation threat as long as it is well safeguarded and the Russian-supplied fuel is repatriated in accordance with a 2005 agreement. A fuel-fabrication facility at Esfahan, the completion of which Ahmadinejad announced in April 2009, saying it gave Iran 'control of the entire nuclear fuel cycle', was innocuous from a proliferation perspective.

Other aspects of Iran's nuclear programme, however, continued to raise suspicion. In addition to concerns about the dual-use capabilities of the Natanz and Arak facilities, other nations continued to criticise Tehran's failure to cooperate with the IAEA investigation of past Iranian nuclear activities and its verification of new undertakings. Iran continued to reject its treaty obligation to provide advance declarations of new nuclear facilities and to allow inspectors regular access to facilities under construction, including the Arak research reactor. In June, it rejected an IAEA request to install more surveillance cameras at Natanz to adequately monitor the expanding number of cascades.

Iran also refused to answer questions about evidence of nuclear-weapons development work prior to late 2003 (when the US intelligence community believes Iran suspended this work). This evidence included information the IAEA said in September 2008 it had obtained about foreign help to Iran regarding experiments on a detonator suitable for an implosion-type weapon. This involved a former Russian weapons expert who visited Iran on his own. According to a US Senate Foreign Relations Committee report of May 2009, foreign (Israeli) intelligence analysts believed that by the time Iran stopped its weapons-development work in late 2003, it had already produced a suitable design, manufactured some components and conducted enough successful explosive tests to set aside the work until it had produced sufficient quantities of enriched uranium. US Director of National Intelligence Dennis Blair testified in March that the United States and Israel had the same basic intelligence information but that the Israelis 'take more of a worst-case approach'.

> Iran continued to reject its treaty obligations

Iran's expanding missile capabilities also provoked international concern. Iran already fielded a *Shahab*-3 missile with the 1-tonne payload capacity and 1.2m airframe diameter necessary to carry a nuclear warhead. Its 1,300km range encompasses Israel, Turkey and Saudi Arabia. The *Shahab*-3 also formed the first stage of the two-stage rocket Iran used to launch its first satellite into low Earth orbit in February 2009, becoming the tenth nation to demonstrate such a capability. Russian President Dmitry Medvedev echoed the concerns of many nations when, in a private meeting with American scholars in the Kremlin, he reportedly expressed alarm in 'very graphic language' over the satellite launch and its demonstration of Iran's 'far-reaching nuclear ambitions'. A French Foreign Ministry spokesman said 'we can't help but link this to the very serious concerns about the development of military nuclear capability'. Perhaps more worrying than Tehran's satellite-launch capability, however, was the November 2008 test firing of a new medium-range ballistic missile, the solid-fuel *Sajjil*. Although its range and payload were similar to those of the *Shahab-3*, a solid-fuel missile of this size is more difficult to build and provides more planning options because it can be launched more quickly with less vulnerability to a pre-emptive strike.

In addition to its nuclear and missile programmes, Iran continued to provoke Western anger through its support for groups in Lebanon, Iraq, Afghanistan and the Palestinian territories that engaged in acts of terrorism. A report published by the US State Department in May 2009 called Iran the 'most active state sponsor of terrorism' in the world. The report said Iran's Islamic Revolutionary Guard Corps' Quds force was the principal means by which Iran supported such groups. Given Washington's relationship with Israel and concerns about terrorism, Iran's military backing for these groups would also have to change if the US and Iran were ever to normalise relations.

Diplomatic stand-off

Iran's progress in both the nuclear and missile fields lent an air of futility to the various international efforts to bring a halt to these programmes. The most significant of these efforts was a repackaged incentives proposal submitted to Iran on 16 June 2008 with a cover letter signed by the foreign ministers of China, France, Germany, Russia, the United Kingdom and United States (the E3+3) along with EU foreign-policy chief Javier Solana. In addition to the nuclear-energy technology and other economic benefits pre-viously offered in 2006, the proposal included cooperation on Afghanistan and drug trafficking and a constructive role for Iran in international affairs, and reaffirmation of the prohibition against the threat or use of force in inter-national relations. Translated into Farsi and made public so that the Iranian people would have no doubt about the opportunities the country was being offered, the package came with a renewed proposal for a so-called 'double freeze' – no additional sanctions and no additional centrifuges – as a basis for a six-week period of 'pre-negotiations', to be followed by a full suspen-sion of sanctions and enrichment during full negotiations.

The proposal, and US Secretary of State Condoleezza Rice's signature on it, initially seemed to find favour in Tehran. Former Foreign Minister

Ali Velayati, a top adviser to the supreme leader, declared that Iran should accept the package, and Iranian state radio held an unprecedented debate on whether to do so. These and other positive signals led the United States to engage with Iran on the nuclear issue for the first time, sending Under Secretary of State William Burns to Geneva on 19 July 2008 with the other E3+3 partners for pre-talks with Iran's chief nuclear negotiator Saeed Jalili. Iran's response was, however, seen as a 'no'. Tehran proposed modalities for starting negotiations, including an extended round of pre-talks, but ignored the key issues of freeze and suspension. That apparent lack of interest contributed to a decision by a George W. Bush administration decision not to follow through with the idea to offer to establish a US consular presence in Tehran.

Accordingly, the Western nations reverted to the sanctions track. On 8 August 2008 the EU amended its common position implementing Security Council sanctions against Iran by calling on the Union's financial institutions to exercise 'restraint' – not just vigilance – on export credits, and decreeing that EU member states inspect Iran-bound cargoes. Additional sanctions also began to be floated in New York, but the Russia–Georgia crisis that month soon overshadowed the Iran issue. Diplomats succeeded only in producing, on 27 September, a toothless fifth Security Council resolution demanding suspension of enrichment but without any new sanctions or deadlines. In the aftermath of the Georgia crisis, Western nations were happy that Russia would agree to any resolution at all. Like three out of four of the previous Security Council resolutions on Iran, Resolution 1835 was adopted unanimously. Still, Iran claimed that most countries were on its side, citing as proof the 30 July declaration of a ministerial conference in Tehran of the 118-member Non-Aligned Movement, which stated that Iran's 'fuel cycle policies must be respected'.

Obama's engagement strategy

Global disenchantment with the United States during the Bush administration may have helped Iran garner diplomatic allies. World views toward the United States changed, however, with the election on 4 November 2008 of Barack Obama, who had signalled an emphasis on diplomacy, including a posture of speaking with adversaries. During the presidential election campaign he had promised engagement with Iran without preconditions and suggested that he would be willing to meet with his Iranian counterpart. Obama followed up those pledges in his inaugural address on 20 January

2009, offering, to unnamed oligarchs, to 'extend a hand if you are willing to unclench your fist'. Two months later, at the start of the Persian New Year, Obama recorded a video address to the Iranian people and leaders, offering a new beginning to diplomatic relations. Speaking with warmth and twice referring to the 'Islamic Republic of Iran', he called on the nation to 'take its rightful place in the community of nations', but also to accept its responsibilities by not seeking to take its place 'through terror or arms'. In April, the United States said it would henceforth be a full participant in international talks with Iran over the nuclear issue, regularising the Bush administration's July 2008 one-time exception to the policy of not joining talks until Iran suspended its enrichment programme. In his 4 June 2009 speech at Cairo University, Obama offered an implicit apology for the US role in overthrowing a democratically elected regime in Iran in the middle of the Cold War, reaffirmed Iran's right to nuclear power if it complied with its responsibilities under the Nuclear Non-Proliferation Treaty, and reiterated his desire to move forward without preconditions to overcome decades of mistrust.

US Secretary of State Hillary Clinton appointed veteran Middle East negotiator Dennis Ross as her special adviser on the Gulf and Southwest Asia, a title that avoided the word 'Iran' so as not to appear over-eager to enter into talks and thereby lose negotiation leverage. Ross coordinated a measured review of policy toward Iran and a quiet, back-channel outreach, and in June moved to the White House with expanded regional responsibilities. Another special envoy, Richard Holbrooke, in charge of policy toward Afghanistan and Pakistan, initiated one of the first bilateral contacts between the US and Iranian governments in many years by chatting with an Iranian representative to an Afghanistan stakeholders conference in The Hague on 31 March. As difficult a problem as Afghanistan might be, it also presented a propitious area for US–Iranian engagement, given a congruence of interest in reducing the opiate trade and instability that threatens both nations. (At least 5% of Iran's adult male population is addicted to opiates, which largely come through its border with Afghanistan.) The problems of radicalism in Pakistan also resonate with Iran, which faces its own Sunni radicalism in the tribal region of Balochistan, where the terrorist group Jundallah in 2008 abducted and executed 16 police officers and conducted a suicide attack that killed four security officers. However, potential cooperation with the United States in countering Islamic terrorism would first have to overcome Iranian accusations that Washington is behind the ethnic incidents in Balochistan.

Obama's policy of dropping preconditions on US discussions with Iran did not mean that the Europeans who had been leading the talks with Iran would similarly drop preconditions. A French Foreign Ministry spokesman repeated in mid April that substantial negotiations with Iran on the future of its nuclear programme could only begin in accordance with the earlier E3+3 position that all uranium enrichment must be halted. As a US State Department spokesman explained when asked how this position meshed with Obama's pledge of no preconditions, 'this issue of suspension of uranium enrichment is an international condition, not an American condition'. Whether it would continue to be a precondition was unclear throughout the spring, and the firmness of the position was not helped when US Senate Foreign Relations Committee Chairman John Kerry in June pronounced the position of no enrichment 'ridiculous'.

> Obama continued Bush's financial squeeze

The Obama focus on engagement was part of a two-track strategy designed to create the conditions for persuading European and other allies to join in upping the pressure on Iran if engagement failed to produce results. In keeping with his election pledge to 'use all elements of American power to pressure Iran' to 'abandon its dangerous nuclear programme', Obama continued Bush's financial squeeze by limiting Iranian access to the international financial sector. In congressional testimony on 22 April, Clinton said that US attempts to reach out to Iran would be joined by the threat of 'crippling' sanctions if Tehran refused to cooperate. Obama retained Treasury Under Secretary Stuart Levey, who had led the Bush administration's banking sanctions and who sharpened the campaign of financial isolation. In April 2009 the Treasury Department imposed sanctions on six Iranian firms and one Chinese individual, all of whom were suspected of involvement with the uranium-enrichment programme. Other Iranian nationals were indicted on charges of exporting restricted aircraft parts to Iran.

Separately, Obama backed new legislation introduced in Congress in April that would impose sanctions on foreign companies that sell or ship refined petroleum to Iran. Restricting the petroleum imports that fuel 30–40% of Iran's road transport is seen as a way of putting real pressure on Iran, including driving up the consumer cost of gasoline. A Senate sponsor of the bill said 'we need to give them a choice: you can do business with Iran's $250 billion economy or our $13 trillion economy, but not both'. Legislation was also introduced in May that would give legal protection to state and local governments that join a campaign to divest their public-pension-fund assets from companies investing more than $20m in Iran's energy sector.

The Obama administration also hoped that the prospect of improved US–Russian relations would encourage Moscow to join in putting pressure on Iran. In a February letter, Obama told Medvedev that if Russia could help stop the Iranian threat, there would be less need to deploy the missile-defence systems in central Europe that Russia so strongly opposes. Medvedev reacted coolly, saying through a spokesman that the letter contained no specific proposals. Russians do not want relations with the United States to be contingent on outcomes over which they may have little control. They note that with less than $3bn in bilateral trade annually, Russia does not even make the list of Iran's top ten trading partners. But the trade they do have includes about $400,000 a year in defence sales, which is of great importance to Iran's military.

Notwithstanding the Treasury Department's continued pressure, Obama decided to hold fire on a full-scale sanctions push until his outreach strategy – to both Russia and Iran – had a chance to succeed. Israel went along with this sequence of sweeter carrots before stronger sticks, but argued that the interval should be time-limited and short. When incoming Israeli Prime Minister Benjamin Netanyahu visited Washington in late May, he argued that it should be no longer than three months after the June Iran election. Key Persian Gulf states also expressed concern about the efficacy of diplomacy to stop Iran's nuclear activities and involvement in its neighbour's affairs. In response to Netanyahu, Obama refused to impose an 'artificial deadline', but agreed that outreach could not be open-ended while Iran continued to enhance its nuclear capabilities, and that by year's end he would have a good idea of whether Iran was making a 'good-faith effort to resolve differences'.

How to deal with the election controversy became a political football in the United States, as Republican Party politicians and commentators criticised Obama for not siding more forcefully with the protesters. For days after the election, he withheld comment on the results themselves, only gradually condemning the brutal crackdown, so as not to give the government any excuse to cast the issue as other than an internal debate. Sticking to a pro-engagement strategy that included a pre-election letter to Khamenei reiterating his public offer of talks with Iran, Obama also knew that any chance of finding a solution to the nuclear issue would require working with those in Iran who retained power. Depriving the regime of a foreign enemy would also allow the societal differences to deepen.

Israel's stance

How Israel would deal with Iran's growing nuclear capability remained one of the key security questions throughout the year. According to the *New York Times*, Israel in spring 2008 asked US permission to fly over Iraq to bomb the Natanz nuclear facilities and for the United States to sell Israel bunker-busting bombs for such an operation. The story said Bush rejected both requests, and that the White House never concluded whether Israel had decided to carry out the strike before the United States protested, or whether it was trying to goad the White House into taking decisive action before Bush left office. As compensation for rejecting the requests, the White House reportedly briefed Israeli officials on new US efforts to sabotage Iran's nuclear infrastructure.

Israel's perception that it was under time pressure to strike was somewhat relieved by Moscow's decision to put on hold the sale of S-300 advanced air-defence systems to Iran, which would provide a formidable shield against air-strikes on the nuclear facilities. When Netanyahu came to power in late March 2009, he was determined to press America harder to deal with the Iran issue. In an interview with *Atlantic* magazine shortly before taking office, he said if Obama did not stop Tehran from acquiring nuclear weapons, Israel might be forced to attack Iran's nuclear facilities itself. Politicians who spoke with Netanyahu said he had made up his mind to destroy Iran's nuclear installations, and most of the public seemed to agree it would be necessary. In a May 2009 opinion survey, 66% of Israelis polled said they approved of military action against Iran. But many Israelis questioned whether their air force could successfully carry out air-strikes without US involvement, which was even less likely to be forthcoming under Obama than under Bush. US Secretary of Defense Robert Gates testified in Congress on 30 April that bombing Iran would not solve the problem; it would only delay the nuclear programme while hardening the regime's resolve and making the programme more covert. In 2007, Gates had said that bombing Iran would 'create generations of jihadists'. At the beginning of May, CIA chief Leon Panetta reportedly held secret talks with senior Israeli officials who reassured him that Israel would not surprise the United States with a strike on Iran, although neither would it take the option of military action off the table.

In addition to the question of how much time to give to negotiations, Israel and the United States developed differences over how to characterise the Iranian worst-case outcome and how resolving it should be linked, if at all, to the Palestinian issue. In statements at the White House in May, Netanyahu emphasised the danger of Iran developing nuclear-weapons 'capabilities', whereas Obama referred to preventing Iran from 'obtaining a nuclear weapon'. The US president repeated that formulation in his speech at Cairo University. In the other area of difference, the Obama administration urged Israel to seek resolution of the Palestinian conflict as a useful step toward addressing the Iranian nuclear threat. Netanyahu's new government saw the linkage in the reverse sequence, arguing that the road to Jerusalem led through Iran. Top Israeli officials said they could not move ahead on the core issues of peace talks with the Palestinians until Iran's influence in the region was curtailed by stopping its pursuit of nuclear weapons. The chicken-and-egg issue was resolved when Netanyahu, at his May meeting at the White House, committed to 'simultaneous and parallel' pursuit of Arab–Israeli peacemaking and steps to prevent Iranian acquisition of a nuclear-weapons capability.

Regional relations

Iran's drive for a nuclear-weapons capability reinforced anxieties among many of its neighbours about what they see as hegemonic instincts. After visiting Cairo and Amman in early May, Netanyahu asserted that there was unanimity of views between the Arab world and Israel regarding the dangers which Iran represented in the region. He had several reasons to highlight Iranian troublemaking, especially after Ahmadinejad just weeks before had launched an anti-Israeli tirade at a UN anti-racism conference that caused 30 diplomats present to walk out. Although the Israelis overstated the degree of unity against Iran in the region, there was no doubting the increasing Arab sense of concern. Worries about Iran's nuclear programme itself were coupled with fears that Washington might cut a deal with Tehran at the expense of the Arabs.

Iran's neighbours had other reasons to get their backs up. Former Iranian parliament speaker Ali Akbar Nateq Nori, who holds a senior position in Khamenei's office, sparked a firestorm of protest from Arab leaders in February 2009 when he referred to Bahrain as Iran's 14th province. Morocco severed ties with Iran over the incident and claimed that Iran's promotion of Shia Islam was interfering in Morocco's domestic affairs. Egyptian–Iranian

relations took a downturn in April when Cairo arrested members of an
Iranian-funded Hizbullah cell who were suspected of planning attacks on
Egyptian soil and smuggling weapons into Gaza. Iran is the main supporter
of Hamas, supplying both weapons and training, although it probably did
not instigate the rocket attacks that prompted Israel's incursion into Gaza in
January. In Baghdad, Iran failed to persuade the Iraqi leadership in December
2008 not to sign a security agreement with the United States that allowed for
continued stationing of US forces. Iranian influence in Iraq waned in proportion to a growing sense of Iraqi confidence and nationalism. In Afghanistan,
Iran maintained friendly relations with the Karzai government but opposed
Afghan reconciliation talks with the Taliban.

Syria was one of the few neighbours with whom Iran deepened relations
during the past year. When Ahmadinejad visited Damascus in early May
2009, Syrian President Bashar al-Assad defended his long-standing alliance
with Iran and said a strategic relationship between the two countries contributed to Middle East stability. Neither president referred to the US Navy
interception in January of an Iranian-chartered vessel transiting the Red Sea
en route to Syria that was found to be carrying components for mortars and
thousands of cases of powder, propellant and shell casings in contravention
of the March 2008 UN Security Council Resolution 1747 that prohibited the
transfer of any arms by Iran. The sustainability of the Iran–Syria alliance,
however, came under pressure as the United States opened talks with Syria
for the first time in years and Syria probed for prospects of resuming peace
negotiations with Israel.

Iran's response to Obama

Still facing both carrots and sticks, Iran seemed uncertain how to respond to
Obama's outreach. Immediately after the US election, Ahmadinejad sent an
unprecedented letter of congratulation, which initially provoked a backlash
among hardliners who were cautious about what they saw as an uncoordinated attempt at reconciliation but who later came around to arguing that if
there was to be an opening with the United States, the hardliners should take
credit for it. Many Iranian officials remained dismayed that Obama never
responded directly. Maintaining a cautious approach, Tehran sent to the
Afghanistan conference in The Hague a relatively low-level official whose
conversation with Holbrooke was limited to awkward niceties. The reply to
Ross's quiet outreach was to keep it on ice on until after the Iranian election.
In response to Obama's Persian New Year message, Khamenei coldly pro-

nounced that 'words are not enough', and that the United States needed to change its policies if it expected Iran to do the same. Having previously said he would decide when the time was right for engagement with the United States, he appeared worried that Obama was pre-empting that decision. In mid April, Ahmadinejad said Iran was preparing a new package for negotiations on global issues such as disarmament and UN Security Council reform, but that it would not address Iran's nuclear activities. 'The time for discussions over the nuclear program has come to an end, and the clock will not go back', he insisted. Henceforth, Iran would discuss nuclear issues only with the IAEA.

Human-rights violations

Iran's ambivalence over how to respond to Obama's effort to change the atmosphere was reflected in the January 2009 arrest of Iranian-American journalist Roxana Saberi for buying wine, her April sentencing after a closed-door trial to eight years' imprisonment for trumped-up charges of spying, and her subsequent release in May. Although there are competing theories as to what was transpiring behind the scenes, judiciary hardliners seemed to be intent on using her to undermine prospects for engagement lest it remove the pretext of an American enemy that underlines the regime's *raison d'être*. But Ahmadinejad, possibly seeing the case in terms of his own chances to land the American prize, intervened to instruct the chief prosecutor to allow Saberi the opportunity for a full defence.

Whether or not Saberi's case reflected an internal political struggle or possibly an effort to create and then defuse a crisis for the sake of future negotiation advantage, her arrest was consistent with Iran's harsh treatment of reform-minded domestic journalists, human-rights activists and other potential regime opponents. As of April, nine journalists and bloggers were facing charges including espionage. In August 2008, two doctor brothers were arrested as they headed to an international AIDS conference to be awarded prizes for their work with drug-addicted AIDS victims. They were convicted for foreign collaboration promoting the 'soft overthrow' of the Islamic Republic. Human-rights activist and Nobel laureate Shirin Ebadi, who helped defend Saberi, had her office raided in December and her Centre for Protecting Human Rights closed down. Esha Momeni, another young Iranian-American woman, was arrested in October 2008 while doing academic research, and by May was still not allowed to leave Iran. In December, Iran detained and interrogated a prominent American academic, Glenn

Schweitzer, head of the National Academies of Sciences' Eurasian programme, which prompted the academies to suspend scientific exchanges. Amnesty International reported 346 executions in Iran in 2008 and criticised the nation for persistent human-rights violations. Mousavi's support for a civil-rights charter and a declaration on the rights of ethnic and religious minorities contributed to the enthusiasm he generated among reformists.

Unlikely prospects for rapprochement

Ahmadinejad's re-election frustrated those at home and abroad who had hoped that a new president in Tehran would be able to work with the new president in Washington. Although all the candidates had vowed to continue the nuclear programme, their focus on the need for sound management of foreign policy sparked Western hopes that an unprejudiced weighing of the costs and benefits of uranium enrichment would give a new president reason to seek some kind of accommodation. Such hopes were probably overblown to start with, given the Iranian president's relative lack of authority in contrast to the all-embracing powers of the supreme leader. At best, a more moderate Iranian president would only help shape the public debate and marginally shift the alignment of factions in the regime elite.

Khamenei and Ahmadinejad seemed likely to want to follow through on their earlier expressions of interest in engaging with the United States, once they deemed it safe to do so without rekindling reformist momentum. For his part, Obama might find it more difficult to treat with respect an Iranian president whose legitimacy and human-rights record was newly under question. In any case, no engagement could be effective in overcoming the nuclear impasse without compromise on substance. Given the unwillingness of Iran's leadership to brook compromise on any aspect of the nuclear programme for the past four years, there was little reason for optimism that the next four years would be any different.

Middle East: New US Impetus Faces Old Challenges

For four years to 2009, an Israeli administration willing to consider game-changing initiatives had coincided with a US administration too distracted to provide the mediation necessary to transform the impulse into a sustainable advance. In 2009, following a pattern that has occurred with some regularity over the past three decades, a US administration committed to bold action on the Arab–Israeli front came into office just as a new Israeli administration opposed to dramatic change was elected. This bilateral dissonance was not the only problematic factor. Progress was also stymied by the trajectory of Palestinian politics, which continued to point to a clash for leadership between the Islamist militant group Hamas and its more established secular rival Fatah. Both factions appeared more interested in settling their respective claims to power within Palestine than in developing a coherent programme for negotiating with Israel. The other obstacle was the injection of Iran as a pivotal factor in the Israeli–Palestinian conflict by Israel, the United States and even Iran, in different but mutually reinforcing ways.

Post-Annapolis: a stalled peace

By mid summer 2008, what little momentum had been generated by the November 2007 Annapolis conference convened by President George W. Bush seemed to have dissipated. The conference had called for a framework agreement to be signed by both parties by the end of 2008, but this opportunity had largely been overtaken by events: continued haggling over the outlines of a peace agreement, the split between Fatah and Hamas, continued violence and Israel's internal political crisis.

The Bush administration had made several attempts to shore up bilateral talks between Israeli Prime Minister Ehud Olmert and Palestinian Authority (PA) President Mahmoud Abbas during its final year. US Secretary of State Condoleezza Rice travelled to the region several times, monitoring the progress of working groups and meeting with leaders individually. Her last visit in November 2008 was to the West Bank city of Jenin, which saw the most brutal fighting during *Defensive Shield*, the Israeli incursion in 2002. But by year's end, Bush administration efforts focused mainly on the building of reliable Palestinian institutions and bolstering PA Prime Minister Salaam Fayyad. The first battalion of a Palestinian security force, expected to number 50,000, arrived in Jordan for US training in 2008. Washington also funnelled additional aid into the West Bank to improve infrastructure and governance.

Despite the Bush administration's belated interest in the peace process, wide gaps still existed between Israel and the PA. Three issues effectively derailed bilateral talks between Olmert and Abbas. First, in May 2008, a ban on construction of settlements in the West Bank was abrogated when the Israeli Defense Ministry approved 22 new homes for settlers near the border with Jordan. The White House criticised the move as undermining 'confidence across the board'. Secondly, the issue of sovereignty over Jerusalem proved again to be a non-starter. Olmert refused to deal with it, fearing a domestic backlash, which he lacked the confidence – and credibility – to manage. For the Palestinians, any agreement without Jerusalem was unacceptable.

Thirdly, and most crucially, the overarching Israeli and Palestinian approaches to negotiations remained antithetical. For Abbas and his negotiators, either there would be a comprehensive agreement covering Jerusalem, borders and the right of refugees to return, or no agreement at all. Israel favoured leaving so-called 'core issues' to an unspecified future wherein Palestinian violence and incitement would be curtailed by responsible Palestinian institutions. Israeli leaders were nevertheless thinking about an endgame. Just before Olmert's resignation in September 2008, the Israeli newspaper *Haaretz* published what it claimed was the latest Israeli proposal. Israel offered a withdrawal from 93% of the West Bank and from a narrow piece of land along the Gaza Strip. Israel would keep the major settlement blocs, including those near Jerusalem and some along the Israeli border. The land swap and notional corridor between Gaza and the West Bank would, according to Israeli calculations, leave Palestinians with 98.5% of the land currently claimed by Palestinians. In terms of area, this would improve upon the Israeli offer made at Taba, Egypt in early 2001. The evacuation of additional settlers and the free passage for Palestinians between Gaza and the West Bank would be contingent on the Palestinians' ability to maintain order and carry out their commitments.

Later in the month, Olmert confided to the Israeli newspaper *Yediot Aharonot* that the country 'should withdraw from almost all of the territories, including in east Jerusalem and in the Golan Heights', but that an agreement had to come first before any practical steps were taken. Abbas's negotiators believed the offer to be disingenuous, but, in any case, unacceptable, since it would still impair West Bank contiguity, leave the status of Jerusalem unresolved, and fail to conform to the June 1967 border. Thus, despite the promises of a renewed bilateral process and the personal relationship between the Israeli prime minister and the Palestinian president, even the contours of an agreement remained elusive at the end of 2008.

The June ceasefire

Yet another tenuous ceasefire (*tahdiyah*) in Gaza between Hamas and Israel commenced on 19 June 2008. For months, Israeli towns bordering Gaza had been showered with rocket and mortar attacks by Hamas and other

Palestinian militant groups. Retaliatory Israel Defense Forces (IDF) incursions into Gaza supplied the rationale for yet more attacks. Much like previous ceasefire arrangements, neither side could trust the other to show restraint. Israel's commitment to preventive action was used by Hamas to justify arms smuggling through border tunnels, which in turn provoked Israeli air-strikes.

Brokered by the head of the Egyptian intelligence services, General Omar Suleiman, in indirect talks covering on-the-ground issues such as security, border crossings, Israel's blockade and prisoner exchanges, the terms of the truce were that Hamas would end its rocket attacks against Israel provided Israel would end its military incursions. Israel agreed to ease restrictions on the movement of some goods through Israel's border and considered opening the Rafah crossing with Egypt. Arrangements made on these topics were to last six months, though negotiations continued over prisoners and border crossings.

Military stalemate appeared at the time to set the table for a political settlement. For Olmert, the ceasefire would dampen criticism of his government's inability to deal with Hamas's attacks and allow him to focus on his own political scandal involving his alleged acceptance of some $150,000 from an American businessman, which had prompted calls for him to step down and call elections. For Hamas, attacks against Israel had yet to provoke a massive response, allowing it to consolidate control and affirm its legitimacy as a resistance movement. A two-year-old economic and military blockade of the Gaza Strip also left the economy in ruins: per capita GDP was around one-third lower than in 1999, poverty neared 50%, and unemployment hovered around 40%.

Domestic politics, international issues

While the ceasefire held through October, political scandal and elections attracted the major headlines in Israel. Olmert stepped down on 30 July in the wake of his pending indictment and a May report harshly critical of his government's handling of the 2006 'summer war' against the Lebanese Shia militia Hizbullah. He was replaced as Kadima party leader by Foreign Minister Tzipi Livni following a party vote on 17 September. Israeli President Shimon Peres then invited Livni to form a new coalition government by early November. Labor and the ultra-orthodox party Shas were Kadima's partners in the Knesset, but Shas demands in a new coalition proved insurmountable. The party's leaders refused to compromise on their demand for

$280 million in child allowances and a promise from Livni that there would be no negotiations over the division of Jerusalem. With the loss of one of the major religious parties, Livni announced her failure to form a government in late October, opening the way for general elections in February 2009. The Likud under Benjamin Netanyahu and Kadima under Livni were now in competition for a narrow band of seats in the Knesset. Ehud Barak's Labor Party was rapidly marginalised, as leading personalities quit in favour of the centrist Kadima and more leftist parties. The demise of Labor ended an era. Barak, its standard bearer, would opt to become Netanyahu's defence minister.

The major election issues were initially the economy and Iran. Autumn politicking took place under the pall of the global financial crisis. Domestic credit markets in Israel did not freeze as they did elsewhere, but stock markets fell to a two-year low and the fiscal deficit widened. Real GDP growth, which had held strong at around 5% between 2004 and 2008, fell precipitously to a projected 0.4% in 2009. Budget constraints and an uncertain financial environment threatened to lead to tough decisions on defence spending, forcing Israel to choose between preparation for future ground wars or a looming general conflict with Iran.

Speculation over Israel's response to Iran boiled over in summer 2008. Israeli military officers discussed the possibility of an Israeli air-strike against Iranian nuclear facilities in June. An Israeli Air Force exercise on 20 June took place 1,500km west of Israel in the Mediterranean in an apparent move to demonstrate the country's ability to strike the Iranian reactor in Natanz, approximately 1,500km to the east. Soon afterwards, Israeli Transportation Minister Shaul Mofaz warned that a strike against Iran to stop its nuclear programme 'will be unavoidable'. Iran threw fuel on the fire on 9 July when it tested nine medium-range ballistic missiles, at least one of which could reach Israel. However, the extent to which Iran had refined its ability to mount a nuclear warhead on such a missile remained unclear. In a controversial National Intelligence Estimate released the previous year, the US intelligence community reported that Iran had stopped designing nuclear weapons in 2003. Olmert contested this conclusion and said he believed Iran's nuclear programme was ongoing.

There was a noticeable difference between US and Israeli perceptions of the Iranian threat. The Bush administration publicly stated its support for Israel and proclaimed that the military option was 'on the table', but resisted committing to an Israeli timeline. While Israeli leaders were escalating their rhetoric during the summer months, Admiral Mike Mullen, chairman of the Joint Chiefs of Staff, warned that attacking Iran would have consequences that were 'very difficult to predict' and that opening a third front would be 'extremely stressful' for US forces. Barak told Israeli Army Radio in August 2008 that the United States did not 'see an action against Iran as the right thing to do'. The *New York Times* reported that Bush had rejected the IDF's request for specialised bunker-busting bombs and permission to fly over Iraq to reach Natanz.

Barack Obama's victory in the US presidential election caused concern about changes in US policy towards Iran. Obama supported unconditional talks with Tehran, an idea that Livni believed could be interpreted as a sign of weakness. Livni thought negotiations could be accompanied by tighter sanctions, but that the military threat should not be taken off the table. Netanyahu emphasised the threat from Iran. Though the economic crisis would ultimately be reversed, he said, an Iran with nuclear weapons could not. Israel would have to deal with them, he added, 'neutralising the power of the mother regime' of Hizbullah and Hamas.

Operation Cast Lead

These issues were pushed aside during Israel's 22-day offensive against Hamas in Gaza in December and January. Both sides had remained on edge after the June ceasefire, which had held for nearly five months despite periodic rocket attacks, mainly from non-Hamas militants. Only two rockets were fired in October, but by November the situation was unravelling and the rocket fire increased. Election politics in Israel were in full swing, Hamas–Fatah tensions were boiling over after waves of arrests despite Egyptian-led mediation talks in Cairo, and another cycle of violence began between Israeli military units and Hamas militants.

On 4 November, the first armed clash since June between a raiding IDF unit and Hamas forces left one senior Hamas commander dead. Palestinian militants fired dozens of rockets and mortars in retaliation and additional IDF incursions to close border tunnels effectively annulled the ceasefire. Israel promptly shut off most supply and goods shipments to Gaza on 5 November, causing international concern and prompting more rocket attacks. On 6 November, the Bush administration announced that it would leave the Israeli–Palestinian conflict to President-elect Barack Obama. Hamas cancelled its unity talks with Fatah in Cairo the following week. Both sides initially professed a willingness to resume the truce, but several factors made this untenable. Hamas faced criticism from smaller militant factions, and there were few signs that Israel would lift its blockade of Gaza. Pressure from militants within the movement about the border crossings, Israeli incursions, Fatah's popularity and the failure of reconciliation talks probably left Hamas eager to reassert its status as the 'heroic resister'.

Especially after the failure of reconciliation talks with Fatah, Hamas calculated that a ceasefire was no longer in its interest. With the expiration of the Israel–Hamas ceasefire approaching on 19 December, Hamas leader Khaled Meshal declared that 'there will be no renewal of the calm after it expires'. He and Ismail Haniyeh, Hamas's leader in Gaza, blamed Israel for not respecting the truce and called for it to raise its three-year-long siege of the Gaza Strip and open Gaza's borders. Around 330 rockets and mortar shells had been fired during the six-month ceasefire. In a single week after the deadline passed, almost half that number were launched into southern Israel.

Israel initiated its aerial assault on Gaza on 27 December with the declared aims of reducing rocket attacks and 'restoring Israeli deterrence'. The latter goal alluded to the damage to the Israeli deterrent produced by the 2006 war against Hizbullah, which was commonly believed to be a victory for the Lebanese terrorist group and a blow to the IDF's putative superiority. These in turn were believed to have fuelled Hamas's determination to bleed Israeli forces and chip away at the Israeli civilian population's morale. Beyond these stated objectives, Israeli leaders were not clear about the desired outcome of the war or how long the conflict would last. They hoped that Egypt would play a greater role in securing the southern border and that the PA could help control aid into Gaza, but eschewed re-occupation and installing Fatah in Gaza because of the potential for significant casualties, the PA's shaky condition and the fact that Hamas's destruction would be far from certain.

Israel's war aims were also coloured by national elections scheduled for 10 February. In late November, Likud launched its first attack against Kadima, claiming it was not doing enough to respond to Hamas rockets. Netanyahu called for a war of annihilation against Hamas, which would 'restore our national honour'. Kadima and Labor leaders, worried about Likud's advances in the polls, subsequently delivered tough speeches warning of a punishing blow against Hamas. Even the left-of-centre party most closely identified with the peace movement, Meretz, eventually endorsed *Operation Cast Lead*. In the week prior to the Israeli operation, Prime Minister Olmert (who was still in office pending the general election) cautioned against a full-scale ground invasion, but was drowned out by calls from his own foreign minister, Livni, to 'topple the Hamas regime' and from Likud's Netanyahu to embark on a more 'active policy of attack'.

The IDF's broad bombing campaign and ground invasion aimed to knock out as much of Hamas's command-and-control capabilities as possible. Targets included Gaza infrastructure, weapons caches, military facilities, individual leaders and smuggling tunnels along the Egyptian border. The ground invasion, which began on 3 January, proceeded from the northern part of Gaza and surrounded Gaza City within a few days. Hamas rocket and mortar fire persisted, but became less frequent as the Israeli army tightened the noose. After firing some 600 rockets into Israel and losing 1,200 to IDF air and ground forces, Hamas only had about 1,200 rockets at the time of the ceasefire in January 2009. The IDF seemed to have redeemed its poor performance in 2006, but the political situation sill remained unresolved.

> **Olmert cautioned against a full-scale ground invasion**

Ignoring a 14–0 vote by the UN Security Council calling for a halt to the conflict, Israel and Hamas continued to fight into mid January. Meshal insisted that Israel withdraw its troops, lift its blockade of Gaza and open the Rafah crossing. There were rumours of tension between Meshal's hardline supporters in Damascus and the beleaguered Haniyeh in Gaza. But these proved inconsequential, as Israel announced a unilateral ceasefire on 17 January after signing the US–Israel Memorandum of Understanding, which entailed extensive US and NATO assistance to stop weapons shipments from crossing into Gaza. Hamas followed with its own independent ceasefire on 21 January, demanding that Israel lift its 18-month economic embargo on Gaza and border crossings for regular commerce. Israel insisted that the resolution of the case of a captured Israeli soldier, Gilad Shalit, be tied to the full operation of the border crossings and called for all aid to be channelled through the PA. A genuine ceasefire proved unachievable, however, as rocket fire and Israeli military strikes carried on into the spring.

The three-week offensive caused tremendous damage to Gaza's infrastructure – extending to 14,000 homes, 68 government buildings and 31 offices of non-governmental organisations (NGOs) – and led to the death of at least 1,300 Palestinians (at least 700 of them civilians). In contrast, only 13 Israelis were reported killed. This lopsided casualty count flowed directly from Israel's military strategy to keep IDF casualties to an absolute minimum through the heavy use of relatively indiscriminate firepower that inevitably generated high casualties on the Palestinian side. Hamas's proclivity to deploy militants among civilians to force its adversary to sacrifice the moral high ground further contributed to the heavy toll among non-combatants.

Following this violence, about half of Gaza's population was dependent on UN food aid. As of mid 2009, thousands remained homeless. Besides food and vital medicine, few raw materials could enter Gaza to build new homes. Israel's control over Gaza's economy was underscored by a World Bank report warning that Gaza was now completely dependent on water resources controlled by Israel. Despite an obvious humanitarian crisis, NGOs still had difficulty obtaining access to the Gaza Strip and continued violence undermined the new ceasefire. By March, $5.2 billion had been pledged to Abbas and the PA to rebuild Gaza. Donors intentionally avoided giving money to Hamas, while the United States pledged $900m to shore up the PA and help rebuild Gaza.

The Israeli election

Ultimately, the Gaza War determined the election. Political posturing by the major Israeli candidates resumed soon after the ceasefire was declared. Previous statements may have raised expectations about regime change, as many in Israel were clearly disappointed that Hamas had not been crushed. In an implicit criticism of Olmert and Livni's response to Hamas, Netanyahu said on 19 January that Israel needed 'a strong, unwavering, persistent hand until the threat is eliminated'. Throughout the conflict, he successfully promoted the view that anything less than the removal of Hamas in Gaza was a failure. Right-wing groups were buoyed by this perception and, though the personal approval ratings for all the major candidates increased after the offensive, it appeared to benefit the right-wing parties – including Netanyahu's Likud – most heavily.

The election results proved inconclusive, however, and seven weeks of horse-trading ensued. Kadima came in first with 28 seats over Likud's 27, but the latter could count on the religious and conservative parties for support. The Russian-immigrant-based party Yisrael Beiteinu was promised five cabinet posts, including the foreign ministry for the party's leader, Avigdor Lieberman. Labor narrowly agreed to join Netanyahu's government, allowing Ehud Barak to remain as defence minister. Livni demanded an equal coalition partnership, giving Kadima control of the prime minister's office during the second half of the government's term, and insisted that Netanyahu commit to the creation of a Palestinian state. Both demands were refused. After seven weeks of coalition negotiations, Netanyahu became prime minister on 31 March.

The end of the two-state solution?

By the end of the Gaza War, a rising chorus of voices in the United States, Israel, Europe and the Arab world suggested that the idea of a two-state solution was dead. A *Christian Science Monitor* headline in February read 'Window Closing for a Two-state Solution in the Middle East'. Op-eds in the *New York Times* suggested abandoning the two-state model for a one-state (Muammar Gadhafi), three-state (John Bolton), and even a five-state (Thomas L. Friedman) solution. The Begin–Sadat Center of Bar-Ilan University in Israel published a January report concluding that 'the two-state solution has died as a viable option'. 'The two-state solution is disappearing', said Mansour Tahboub, senior editor, at the West Bank newspaper *Al-Ayyam*. The editor of the London-based pan-Arab daily *al-Quds al-Arabi* wrote that the Gaza War effectively 'cancelled all that preceded it in futile negotiations, a false peace process, defeatist leaders, and the so-called two-state solution'.

These speculations were due in significant part to the election of Netanyahu, who had refused to promise a Palestinian state and resolutely refrained from speaking publicly about a two-state solution. An aide to Netanyahu even called the concept of a Palestinian state 'childish and stupid'. At the same time, while Foreign Minister Lieberman achieved some notoriety by rejecting the Annapolis peace process, he expressed support for the 2003 'Road Map', which could lead to Palestinian statehood. In June 2009, Netanyahu shifted his position to say that Israel could accept a Palestinian state, but only one that was completely demilitarised and subject to a number of other conditions. The bottom line appeared to be that there remained a lack of political will in both Israel and Palestine to forge a two-state solution owing to mutual mistrust, political disarray and the desire of some intentionally to sabotage such an eventuality.

Another oft-cited and formidable hurdle was Israeli settlement construction. Even if frozen and partially dismantled, settlements had so overrun the West Bank that a truly Palestinian state could only be a concept, not a reality. According to Rashid Khalidi, 'the amount of concrete that has been poured, the barriers, the bypass roads, the expansion of the settlements mean that you have a Swiss cheese in the West Bank'. Avraham Burg, a former speaker of the Knesset, saw both societies as 'kidnapped by religious vision', with Israeli settlers and Hamas only believing in one state for themselves. The Obama administration, however, broke from past American reticence on the issue. Secretary of State Hillary Clinton said to reporters in May 2009 that the administration 'wants to see a stop to settlements – not some settlements, not outposts, not natural growth exceptions'. This triggered a response from Barak, who dismissed settlements as an issue: 'Ninety-five percent of people will tell you it cannot be that someone in the world honestly thinks an agreement with the Palestinians will stand or fall over this'.

The Gaza War also impeded Hamas–Fatah reconciliation. Polling by the Palestinian Center for Policy and Survey Research indicated that Hamas's popularity rating increased from 28% to 33% between December 2008 and March 2009. The poll also measured Palestinians' preference in a presidential election. Although Mahmoud Abbas's popularity declined only from 48% to 45%, besieged Hamas leader Ismail Haniyeh's popularity rose from 38% to 47% over the same three-month period. Egyptian-mediated reconciliation talks resumed after the war, but stalled repeatedly over issues such as the terms for a unity government, a formula for holding new Palestinian legislative and presidential elections and security arrangements. In January 2010, the mandates for Abbas's presidency and for the Hamas-controlled parliament were to expire. Without an agreement by then, the lack of a legitimate Palestinian government and, consequently, a reliable negotiating partner for Israel would make an independent Palestinian state seem even further out of reach.

The US and Israel

The tremendous pessimism in the Middle East following the Gaza War stood in stark contrast to the optimism in the United States following the American presidential elections. America's first African-American president, Barack Hussein Obama, was also the first president with a familial connection to Islam. His father was a Muslim from Kenya, and Obama lived in Indonesia briefly as child. Many believed the president had the potential to radically change the deplorable state of US–Muslim relations, and the administration was very conscious of the opportunity. Obama extended an olive branch to Muslims in his inaugural address, appointed George Mitchell as special envoy for Middle East peace, announced his intention to close the detention centre at Guantanamo Bay, and delivered a historic speech to the Muslim world in Cairo in June 2009. Expectations remained high, but it was too early to tell whether the Obama administration's determination could overcome the post-war malaise.

Obama's campaign promises and outreach to Arab communities worldwide suggested to the new Israeli government that US approval for its policies would not be automatic. But Netanyahu is assertive and shrewd, and in an even more solid political position than he was during his previous tenure as prime minister in the late 1990s. He was unlikely to back down easily. His record as a public official suggested a potential for moderation and opportunism, but he also believed strongly that Israel must defend itself aggressively – pre-emptively if necessary. In a post-election interview, he likened Iran to the Biblical Amalekites, a tribe whose predatory attacks on the weak and infirm among Israelites escaping slavery in Egypt warranted a divine writ of total destruction. Considering both Netanyahu's beliefs and the nature of coalition politics in Israel, which currently favours right-of-centre parties, Washington would have to carefully weigh the implications of any new initiative with the PA, Syria or Iran.

> **The military option posed technical problems**

One of the most critical differences between the United States and Israel has been over how to respond to Iran's nuclear activities. Israeli leaders consider a nuclear-armed Iran an existential threat and refuse to rule out the possibility of a pre-emptive or preventive strike against Iran's nuclear infrastructure. Netanyahu has said that an Islamist nuclear umbrella would inspire fanatics worldwide, leading them to believe they were on 'the ultimate road to triumph'. The Obama administration has stayed silent on the military option, while laying plans for direct engagement after elections in Tehran.

The military option remained technically problematic for Israel. It was not clear that a successful air-strike or missile launch against Iranian facilities was feasible. The precise locations where uranium enrichment was taking place were unknown, and attacking just the major sites at Isfahan, Natanz, and Arak might not be enough. The number of possible targets in Iran ranged from a few hundred to thousands, at least 75 of which were believed to be hardened or underground. Israel already possessed about 100 GBU-28 'bunker buster' bombs, but in 2008 the Bush administration denied it a shipment of GBU-39s, which are smaller, more accurate and therefore more appropriate to the task. Israeli warplanes would need to travel along the Syria–Turkey border, which skirts Iraq, directly over Jordan, or south of Jordan along the border with Saudi Arabia. All of these options involve significant complications and risks, with no assurance of success – realities not readily apparent from Israel's mock-run over the placid eastern Mediterranean last summer. Once in Iran, Israeli Air Force pilots might encounter the vaunted Russian-made S-300V (SA-12 *Giant*) anti-aircraft defence system, should Iran's procurement deal for these weapons go through. Nonetheless, reports said Israel military officials believed there was a reasonably good chance of setting back the Iranian programme for two to five years and felt compelled to act in some way before Iran acquired a nuclear weapon, which it was estimated to be able to do between 2010 and 2015.

These issues were at the forefront of US–Israeli relations, when Obama and Netanyahu met for the first time in Washington on 18 May 2009. The Israeli leader had previously tried to link progress on the peace process to firm commitments from Washington on dealing with Iran. Expectations were that Obama would try to reverse the direction of this linkage, pressing Netanyahu to commit to a Palestinian state and freeze settlement construction. At the meeting, the Israeli prime minister tried to secure an American commitment to a timeline for suspending Iranian uranium enrichment. Obama met him part way by agreeing that the United States would review whether Iran was making a 'good-faith effort to resolve differences' by the end of 2009. The understanding was an implicit Israeli endorsement of a US diplomatic overture to Iran. However, Obama was unable to budge Netanyahu from his opposition to Palestinian statehood or on halting settlement construction. The prime minister agreed only to pursue negotiations with the Palestinians and Syrians without preconditions.

As of mid 2009, Hamas–Fatah unity talks were at an impasse and violence between the two factions was ongoing. The two sides had already set up competing security infrastructures, with Hamas forces dominating Gaza and Fatah loyalists (some of them US trained) prevailing in the West Bank. Egyptian-mediated discussions in 2008 foundered in the wake of intra-factional bombings and tit-for-tat arrests of Hamas members in the West Bank and Fatah members in Gaza. Just before the Gaza War, Hamas was criticised for failing to attend a summit in Egypt unless all Hamas members were released from West Bank jails. Following the Gaza War, controversy enmeshed Abbas when he declared his intention to stay in office after his presidential term had expired in January 2010. Talks occurred intermittently and continued into summer 2009 as the two sides tried to work out a power-sharing arrangement ahead of national elections scheduled for that month. But Hamas remained unlikely to recognise Israel, abide by previous agreements calling for a two-state solution or renounce violence, let alone submit to Fatah's authority.

Uncertain prospects

As 2009 reached its midpoint, Obama, in a speech to the Muslim world broadcast from Cairo, referred explicitly to Israeli 'occupation', the 'daily humiliations' endured by Palestinians, and the need to stop all settlement activity. From an American leader these phrases were new to Muslim ears, even if US officials in the past had privately described the situation in such terms. Obama also drew renewed attention to Palestinian violence and incitement. Both Israelis and Palestinians applauded the speech, with each party ignoring the parts directed critically at them. Whether they could adjust their behaviour in accordance with these criticisms to the extent required to make a solution possible depended a great deal on the staying power that the Obama administration was able to bring to the Middle East's heretofore intractable problems amidst myriad other foreign-policy challenges.

Even if the new American leadership did find the focus to re-energise conflict resolution between the Israelis and the Palestinians, its success would be highly contingent on multiple factors. These included, but were not limited to, the relative political strengths of Fatah and Hamas after the January elections, whether Obama decided to take a conciliatory stance vis-à-vis Hamas in an effort to ensconce it more firmly in non-violent politics, whether the Israeli leadership could then be persuaded to play along, whether the Israeli–Syrian peace process advanced sufficiently to lend momentum to the Israeli–Palestinian track, and whether the United States and its European partners made diplomatic headway with Iran. In this light, grim determination, rather than anything as rosy as guarded optimism, seemed to be the most realistic outlook.

Iraq: Nation Gathers Strength

Iraq in the year to mid 2009 was dominated by two interlinked political and military dynamics. The first was the comparatively successful military aftermath of the 'surge', the increase in US troops which began in February

2007. A series of events triggered by the surge dramatically reduced the internecine violence that had dominated Iraq since 2005. The second dominant dynamic was the rapid rise in the power of Iraq's prime minister, Nuri Kamal al-Maliki. At the end of March 2008, as the US military operations that had accompanied the surge began to wind down, Maliki seized the strategic initiative and deployed Iraqi troops against the Jaish al-Mahdi militia that had controlled areas of the southern city of Basra. The success of this mission encouraged Maliki to challenge the militia's power in Baghdad. Capitalising on a wave of public support for this stance, Maliki re-branded himself a tough Iraqi nationalist, claiming he was going to impose law and order across Iraq whilst reducing American influence. This new approach allowed Maliki to negotiate a very favourable Status of Forces Agreement (SOFA) with the United States, consolidate his hold over the institutions of the Iraqi state and win a convincing victory in Iraq's provincial elections held in January 2009. It also put him in a strong position to win Iraq's next set of national elections in January 2010.

Reduced violence

In September 2008, General David Petraeus left Iraq to take up the leadership of US Central Command. In handing over command of US forces to Lieutenant-General Ray Odierno, Petraeus was effectively signalling the end of the surge. That violence in Iraq has reduced since its peak in early 2007 is beyond dispute. In January 2007, an estimated 3,500 civilians were killed across Iraq, and by June 2009 the monthly figure had dropped to 340. It is more difficult to determine exactly why this dramatic reduction occurred, and whether it is sustainable. The US military's own explanation stresses the change in tactics triggered by the surge: the move away from large military operations targeting the insurgency, to methods that concentrated on protecting Iraqis and putting into effect a new counter-insurgency doctrine. This analysis focuses not only on the sharp increase in US troops numbers but also on their stationing amongst the Iraqi population, in small forts or Joint Security Stations scattered across Baghdad.

Those analysts who have been sceptical about this explanation look instead to the widespread population transfers triggered by the sectarian warfare that dominated Baghdad until 2007. The Shia militias – the Badr Brigade and Jaish al-Mahdi – deliberately set out to drive Sunni residents from mixed neighbourhoods and then from Baghdad altogether. Calculations vary on how many people were displaced in this sectarian warfare but the

US military's estimate is 350,000. Of these, according to an Associated Press survey carried out in March 2009, only 16% are estimated to have returned to their former homes.

There is an argument to suggest that once the surge started in early 2007, the US military inadvertently solidified this population transfer. They replaced makeshift defences erected by communities with concrete blast walls designed to impede the access of both suicide bombers and militias. According to this argument, it was this sectarian division of the city that reduced inter-communal violence. Put crudely, the Shia death squads had won: they created religiously homogeneous communities that were then walled off by the US military. Those backing this explanation would point to an increase in bombings in March and April 2009, suggesting this was caused by the removal of a small number of security walls by the Iraqi government.

> " The Shia death squads had won "

The third explanation for the decline in both civilian and military casualties is the so-called 'Anbar Awakening'. In 2006, a number of residents of the Sunni province of Anbar in western Iraq rose up against the al-Qaeda in Mesopotamia group, driving its members out of their communities. Petraeus, upon his arrival in Iraq, was quick to see the potential of this movement. He set up the Sons of Iraq programme, which paid volunteers to man checkpoints across Baghdad and the northwest of Iraq, effectively encouraging former Sunni insurgents to turn against al-Qaeda in return for support and resources. The Awakening movement undoubtedly reduced the numbers of Iraqis who actively or passively supported the revolt against the Americans in Iraq. However, the sustainability of this phenomenon was open to question, as the Iraqi government has begun to disarm and disband the Sons of Iraq organisations and arrest key leaders.

The fourth reason for the decline in violence was the role that the radical Shia politician Moqtada al-Sadr and his militia, the Jaish al-Mahdi, played during the surge. As the surge began, al-Sadr quickly realised he and his forces would be one of its key targets. In response he demobilised his fighters and fled to Iran. After intra-Shi'ite violence between the Jaish al-Mahdi and the Badr Brigade he declared an outright ceasefire in August 2007. This allowed both US and Iraqi forces to target the more radical and violent operatives in al-Sadr's movement and break their capacity for widespread violence. This policy has been so successful that the Jaish al-Mahdi, responsible for the majority of sectarian violence in 2006–07, has lost a great deal of operational capacity and popular support.

However, Petraeus was always clear that the surge's main aim was not military but political: that is, the delivery of some kind of political reconciliation across Iraq. This grand political bargain has not emerged and there were no signs that it would do so in the medium term. The lack of a political settlement has shaped the changing nature of violence across Iraq, and especially in Baghdad. With the start of the surge in February 2007, violence was rapidly reduced and at mid June 2009 was 80–90% lower than at its peak. However, because there has never been a comprehensive political settlement, the mass sectarian killings during 2005–07 were replaced in 2008 by targeted political assassinations. Small magnetic bombs and guns with silencers were used to kill prominent judges, civil servants and political activists, indicating not only clear political motive but also an extensive and organised network with access to real-time intelligence. April 2009 also saw a return of mass-casualty car bombings, presumably orchestrated by al-Qaeda in Mesopotamia. Six car bombs exploded in Baghdad in January, four in February and three in March. These were followed by 12 in April, which killed a total of 200 people. This indicated two facts: that political contests were still being settled by murder, and that al-Qaeda in Mesopotamia had reconstituted its capacity to inflict mass-casualty attacks in and around the capital.

Maliki's rise and US forces
Nuri al-Maliki became prime minister after months of negotiations in spring 2006. For the first two years, his premiership was chronically weak, beset by numerous plots to unseat him, a set of powerful cabinet ministers over whom he had little control and a widespread perception that he was little more than an American puppet. However, the extent to which he had consolidated power in the office of the prime minister became apparent in March 2008. Maliki moved 30,000 Iraq troops south to Basra to retake the city from the Jaish al-Mahdi militia. They met much stronger opposition than had been anticipated, and defeat was only avoided by heavy reliance on American combat advisers and air power. However, the eventual re-establishment of government authority in Basra struck a widespread popular chord with an Iraqi population long subject to criminality and sectarian violence. Maliki went on to bolster his new-found popular appeal in May 2008 by regaining control of the Sadr City area in Baghdad, the huge slum that had until then been dominated by the Jaish al-Mahdi.

The prime minister built on this popular support by portraying himself as an Iraqi nationalist and adopting a tough negotiating stance over the SOFA that was required with the United States. The lengthy and at times antagonistic negotiations between Washington and Baghdad were indicative of the transformation of relations during 2008. This process began in 2007, when President George W. Bush and Maliki committed their respective governments to a legal agreement that would formalise long-term relations between the two countries. However, as negotiations dragged on, Maliki increasingly couched his opposition to its more objectionable clauses in terms of Iraqi national sovereignty. The popular approval that this won encouraged him to take an even tougher negotiating stance.

By autumn 2008, negotiations had reached a standstill. Maliki was happy to use the SOFA to demonstrate his nationalist credentials and independence from Washington, safe in the knowledge that an Obama presidency would give him a similar if not better agreement. The American presidential electoral cycle and the growing confidence of the Iraqi prime minister combined to give much greater leverage to the Iraqi side. The final agreement saw the Iraqi government achieve the majority of its demands, with the United States making large concessions in order to gain a settlement.

The most important concession extracted from the United States was an unambiguous timetable for US troop withdrawal. The first step agreed was that all US combat forces would withdraw from Iraqi cities, towns and villages to a limited number of bases by 30 June 2009. This was likely to create few problems in most Iraqi provinces, where responsibility for security had already been handed to the Iraqi government over the past two years. However, there was a danger that it could lead to increased violence in Baghdad, the northern city of Mosul and the unstable province of Diyala, east of the capital. After the withdrawal to bases in June 2009, the agreement gave US forces two and a half years to leave the country entirely. It unambiguously stated: 'All US forces are to withdraw from all Iraqi territory, water and airspace no later than 31 December 2011'.

From June 2009 to December 2011, the US government will continue to have legal jurisdiction over its military and civilian personnel whilst they are on their bases. However, the Iraqi government has the right to exercise jurisdiction over them when they are suspected of committing major or premeditated crimes outside their bases. In addition, the Iraqi government won jurisdiction over private military contractors employed by the United States, who have been a source of deep resentment amongst Iraqis.

The SOFA imposed a rigorous set of regulations under which US military operations were now to be conducted. A Joint Military Operations Coordination Committee was set up to oversee all activities outside US bases – in effect requiring all US military operations to be authorised by the Iraqi government. US forces will not be permitted to search houses unless an Iraqi judicial order has been issued. Of greatest immediate significance was Article 22, which stated that US forces would not be allowed to hold Iraqi prisoners for more than 24 hours before turning them over to the Iraqi government. As of September 2008, US forces were holding 18,900 Iraqi prisoners. The United States could not release the majority of these into Iraqi custody because this would overwhelm an already poorly functioning prison service. So the majority of those in US custody were gradually being released.

Provincial election victory

Maliki used his new-found Iraqi nationalism and his role as the champion of a strong Iraqi state to win the December provincial elections. He named his coalition Dawlat al-Qanoun (State of Law) to remind the population that the prime minister's policies and actions had brought increased law and order to Iraq. Well-known independent Shia politicians like the oil minister, Hussain Shahristani, and the ex-national security adviser, Qasem Daoud, also joined Maliki's coalition to broaden its popular appeal.

On the campaign trail Maliki stressed the success of the military campaigns in Basra and Sadr City as well as his role in challenging the Kurdish Regional Government's attempts to gain control over areas along its boundary with the rest of Iraq. In a key campaign speech, he set himself against the decentralised federal agenda of his main rivals for the Shia vote, the Islamic Supreme Council of Iraq (ISCI) and its partners in government, the Kurdistan Democratic Party and the Patriotic Union of Kurdistan.

This statist approach saw Maliki's coalition win the largest slice of the popular vote in nine out of the 14 participating provinces. Once the seats were allocated, State of Law won outright majorities in both Baghdad and Basra. It only failed to win Sunni-dominated Anbar, mainly Sunni Salah Al-Din, Shia-dominated Karbala, and the mixed provinces of Diyala and Nineva.

The extent of Maliki's success can be judged by the poor performance of ISCI, which tried to repeat the success that an overtly religious approach had given it in 2005. This time, its coalition did not have the backing of Iraq's most senior Shia religious figure, Grand Ayatollah Ali al-Sistani. Reportedly disillusioned with government corruption and inefficiency over the past four years, al-Sistani limited his involvement in the election to insisting that it was every adult's duty to vote. That left the ISCI coalition, Qaimat Shahid al-Mihrab wa al-Quwatt al-Mustaqilla (the Martyr of Mihrab and Independent Forces list) to run a campaign based heavily on religious symbolism and its pledge to move towards greater decentralised federalism.

This approach badly misjudged the mood of a country that had only recently emerged from extensive violence justified in the name of sectarian appeals to religious and ethnic identity. In Baghdad, ISCI took just 5.4% of the vote, compared to 39% in 2005. In the Shia religious heartlands of Najaf and Karbala its share was 14.8% and 6.4% respectively, down from 45% and 35% in 2005.

Moqtada al-Sadr's Sadrist Current was effectively banned from participating in January's elections by laws making it illegal for any organisation with a militia to take part. (These laws were not applied in the case of militias belonging to ISCI and both main Kurdish parties.) In the January elections, therefore, key Sadrist politicians were left to back smaller coalitions of independent politicians through which they could later make their influence felt.

Politicians seeking to represent Iraq's Sunnis had boycotted the 2005 provincial elections but found their actions had effectively marginalised their ability to influence politics. This time they worked hard to mobilise their target constituency. In Baghdad, the specifically Sunni coalition Tawafuq (the National Accordance Front) won 9% of the votes and seven of the 57 seats on the council. However, Sunnis also voted for Ayad Allawi's overtly secular National Iraqi list, which won 8.6% of the vote and five seats on the Baghdad council.

The parties seeking to represent Sunnis were adept at maximising their vote in areas that have seen Arab–Kurdish tensions. In the northern province of Nineva, bordering both the Kurdistan Regional Government's area and Syria, one leading Sunni group, the National Hadba Gathering, gained nearly half of the vote and pushed the Kurdish list, with around a third of the vote, into second place. In Diyala province, east of Baghdad near the Iranian border, the Sunni National Accord Front edged out the Kurdish Alliance with 21.1% of the vote compared to 17.2%.

Anbar province had been the epicentre of the Sunni insurgency, but also the birthplace of the anti-al-Qaeda Awakening movement. Anbar is unusually homogeneous, being dominated by Sunni Arabs. Nevertheless, the provincial elections were hard fought. The 2005 winner, the Iraqi Islamic Party (IIP), tried to fight off a sustained challenge from one group representing the Awakening and one of its leaders, Sheikh Ahmed Abu Risha, and a second group run by the national politician Saleh Mutlaq. The result saw Mutlaq's party secure 17.6% of the vote, Abu Risha, 17.1% and the IIP 15.9%. The fractious nature of the campaign and the relatively low turnout at 40% – nevertheless up enormously from 2% in 2005 – reflected Anbar's fragile politics and the need for it to be integrated more fully into national politics.

The December provincial elections were a success, signalling a move away from the violent zero-sum sectarian politics that dominated Iraq from 2004 until 2007. The participation of specifically Sunni groups and those seeking to mobilise a wider non-sectarian coalition highlighted the fact that the Sunni community had largely moved away from rejecting the post-Ba'athist political settlement and the use of violence to bring it down. The vote secured by Maliki's coalition was large enough to encourage his agenda of securing stability, law, order and a strong centralised state, but small enough to require him to govern via provincial coalitions.

Outstanding issues

Maliki's successful consolidation of power, his popular negotiating stance with the United States and his victory in the provincial elections did, however, leave three big issues still to be resolved: the capacity of the Iraqi army, the future of the Sons of Iraq movement, and relations between the national government in Baghdad and the Kurdistan Regional Government based in the northern city of Irbil.

With US forces scheduled to leave Iraqi soil by December 2011, the future stability of Iraq rests on the capacity and coherence of the Iraqi armed forces. By December 2008, the Iraqi army had 262,000 soldiers on its payroll, organised into 14 divisions, mainly equipped for counter-insurgency. The Ministry of Interior had 480,000 employees and planned to add another 67,000 police officers to its payroll over 2009.

Over the past year, Lieutenant-General James Dubik, the US officer responsible for training the Iraqi army, has been generally upbeat about its capacity to guarantee the stability of the country. Analysts argued that after their re-creation in 2003 and rapid expansion since, the armed forces lacked a strong set of junior and non-commissioned officers who could lead their troops into combat. Dubik argued that the quality of the troops had rapidly improved, though he admitted that the quality of leadership was uneven and the army still suffered from sectarianism.

The Iraqi government itself acknowledged that, for their armed forces to be truly independent, large-scale investment was needed in heavy armour, attack aircraft and patrol boats. In 2008, with oil at $140 a barrel, Iraq set aside $6 billion to purchase patrol boats for the navy, M1A1M *Abrams* tanks for the army and F-16 fighters for the air force. This would have given the air force its first real ground-attack capacity and the navy the ability to defend Iraq's crucial offshore oil terminals in the Gulf. However, with the sharp decline in oil prices in 2009, the Ministries of Defence and Interior saw their budgets cut by 50%. This meant that Iraq would be dependent upon the United States for air and fire support long after 2011. The prime minister's spokesman, Ali al-Dabbagh, frankly admitted: 'We do understand that the Iraqi military is not going to get built out in the three years. We do need many more years. It might be 10 years.' The furore that this statement caused in Baghdad was indicative of the high levels of mistrust towards the United States that remained amongst Iraq's ruling elite.

> Maliki was pursuing a divide-and-rule policy

The second potential challenge to the authority of both the Iraqi prime minister and beyond him the Iraqi state was the Sons of Iraq organisations (SoIs). In 2007, in an attempt to impose order on the country, the US military recognised a series of ad hoc military groupings across the country, paying their 103,000 members between $200 and $300 a month to man checkpoints and supply information about al-Qaeda and militia activity. Many members of these local groups were ex-soldiers and they hoped membership of the Sons of Iraq would lead to re-employment by the armed services.

The Iraqi government has had deep misgivings about the Sons of Iraq since their formation. It attempted to control or at least monitor their activities by setting up a Committee of National Reconciliation in 2007, to oversee state relations with the SoIs. In September 2008, after heavy lobbying from the Americans, Maliki committed the government to integrating 20% of the SoIs into the Iraqi security services. However, by the middle of 2009, only 5,200 had been given security jobs and the reconciliation committee itself had become inactive. It had become apparent that Maliki was pursuing a divide-and-rule policy. Some former leaders of the SoIs had been employed by the prime minister's office whilst others were being arrested and allegedly mistreated by the security services. It was estimated by US forces in Iraq that 217 SoIs were arrested by the Iraqi government in 2008.

Although the recent rise in al-Qaeda-related violence in and around Baghdad might well have been linked to the government's crackdown on the Sons of Iraq, Maliki's policy did not produce the reinvigoration of the insurgency many had predicted. The US military was careful to take a great deal of information from SoI members before it paid them. The US military and Iraqi government now have biometric data, fingerprints and iris scans of all the SoI, making it almost impossible for them to return to anti-government violence. The second explanation for the comparative ease with which the government broke the Sons of Iraq was their lack of organisation or social coherence. What was originally described as an 'awakening' or 'tribal revolt' was in fact the result of sporadic localised responses to al-Qaeda brutality. What gave the Sons of Iraq organisational coherence was US support and funding, and once that was removed, the movement quickly dispersed.

The final challenge to Maliki's growing authority emerged as the violence across Iraq declined and the state's power grew: relations between Baghdad and the Kurdistan Regional Government (KRG) based in the northern city of Irbil. Since the removal of the Ba'athist regime in Baghdad in 2003, the KRG had fought a hard diplomatic campaign to accrue as much power as possible. This strategy reached its peak with the drafting in 2005 of an Iraqi constitution that was very favourable to it. Alongside this diplomatic strategy, the two Kurdish parties used their militias, the Peshmerga, to unofficially expand the territorial reach of the regional government. Along the Baghdad side of the 500-kilometre border between the KRG and the rest of Iraq, Peshmerga forces had been occupying villages beyond the jurisdiction of their regional government. First, militia forces would enter a chosen village, then the two Kurdish parties would set up offices before the area was de facto integrated into the KRG. This policy resulted in as much as 7% of Iraqi territory being taken by the KRG, with Kurdish checkpoints and militia members operating 120km south of the regional border. Unsurprisingly, this creeping annexation alienated large numbers of non-Kurdish residents and directly contributed to the rise in sectarian-motivated violence across northern Iraq.

After the success of Maliki's military campaigns in Basra, Baghdad and Mosul, he moved the Iraqi army into the unstable province of Diyala, northeast of Baghdad. Although the stated target of this campaign was al-Qaeda, Iraqi soldiers quickly came into contact with Peshmerga forces operating in northern Diyala, well south of the KRG's border. Tensions reached their peak in August 2008 in the oil-rich town of Khanaqin, 25km south of the KRG's territory. Iraqi soldiers and Peshmerga were manning checkpoints in close proximity to each other; hostilities were avoided by the speedy intervention of US forces and the negotiated withdrawal of the Kurdish militias.

The disputed oil-rich city of Kirkuk is often seen as the most likely point of conflict between Baghdad and Irbil. However, events in August 2008 showed that the KRG's policy of expanding its borders and a resurgent Iraqi government meant conflict could come at any point along the 500km border. This was especially the case as United Nations efforts to resolve the situation had been rejected by all sides.

In 2008–09, Maliki's grip tightened over both the coercive and political institutions of the state. His success in the provincial elections indicated that he had developed the ideological and organisational capacity to win the next set of national elections in 2010. If this were to happen, Iraq might well have found another strong man, using both overt and covert means to dominate the state and society as it enters a post-conflict period. The centralisation of power in the office of the prime minister was occurring at the same time US troop numbers and hence influence were declining across the whole of the country. With 340 people a month still being murdered and mass-casualty attacks occurring regularly in and around Baghdad, Iraq was still a very dangerous and unstable country. However, compared to the peak of sectarian violence in 2007, it was clear that the institutions of the Iraqi state had gained enough power to impose a rough and ready order on the country. If Maliki were to continue to increase his grip on power over the next two years, the reigniting of Iraq's sectarian conflict would be unlikely. However, the sustainability of country's newly created democracy remained in question.

Saudi Arabia and the Gulf: Cautious Modernisation

On 14 February 2009, King Abdullah bin Abdulaziz Al Saud announced far-reaching changes to Saudi Arabia's administrative and judicial structures. Several hardline conservatives were removed from key positions, and the first female government minister was appointed. By embarking on the reforms, the Saudi ruler indicated his desire to reappraise internal relationships, including close traditional ties between the government and the clerical establishment.

The degree of change in the Saudi establishment should not, however, be exaggerated. On 27 March the king designated his half-brother and long-time interior minister, Prince Nayef bin Abdulaziz, as second deputy prime minister, a position that would normally place him second in line to the throne. The elevation was necessitated by the serious illness of the heir apparent, Prince Sultan bin Abdulaziz Al Saud. As interior minister, Nayef had been successful at curbing radical Islamist terrorist groups, but had also overseen arbitrary imprisonments and strict interpretations of sharia law. The kingdom's Shia minority and its liberal voices – many of them past inmates of Nayef's prisons – remained edgy.

Nevertheless, the changes introduced by King Abdullah demonstrated his keen awareness of the trials facing Saudi society, stemming partly from the collapse of oil prices and global recession. The price of oil fell from a high of about $140 a barrel in mid 2008 to less than $50 a barrel, though by mid 2009 it was approaching $70. While the kingdom, the world's largest oil producer, had received a significant windfall from the spike in prices, previous budget deficits and anticipated expenditures reduced its cushion against the economic downturn. With global recession threatening to trigger a sharp fall in demand for Saudi oil, the kingdom's priority was to retain market share so as to weather the fall in the value of its investments and reduced foreign investment in the energy sector. As food prices rose in 2008, domestic inflation climbed into double digits. To meet this challenge, and wary of wasting costly desalinated water for rice, Riyadh invested in rice farms in Thailand and planned similar arrangements in Pakistan and Sudan.

The international agenda

Saudi diplomatic initiatives on Lebanon, Iraq and the Israeli–Palestinian conflict yielded disappointment. While the king stood by the 1989 Taif Accords that ended the Lebanese Civil War, his firm commitment to the Lebanese Sunni community pitted the kingdom against Iran and Lebanese Shi'ites, including Hizbullah, the armed militant group that had gained increasing power in Lebanese politics and government. Although Saudi Arabia contributed substantially to the reconstruction of south Lebanon after the 2006 war between Israel and Hizbullah, it was not seen by the country's Shi'ites as a neutral arbiter. In mid 2008, it ceded the role of Lebanon's primary peace broker to Qatar.

In Palestine, Abdullah promoted a power-sharing agreement between Hamas, the militant Palestinian Islamist group, and Fatah, its secular rival, in 2007, only to see his efforts unravel after Hamas ousted Fatah in a bloody coup in Gaza, which led to an even more violent military conflict between Hamas and Israel in late 2008. Iranian–Qatari mediation eventually secured a ceasefire in Gaza, again sidelining Saudi diplomacy. In Iraq, the Shia majority did not trust Sunnis in general and Riyadh in particular to be objective regional interlocutors, which precluded Riyadh from playing a useful role.

The Saudis had hopes of greater success in supporting a negotiated solution in Afghanistan, where President Hamid Karzai and Western diplomats recognised that there could be no straightforward military solution to the Taliban guerrilla problem. Riyadh positioned itself to serve as a mediator in talks that could occur after Afghanistan's 2009 elections, with the purpose – from its point of view – of curbing Iranian influence. Abdullah also advanced political reconciliation with Syrian President Bashar al-Assad in January 2009 at the Kuwait Economic Conference and, with Egypt, forged the League of Arab States' grudging agreement to provide aid to Palestinian refugees in Gaza at the league's Doha Summit in March 2009.

Although the election of Benjamin Netanyahu as Israeli prime minister appeared to dampen prospects for a two-state solution to the Israeli–Palestinian conflict, the public commitment of the new administration of US President Barack Obama to such a solution along the lines proposed by Saudi Arabia in March 2002 appeared to ensure a Saudi role in the resolution of the conflict. More generally, it seemed likely that a close bilateral relationship with the United States would continue, given America's ongoing need for counter-terrorism cooperation in the region (which military draw-down in Iraq might amplify), as well as the ongoing importance of its strategic oil relationship with Riyadh. Abdullah's tilt towards political reforms was broadly consistent with the more modest form of US democracy promotion that has prevailed since the latter part of President George W. Bush's second term. It was notable that Obama visited Saudi Arabia in June 2009 before making a speech in Cairo that sought to rebuild trust in America across the Muslim world.

Religious and political reforms

The Saudi monarch ushered in key reforms in February 2009 by revamping the Council of Ulama, the body that advises on every aspect of law and governance in the kingdom. To establish greater Sunni tolerance, he expanded its membership and, in an important shift, invited members other than Hanbali theological scholars, including those of the Maliki, Hanafi and Shafi'i schools, to join in the deliberations. While no Shia clerics were included in this latest roster, observers anticipated that even they would eventually take their seats at council tables.

The most significant changes targeted the judiciary, where leading practitioners perceived the ruler as a maverick whose views seldom coincided with theirs. By firing Ibrahim al-Ghaith, the head of the Commission for the Promotion of Virtue and the Prevention of Vice – the so-called *mutawa'in* or religious police – Abdullah reminded his subjects that Saudis desired uniformity in the application of law. Ghaith's successor, Abdul Aziz bin Humayn, declared that it was his duty to implement the monarch's agenda, pledging to 'achieve the aspirations of the rulers'. This recognition of Abdullah's primacy was a clear departure from earlier practice. Furthermore, Abdullah concluded that some of those charged with enforcing public morality did not treat people with sufficient respect. By enjoining the *mutawa'in* to recognise basic freedoms, Abdullah signalled that he wanted a commission that connected with society instead of living in isolation from it, and operated in accordance with the law. An additional effort was made to rehabilitate an estimated 4,000 'deviant' clerics and hire moderate religious scholars to debate those with more extreme views.

In Abdullah's view, religious authorities had committed several grave errors, which weakened their positions. Sheikh Saleh al-Luhaidan, chief justice of the Supreme Judicial Council and the most powerful cleric in the kingdom, had refused to implement the monarch's 2007 reform decree requiring that sharia law be codified. He embarrassed Abdullah during Ramadan in 2008 when he declared that officials who encouraged the broadcast of 'immoral' television programmes could be executed. Moreover, in 2002, *mutawa'in* guards had refused to allow firemen to enter a burning girls' school in Mecca, and 15 female students died. In the 'Qatif Girl' gang-rape case in 2007, heavy sentences were imposed on the two victims as well as the seven rapists. Abdullah shared the public's revulsion at such drastic interpretations of the law and vowed to rectify the problem. Towards that end, he dismissed Luhaidan in February 2009, signalling that the courts and the morality police would now face thorough modernisation and moderation.

Augmenting the picture of a country seeking cautiously to present a more moderate face of Islam, King Abdullah convened, jointly with Spain, a Muslim World League conference in July 2008 to encourage inter-cultural dialogue. The meeting in Madrid featured nearly 300 delegates representing the world's major faiths – Judaism, Christianity, Islam, Buddhism, Hinduism and others. The Saudi monarch said that 'we all believe in one God, who sent messengers for the good of humanity in this world and the hereafter'. He emphasised that 'differences must not lead to conflict and confrontation', because whatever 'tragedies that have occurred in human history were not attributable to religion, but were the result of extremism with which some adherents of every divinely revealed religion, and of every political ideology, have been afflicted'.

Abdullah presented himself as an opponent of extremism, which he often describes as 'deviancy' from Islam. He urged all Muslims, including the ultra-conservative clergy in the kingdom, to welcome dialogue with other faiths. While Saudi Arabia bans all non-Muslim houses of worship, Saudi conservatives who seek refuge in archaic norms plainly irritate Abdullah, and the Muslim World League, under his guidance, no longer propagates hardline interpretations of sharia law and encourages the spread of a tolerant message.

> Abdullah opposed extremism and urged dialogue

Beyond the reorganisation within the judiciary, Abdullah made several significant new ministerial appointments. Noura al-Fayez was named deputy minister of education, becoming the first woman in Saudi history to occupy such a high-ranking position in government. Also highly significant was the promotion of Prince Faisal bin Abdullah bin Mohammed, who had been assistant director of intelligence, to be minister of education. Known for his active involvement in anti-extremist security operations, Faisal is the ruler's son-in-law and has the monarch's ear on key matters. Both men understand that the Saudi educational system is laden with extremely conservative thinkers who do not share a reformist vision. Abdullah and Faisal appear to accept that rote learning and religious education are no longer sufficient, and that Saudi youth must acquire technological skills to compete for jobs. Faisal's challenge will be to weed out teachers who refuse to comply with a revised curriculum that emphasises tolerance.

Abdullah also appeared to understand that – given the strategic tension between largely Sunni Saudi Arabia and predominantly Shia Iran – Saudi Arabia could not afford to alienate its Shia citizens, and had to avoid the kind of sectarian strife that had arisen in Bahrain, Kuwait, Iraq and Lebanon.

Accordingly, he increased Shia representation in the Shura Council, the country's legislative body, though he did not make any significant move to integrate the judiciary with Shia clerics.

Five years into his rule, King Abdullah has demonstrated an appetite for change, first with the 2007 Succession Law – establishing a committee, the Allegiance Commission, which would meet immediately on the death of a monarch to decide on his successor – and in 2009 with the dramatic shifts in the judiciary. Abdullah's relative activism by comparison with his predecessors led observers to expect that he would next call for municipal elections, and could perhaps encourage female voting as well as promoting freedom of association and a fairer distribution of wealth.

In May 2009, however, the Saudi government announced that elections would be delayed by at least two years. A week before the announcement, a group of 77 reform activists had sent a letter to King Abdullah and other members of the royal family requesting that the government adopt an elected parliament with legislative authority, agree to term limits for members of the royal family in appointed positions, and appoint someone outside the royal family to be prime minister. Implicitly, the reformers were asking for the establishment of a constitutional monarchy accountable to the public. While Abdullah may have some sympathy for such a dispensation, the postponement of the elections, alongside the strictly limited powers of the new local councils and resulting apathy towards them, also signified the royal family's deep ambivalence about reform and appeared to confirm that it would proceed only slowly and fitfully.

Gulf states: economic challenges

The five other members of the Gulf Co-operation Council (GCC) – Bahrain, Kuwait, Oman, Qatar and the United Arab Emirates (UAE) – struggled over the past year to address the fallout of the worldwide financial crisis.

In the UAE, Dubai found itself in particular economic difficulties as financial markets feared a default on its high short-term debts. Previously booming property prices slumped, developments were abandoned and foreign investors withdrew. In February, the UAE central bank, located in Abu Dhabi, lent Dubai $10bn to help with debt repayments and restore confidence. Dubai, lacking oil wealth, relies on trade, financial services and tourism, and had seen a boom in foreign investment and commercial development. As banks across the world faced funding difficulties in the money markets, the UAE government also made up to $32bn available to banks in all seven emirates and agreed to rescue Dubai's two mortgage companies, Amlak and Tamweel.

A much-touted agreement on a monetary union among GCC states was postponed because neither the name of the unified currency nor the head-quarters of the central bank could be agreed on. Efforts to stimulate economic activity included plans for a unified railway system to link Kuwait to Oman, improvements to water systems and electricity grids.

Leaders remained preoccupied with security – and especially with Iran's nuclear programme – and discussed enhancements to existing mul-tilateral arrangements. Furthermore, though a major oil producer, the UAE was concerned about rising energy demand. Thus, an important strategic development was an agreement between the UAE and the United States on civil nuclear cooperation. This was reached in the final days of the Bush administration, but Obama gave it his support, persuaded that it would be a 'model for promoting peaceful nuclear energy while guarding against weapons proliferation'. Under the accord, which requires US congres-sional approval, the UAE promises not to enrich uranium or reprocess spent nuclear fuel, and pledges to purchase nuclear fuel for reactors from American suppliers. Washington insisted, and Abu Dhabi concurred, that the UAE sign the Nuclear Non-Proliferation Treaty as well as adopting International Atomic Energy Agency safeguards. In April 2009, however, doubt was cast on the deal when videos surfaced that allegedly showed Sheikh Issa bin Zayed, a member of the royal family, engaged in the torture of an Afghan worker. Meanwhile, Washington was engaged in similar dis-cussions with the governments of Saudi Arabia, Jordan and Bahrain, while France, which opened a new naval base in Abu Dhabi in May 2009, signed a separate accord with Abu Dhabi in January 2008. Other nuclear powers also appeared ready to extend assistance in developing nuclear energy for peaceful ends.

Qatar adopted an active and substantially conciliatory posture in regional diplomacy in 2008, coaxing Lebanon's bickering politicians to end their crippling power struggle, mediating between insurgent clansmen and the government of Yemen, seeking to heal a rift between Hamas and Fatah over the Israeli assault on Gaza, and even hosting warring Sudanese factions for high-level negotiations in Doha. At the same time, what were perceived as the pro-Tehran tendencies of Qatar's ruler, Sheikh Hamad bin Khalifa al-Thani, irritated other Arab leaders. Egyptian President Hosni Mubarak skipped the March 2009 League of Arab States summit in Qatar.

In Bahrain, intensifying Sunni–Shia sectarianism – stemming from the fact that a Sunni elite rules a Shia majority – produced serious clashes. Shia protests against discrimination and civil-rights abuses were violently put down, which resulted in the death of a Pakistani worker. The police arrested 23 opposition organisers, including two popular figures, Hasan Mushaima and Sheikh Mohammed Habib al-Moqdad, a Shia cleric. Prosecutors claimed the two men were trying to destabilise the government and were planning terrorist attacks. King Hamad bin Isa Al Khalifa issued pardons to 178 prisoners to defuse rising political tensions. But sectarian friction did not end, as several more alleged conspirators were arrested in early May 2009.

In the shadow of Iran

Iran's persistent pursuit of a nuclear capability continued to overshadow the Gulf region. While the idea of a nuclear Gulf region was anathema to many, most Gulf leaders believed that major powers would not perpetually protect GCC countries and that the eventuality of a nuclear Iran might call for an Arab deterrent. They could not ignore indications of hostile Iranian ambition, such as the pledge of Ali Shamkhani, military adviser to Iranian supreme leader Ayatollah Ali Khamenei, to 'burn the region, its military bases, even the oil wells of GCC states, if Iran ever came under an American military attack'.

The expressed collective preference of Gulf Arab rulers was for Tehran to join them in developing strong ties based on mutual respect, common interests and non-interference in the domestic affairs of neighbouring nations. Although Iran has periodically joined the chorus for lower tensions, the consensus perception in the region was that it has nevertheless pursued wholesale regional primacy while upbraiding GCC governments for nascent alliances with major Western powers.

In 2008, GCC Secretary-General Abdul Rahman Al Atiyyah retorted with unusual bluntness to remarks by Iran's Deputy Foreign Minister for Education and Research Manouchehr Mohammadi questioning the legitimacy of Arab ruling regimes, pointing out that Gulf states were 'very disappointed and deeply concerned' over his 'irresponsible and blatant' rhetoric. Iran has made political inroads in areas – in particular, Iraq, Lebanon and the Israeli–Palestinian conflict – which Gulf leaders consider to be Arab problems. And Iran's involvement in all three areas – including financial and operational support to Shia militias in Iraq, Hizbullah in Lebanon, and

Hamas in the Palestinian territories – is seen in the Gulf as destabilising rather than constructive.

Against this display of Persian power, GCC regimes may well decide that they must seek the protection of a Western nuclear umbrella, or else acquire nuclear capabilities themselves. A principal objective of the United States and Europe in working to prevent Iran acquiring nuclear-weapons capability is to forestall the necessity of Gulf states making any such choice. Only if the American and European efforts are successful will GCC capitals be able to devote primary concentration to the more constructive and progressive areas of political reform, conflict resolution and economic security.

Chapter 8

Africa

Even before taking the impact of global recession into account, the year from mid 2008 was a turbulent period in Africa. Coups and putsches, which had gone out of style, made a comeback, with army takeovers in Mauritania and Guinea, a presidential assassination in Guinea-Bissau and a military-backed overthrow of the government in Madagascar. NATO, the European Union and a cluster of other countries rushed to send warships to counter growing piracy off Somalia (on the route to and from the Suez Canal) which was directly threatening Western and Asian economic interests. However, there was little appetite for committing international forces to Somalia itself, especially in view of competing demands already being made for peace-keepers in Darfur and the Democratic Republic of the Congo. Divergences emerged between Western and African views, notably over support for Zimbabwe's compromise government and the war-crimes indictment of Sudan's President Omar al-Bashir. At the same time, the kind of leadership South Africa, Nigeria and others had shown earlier in the decade in promoting an African revival was no longer visible. South African political energies were largely taken up by internal battles within the ruling African National Congress (ANC) ahead of populist Jacob Zuma's accession to the presidency in May 2009.

Realisation of what the global financial and economic crisis would mean for Africa was slow to dawn. African countries had little exposure to the credit losses sustained by international banks and institutions, and some, such as Ghana and Uganda (which were poised to start oil production), had brighter prospects. It became increasingly clear by early 2009, however, that the continent would be hit on multiple fronts by a slump in commodity prices affecting the bulk of its exports, dwindling flows of foreign invest-

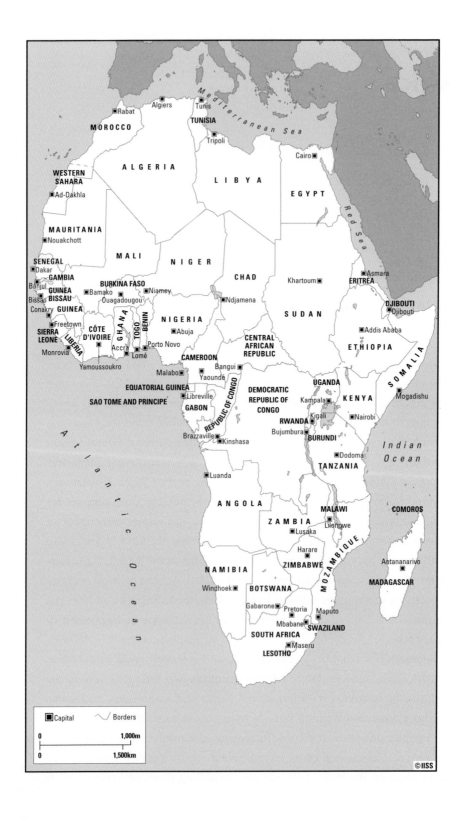

ment and emigrants' remittances, and much tighter availability of credit. China, while not calling off its investment spree, became more cautious. Although Africa was due to receive a large share of the extra resources allocated to the World Bank and other multilateral funders at the G20 summit in London in April, overall aid by 2010 was set to fall well short of the levels promised. Sub-Saharan Africa had no prospect of achieving the main UN Millennium Development Goal of reducing the proportion of people living in extreme poverty by half (compared to 1990) by 2015. In absolute numbers, the number of poor was expected to increase, and many countries faced the risk of unrest in poor urban areas. The weaknesses of small and narrowly based economies, which had been masked by the commodity boom, were again exposed. Regional growth, still around 5% in 2008, was expected to fall to less than half that level in 2009, below the rate of population increase, and African governments were generally ill equipped to counteract the effects of the downturn.

Crossroads in South Africa

Over the past year South Africa had three presidents and saw the culmination of its biggest political crisis since the end of apartheid in 1994. The period leading up to its elections in April 2009, the fourth of the post-apartheid era, was the most eventful in the ANC's time in power. Although its majority was never in doubt, it faced the likelihood of further internal strains as President Jacob Zuma's new administration set about trying to meet public demands in an economy tipping towards its first recession since the end of white rule.

As a broad movement, the ANC always contained conflicting tendencies. Inheriting a nearly bankrupt state 15 years ago, the government turned to free-market policies and reliance on the private sector, opening a rift with the more traditional left that sought greater interventionism and public ownership. As a disciplined organisation that had spent decades operating clandestinely, however, the ANC managed to keep its internal differences largely behind closed doors. What was unusual about the feuding of the past two years was the extent to which the animosity between different factions and personalities was played out in the public arena. So absorbed was South Africa during this period by the personality-driven power struggle that less attention was given to the discussion of policies to cope with growing social pressures.

From Mbeki to Zuma

For nine months up to Thabo Mbeki's dramatic ouster as president in September 2008, South Africa had two centres of power: the national presidency and the ANC leadership. The latter had been conclusively won by Zuma, a colourful figure with a distinctly more rough-hewn style and a contested reputation. Mbeki's decision to stand against Zuma for a further term as ANC leader, even though he could not run again for the presidency, proved to be a massive blunder. By blocking the possibility of promoting an alternative candidate, it cleared the way for Zuma, whom Mbeki had dismissed as deputy president in 2005, to lead the ANC into the elections. Zuma's supporters were in triumphant mood, already convinced that legal cases against him were part of a conspiracy. This belief was reinforced when prosecutors, just after Zuma's leadership victory, revived charges of fraud, corruption, racketeering, money laundering and tax evasion in connection with a 1999 arms deal. In September a High Court judge in Pietermaritzburg discarded the charges as unlawful on procedural grounds. While not dealing with Zuma's guilt or innocence, he suggested that Mbeki and government ministers might have interfered and colluded with prosecutors. The ANC's national executive committee decided this was enough to 'recall' Mbeki from the presidency. Although he firmly denied meddling with the legal process, Mbeki dutifully resigned the next day. The special unit – known as the Scorpions – of the National Prosecution Authority (NPA) that had conducted the investigation was disbanded.

The ejection of Mbeki was not Zuma's wish. Even if he had wanted to take over prematurely he was not in a position to do so, since he had given up his parliamentary seat. Elections were seven months away, and he now faced an open split in the party. However, a wave of hostility had been building up against Mbeki. Widely regarded as aloof and disconnected from the concerns of ordinary people, Mbeki was blamed for failing to recognise the urgency and scale of problems such as violent crime and for a confusing stance on HIV/AIDS. Although South Africa now has the world's biggest programme of anti-retroviral therapy, a study by Harvard University researchers published in November 2008 concluded that more than 330,000 deaths could have been prevented by providing public treatment earlier. Recently, Mbeki was accused of reacting late to power shortages and the outbreak in early

2008 of xenophobic violence against African migrants. He was also seen as using Black Economic Empowerment, a wide-ranging scheme to promote the involvement of non-white racial groups in business ownership, management and jobs, to build a new, politically connected elite. His nine years in office brought moderate growth and greatly increased access to affordable housing, electricity and basic water supplies, but government programmes were unable to keep pace with rising needs. Inequality increased, especially within the 80% majority black population.

The perceived victimisation of rivals united opposition to Mbeki inside the party, not only from the well-organised left, including the ANC's Congress of South African Trade Unions (COSATU) and South African Communist Party (SACP) partners, but also from senior party business figures. As caretaker president the ANC chose its left-leaning deputy leader Kgalema Motlanthe, who had also served as secretary-general under Mbeki. Under South Africa's system of indirect election to the presidency, Motlanthe was duly voted in by parliament.

Zuma's supporters, however, had overplayed their hand. A group of Mbeki stalwarts left to form a new party, Congress of the People (COPE), led by Musiuoa Lekota, a former defence minister and ANC national chairperson, and Mbhazima Shilowa, ex-leader of COSATU, who resigned as premier of Gauteng province, South Africa's economic powerhouse. Launched formally in December, COPE appealed mainly to members of the black middle class who shared the apprehensions of many in the white, mixed-race and Asian minorities about the prospect of a Zuma presidency.

In January, the Supreme Court of Appeal set aside the ruling in the arms affair that had caused Mbeki's downfall. Finding that the judge had overstepped his authority, it effectively reinstated the charges. It appeared quite likely at this stage that the charges would follow Zuma into office. His lawyers wanted to prove that he had no criminal intent and that persisting with the prosecution was against the public interest. It was evident, however, that Zuma had a case to answer, even if he was not necessarily a leading beneficiary of the $5bn deal, which involved companies from Germany, the United Kingdom, Sweden, Italy, France and South Africa. The charges centred on 783 payments he was alleged to have received over a decade, amounting to about $500,000, from a friend and financial adviser who had a direct interest in a defence subcontractor and who was convicted in 2005 of soliciting a bribe for Zuma from a French partner to shield it from investigation.

In April 2009, with just over two weeks to go before the elections, acting NPA head Mokotedi Mpshe withdrew the charges against Zuma. He made clear that this decision had nothing to do with arguments about the substantive merits of the case, but was based on evidence that the legal process had been manipulated for purposes 'extraneous to the prosecution itself'. He quoted transcripts of recordings of telephone conversations between a former NPA head and the then chief of the Scorpions, in which they discussed the appropriate timing of the charges. Mpshe concluded that it was 'neither possible nor desirable' to continue with the prosecution. In a storm of debate about what this meant for the standing of South Africa's legal system, the main Democratic Alliance (DA) opposition applied for a full judicial review of the decision.

Rank-and-file ANC supporters appeared remarkably unfazed by Zuma's legal troubles. Julius Malema, firebrand president of the ANC Youth League, told a rally in the run-up to the election: 'if Zuma is corrupt, then we want him with all his corruption'. The elections on 22 April might have been expected to be troubled, but went ahead with very few incidents and high participation, providing a model for Africa in the way they were conducted. The ANC, the only party to run a genuinely national campaign, won almost 66% of the vote. With record voter registration, its total vote tally was higher than either of the two previous occasions, exceeded only by the massive turnout of support for the first post-apartheid elections in 1994. The result showed that, despite the new competition, poor black South Africans still identified overwhelmingly with the ANC. This was unsurprising in the regional context. The continued hegemony of monolithic liberation parties in other Southern African countries was reflected in legislative elections held in Angola in September 2008, after a gap of 16 years, and was set to be confirmed in elections in late 2009 in Mozambique and Namibia.

It was the first time, however, that the ANC's share of the vote had fallen, after edging up to almost 70% five years earlier. Its parliamentary strength fell to fractionally below the two-thirds majority required to amend the constitution. A steeper fall in most areas was masked by Zuma's strong pull among his own Zulu ethnic group, the country's largest, which had not had an ANC leader for more than 40 years. The only one of South Africa's nine provinces where the party gained ground was Zuma's home territory of KwaZulu-Natal. The DA, which chose not to field a candidate for the national presidency, increased its share of the vote from one in eight to one in six and seized an outright win in Western Cape, a province where more than 70%

of the population was mixed-race or white. The party's leader Helen Zille, a dynamic and popular mayor of Cape Town, moved to take over as the province's premier, ousting the ANC from the government.

COPE captured many fewer ANC voters than it expected. Its vote share of over 7% made it the third party but was only half its hoped-for result, after a poor campaign marred by infighting. In an attempt to distinguish itself from the scandal-tainted ANC it chose Bishop Mvume Dandala, former head of the Methodist Church of Southern Africa and president of the South African Council of Churches, a political novice, as its presidential candidate. The main impact of COPE's entry into the race, as it turned out, was to galvanise the ANC. Running a formidable campaign, the ANC brought former president and national icon Nelson Mandela out of retirement to help mobilise its voters. The fact that Zuma would not be taking over directly from Mbeki made it easier to throw onto Mbeki all the blame for the ANC's previous failings. Zuma, a polygamous Zulu traditionalist with little formal education, who had spent ten years in prison alongside Mandela and was at one stage the ANC's intelligence chief, successfully projected himself as someone who could communicate with poor people and understand their concerns. His campaign homed in on the issues of crime, health and education. In the build-up to the elections, he showed himself to be pragmatic and approachable, able to adapt his discourse to different interest groups. In government, however, these different interests would be harder to reconcile.

> " Since 2004 economic policy had shifted to the left "

Despite populist rhetoric and the inclusion of leftist ministers in a broad-ranging cabinet, it appeared unlikely that the new government would make radical changes either in its handling of the economy, at least in the initial stage, or in foreign policy, to which Zuma was expected to devote less energy than Mbeki. Since 2004, economic policy had already shifted towards the left, with a big push in public investment and a drive to cut poverty and joblessness. Growth accelerated to about 5% a year, faster than in the first decade of ANC government or the decade before that, before it was derailed by the global crisis. Although building work on infrastructure for the 2010 football World Cup in South Africa promised to mitigate the recession, the economy shrank in the first months of 2009 at an annualised rate of more than 6%. The scope for major new redistributive measures was limited, with more than a quarter of the population already receiving state grants. Unemployment, climbing back to more than 30% when people who had given up looking for work were included, was set to rise further. Bad debts were increasing, mining exports were down and manufacturing was already badly damaged by competition from Asia. These were difficult circumstances in which to face heightened expectations among the electorate and widespread demands for more effective delivery of services.

The stage was set for a more substantial realignment in South African politics to take place over the next few years. Further divisions in the ANC could be expected if the government failed to satisfy the demands of its COSATU and SACP partners. Opposition, less dispersed among small parties, was already beginning to coalesce. Had the COPE initiative not misfired, it might have created the basis for the formation of a broader opposition crossing the racial lines that have up to now defined South African politics. The DA, although not without black support, had yet to overcome its image as a party of white and mixed-raced interests.

On taking office, the new president adopted a conciliatory stance, trying to calm political tempers. Despite fears about political pressures on the justice system and the media, stoked by earlier remarks made by Zuma and some of his supporters, events showed South Africa's public and civil institutions to be robust. However, under an untried president, the country was entering its most uncertain and challenging period since the first stages of democratic transition.

Cohabitation in Zimbabwe

Zimbabwe spent most of the year from mid 2008 in political stalemate as the cliques surrounding President Robert Mugabe fought to defend their positions of power. As a result of continued Southern African Development Community (SADC) mediation between the main parties, an 'inclusive' government was eventually installed in February 2009, with Mugabe remaining as head of state. However, the United States, the United Kingdom and other Western countries, whose support was vital for resuscitating Zimbabwe's collapsed economy, were not convinced that the deal marked a genuine change of course that could deliver better government and guarantee respect for human rights. The power-sharing arrangement rested on two pillars with different degrees of democratic legitimacy: a narrowly balanced parliament, which had been elected 11 months earlier in the most transparent contest of recent years, and the presidency, decided in a parody of a run-off vote dominated by a campaign of violent intimidation. Having come close to unseating Mugabe in the first round, opposition leader Morgan Tsvangirai had withdrawn his candidacy, after himself being detained several times while electioneering.

Thabo Mbeki, South African president at the time, resumed his role as SADC mediator in July 2008, shortly after Mugabe's re-inauguration. The talks between Mugabe's Zimbabwe African National Union–Patriotic Front (ZANU-PF), which had lost its parliamentary majority for the first time since coming to power in 1980, and the two factions of the Movement for Democratic Change (MDC) opposition resulted in September in a framework power-sharing deal called the Global Political Agreement, assigning a new post of prime minister to Tsvangirai. The deal envisaged a form of cohabitation in which the same government members would form both a cabinet and a council of ministers, with Mugabe chairing the former for strategic decisions and Tsvangirai the latter for day-to-day operations. A non-negotiable part of the agreement was a reaffirmation of the Mugabe regime's controversial land policy. The seizure of most white-owned farms was declared irreversible, and the UK, as the former colonial power, was called on to take responsibility for paying compensation to the roughly 4,000 farmers concerned. The agreement avoided some important issues, notably skirting the question of reforming the security sector. It provided for ministerial positions to be distributed in proportion to parties' share of parliamentary seats, but left open how specific portfolios were to be allocated. As negotiations became deadlocked over the following months, scepticism grew, both in Zimbabwe and abroad, about the commitment of Mugabe and his hardcore supporters to the reforms that had been agreed.

In the meantime, the economy continued to disintegrate, along with public services such as education and health, for which Zimbabwe previously had a strong record. The collapse of basic water and medical infrastructure was exposed when cholera broke out in August 2008, spreading from urban to rural areas, where it was harder to contain, and reaching into neighbouring countries. By May 2009, when the epidemic appeared under control, more than 4,200 had died from the disease. At the same time, by the reckoning of international agencies, half the population was in need of food aid. Economic output was 40% smaller than in 2000, with agricultural production reduced by more than half. Factories were mostly idle and most skilled and qualified

Zimbabweans were working abroad. As the government carried on printing money to finance its deficit, inflation rose to such dizzying proportions that authorities gave up trying to calculate it after July 2008, when the official annual rate reached 231,000,000%. Teachers and civil servants on shrinking salaries began staying away from work, unable to afford the transport to get there, and lower army ranks became restive. Late in the year, many food-stuffs and other basic products could no longer be found in stores, partly as a result of government price controls, which meant that shopkeepers could no longer sell them at a profit. Wholesale distributors withheld supplies, not wanting payment in a currency that was losing value hourly, while ordinary Zimbabweans hoarded what they could buy for re-sale on the informal market, the country's one thriving economic activity.

Discussions on forming the inclusive government were stalling. Although the September agreement called on prosecuting authorities to speed up the handling of cases of people remanded on politically related changes, further arrests and abductions of political and human-rights activists took place in late 2008. Western governments increasingly doubted the value of any form of power-sharing as long as Mugabe remained in office. The United States, the UK and the EU all called for him to go. The 15-nation SADC, while critical of the manner of Mugabe's re-election, would not venture so far, but began to show divisions on the issue, with scathing condemnation of Mugabe from Botswana and Zambia. The continued flow of migrants into neighbouring countries and the cholera epidemic accentuated the regional dimension of Zimbabwe's prolonged political crisis. Even the South African government, which had long faced domestic and international censure for shielding the Mugabe regime, became frustrated with the delay in negotiations and held back a package of farm assistance. Many within Tsvangirai's MDC were against going ahead with a coalition, fearing it would turn out to be a trap. Comparisons were made with the fate, 21 years earlier, of the Zimbabwe African People's Union led by Joshua Nkomo, which was swallowed up by Mugabe's ZANU after signing a unity pact. There were significant differences, though, in that the MDC was a more broadly based, less regional party, and Mugabe was now a much more discredited figure.

When Tsvangirai finally agreed on a joint government on 11 February it came as something of a surprise. He was, however, not in a strong position.

> The US, UK and EU all called for Mugabe to go

He had failed to get the African Union (AU) or UN to take over the SADC mediation process. South Africa, always believing that any new dispensation in Zimbabwe would have to involve ZANU-PF, had kept up pressure for a settlement. While Tsvangirai might have counted on the deteriorating economic situation forcing ZANU-PF to compromise, it was also weakening his own trade-union base. In the absence of an agreement, ZANU-PF might have been able to carry on in power and inflict further retribution on its opponents. Although Tsvangirai's faction and the smaller splinter party within the MDC had a small majority of ministerial posts, the key jobs other than finance, including defence, justice, foreign affairs and sensitive areas such as media and land, went to ZANU-PF. Knowing from the outset that ZANU-PF would want to keep control of the armed forces, the MDC tried to obtain other security responsibilities, but had to make do with an interim compromise over home affairs (the department overseeing the police), to which the two main sides appointed a minister each. Earlier, the MDC had rejected this solution as unworkable.

The formation of the new government coincided with a fresh wave of invasions of white-owned farms (90% of which had already been seized at the start of the decade) by groups loyal to Mugabe. On the day the new cabinet was sworn in, the MDC's nominee as deputy agriculture minister, Roy Bennett, a white former coffee farmer, was arrested at an airport outside Harare and charged with terrorism-related offences. Both developments were interpreted as demonstrations of force by ZANU-PF diehards opposed to ceding any part of the party's authority. Resistance at senior levels was based in part on self-interest, including fear of eventual prosecution, but also reflected a firmly held belief among ZANU-PF ideologues (shared by counterparts in other national liberation parties in Southern Africa) in their movement's unique entitlement to power. The hard core of resistance was the notorious Joint Operations Command, comprising the army, air force, intelligence, prison service and police chiefs. Although the command was officially replaced in February 2009 by a new National Security Council, bringing in ministers from both sides, the security chiefs continued to wield extensive power.

While the coalition deal seemed to give only restricted scope to the MDC, the climate in Zimbabwe underwent marked improvement in early 2009. The Zimbabwe dollar was abandoned and hyperinflation came to an end. Many businesses and services were already insisting on payment in hard currency. Two weeks before the new government was announced, the authorities decided to allow the use of foreign currencies for all transactions. The US dollar and South African rand took over what was now officially a 'multi-currency' economy. Prices, redenominated in US instead of Zimbabwe dollars, soon started falling, and formerly scarce goods became available again. Tsvangirai, on taking office, promised hard-currency payments to all public employees, including the army and police, a risky step considering the limited amount of foreign exchange at the government's disposal. The measure succeeded in getting schools and other government services functioning again, although unions soon began pressing for much higher minimum salaries than the token amounts being paid.

The government rushed out a wide-ranging short-term recovery plan. This was a bad time, however, for trying to revive the economy, with depressed prices for vital export commodities such as platinum. Reconstruction was impossible without a resumption of substantial international funding for the Zimbabwe treasury. Tsvangirai pleaded for donors to relax their stance, but the United States, the EU and other Western countries were reluctant to ease Zimbabwe's access to grants and loans, or consider lifting sanctions imposed against individuals and businesses connected with the Mugabe regime, until they saw more conclusive evidence of change. The International Monetary Fund said Zimbabwe would not be eligible for new funding until it cleared its arrears with multilateral institutions. South Africa and other SADC neighbours lent support, but did not have the capacity to provide the $8.5bn the government was asking for. Nor was aid from China, despite its close ties with Mugabe, expected to be sufficient to fill the gap. However, donors began to broaden their criteria for assistance, moving beyond humanitarian relief to support for vital infrastructure such as water and sanitation.

Even though MDC leaders had trouble asserting authority in combating farm invasions and determining senior-level appointments, they appeared not to have been neutralised to the extent that many had anticipated, and had scope for setting the economic agenda. At the same time, wariness on the part of Western governments posed a serious challenge, since it was vital from the MDC's standpoint to be able to show visible benefits from its decision to join the government, and the clock was already ticking. The framework political agreement set an 18-month timetable, starting with the inception of the new government, for drawing up and introducing a new constitution, at which point the deal would be reviewed. For it to continue, all three parties would need to agree. Although it could in principle last until the completion of Mugabe's term in 2013, pressure was likely to build up in the MDC to return to the polls at the earliest opportunity, possibly in early 2011. Whether the deal would survive even for two years was far from certain; it depended very much on the survival of both Mugabe, now 85, and Tsvangirai. In neither case was there an obvious successor who could hold divergent forces in their parties together. While the general mood and the outlook for power-sharing appeared more positive than many had expected at the outset, it remained a fragile, uncertain and uneasy arrangement.

Somalia: Anarchy and Piracy

A sharp escalation in ship hijackings by Somali pirates on one of the world's most important trade routes, and the engagement of a range of different naval forces in the region, thrust Somalia into the spotlight. The first incidents involving US-flagged merchant ships in April 2009 made the issue more urgent for the Obama administration, which promised stronger action to confront piracy and enforce the rule of law. The maritime threat was, however, just one symptom of Somalia's prolonged instability, unresolved after 18 years without effective national government. While the international community concentrated on measures to reduce the risk to shipping, including support for in-country policing, no short-term solutions were in the offing for Somalia's wider troubles. The outlook for its five-year-old, internationally backed transitional government, meant to prepare the way for a Western-style democracy but struggling to take root in the country's clan-based society, was uncertain. This was despite a tentative boost to hopes for reconciliation in early 2009. Withdrawal by the Ethiopian army, which spent two years trying to prop up the isolated transitional leadership, removed a major source of tension. A UN-sponsored pact made progress towards broadening the government's weak political base, under a new Islamist president. By then, however, radical Islamist insurgents already held sway over most of southern Somalia, drawing fighters and support from outside. With an inadequate AU mission increasingly bogged down in the capital Mogadishu, and with little willingness in other countries to commit to a major new UN peacekeeping operation, a viable security-building plan was the biggest missing piece of the puzzle.

Most of the piracy stemmed from Puntland, the semi-autonomous region at the tip of the Horn of Africa, between Somalia's more populated central and southern zones and the secessionist state of Somaliland to the north-west. While standing apart from the worst of the country's civil warfare, Puntland showed signs of degenerating into a virtual gangster state, giving free rein to criminal networks. It became clear that efforts to tackle piracy at sea, with whatever resources and however well coordinated, would have little chance of eliminating the threat as long as criminal groups were able to hold ships and crew captive along the coast. The problem was bound up with the absence of effective or reliable state authority and the lack of comparably attractive sources of legitimate income.

A concentration of international naval forces in the Gulf of Aden, the access route from the Indian Ocean to the Red Sea and the Suez Canal, led pirates to shift their activity towards the southeast, further offshore from Somalia and off the coasts of Kenya and Tanzania, and to adopt more aggressive tactics. However, while the lucrative hijack ransom industry was linked to business interests outside Somalia, there was as yet no evidence of involvement by extremist Islamist organisations. If such a connection were proved to exist, the dimensions of the issue and the US response to it could change dramatically.

The dangerous coast

The waters off Somalia were the most hazardous shipping lanes in the world for piracy in 2008, and continued to be so in 2009 as dozens of warships from various nations converged on the region (see Strategic Geography, pp. VI–VII). Not only were attacks more frequent, but pirates also became much more ambitious in their range of operation and the size of ships they targeted. Most of the seizures of ships around the world in 2008 occurred off Somalia. More than 100 incidents were reported during the year, including more than 40 successful hijackings (ranging from private yachts to chemical carriers) and several clashes with foreign naval forces.

Piracy on the Somali coast was not new. Action by local fisherman, demanding levies from foreign trawlers accused of illegal tuna fishing, built up during the 1990s into a well-organised business centred on the fishing port of Eyl in northern Puntland. While pirates continued to use small motorised wooden or fibreglass boats, recent attacks showed they had become better armed and more sophisticated. Equipped with automatic weapons, rocket-propelled grenades and GPS navigation systems, they evidently had intelligence about shipping movements and were capable of tracking warships. The increase in their capability was brought home when the *Sirius Star*, a 330-metre Saudi

Arabian-owned supertanker carrying 2m barrels of crude oil, was hijacked in November more than 400 nautical miles offshore, and held for two months before being released in exchange for ransom. Piracy was now posing a serious threat to a major oil route to Europe and the United States. With up to about 20,000 ships normally using the Suez Canal each year, shipowners had to choose between paying steep additional insurance premiums and taking the much longer route around the Cape of Good Hope. This added to the problems they already faced as a result of shrinking trade volumes and plummeting shipping rates. Ransoms paid during the year probably amounted to $50m, but the overall cost to shippers and insurers of securing the release of vessels and crew could have been three times that figure.

Pressure for tougher international action gathered strength in the second half of 2008. In a series of resolutions, the UN Security Council laid down a clearer legal basis for intervention, authorising foreign navies to breach territorial limits in pursuit of pirates and empowering forces to pursue them on land. In October, NATO assigned warships from a standing naval group for close protection and deterrence patrols, supported by helicopters. In December, the EU launched *Operation Atalanta*, its first-ever naval mission, to combat Somali piracy and escort shipments for the UN's World Food Programme, a task previously carried out in turns by individual navies. The new force, EU NAVFOR Somalia, coordinated at the UK naval command centre at Northwood, outside London, was planned to last one year with eight EU nations plus Norway due to contribute warships and maritime-patrol aircraft. The mission, in cooperation with the International Maritime Bureau and liaising with NATO and other naval forces, set up a transit corridor for merchant ships to travel in groups through the Gulf of Aden, between Somalia and Yemen. In January, the United States formed a new multinational combined task force, CTF-151, with a specific anti-piracy brief, in addition to the existing CTF-150, created primarily for counter-terrorism purposes. Other countries sending naval vessels, mainly to protect their own merchant ships, included China (in its first active deployment overseas since the foundation of the People's Republic), Japan, South Korea, Russia and Iran. Altogether more than 20 nations either had warships in the region or were preparing to send them. To resolve complex jurisdictional issues surrounding the prosecution of captured pirates, Britain, the United States and later the EU reached agreements with Kenya for trials to be held there.

About seven different groups, including one based in Yemen's Socotra archipelago, were believed to be operating in a nexus of piracy, gun-running and people-smuggling. As naval patrols intensified in the Gulf of Aden, pirates changed tactics, increasingly targeting vessels off the eastern coast and further into the Indian Ocean. While the Gulf of Aden continued to be the scene of opportunistic attacks, the increased range of piracy began to raise questions about the safety of shipping even when it avoided the Suez route. In addition to larger ships, fishing vessels and dhows were still being captured, possibly for use as 'mother ships' for pirate attacks hundreds of miles offshore. Captured vessels were mostly taken to Puntland's Indian Ocean coast, with sometimes more than 15 being held simultaneously.

After a lull at the start of 2009, there was a fresh surge in hijack attempts. A series of events in April propelled the piracy issue to the forefront of world attention. France, which like the United States has forces positioned in Djibouti, at the junction of the Gulf of Aden and the Red Sea, displayed its muscular approach by parachuting 70 commandos to rescue a sailing boat. Four hostages were freed but the boat's owner and two pirates were killed. The operation followed two successful French raids in 2008 in response to similar incidents. Two days later, an American merchant captain, taken hostage in an attempted hijacking of US-registered container ship *Maersk Alabama*, was freed by US Navy SEALs, who shot three pirates holding him. Following the incident, the first attack on a US-flagged vessel, US Secretary of State Hillary Clinton said Washington would press Somali authorities to crack down on pirates' land bases and would seek ways of tracking and freezing ransom payments.

Despite the greatly increased international naval presence, the shift in pirate activity to the open expanses of the Indian Ocean made it much more difficult for warships to intervene in time. The EU had to consider whether to reposition part of its force, sacrificing some of its protection in the Gulf of Aden. More reliance was placed on ships' crews taking protective measures such as evasive manoeuvres, use of pressurised hoses against boarders and lock-down routines to delay access to control of vessels. However, while the commander of US naval forces in the region called for armed guards aboard ships, international maritime bodies and EU officials were concerned that this might only escalate the level of violence and result in reprisal attacks.

A new balance of power

In the course of 2008 it became more and more evident that Somalia had reached a political impasse. Radical Islamist insurgents were gaining ground and the security situation in many parts of the country was, if anything, getting worse. The presence of the Ethiopian army in Somalia for a second year was uniting opposition against the fragile government it was sent to save.

A preliminary peace plan, brokered by the UN at talks in Djibouti between representatives of the internationally supported Transitional Federal Government (TFG) and the exiled opposition, had a difficult start. The 15th attempt at peace since the implosion of central government in 1991, it caused problems with hardliners on both sides. The opposition Alliance for the Re-liberation of Somalia (ARS), a coalition including Islamist leaders chased from Somalia by Ethiopian forces at the end of 2006, split in two, with a rejectionist faction staying in the Eritrean capital Asmara. Somali President Abdullah Yusuf Ahmed, a former warlord appointed when the TFG was established, tried to block the proposed accommodation, provoking a show-down with other countries in the regional Intergovernmental Authority on Development and his prime minister, Nur Adde. Isolated, Yusuf resigned in late December.

The peace plan called for a phased withdrawal of Ethiopian troops under cover of a UN stabilisation force. The UN force never materialised, but Ethiopia, which had become impatient with Yusuf's stalling, decided to leave the TFG to its own devices. It completed withdrawal in January, pulling back first from its main bases in Mogadishu and then, two weeks later, from Baidoa, the seat of the transitional parliament. The town was overrun within hours by radical Islamists. The unelected parliament, meeting in Djibouti, voted to double its seats to 550, making room for 200 members from the moderate branch of the ARS, and extended its transitional mandate by two years to 2011, putting off elections. From a slate of presidential candidates, the expanded parliament opted for the ARS's Sheikh Sharif Ahmed. A respected cleric, he was the former chairman of the Union of Islamic Courts, a coalition of Islamists, businessmen and clan elders which for six months in 2006 exercised effective control in Mogadishu and most of southern and central Somalia, managing to establish relative order.

The wheel appeared almost to have turned full circle, but key players had changed places. The Islamic Courts leader was now heading the TFG, and the organisation's former armed youth wing al-Shabaab, a fiercely radi-calised movement with a strong nationalist element spanning clan divisions, was now in charge in most of south-central Somalia. Despite the govern-ment's broader political base, the new president was initially in an even weaker position than his predecessor, with no significant forces under his control nor the backing of foreign troops, other than Ugandan and Burundian peacekeepers of the African Union Mission in Somalia (AMISOM) concentrated in Mogadishu. By early 2009, two years after its initial deployment, AMISOM had barely managed to reach half its planned strength of 8,000. Most government soldiers had deserted, many taking their weapons with them. Forces grouped under the banner of al-Shabaab, including several hundred foreign fighters, controlled the six southernmost regions, limiting the government's effective rule to part of Mogadishu and a few other areas. Returning to a much more radicalised country, Sharif began reaching out to more militant factions in an effort to widen the reconciliation process.

> The US agenda for combating extremism lay in ruins

The agenda pursued over the previous three years by the United States for combating extremism in Somalia lay in ruins. One after another, US policies backfired. An alliance of clan warlords, backed by Washington as a bulwark against Islamist militancy, was swept aside by the Islamic Courts. Ethiopia's subsequent invasion, carried out with US acquiescence, ousted the Islamic Courts but set off an insurgency. The designation of al-Shabaab as a foreign terrorist organisation proved counterproductive, enhancing its status. Unilateral US air and missile strikes against 'high value' al-Qaeda suspects in Somalia (one killed al-Shabaab commander Aden Hashi Ayro in 2008) served as a jihadi recruiting aid.

In late 2008 the outgoing US administration of President George W. Bush pushed for a UN peacekeeping force, but UN Secretary-General Ban Ki Moon said the time was not right and no country was prepared to lead a new mission in Somalia. The UK and France opposed sending UN peacekeepers, and Obama's UN ambassador Susan Rice also voiced scepticism. The country saw continued outbreaks of fighting, involving rival militias, government police and AU troops; further abductions and killings of aid workers and journalists; and an increase in suicide bombings, a relatively recent phenomenon in Somalia. Coordinated car bombs in October killed at least 30 people in Bosaso in northern Puntland and Hargeisa, capital of Somaliland, where an Ethiopian consular office, a UN Development Programme compound and the presidential palace were targeted. In February 2009 a bomb in Mogadishu killed 11 Burundian AMISOM soldiers. An offensive by al-Shabaab and allied fighters of Hizbul Islam, a recently formed group, in the capital in May 2009 provoked a renewed exodus of Mogadishu residents, many of whom had returned to their homes in previous months. There were already some 1.3m displaced people inside Somalia and 500,000 refugees across its borders, the majority concentrated in Dadaab, northeastern Kenya, where numbers continued to swell. The worsening conflict prompted a call by the AU for the UN Security Council to impose sanctions against Eritrea for channelling support to the extremists.

The strength of radical Islamist-nationalist influence increased fears about an extension of conflict to Somali-speaking regions of Ethiopia and Kenya. Ethiopia's concern about insurgency in its Ogaden region had been an important factor in its decision to invade Somalia at the end of 2006. While it managed to interdict an arms supply route through northern Somalia, the territory stretching from the southern port of Kismayo to the Ogaden border was now in al-Shabaab hands. A further cause for international concern lay in the influx of foreign recruits, from Muslim communities in East Africa and further afield, and the operation of training camps in al-Shabaab's area of control. Although this activity was small compared to Afghanistan under Taliban rule, it created a potential platform for the export of terrorism.

Persisting Intra-state Crises

While major hostilities have become rarer in Africa during this decade the continent has remained a hotbed for internal conflicts, some defying attempts at resolution, others re-emerging or spreading to new zones. International peacekeeping has had patchy success. By mid 2009 deployments in areas on the western border of Sudan and in the Democratic Republic of the Congo (DRC) accounted for more than half of all UN peacekeepers around the world. Together with the continuing chaos in Somalia, these enduring and complex crises posed a difficult challenge to the international community in setting priorities for engagement in the region, raising the risk that none would command sustained attention.

While these conflicts have multiple and varying origins, a common feature is the ease with which militia groups are able to mobilise and impose them-selves as political forces. In sub-Saharan countries these militias, typically starting as self-defence groups, are mostly formed along ethnic lines without well-defined ideological aims, attracting disaffected youth in communities where economic grievances tend to be viewed in ethnic terms. Weapons are readily obtainable throughout the continent. Sometimes roaming across national frontiers, armed groups are variously maintained by expatriate funding, covert support from neighbouring countries, collection of levies and control of economic activities in their areas of operation.

Efforts by regional and sub-regional bodies to promote greater stability were set back during the past year by a resurgence of *coups d'état*. The AU's firm stance against unconstitutional changes of government prompted it to suspend three of its 53 members (Mauritania, Guinea and Madagascar) between August 2008 and March 2009. Although one of the AU's main aims is to entrench the principles of democratic legitimacy, the organisation has been unable to prevent incumbent African leaders from manipulating constitutional rules to keep themselves in office. In February 2009, somewhat contradictorily, it chose Muammar Gadhafi, in his 40th year as Libya's unelected leader, to take over its rotating chairmanship. Following the earlier example of Uganda and Chad, Algeria became the latest African country to remove presidential term limits. The decision, taken by a show of hands in parliament without debate, cleared the way for President Abdelaziz Bouteflika's unsurprising re-election in April 2009. In neighbouring Niger, President Mamadou Tandja also tried to secure a further term by changing the rules through a referendum, even though the country's highest court judged his plan to be unconstitutional. While almost all of Africa has acquired the trappings of elected government, ruling factions in a number of countries have continued to undermine the independence of judiciaries, electoral authorities and other key institutions to protect their control. Lack of confidence in the integrity of public institutions has been an important factor aggravating tensions and perpetuating instability in much of the continent.

Sudan: closer to the brink

Prospects for the resolution of Sudan's complex regional differences became increasingly murky over the past year. The concentration of international concern on the devastated western region of Darfur distracted attention from the danger of wider breakdown. The four-year-old transitional power-sharing agreement, which brought an end to Sudan's long north–south war, was at risk of unravelling as the 2011 deadline loomed closer for the south's promised referendum on secession. Further conflicts were brewing in outlying regions, although no regional opposition appeared likely to have sufficient strength to overturn the balance of power in Khartoum.

In the absence of willingness by the US and other Western governments to intervene directly in Darfur, efforts to exert pressure on the Sudanese regime focused on action by the International Criminal Court (ICC). But the issuing of an arrest warrant for President Omar al-Bashir in March 2009, and the regime's reaction to it, complicated matters, aggravated the difficulties of humanitarian relief and possibly contributed to the postponement of scheduled elections. The move also showed up divisions between Western governments, which supported the action, and those opposing it, including leading countries in the region (such as Egypt), as well as China (the major investor in Sudanese oil) and other commercial partners in Asia. Despite shared concern about the consequences of Sudan's potential disintegration, the concerted diplomatic approach seen in the run-up to the north–south Comprehensive Peace Agreement (CPA) in 2005 was conspicuously lacking,

Bashir's indictment was the first such high-profile decision by the ICC, although war-crimes charges had previously been brought by ad hoc tribunals against sitting heads of state such as Yugoslavia's Slobodan Milosevic in 1999 and Liberia's Charles Taylor in 2003. Both had been sent for trial at The Hague after being forced from office. While Sudan's allies saw the move against Bashir as a threat to stability, there was little immediate prospect of the warrant being enforced.

The ICC panel of judges cited allegations of war crimes and crimes against humanity in the counter-insurgency campaign in Darfur, but omitted a charge of genocide originally sought by the chief prosecutor. The court overrode objections by the Arab League and the AU, which pleaded for a delay. African leaders argued that a formal indictment would damage chances of conciliation. Under the ICC treaty, an option remained for the UN Security Council to exercise leverage on the regime by requesting a 12-month deferral of proceedings in exchange for firm commitments on a peace process.

Fears that the arrest warrant would lead to a hardening of the Sudanese leadership's position were borne out when it responded by ordering 12 foreign aid organisations and a US development services company to end activities in northern Sudan, including Darfur, accusing them of feeding information to the ICC. Three local relief organisations were also dissolved. This drastic setback to humanitarian operations prompted a breakdown of peace talks (mediated by Qatar) between the government and the Justice and Equality Movement, now the strongest of Darfur's fragmented rebel groups. However, the government later agreed to let some of the aid organisations back to the region.

Latent conflicts threatened to erupt in other peripheral zones of northern Sudan. A crisis in the oil-producing area of Abyei, on the border with Southern Sudan, was successfully defused after heavy fighting in May 2008, with northern and southern military units replaced by a joint force. But the potential for hostilities remained high both there and in southern Kordofan, another of the disputed areas that were sticking points during the CPA negotiations and had been made subject to special arrangements. Among the victims of spreading unrest in this region were nine Chinese oil company employees kidnapped in October 2008, five of whom were killed.

The CPA established both a framework for sharing power and wealth and a precedent for other deals, such as those reached in 2006 for Darfur (where only one rebel faction signed up) and eastern Sudan, though it was unclear how far the CPA formula could help resolve other regional disputes. Implementation of the agreement has been patchy. About half the 4m people displaced from the south were reckoned to have returned by early 2008. New joint governing structures were put in place, troops redeployed and revenues split according to plan, although reduced oil prices and high security spending eroded the capacity for domestically funded development. Other parts of the plan were delayed, notably demarcation of the north–south border, which affects oil rights. More ambitious parts of the deal, including the highly sensitive issue of access to land, were still pending. Little progress had been made in such areas as press freedom.

> **The potential for hostilities remained high**

Under the agreement multiple elections should have taken place in 2009, for the presidency and parliament at both national level and in Southern Sudan, and for governorships and legislatures in all 25 states. But after delays in preparations they were rescheduled to February 2010. The National Congress Party, dominant partner in the power-sharing government in Khartoum, sought allies to ensure consolidation of control ahead of the referendum in Southern Sudan. The southern partner, the Sudan People's Liberation Movement (SPLM), was ambiguous about the issue of separation. Senior figures argued that the CPA, if properly implemented, could provide a basis for maintaining ties, and some feared the elections could weaken its position in the national government. At the same time, numerous reports suggested that the SPLM-led autonomous government in the south has been re-arming. These reports were reinforced when a Ukrainian-operated ship, the *Faina*, was seized by pirates off Somalia in September 2008 with a listed cargo of 33 Soviet-era T-72 tanks, together with grenade launchers, anti-aircraft guns, ammunition and spare parts, bound for the Kenyan port of Mombasa. Ukrainian and Kenyan officials insisted that the shipment, eventually landed in February 2009, was for Kenya, but the cargo manifest indicated that it was destined for Southern Sudan.

While the idea of separation generated little if any enthusiasm on the part of outside governments, the chances of making unity sufficiently attractive to sway southern voters in the 2011 referendum appeared remote. But politicians in Khartoum were reluctant to contemplate what would follow a secession vote. The south's independence would deprive the north of control over most oil production, but the south depends on the north's pipeline and port facilities. Renewed confrontation could not be ruled out.

International diplomatic efforts over the last two years were in large measure focused on mounting peacekeeping operations, with the UN now running three different missions in Sudan and across its western borders. Deployment of the largest of these, the joint UN–AU Mission in Darfur (UNAMID), was plagued by Sudanese government obstruction and a shortage of willing contributors of troops, armoured vehicles, reconnaissance aircraft and helicopters. In early 2009, a year after it was supposed to reach full strength, it had barely 15,000 of the planned 26,000 troops and police. Under criticism for inaction over Darfur, the outgoing Bush administration made a late gesture in January 2009 by pledging heavy air transport to airlift vehicles and equipment for UNAMID. But the peacekeepers had limited impact, as further attacks increased the number of people displaced by violence in the region to an estimated 2.7m. With senior members of the Obama team having previously advocated a more forceful role in Darfur, pressure was expected to increase for measures such as enforcement of a no-fly zone to protect relief efforts, potentially adding a new dimension to the conflict.

In March 2009 the EU handed over to the UN its mission in refugee areas of eastern Chad (bordering Darfur) and in the northeast of the Central African Republic. Regarded as a model for bridging operations deployed quickly ahead of full-scale peacekeeping, the year-long EUFOR mission was the largest yet carried out by the EU in Africa, with more than 3,000 troops, principally from France. Many were re-hatted as part of the UN Mission in the Central African Republic and Chad (MINURCAT), which was due to increase its strength to 5,000 by the end of 2009. Despite the role played by the force in protecting refugee camps, the situation in the region remained precarious. Chad's long-running internal power struggle risked flaring up again, and cross-border movements continued to be uncontrolled. The expulsion of aid organisations in Darfur appeared likely to increase the flow of refugees, increasing the capacity of Darfur rebels to recruit in camps on Chad's side of the border. Although Chad and Sudan repaired their broken relations in November 2008, rebel movements in both countries continued to draw on cross-frontier support.

Congo's lawless east

Wider problems of state authority and governance in the DRC were over-shadowed in the second half of 2008 and early 2009 by renewed fighting in the country's eastern provinces. More than six years after the end of a war that drew in soldiers from six other African nations, the DRC continued to suffer the effects of conflicts originating in bordering countries of the Great Lakes region. For a period in early 2009 it once again had combat troops from three neighbouring armies overtly engaged on its soil, acting jointly with its own DRC Armed Forces (FARDC). The circumstances of these operations testified to significant shortcomings, both in the building of effective unified national security forces and in the capacity of the United Nations Mission in the DRC (MONUC), the largest of all current UN peacekeeping missions, to carry out its mandated task of protecting civilians.

After previous unsuccessful attempts, the progress made in improving international cooperation in the region and disentangling some of the elements of conflict was not to be underestimated. But this took place only after a renewed escalation in fighting. The turmoil reflected the limited ability of President Joseph Kabila's government in Kinshasa to project its authority in the east, the failure of earlier plans for dismantling militia groups and the continued involvement of armed factions in exploiting mineral and forestry resources. A deal signed in January 2008 between the government and 22 armed groups in the provinces of North and South Kivu was meant to bring a full ceasefire and disarmament of non-state militias, but it came apart during the year.

The National Congress for the Defence of the People (CNDP), a well-organised force aligned with the region's Rwandan-origin Tutsi community and led by Laurent Nkunda, a renegade Congolese general, had signed up to the deal, which included demobilisation or integration of forces into the national army. But the peace plan did not bring in the DRC-based Democratic Liberation Forces of Rwanda (FDLR), made up of ethnic Hutus (including members of militias implicated in Rwanda's 1994 genocide who subsequently fled across the border). Nkunda refused to disarm while the FDLR was still active in the region. Fighting resumed in August between his forces and government troops, the FDLR and local pro-government militias. It reached a peak in October when the CNDP, better trained and equipped than the FARDC, took control of large areas of North Kivu. As FARDC troops fled, MONUC was forced into engaging directly, using attack helicopters to try to block the advance. The CNDP twice overran a major army camp, seized the headquarters of Virunga National Park on the borders of Uganda and Rwanda and was poised to capture Goma, North Kivu's provincial capital. Angry Goma residents, blaming MONUC for failing to defend them, stoned peacekeepers' bases. The number of people forced from their homes in the province rose to about 850,000, many of them displaced several times.

The loss of territory exposed poor discipline and morale in the FARDC and led to the replacement of its chief of staff. The fighting also highlighted MONUC's limited ability to protect civilian commu- nities outside a few urban areas. In November, the UN Security Council authorised an extra 3,000 troops in addition to the 17,000 already deployed across the

> The fighting highlighted MONUC's limited ability to protect civilians

DRC, a third in North Kivu. At the UN's request, the EU considered organ- ising an interim military force, following the example of its first African operation in the adjacent Ituri province in 2003. France, which headed that first mission, initially backed the proposal but changed its position. The UK and Germany were opposed, and Belgium, as the former colonial power, was reluctant to take the lead.

At the same time, however, the UN, US and EU kept up pressure on the DRC and Rwanda to revive attempts at a joint approach. A UN panel report in December produced damning evidence of Rwandan financial and military support, including equipment and personnel, for Nkunda's CNDP rebels. It also accused the DRC of collaborating with the FDLR. To extri- cate themselves from this mess, the foreign ministers of the two countries signed an agreement in December, essentially allowing Rwanda to go after the FDLR in exchange for dealing with Nkunda.

The solution with respect to Nkunda, who had inflamed matters by declaring national ambitions, came the following month after a split in the CNDP. Its second-in-command, Bosco Ntaganda, said Nkunda had been dismissed as leader, and went on to announce a ceasefire with the government. The split made Ntaganda, wanted by the ICC on charges of conscripting child soldiers, a key player in peace plans. His role effectively shielded him from any move by the DRC, which unlike Sudan was a party to the ICC, to arrest and surrender him for trial as in theory it was obliged to do.

Under the plan agreed with the DRC government, several thousand Rwandan troops crossed the border on 20 January to flush out the FDLR from its strongholds in a joint operation with the DRC, for which MONUC offered transport and medical support. Two days later Nkunda was arrested in western Rwanda.

Previously stalled talks in Nairobi under UN auspices with former Nigerian president Olusegun Obasanjo acting as chief mediator led to a fresh peace deal in Goma in March, under which the CNDP said it would transform itself into a political party and the government pledged an amnesty and the release of prisoners.

The Rwandan intervention against the FDLR followed the entry of Ugandan forces in mid December 2008 under a separate joint-operation agreement with the DRC which also involved the forces of self-governing Southern Sudan. This was aimed at rooting out the Lord's Resistance Army (LRA), a smaller but stubborn group of marauding rebels notorious for its brutality and the systematic abduction of children. Previously active in northern Uganda, using bases in Southern Sudan, the LRA began moving into the remote northeast corner of the DRC in 2005, basing itself in Garamba National Park. With a strength estimated at 500–700 active members, it had split into smaller groups, roaming as far as the southeast of the Central African Republic. The operation was prompted by LRA leader Joseph Kony's repeated failure to appear for the signature of a final peace agreement, which had been last scheduled in November.

Both operations provoked political controversy in light of Rwanda's two invasions of the DRC in the late 1990s and the role of Uganda in the northeast until its official withdrawal in 2003. Rwandan forces pulled back in February, after a month, and the Ugandans finally left in March, under pressure from the DRC government. While both Rwanda and Uganda claimed to have seriously weakened their opponents, the results were questionable. Congolese officers said about 150 FDLR were killed, of an estimated strength of 6,500.

Hundreds of FDLR fighters applied for repatriation to Rwanda. But immediately after the Rwandans withdrew the group moved back into former positions, carried out further attacks, forced more people from their homes and spread the zone of conflict further south into South Kivu. Uganda said at the end of its operation that it had destroyed most of the LRA's bases. But it failed to capture Kony, while LRA reprisals following the entry of Ugandan troops were blamed for the deaths of 900 civilians in the DRC and the Western Equatoria region of Southern Sudan. By the time MONUC dispatched troops to the area, tens of thousands had fled their villages. While peacekeeping reinforcements promised to provide some widening of protection, the crisis of security in the region was far from over.

Fresh upsets in West Africa

Mauritania's attempt to break away from its post-independence record of military and authoritarian rule was interrupted in August 2008 when top military officers who had just been sacked overthrew the elected government. The takeover was the culmination of a political crisis precipitated by a parliamentary vote of no confidence. It took place three years almost to the day after Mauritania's previous coup, which had paved the way for a democratic transition and the country's first genuinely open presidential election. President Sidi Ould Cheikh Abdallahi, in power for barely a year, was placed under house arrest, as were the prime minister and interior minister. Amid widespread international condemnation, the AU suspended Mauritania and imposed sanctions against the coup leaders. General Mohamed Ould Abdel Aziz, who had been dismissed as commander of the presidential guard, took over as head of a high state council composed of military officers. Under strong pressure to return the country to civilian rule, he stood down in April 2009 to run for election as president.

The coup created a dilemma for Washington, which cut off all non-humanitarian aid, including military and counter-terrorism assistance aimed at combating armed extremists in the region. The Algerian-based group al-Qaeda in the Islamic Maghreb (AQIM) responded to the coup by declaring a holy war in Mauritania and the following month ambushed an army patrol in the north of the country, near the border with Moroccan-controlled Western Sahara. The decapitated bodies of 11 soldiers and a civilian guide were dumped in the desert. AQIM activity also heightened insecurity in Niger and Mali. A British hostage, one of four European tourists abducted in January 2009 near the border between the two countries, was reported in June to have been killed by the group, which demanded the release from detention in the UK of radical Islamic cleric Abu Qatada. A resurgence of

Tuareg rebellions in northern Niger and Mali was met by government offensives, but separate mediation by Algeria and Libya achieved some progress towards peace in early 2009.

A second military takeover in 2008 came in Guinea in December, hours after the death of President Lansana Conté, who had been in power for almost 25 years. The army intervention was neither very surprising nor, for many Guineans, unwelcome. Although the country was comparatively tranquil during the violence that engulfed its neighbours Liberia, Sierra Leone and Côte d'Ivoire in the 1990s and early 2000s, the final period of Conté's army-based rule was marked by simmering unrest. Tension remained high following a 2007 popular uprising in Conakry, the capital, when more than 150 were killed, and legislative elections were repeatedly put off. The coup, like Mauritania's, took place without bloodshed. Led by Captain Moussa Dadis Camara, an obscure logistics officer, it carried support from the army's middle ranks. The takeover caused Guinea to be suspended from the AU and the regional Economic Community of West African States (ECOWAS), and was condemned by the EU and US, which pared down its aid. Senegal's President Abdoulaye Wade, however, urged recognition of the new leadership.

> "The coup raised concerns about spreading regional instability"

A new government of military officers and non-party technocrats was named, with a banker, Kabiné Komara, as prime minister. Top commanders in the army, which had provided the foundation of Conté's authority, were forced to retire and a wave of arrests took place related to corruption allegations, including several former mining ministers.

Elections were first promised for the end of 2010 but the date was brought forward to December 2009. The government faced a hard task meeting popular demands for reform, with less aid coming in and a fall in prices for bauxite, the country's dominant export.

The coup raised concerns about spreading regional instability, with several neighbouring countries struggling to overcome the legacy of conflicts. France started reducing its military presence in Côte d'Ivoire, arguing that the security situation had improved, but there were further delays to presidential elections, which should have been held in 2005. In Liberia, the UN began a drawdown of its peacekeeping force in the second half of 2008, but discontent among large numbers of former civil-war combatants continued to be a cause for concern.

Guinea-Bissau, on Guinea's opposite border, was the scene of a double assassination in March 2009, ending a long feud between President João Bernardo 'Nino' Vieira and Armed Forces Chief of Staff Lieutenant-General Batista Tagmé Na Waié. The military chief, who had taken over the post when mutinous soldiers murdered his predecessor, was killed by a bomb detonated under a staircase at military headquarters. Less than 12 hours later, a group of soldiers attacked the president's house and shot and hacked him to death. After initial confusion, a semblance of normality returned with the installation of a caretaker head of state and the scheduling of a presidential election. But tension rose sharply again in June with the fatal shootings of two of Vieira's close allies, one a candidate in the election and the other a former defence minister, who were both accused of involvement in an alleged coup plot. The impoverished forrmer Portuguese territory remained vulnerable to ethnically based rivalries and military interference in its political life. The events were symptomatic of chronic weaknesses, made worse by high-level corruption and involvement in international drug traffic between South America and Europe.

In Ghana, peaceful legislative and presidential contests in December 2008 brought the country's second change of government through elections. Opposition candidate John Atta Mills, standing for the third time, won a narrow run-off vote against former Foreign Minister Nana Kufo-Addo. However, with the National Democratic Congress back in power, Ghana faced a difficult test in how it would manage revenues from offshore oil, expected to start flowing in 2010 or 2011 following one of the region's biggest recent offshore discoveries.

Oil-related troubles persisted during the year in Nigeria, West Africa's regional giant. While the country suffered violent outbreaks elsewhere, notably in the central city of Jos where several hundred people died in riots between Christians and Muslims after November 2008 local elections, security worries related mainly to the Niger Delta and nearby waters, which continued to be the scene of bombings, kidnappings and sabotage. While Nigerian production setbacks made less impact on the world oil market because of the decline in demand, their effect on domestic revenues was all the greater at a time of lower prices. A combination of reduced OPEC quotas and production shut-ins, partly caused by well-organised militant attacks and criminal activity, saw Nigeria overtaken by Angola as Africa's largest oil producer. In early 2009, President Umaru Yar'Adua said daily output was down to 1.6m barrels, well below the 2008 average of 2m, which was already one-third less than Nigeria's capacity.

While the government tried to pursue dialogue to pacify the oil producing region, it also stepped up its military campaign against the Movement for
the Emancipation of the Niger Delta (MEND), the main group fighting over
the use of oil resources. The group announced a ceasefire in late September
2008 but revoked it four months later, and in May 2009 government forces
launched a major operation using gunboats, helicopters and ground troops
to destroy militant encampments. Attacks against an increasingly wide
range of targets by insurgent and criminal groups posed a growing threat to
shipping and oil installations throughout the region.

Kenya's flawed peace

The aftershock of Kenya's post-election crisis in early 2008 continued to be
felt well after the violence had subsided. The country's image as a vibrant
and promising democracy and regional leader was badly dented. Many of
the several hundred thousand people displaced by the upheaval, which left
more than 1,200 dead in two months, were still waiting to be resettled a
year later. Relatively strong growth in East Africa's largest and most diversified economy was severely reduced in 2008 by the impact of the violence on
agriculture and tourism, and prospects for recovery in 2009 were dashed,
first by a drought which caused serious food shortages, and secondly by the
worldwide downturn.

The coalition formed as a way out of the political crisis made little
progress by mid 2009 towards building trust in the country's public institutions. There were delays in establishing an interim replacement for the
discredited electoral authority and resistance to thoroughgoing reform of the
tainted judicial system. In a country where party loyalties are largely determined by ethnicity, political leaders rarely showed any sign of rising above
narrow group interests. Western donors became increasingly impatient with
the slow pace of change and dismayed by the comeback of political crony-
ism and high-level corruption.

The compromise agreement to resolve the disputed outcome of the
December 2007 presidential election, reached after a lengthy mediation
process headed by Kofi Annan, the former UN secretary-general, put in
place an unwieldy double government comprising more than 90 ministers
and assistant ministers from the contending sides. President Mwai Kibaki,
retaining his post for a second term, was clearly intent on completing a full
five-year mandate, but the coalition appeared no more secure than previous governing partnerships. It soon became clear that his election opponent

Raila Odinga, in the ill-defined post of prime minister, had the worse side of the bargain. Bitter rivalries persisted in the coalition, especially over official appointments. Cracks also started to appear within Odinga's Orange Democratic Movement, which emerged from the 2007 contest with by far the greatest number of parliamentary seats, as possible new alliances began taking shape for the next elections due in 2012.

Work on a new constitution, which would provide the framework for other reforms, was again delayed. During Kibaki's first term, constitutional-reform plans had run aground, mainly over the extent of presidential powers. Under the new coalition, a fresh draft was promised within a year, but the deadline was deferred to March 2010. If the process were delayed any further, constitutional issues would risk becoming entangled with political tussles in the run-up to elections.

The government did go ahead with a series of steps resulting from the mediation talks. Legislation was passed to formalise the power-sharing arrangement. Separate independent inquiries were set up on the conduct of the elections and the violence, and produced their reports in September and October. Towards the end of 2008, laws were enacted setting up a truth, justice and reconciliation commission and criminalising tribal discrimination. But questions remained about the commitment of government leaders to implementing some of the recommendations, especially prosecution of those accused of inciting, financing and organising the inter-ethnic attacks. Similar inquiries had been held after previous violence surrounding elections in 1992 and 1997, but nobody was punished. The 2008 inquiry, known as the Waki Commission, called for the establishment of a special tribunal with Kenyan and foreign judges, failing which a list of suspects would be passed to the ICC. Both Kibaki and Odinga supported the local option, but opponents argued that Kenyan trials would be vulnerable to political manipulation and pressure on witnesses. A constitutional amendment, a preliminary step towards setting up a special court, was blocked by parliament in February 2009. The United States, the leading bilateral donor, continued to press for a Kenyan tribunal.

A further inquiry by UN special rapporteur Philip Alston into extra-judicial killings condemned a lack of police accountability. This applied not only to post-election clashes but also to the alleged use of police death squads and accusations of abuses during a police and army campaign in March and August 2008 against a militia group, the Saboat Land Defence Force, in western Kenya. Official hackles were raised when he called for the sacking of the police commissioner and the resignation of the attorney-general.

While the events of 2008 were not without precedent, the violence was much more intense and more widely spread than on previous occasions, involving both urban and rural communities. It showed the ease with which sentiment among different ethnic groups could be drummed up for political ends, and revealed a high state of preparedness. By mid 2009 this preparedness had increased, and grievances were likely to be magnified in a struggling economy. As the Waki Commission report warned, 'ethnic fears and hatred have been elevated in importance and could turn violent again even more easily than has happened in the past'.

Madagascar's populist revolt

Weeks of turmoil in Antananarivo, Madagascar's capital, in early 2009 brought the country close to civil war and left more than 130 dead. Initial efforts by the UN and AU to mediate in the power struggle were fruitless. After alienating much of the army, President Marc Ravalomanana was toppled, two years into his second term, by his rival Andry Rajoelina. Prospects for economic development, on an island that since the 1970s had been among Africa's poorest countries, were once more thrown into doubt.

The events echoed the manner in which Ravalomanana himself came to power seven years earlier, when he declared himself the winner of a disputed presidential election, using his position as the capital's mayor to rally support. That standoff lasted for six months, ending with the forced exile of the incumbent Didier Ratsiraka. In the following years Madagascar underwent a sharp economic recovery. The World Bank saw hopeful signs that it was breaking away from its history of mismanagement and periodic crises. The president, however, faced accusations of accumulating power for himself and mixing business and political interests.

Rajoelina, an events organiser and broadcasting entrepreneur, entered national politics by becoming mayor. The confrontation began in December 2008, when his television station was closed down after showing an interview with Ratsiraka. Rajoelina became a catalyst for protests against rising food prices, alleged misspending and government land policies. These turned violent in late January with attacks on the premises of state television, a private channel linked to Ravalomanana and his family's supermarket business. In early February, the government removed Rajoelina from his post. A few days later, presidential guards fired on demonstrators, killing about 30 and prompting the defence minister to resign. Talks between the two sides failed. Soldiers began to mutiny, and the army chief of staff and new defence minister were both ousted. Rajoelina, after briefly sheltering in the French Embassy, demanded Ravalomanana's departure. On 16 March, while the president stayed in his official residence outside town, a group of soldiers seized the presidential palace. In a radio address the next day, Ravalomanana announced he was handing over to a *directoire* of senior military officers, but the officers refused and said they were handing over instead to the 34-year-old Rajoelina.

Although Madagascar's constitutional court 'validated' the transfer of power, the country was suspended by both the AU and SADC. Norway and the United States halted most aid. France, the biggest bilateral donor, which had poor relations with Ravalomanana, followed the EU in condemning the takeover as a *coup d'état*, but maintained its assistance programme. While Ravalomanana took refuge in Swaziland, a series of counter-protests by his supporters suggested that trouble was not over. Rajoelina, heading a High Transitional Authority, responded to international pressure by bringing forward his initial two-year deadline for elections, but the timing was uncertain.

For the AU, which had been planning its mid-year summit in Madagascar, the crisis demonstrated the limited traction it could exert in its efforts to defend constitutional order and a more settled environment for African development. Madagascar presented an all-too-familiar story of poor governance and endemic instability fuelled by poverty, gross inequality and scarce job opportunities. This trend was unfortunately likely to get worse as the full impact of the global economic contraction was felt on the continent. The downturn, which hit Africa later than developed regions, threatened to undo some of the advances of the previous few years. In a deteriorating social climate, the processes of economic reform and liberalisation that accompanied recent growth in many African countries were now in question, and there was a clear risk of a resurgence of authoritarianism.

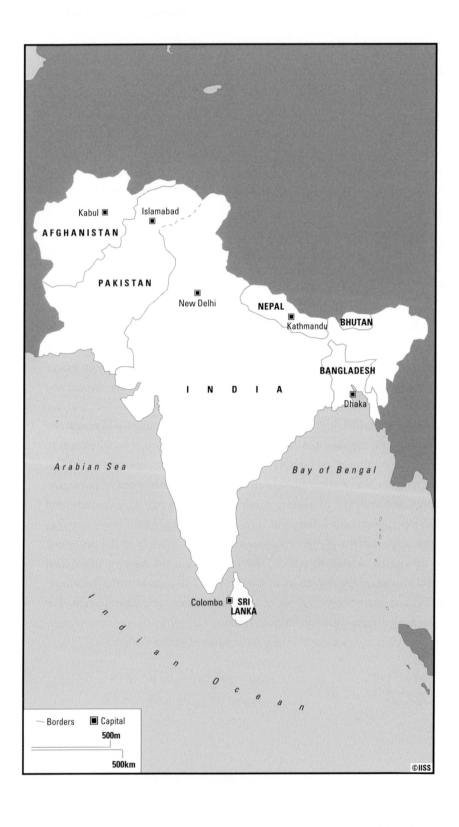

AFGHANISTAN

Kabul ■

Islamabad ■

PAKISTAN

New Delhi ■

NEPAL

Kathmandu ■

BHUTAN

BANGLADESH

I N D I A

Dhaka ■

Arabian Sea

Bay of Bengal

Colombo ■ SRI LANKA

Indian Ocean

— Borders   ■ Capital
500m
500km

©IISS

Chapter 9

South Asia and Afghanistan

The year to mid 2009 saw a number of important developments in South Asia, and was especially marked by political turmoil and escalating violence in Pakistan. A 26-year-long civil war ended in Sri Lanka and democracy resumed in Bangladesh, but threats to the region were underlined by a terrorist attack on the Indian city of Mumbai, and by the bitter conflict in Afghanistan, which was no nearer to resolution.

For several years, international forces' efforts to battle Taliban insurgents in Afghanistan have been hampered by the flow of fighters across the border from Pakistan. The incoming Obama administration in Washington, taking the view that the problems of the two countries were closely linked, conceived a new policy under which both military and civilian efforts were stepped up in Afghanistan – with 21,000 more US troops – and more aid was to be pumped into Pakistan. However, the prospects of achieving success (however defined) in Afghanistan remained in considerable doubt, and developments in Pakistan were causing mounting international concern. The United States stepped up attacks on militants by missile-armed unmanned aerial vehicles in the mountainous tribal areas of Pakistan, where Osama bin Laden and other leaders of the al-Qaeda terrorist group were believed to be hiding, eight years after the 11 September 2001 terrorist attacks.

The prospects for Pakistan were worrisome, and not improved by the shakiness of its government. Following the ousting of Pervez Musharraf as president, his successor, Asif Ali Zardari, lost popularity due to economic problems and weak leadership. The spread of militant Islamist violence across the country posed a growing threat to the nation. After extremists gained ground when they were allowed to impose sharia law in parts of North-West Frontier Province, they were driven back by a major military offensive. The threat of terrorism originating in Pakistan was highlighted when a ten-man group, which had come to India by sea from Pakistan and was linked to the Lashkar-e-Tayiba terrorist group, killed at least 166 people in a 60-hour rampage through Mumbai.

A difficult period of reconciliation lay ahead in Sri Lanka after the army completed a concentrated offensive by capturing all the areas long controlled by Tamil Tiger rebels and killing their leader Velupillai Prabhakaran. In Bangladesh, two years of military-backed rule ended with the holding of general elections in which Sheikh Hasina's Grand Alliance won a landslide victory. Nepal's difficulties in implementing the peace process that had ended a ten-year Maoist insurgency were underlined by political arguments that resulted in the replacement of one coalition government with another.

In India, the Congress party-led coalition was re-elected in May with a clear victory, confounding expectations of a hung parliament. Prime Minister Manmohan Singh had previously faced down leftist opposition and pushed through a landmark civil nuclear agreement with the United States. For the first time since the mid 1970s, India was permitted to acquire fuel supplies and equipment for its civilian nuclear reactors to counter growing energy shortages, in return for placing them under international safeguards. Amid global recession, India continued to be seen as a beacon of economic light, as it was forecast to show healthy – albeit reduced – growth in 2009.

Pakistan: Political Fragility

Pakistan's chronic political turmoil was not ended by the election in February 2008 of a coalition government headed by the Pakistan People's Party (PPP), which had been led by Benazir Bhutto until her assassination in December 2007. Against the background of continual political wrangling amongst the establishment, a series of terrorist attacks made the growing threat from radical Islamist groups ever more apparent, and the armed forces were eventually moved to launch offensives to regain large areas of territory which had been lost to government control.

The first challenge for the new government was to oust Pervez Musharraf, who remained as president although he had given up leadership of the army and allowed democratic elections. On 18 August 2008, facing the threat of impeachment by parliament, he resigned the presidency. The ruling coalition, comprised of parties which had long bitterly opposed one another, only lasted another week after this victory: the Pakistan Muslim League-Nawaz (PML-N), led by former Prime Minister Nawaz Sharif, withdrew because judges ousted by Musharraf had not been reinstated. The PPP, however, still retained a simple majority (193 of 342 national assembly seats) with the support of smaller parties and independents. The way was clear for Bhutto's widower Asif Ali Zardari, who had assumed the PPP leadership, to secure the presidency with 482 votes of the 702-member electoral college of federal and provincial legislators. On 9 September he was sworn in, completing the country's turbulent transition to democracy after nine years of military rule.

Zardari's government, however, remained shaky. His popularity declined due to growing economic problems and weak leadership, and he faced opposition from Sharif as well as from a movement of lawyers who backed the ousted judges. An attempt to use the judiciary to remove Sharif and his brother Shahbaz Sharif, chief minister of Punjab province, back-fired. A 25 February Supreme Court ruling disqualifying both brothers from holding elected office or running for election in view of past convictions led to nationwide protests. These were exacerbated by the imposition of central rule in Punjab and the dismissal of Shahbaz Sharif as chief minister. But on 30 March the Supreme Court imposed a stay order on the disqualification notice of Shahbaz Sharif and restored him as chief minister, and on 26 May reversed its earlier decision and declared that both brothers were eligible to contest elections and hold public office.

The lawyers' movement, which had played a large role in sparking public opposition to Musharraf after he suspended Chief Justice Iftikhar Muhammad Chaudhry in 2007, was dissatisfied that only a few of the over 60 judges sacked by Musharraf were reinstated. In early March the govern-ment began arresting lawyers and opposition leaders, and violent street protests took place starting with a lawyers' 'long march' to Islamabad in March 2009. On 14 March both Nawaz Sharif and Chaudhry Aitzaz Ahsan, former president of the Supreme Court Bar Association, defied house arrest to lead a march demanding the reinstatement of the chief justice. Bowing to pressure from the army, which was alarmed at the growing public unrest, Prime Minister Yousaf Raza Gilani announced on 16 March that all deposed judges would be reinstated. On 22 March Chaudhry duly resumed his posi-tion as chief justice.

Financial and economic frailty posed a further challenge. Already weak-ened by high fuel and food prices, the economy suffered severely from the

2008 financial crisis and was forced to accept a $7.6bn bailout package from the International Monetary Fund, under which it pledged to reduce its fiscal deficit. At a donors' conference in Japan co-hosted by the World Bank in April 2009, international donors pledged $5bn to help stabilise Pakistan.

Long-running political wrangles within the Pakistani establishment seemed likely to continue as the PPP and the PML-N differed over changes to the seventeenth amendment to the constitution, which provides for an executive president and a titular prime minister. Zardari showed no sign of giving up executive power by voting to repeal the amendment, even though the parties had promised in a joint charter in 2006 to rectify the imbalance between the powers of the president and prime minister. General Ashfaq Kayani, who succeeded Musharraf as army chief in November 2007, continued to play a powerful but discreet role. While reducing the army's role in civilian affairs, he strengthened his own position by shuffling top army officers and appointing Lieutenant-General Ahmed Shuja Pasha, a former director general of military operations, as director general of the Inter-Services Intelligence (ISI) agency. He scotched an attempt by the Zardari government to transfer administrative control of the ISI and the civilian Intelligence Bureau to the Interior Ministry, headed by Rehman Malik, a former chief of the civilian federal investigation agency.

Growing militancy and terrorism

Against this background of chronic political and economic fragility, the spread of Islamist militancy and terrorism from the Federally Administered Tribal Areas (FATA) bordering Afghanistan to the adjoining areas of the North-West Frontier Province (NWFP) posed a grave and growing challenge. On the one hand, there was mounting concern in Washington over the rise of attacks in Afghanistan by the Afghan Taliban, attributed largely to their use of Pakistan's tribal areas as a sanctuary from which to launch incursions. On the other, the Tehrik-e-Taliban Pakistan (TTP or Pakistan Taliban) held growing sway and posed a series threat to Pakistan's own national security.

The incoming administration of US President Barack Obama took the view that the problems of Afghanistan and Pakistan needed to be addressed by a single strategy. Richard Holbrooke, an experienced US official with a reputation for toughness stemming from the Bosnian peace process, was named as special representative for Afghanistan and Pakistan as soon as Obama was inaugurated. In March a new 'Afghanistan–Pakistan' policy was unveiled, emphasising the need for a comprehensive regional approach to target the al-Qaeda and Taliban leadership along the Afghanistan–Pakistan border, including better coordination with Pakistan. As well as sending more troops to Afghanistan, the United States stepped up its logistical and training support to Pakistani security forces, while tripling non-military aid to Pakistan to $1.5bn annually until 2014.

Although Pakistan had deployed 120,000 army and Frontier Corps troops to the border regions, they had been unable or unwilling to effectively counter Afghan and Pakistan Taliban militants. Bilateral relations sank to a new low in mid 2008 as Afghan President Hamid Karzai threatened to send troops across the border to fight the Afghan Taliban. President George W. Bush reportedly authorised covert cross-border attacks targeting al-Qaeda operatives in the tribal areas. On 3 September 2008, an American ground attack on a village near Angoor Adda in South Waziristan, near the Afghan border, caused public outrage in Pakistan. No further such incursions were reported, but there was a sharp increase, which continued into 2009, in the number of strikes by missiles fired from unmanned aerial vehicles against suspected militant targets in Pakistan.

In August 2008, Pakistani security forces began a major operation against al-Qaeda and TTP militants in the Bajaur Agency in FATA – a campaign that was continuing at mid 2009. Some 230,000 people were displaced from their homes. Government-backed tribal *lashkars* (militias) also began to mount offensives against the Pakistan Taliban, but suffered a major setback with a bomb attack on an anti-Taliban *jirga* (council) in the Khadezai area of Upper Orakzai Agency in October, which killed 85 people.

Following the launch of this operation, the Pakistan Taliban escalated its campaign of terrorist violence across Pakistan. The TTP was led by Baitullah Mehsud, who was responsible for a large number of terrorist attacks, including Bhutto's assassination. A Taliban fighter against the Soviets in Afghanistan, he rose to prominence in 2006 as a ruthless and much-feared militant Pashtun leader in South Waziristan. In 2008 he formed the TTP, believed to be a loose coalition of militant leaders from FATA. The group was responsible for a marked rise in suicide bombings and attacks on security forces. On 20 September, a truck bomb destroyed the landmark Marriott Hotel in Islamabad, popular with foreigners and the Pakistani elite, killing 54 people including the Czech ambassador. On 3 March gunmen attacked the Sri Lankan cricket team's bus in Lahore, killing six policemen and a driver. On 9 June, 18 people were killed in an attack on the Pearl Continental Hotel in Peshawar.

The deadliest attack against the Pakistani defence establishment took place on 21 August 2008, when two suicide blasts killed 70 people at the gates of the country's main ordnance factory in Wah, 45km from Islamabad. This led to an official ban on the TTP, which claimed responsibility. An eight-hour attack on a police-training centre in the Lahore suburb of Manawan on 30 March 2009 killed 12 people. On 4 April, a suicide attack killed eight paramilitary troops in Islamabad, and on 27 May 30 people were killed in a bomb blast outside the building of the emergency police service, near that of the ISI in Lahore. Terror attacks continued in the tribal areas and NWFP. On 6 September 2008 a suicide car bomb killed 30 at a police checkpoint in Peshawar, and on 5 June 2009 an explosion killed 40 people in a mosque in NWFP. Several sectarian attacks also took place, including a suicide attack on a Shia mosque in Dera Ghazi Khan, Punjab, which killed 24 people. A fortnight later at least 30 were killed in a suicide bomb blast at a Shia procession mourning the murder of Shia leader Sher Zeman in Dera Ismail Khan, NWFP.

Meanwhile, the growing influence of the TTP in the Swat Valley of the NWFP, until recently a popular tourist destination, caused serious concern. Even as the TTP prosecuted its campaign of suicide attacks across the country, it was terrorising the local population of Swat by burning schools, closing down music and video stores and other businesses it felt were 'un-Islamic', and damaging public buildings. A video of a teenage girl being flogged by extremists in Swat was broadcast nationally in early April, sparking widespread condemnation. In an attempt to curtail TTP excesses, the beleaguered NWFP administration signed an agreement on 16 February with Sufi Mohammed, a pro-Taliban leader of the outlawed Tehrik-e-Nifaz-e-Shariat-e-Mohammadi (TNSM) militant group, whose son-in-law Maulana Fazlullah was linked to the TTP. This allowed the imposition of sharia law in the Swat valley and the Malakand division, which comprises a third of the NWFP, in return for an end to the Taliban insurgency in the area. On 24 February the TTP agreed to a ceasefire.

Although this agreement raised international concern that the Malakand division would become another safe haven for the Afghan Taliban and al-Qaeda, the NWFP government, backed by Zardari, was determined to implement it. On 13 April Zardari signed the Nizam-e-Adl Regulation 2009 implementing sharia law in Malakand division. But in a blatant violation of the deal the Taliban militants refused on 15 April to disarm. On 22 April, they took control of parts of Buner, adjacent to Swat, only some 100km northwest of Islamabad.

This finally led to a change of policy. On 28 April Pakistani troops began a major military offensive against the TTP in the Malakand division, beginning with Lower Dir district and then Buner and Swat. Combat aircraft were used in NWFP for the first time, along with helicopter gunships and artillery. Fierce fighting took place in May and June. Some two million people were forced to flee their homes. The military claimed successes and in mid June 2009 the defence minister announced that the offensive was nearly over. The army said it was shifting the focus of its offensive to the South Waziristan region of the FATA and targeting Mehsud, in what was expected to be a far more difficult and protracted operation.

Meanwhile, the government continued to face an insurgency in the southwestern province of Baluchistan. The three major armed Baluchi groups announced on 4 January 2009 the end of a unilateral ceasefire which had been declared in September 2008. On 2 February an American national heading the UN refugee agency's office in Baluchistan, John Solecki, was kidnapped by a previously unknown group, the Baluch Liberation United Front, and held hostage for two months before being released, reportedly in exchange for Baluchi nationalists held by the security services. Following Zardari's refusal to grant a general amnesty to Baluchi nationalists, they rejected the government's 'reconciliation policy'. The discovery in April of the bodies of three Baluchi nationalist leaders in Turbat district, who had reportedly been seized by the intelligence services, sparked protests in which 20 people were killed.

The serious challenges that nuclear-armed Pakistan faced, including the spread of violent Islamist militancy, had broader strategic implications. However, the cohesion of its large army remained a powerful stabilising factor. International worries over nuclear weapons falling into the hands of the Taliban, or of Pakistan becoming a failed state, appeared premature.

Afghanistan: Insurgency Grows

The eight-year-old conflict in Afghanistan saw no real sign of sustainable progress in any area of the international stabilisation effort. The writ of the central government remained weak as President Hamid Karzai approached the end of his first term in office. International leaders expressed concern over the lack of progress at a conference convened by the United Nations at

The Hague on 31 March 2009, but showed solidarity for continued support to Afghanistan.

According to data from official and non-governmental sources, violence increased in most provinces in the south and east. It also spread to the west, and there was a rise in insurgent activity in some northern provinces. The UN reported 857 violent incidents a month in the second half of 2008 compared to 625 incidents a month in the first half of that year. A mild winter allowed higher than normal insurgent activity and movement through the winter months. The upsurge in activity most likely reflected a Taliban objective of disrupting the 2009 presidential election so as further to damage the credibility of the government and its international allies.

The elections were scheduled for 20 August 2009. In the absence of a united opposition it was widely thought that Karzai would win another term, an expectation strengthened when the Afghan Supreme Court ruled that, although constitutionally he should have stood down on 21 May to allow a fair campaign, he could stay in office given the unstable conditions in the country. The extension of his tenure drew accusations that it gave him an unfair advantage and he would be able to dominate the media and use development and aid projects to garner votes.

Widespread fears amongst officials and the international community that voter turnout would be low diminished with the announcement in March 2009 that 15.6 million Afghans (38% of them women) had registered to vote. The remaining challenge for a successful ballot was that threats to security would prevent voters reaching the polling stations. A programme under the aegis of the UN Assistance Mission in Afghanistan (UNAMA) was instituted to train up to 35,000 police officers for election security duties.

The candidate and party list showed that politics in Afghanistan remained ethnically and religiously polarised, with few signs of a party-political system emerging. The leaders of the former Northern Alliance, who had made up the United National Front political grouping, split and registered their candidacies separately, ending the only meaningful attempt to form a coalition of candidates of different ethnicities. Of the 41 registered presidential candidates, former Minister of Foreign Affairs Abdullah Abdullah, former Finance Minister Ashraf Ghani and former US Ambassador to Kabul Zalmay Khalilzad were considered to have the best chance of beating Karzai. The governor of Nangahar province, Gul Agha Sherzai, withdrew his candidacy at the request of the president. The debate surrounding the elections also dwelt on the creation of an executive vice-presidential post to bolster the president's authority. Khalilzad's name was most associated with this appointment, raising the prospect of greater US influence and control.

The continued insurgency

The Taliban-led insurgency heated up, and there was evidence of greater involvement by foreign fighters. Insurgents also adopted new tactics and technological approaches. One attack in Kabul on 11 February 2009 showed the continued ability of armed insurgents to move with relative freedom and to mount coordinated attacks in the capital. Suicide bombers and gunmen attacked the Ministries of Justice and Education and the Department of Prisons in a direct challenge to the authorities. Meanwhile, at the provincial and regional level the target of choice was the Afghan National Police (ANP), which remained vulnerable and poorly trained and equipped.

As well as continued high use of improvised explosive devices, including suicide attacks, there was increasing use by the Taliban and other insurgent groups of indirect-fire weapons, particularly mortars. Concerns among Afghan and international forces were raised when it was reported that the Taliban might have obtained the SA-14 surface-to-air missile system through Iran. System components were allegedly found by US troops in western Afghanistan. In a separate incident Coalition forces found and destroyed Russian-made ZPU-1 anti-aircraft guns in Helmand province.

The increasing activities of an al-Qaeda affiliate, Lashkar al-Zil ('Shadow Army'), highlighted the possibility of greater links between jihadist groups active in the insurgency in Pakistan and insurgent groups operating in Afghanistan. Lashkar al-Zil was widely believed to have carried out attacks in most provinces in the east and south of Afghanistan during the year, as well as to have taken part in insurgent operations in the Swat Valley in Pakistan.

Attempts to cut down on funding for the insurgency continued to focus on income from the trade in illegal drugs. According to the UN Office on Drugs and Crime (UNODC), the cultivation of opium poppy in Afghanistan decreased by 19% in 2008 and 18 provinces were poppy free, compared with 13 in the previous year. Despite this trend, in May 2009 the chairman of the US Joint Chiefs of Staff, Admiral Michael Mullen, said the international community was losing the battle against the production of illicit drugs in Afghanistan. According to UNODC, the reduction in cultivation did not translate into a commensurate reduction in yield. There was general recognition that focusing on the destruction of the poppy crop was the wrong strategy and greater emphasis had to be put on dealing with other parts of the trade. Mullen specifically mentioned the need to deal with drug lords controlling smuggling routes and networks. His remarks were supported by others, including a World Bank official who argued that the current strategy only harmed impoverished farmers and emphasised the need to deal with the traffickers and corrupt officials who helped them. Antonio Maria Costa, head of UNODC, went further, saying that eradication efforts in Afghanistan were 'incompetent and inefficient' and efforts to control the movement of drugs across borders should be increased. Costa emphasised the need to attack the business model of the traffickers to create disruption in the market and a surplus in the country that would cause the price to fall and make cultivation of poppy less lucrative for farmers.

> "Destruction of the poppy crop was the wrong strategy"

There was general recognition of a need to find alternatives to the poppy crop and to target traffickers and heroin factories. As one response to the change in strategy, the NATO International Security Assistance Force (ISAF) adopted a new mission in October 2008 to disrupt the facilities and facilitators of the drugs trade. The control of borders to combat traffickers was complicated by the scale of the problem, the diversity of routes and methods of transportation, and the armed capability of traffickers, which in some cases was greater than that of border forces. Iran started to build fortified positions on its border with Afghanistan in recognition of the scale of the problem and it was proposed that joint Iranian–Afghan border patrols should be instituted to curb the main flow of heroin from Afghanistan.

The security of Afghanistan's borders remained a priority, both to interdict illicit cross-border trade and, in the case of the 1,900km eastern border with Pakistan, to cut down on the movement of insurgents from the North-West Frontier Province (NWFP) and Federally Administered Tribal Areas (FATA). *Operation Lionheart* began in autumn 2008 as a coordinated US–Pakistani effort to cut off insurgent escape routes from Bajaur and Mohmand districts in Pakistan into Kunar province in Afghanistan. There was also a drive to boost the numbers of the Afghan National Border Police (ANBP) from 12,000 to its established strength of about 18,000.

A new US strategy

The US reaction to the growing insurgency was a new strategy aimed, in the first instance, at ensuring the elections could take place, and secondly that tactical progress could be sustained. The counter-insurgency campaign continued to be dogged by an inability to hold captured territory due to insufficient troop numbers. Following his inauguration as US president, Barack Obama announced on 22 January 2009 that his administration was re-focusing attention and resources on Afghanistan and Pakistan. This was followed by an announcement of a 'surge' of 17,000 troops to be deployed to the south and east of Afghanistan with an additional 4,000 troops dedicated to the training of the Afghan National Army (ANA). By the end of 2009 the US aimed to have increased its troop strength in Afghanistan to around 64,000. Apart from the considerable increase in numbers of US troops other NATO member states also committed extra military resources and assistance to Afghanistan, but with limitations. At NATO's 60th anniversary summit in April 2009 European member states pledged to deploy some 5,000 more troops: 3,000 designated only for security during the elections, nearly 2,000 for training the ANA, and 400 for police training. The extra deployments and increase in operational tempo coincided with an increase in casualties. In the first half of 2009 65 US soldiers were killed, compared with 36 in the first half of 2008. UK fatalities rose from 20 in the first half of 2008 to 32 in the first half of 2009. Boosting the capability and strength of the ANA and accelerating its training so that Afghanistan could take charge of its own security was seen as critical. The ANA was to be developed from a strength of about 80,000 to 134,000 troops by 2011. But in line with the drive to build up the strength of the ANP and ANBP, Obama called for that number to be doubled to about 260,000.

Efforts to improve the capacity of the ANP and build its strength to around 80,000 by 2011 remained uncoordinated and were seen as secondary to building the ANA. Corruption in the ANP and Interior Ministry also hindered capacity-building and trust, but the appointment of Hanif Atmar as minister of the interior raised hopes of a crackdown on corruption. Atmar had a reputation for rooting out inefficiency and corruption. The EU's police-training mission (EUPOL) struggled to find enough trainers to fill its established strength of 240 personnel and was seen as too small – the United States had requested up to 3,000 police trainers – to make a significant contribution to the mission. It became apparent that the United States would once again carry the burden. The US Focused District Development (FDD) programme, set up in 2007 to accelerate the training of the ANP, expanded its activities accordingly whilst EUPOL played a minor role and some ISAF Provincial Reconstruction Teams also ran small-scale training programmes. It was widely held that to better co-ordinate the various programmes they should all be placed under FDD control.

Another move to boost Afghan security capacity was the announcement that armed security elements known as Public Protection Forces (PPFs) were being formed at the local level. The new initiative was a reversal of the previous policy of the international community, which had been against the arming of local militias. The local forces were seen as analogous to the militias known as 'Awakening Councils' in Iraq created under the direction of General David Petraeus, now commander-in-chief US Central Command. The initial phase of the programme was to train 8,000 personnel by July 2009 in 40 out of 365 districts, with approximately 200 PPF personnel in each. The training by US troops started in Wardak, a province close to Kabul which had a large Taliban presence and was thus a priority for the PPF programme. There was, however, some concern that the PPF might detract from efforts to create a proper national police force.

> Obama's strategy recognised connections in a way Bush had not

Obama's strategy recognised the connections between and common problems of Pakistan and Afghanistan in a way the Bush administration's strategy had not. In a departure from previous policy there was more flexibility on the issue of possible negotiations with moderate Taliban elements. Obama appointed Richard Holbrooke as his special representative for Afghanistan and Pakistan. Holbrooke advised the president on the need to negotiate with moderate Taliban, and US Vice President Joe Biden indicated in a March statement that Washington saw negotiations as possible, although there was general agreement that this could not include the hardline leadership such as the Quetta Shura and Mullah Mohammad Omar.

The careful selection of key personnel was a focus of the new strategy. Besides Holbrooke as his special representative, Obama appointed Lieutenant-General Karl Eikenberry, former commander of Combined Force Command–Afghanistan, as US ambassador to Kabul. In what was seen as an attempt to give further impetus to the counter-insurgency campaign, the 'surge' was accompanied by the unexpected early removal of General David McKiernan from command of ISAF. McKiernan was effectively sacked when US Secretary of Defense Robert Gates flew to Kabul and announced on 11 May 2009 that Lieutenant-General Stanley McChrystal would take over from McKiernan, who was only 11 months into his tour of duty. The change of command was seen as part of a US effort to accelerate change and raise the tempo of military operations. Congress was indicating that funding for Afghanistan would be dependent on some visible progress. The choice of McChrystal, an experienced special-forces officer, who relinquished command of Joint Special Operations Command (SOCOM) to take over in Afghanistan, was seen as one means of achieving this. He was most likely the personal choice of Petraeus, under whose command McChrystal had been deployed in Iraq. However, there was concern that appointing a commander with McChrystal's background and reputation could result in a disproportionate use of force and an increase in civilian casualties during the election period, risking a further loss of public support for the Afghan government and its allies.

On taking over in June 2009, McChrystal commanded NATO and US forces totalling 65,000 troops from 42 countries, including an increasing number of American forces which numbered 30,000 in February and were expected by some analysts to rise to as much as 60,000 by the end of 2009.

Civilian casualties

The use of air-strikes and heavy weapons to reduce the risk of ISAF casualties continued to be an important part of military operations. Low casualty rates among non-Afghan troops were also important to maintain domestic political support in the countries with forces deployed in Afghanistan. But, for Karzai, rising civilian casualties from ISAF, ANA and US operations continued to undermine his authority and his electoral campaign. The NGO Afghanistan Rights Monitor estimated that in 2008 over 3,000 civilians had been killed by US, ISAF, or Afghan military action.

The issue of civilian casualties came to a head on 3 May 2009 after a clash between insurgents and Coalition forces in Farah province in western Afghanistan. During the incident in Bala Buluk district which lasted for 7–8 hours Afghan troops and police came under sustained pressure, leading to air-strikes to allow them to withdraw. It was reported that an estimated 86 civilians were killed or injured by Afghan and international forces during actions involving the use of airpower against Taliban insurgents. The International Committee of the Red Cross issued a statement saying that some of the civilian casualties had burns which might have been caused by white-phosphorus munitions. ISAF denied that white phosphorus had been used during the operation. Although the military use of white-phosphorus munitions is not specifically banned under international law, the use of incendiary munitions in civilian areas is banned under the Geneva Conventions. The incident coincided with a three-way meeting in Washington between Obama, Karzai and Pakistani President Asif Ali Zardari and led the Afghan president to criticise his allies for their disproportionate use of force, particularly airpower. Hinting that the Taliban might have deliberately staged the incident to create anti-government propaganda during the Washington meeting, a US military report referred to the use of white-phosphorus munitions by insurgents, citing 44 incidents where there was evidence of its use in improvised explosive devices and some indirect-fire attacks. The issue of civilian casualties continued to hamper attempts to shore up support for Karzai and his international allies who used airpower to keep their own casualties to a minimum. In June the inquiry into the incident reported that serious mistakes had been made in the deployment of allied combat aircraft during the operations in Farah. In a statement to the US Senate Armed Services Committee on 2 June 2009, McChrystal acknowledged the damage to the mission in Afghanistan caused by civilian casualties and pledged to review all rules of engagement and to limit the use of air-strikes.

Logistics for ISAF and US forces were complicated by attacks in December 2008 and March 2009 on depots in Peshawar which held supplies in transit from Karachi to Kabul via the Khyber Pass. Following the attacks, attempts were made to open other supply routes. Agreement was reached with Russia for a rail route from the Baltic via Russia to Central Asia which would carry non-lethal consignments. In a sign that a more pragmatic relationship was developing following the breakdown of relations in 2005, Uzbek authorities agreed to the use of Navoi air base by US aircraft. The arrangement with Tashkent was designed to offset to some extent the planned closure of Manas air base in Kyrgyzstan, which was announced by President Kurmanbek Bakiyev in February 2009, but which was reversed in June when a Kyrgyz parliamentary committee announced it had reached agreement with the United States for the continued use of Manas on a limited basis, restricted to the movement of non-lethal supplies in transit to Afghanistan. Another agreement was reached with Tajikistan for the movement of supplies through either Kulyab or Dushanbe air bases for onward movement to Afghanistan by road. The new routes raised the possibility that they could become targets for insurgent and terrorist groups in Central Asia (see Strategic Geography, pp. X–XI).

Aid and development

International donors retained as their roadmap the Afghan National Development Strategy (ANDS) with its three pillars of security; governance, rule of law and human rights; and economic and social development. These three strands became better coordinated by the creation of three standing committees within the Joint Co-ordination and Monitoring Board, which had previously had to act through a plethora of interest groups. The Integrated Approach Working Group was created in November 2008 with the mandate of coordinating the programmes of the Independent Directorate for Local Governance with UNAMA, ISAF and international donor-led programmes. A key part of the work was the identification of 51 districts as priorities for faster development. Continued international support for ANDS was reiterated at the Hague Conference in March 2009.

Although progress in development remained slow and was hampered by insecurity across much of the country, greater regional interest in Afghanistan created some impetus. Afghan and regional representatives discussed priorities for assistance at an informal ministerial meeting in Paris on 14 December. Uzbekistan agreed to provide electricity to Kabul and parts of northern Afghanistan, and Tajikistan agreed to supply electricity in 2010. Power supplies, however, remained sporadic, with an estimated 50% of the population having no power and only 5% a constant supply.

One area highlighted for urgent development was agriculture, with only half of the nearly eight million arable hectares under cultivation. One reason, apart from security, was the lack of irrigation channels, many of which had been destroyed or neglected through decades of conflict. The improved relations with Central Asian neighbours crucially included agreements on water management.

Despite some positive signs of improved coordination of development efforts, attempts to build the capacity of the Afghan government were strongly criticised. In response to frustration in Washington over the way aid programmes were being carried out in Afghanistan, Obama announced there would be a surge in civilian capacity. The initiative was hampered by a lack of volunteers, but the United States planned to deploy up to 600 civilians with expertise in agriculture, economics, law and other critical areas. There was further concern over the lack of accountability of development aid from international donors. In the United States, following the creation of the Office of the Special Inspector General for Afghanistan Reconstruction in 2008 designed to give Congress more oversight of expenditure, the

Government Accountability Office responded to congressional concern over financial wastage by calling for more oversight of expenditure in all areas of the operation, including security, economic development, counter-narcotics, capacity-building and expenditure on contractors.

The regional dimension

Pakistan remained the biggest source of instability for Afghanistan. The inability or unwillingness of the Pakistani authorities to deal with the leadership of the Afghan Taliban, the Quetta Shura and safe havens in FATA, and mutual accusations of lack of control of militants moving across the Durand Line, ensured a continuing difficult relationship between Kabul and Islamabad. With the visit of Zardari to Kabul in January 2009, however, the relationship between the Afghan and Pakistani presidents improved. Following the visit there was a joint declaration on a 'new visionary chapter' in relations between the two countries 'to counter and eliminate the menaces of militancy, extremism and terrorism from the region'. The upsurge in violence in Pakistan and the robust reaction of Pakistan's security forces offered a chance to change the dynamics of the interconnected insurgencies. Additional aid amounting to approximately $5bn pledged to Pakistan at the Tokyo Donors' Conference in April 2009 was a key component in supporting Islamabad in this effort and emphasised the need to treat Pakistan and Afghanistan as one entity in terms of security supported by development.

Iran's involvement in Afghanistan continued to be ambiguous. Tehran's aid to the western provinces remained a key factor in their development, and cross-border trade between Iran and Afghanistan continued to grow. Iranian construction projects, particularly in Herat province, focused on schools, clinics and a $80m railway to connect Tehran to Afghanistan. But there were indications of a more negative Iranian stance towards the United States and its allies in Afghanistan. Weapons and explosives were discovered in Farah province near the Bakhshabad Dam, a $2.2bn Western-funded project. Afghan border guards also reported arms smugglers crossing into Afghanistan from Iran. It was expected that the new US administration would seek more cooperation from Tehran on the narcotics issue, an area of common interest.

Pakistan continued to view the Afghan–Indian relationship with suspicion, fearing that if the largely Western involvement in Afghanistan diminished or ceased altogether, India would increase and possibly militarise its presence in what Islamabad regards as its 'strategic depth'. India's involvement in Afghanistan steadily increased following the attack on its embassy in Kabul on 7 July 2008, in which two diplomats and 39 others were killed, and India was widely regarded as a strong ally of Afghanistan. New Delhi's support for Kabul remained largely focused on reconstruction and development, although there was also some Indian support for the training of Afghan border guards.

The December conference of regional ministers in Paris raised hopes for greater trans-regional involvement and cooperation in Afghanistan. Russia, concerned over a potential spillover of security threats into Central Asia, increasingly supported the international effort in Afghanistan. The agreement over the overland supply route through Russia and Central Asia into northern Afghanistan and acquiescence to allied supply and transit bases in Central Asia showed Moscow's concern for a successful outcome that would not require deployment of Russian troops. Russia strengthened its bilateral relationship with Afghanistan principally through trade, the promotion of bilateral relations between Kabul and the Central Asian capitals, and some training in counter-narcotics.

At the Hague conference, Chinese Vice Foreign Minister Wu Dawei made a commitment to donate $75m in aid over five years. However, speaking at the IISS Shangri-La Dialogue in Singapore in May, US Secretary of Defense Robert Gates called on China (as well as Europe) to do more in Afghanistan. Beijing's involvement remained mostly at the level of cross-border trade, with one or two mutually beneficial economic-development projects such as the Aynak copper mine project in Logar province. The project to develop the Aynak copper reserves was impeded due to a large Taliban presence in Logar and neighbouring Wardak provinces. Beijing and Kabul relied on US forces in the area to bring the stability needed for the project – the largest investment in the history of Afghanistan – to start. The mine was set to bring much-needed jobs as well as more infrastructure projects, including a railway network.

Conditions for progress

The events of the year to June 2009 revealed little improvement in Afghanistan's overall security and stability. However, in some areas there were signs of a more concerted effort by the international community to bring coherence and coordination to the multi-faceted counter-insurgency and capacity-building effort. The new US strategy focusing on Afghanistan and Pakistan together was the key element. If Pakistan succeeds in quelling

314 | South Asia and Afghanistan

its insurgency emanating from the FATA and NWFP, a more benign environment could emerge in Afghanistan, allowing more sustainable development to take root, but building the capacity of the Afghan national security forces remains crucial to sustainable security and development.

India: Elections Bolster Stability

In India, the position of the ruling Congress-led United Progressive Alliance (UPA) coalition had at times looked precarious as the 2009 general elections approached. Its most serious challenge occurred on 22 July 2008 when it was forced to obtain a vote of confidence in the Lok Sabha (lower house of parliament) following the withdrawal of support by leftist parties over India's intention to proceed with the long-pending nuclear deal with the United States that it had stalled for several months in fear of just such an outcome. With elections looming in both the United States and India, the agreement on cooperation on civil nuclear technology needed to be consummated or it would almost certainly fail. Amidst hectic lobbying and allegations of bribery, the government won the confidence vote by 275–256 with the support of the Samajwadi Party, based in the state of Uttar Pradesh. Following this victory, it obtained better than expected results in four of the six provincial elections held in November and December, overturning the rule of the opposition Bharatiya Janata Party (BJP) in Rajasthan and retaining the National Capital Territory of Delhi. The government therefore felt that the general elections in April and May could enable it to benefit from populist economic measures, and that it could be helped by lower fuel and food prices, which contributed to a fall in inflation.

On the eve of the general elections, both the UPA and the BJP-led National Democratic Alliance (NDA) faced significant desertions by coalition partners. The BJP's second-largest partner, the Orissa-based Biju Janata Dal, joined leftist and other parties in a new 'third' front; while the Congress party's largest partner, the Bihar-based Rashtriya Janata Dal, formed a new alliance, labelled the 'fourth front', with two other regional parties. The five-phase election process was held over four hot weeks in April and May with 428m people voting (a turnout of 60%).

The UPA was returned to power with a clear electoral victory, confounding expectations of a hung parliament. The Congress party, moreover, increased its strength in the Lok Sabha by 42% to 206 seats. Along with its pre-poll alliance partners, it held a near-majority of 263 seats in the 545-member parliament, with additional pledges of support raising this to 322 seats. On 22 May Manmohan Singh, at the age of 76, was sworn in as prime minister for a second consecutive five-year term. The new 79-member council of ministers (of whom 33 are cabinet members) of the second 11-party UPA government, with 25 fresh faces, was a complex mix of castes, experience and regional representatives. It accommodated the demands of the Congress party's two main coalition partners, the West Bengal-based Trinamool Congress and the Tamil Nadu-based Dravida Munnetra Kazhagam, with 19 and 18 seats respectively. Without the need to rely on support from leftist parties, the new government was expected to be more stable than its predecessor.

The Congress party's convincing win was interpreted as a vote for stability and continuity. Its populist economic measures – such as a $15bn farm-loan waiver and a $9bn rural-employment guarantee scheme – paid political dividends, as did nomination of the popular Singh as its candidate for prime minister. There was an unexpected Congress revival in the traditional 'Hindi heartland' of the northern states of Uttar Pradesh, Madhya Pradesh and Rajasthan after campaigning by Rahul Gandhi, son of Congress president Sonia Gandhi and a member of India's most powerful political dynasty. A significant proportion of the 43m new young voters appeared to gravitate towards the party. In a vote for moderation, both left- and right-wing parties lost support. The former made their worst showing in decades and the opposition BJP was reduced from 138 to 116 seats in the Lok Sabha.

Singh's first priority was to revive an Indian economy punctured – though by no means devastated – by the global financial and economic crisis. Following fiscal stimulus measures, economic growth was 6.7% in the 2008/09 financial year ending on 31 March 2009, lower than the recent peak of 9%. The benchmark Sensex index of the Bombay Stock Exchange fell nearly 60% in October 2008 as foreign institutional investors pulled out of the Indian market. However, the election results brought a one-day rise of 17%. Finance Minister Pranab Mukherjee aimed to accelerate economic growth to 7% in 2009/10 with a focus on liberalisation, privatisation and infrastructure development. The government also planned to increase social-sector spending, although the global recession, rising fiscal deficit and differences within the coalition could make this difficult.

While the elections were mostly conducted peacefully, Maoist Naxalites killed over 50 security and election personnel in the three eastern states of Jharkhand, Chhattisgarh and Bihar, and hijacked a passenger train in Jharkhand. They were, however, unable to disrupt the elections in states where they had called for a boycott, with over 50% turnout in Chhattisgarh and Jharkhand. Chhattisgarh continued to suffer attacks on security personnel, and in mid June five states were put on alert to counter a two-day strike called by the Maoists in response to the continuing anti-Maoist security operations in West Bengal.

Attack sours India–Pakistan relations

Tensions with Pakistan were sharply raised by a terrorist attack in Mumbai on 26–29 November. Ten men armed with guns and bombs attacked multiple sites over 60 hours, killing 166 people and wounding over 300. The attacks took place at the main railway terminus, the five-star Oberoi and Taj Mahal hotels, a café frequented by Westerners and a Jewish centre. Nine terrorists were killed and one captured. The attacks showed unprecedented planning and coordination. While much of the killing was indiscriminate, foreign nationals were specifically targeted and 22 were killed.

As evidence showed that the group had arrived by boat from Pakistan, the armed forces of both countries were placed on high alert. However, India showed considerable restraint and there was no military mobilisation, unlike a similar crisis in 2001–02. India named the Lashkar-e-Tayiba (LeT) group and its front organisation Jamaat-ud-Dawa (JuD) as responsible for the attack. Singh called Pakistan the 'epicentre of terrorism' and said the attack had the 'support of some official agencies in Pakistan', something Islamabad denied.

Concerns about terrorism originating from Pakistan had already been aroused by the suicide bombing of the Indian Embassy in Kabul on 7 July 2008 that killed 41 people, including two senior Indian diplomats and three Indian security personnel. This attack was carried out by the Taliban-linked Haqqani network, allegedly linked to Pakistan's ISI. Following the Mumbai attack, international pressure mounted on Pakistan to do more to shut down terrorist groups operating from its territory, and in particular to act against LeT and JuD. LeT had originally been formed as a group opposing Indian sovereignty in the disputed territory of Kashmir, but later acquired a broader Islamist agenda. Though officially banned in Pakistan, it had been widely alleged to have links with the ISI. After the Mumbai attacks, Pakistan took steps against both organisations. On 9 December, Pakistani security forces raided LeT camps and offices. Following the announcement of UN

Security Council sanctions on the JuD on 11 December, Pakistan banned the organisation, carried out further raids and arrested more than 120 people. JuD chief Hafiz Muhammad Saeed was placed under house arrest. On 7 January 2009 Pakistan admitted that the lone surviving terrorist captured by India, Ajmal Amir Kasab, was a Pakistani national; he was later put on trial in Mumbai. A month later Islamabad confirmed that parts of the attack had been planned in Pakistan and that six people were being held in connection with it. By April it had charged nine alleged collaborators, five of whom were in custody. However, India believed that large parts of the network remained untouched, and viewed as a setback Saeed's release by the Lahore High Court in June on grounds of insufficient evidence.

Despite the renewed tension, India sought to re-engage with Pakistan. In her opening address to the newly elected Lok Sabha, President Pratibha Patil indicated that the government would seek to 'reshape' its relationship with Pakistan depending on the 'sincerity of Pakistan's actions'. Singh, at a meeting with Zardari on the sidelines of the Shanghai Cooperation Organisation's June summit in the Russian city of Yekaterinburg, made clear that he was willing to talk to Pakistan on terrorism if it cracked down on groups targeting India.

It was also notable that measures to increase mutual confidence continued across the Line of Control (LoC) dividing Indian-controlled and Pakistan-controlled Kashmir. In October 2008, trade began across the LoC with trucks plying the Srinagar–Muzaffarabad and Poonch–Rawalkot routes. However, the first serious violations of the ceasefire across the LoC since 2003 had taken place in July and August 2008, when both sides reported firing of small arms by the other, even as India noted that infiltration and militant attacks had decreased. India welcomed Zardari's remarks on 6 October that militant Islamic groups operating in Kashmir were 'terrorists', and received a further boost from the remarkably high voter turnout of 60% in the provincial elections in November–December 2008, despite a boycott call by separatists. However, the transfer of forest land for the use of Hindu pilgrims to the Amarnath shrine in the Muslim-majority Kashmir Valley led in August to the largest pro-independence demonstrations in Indian-controlled Kashmir for nearly 20 years. In June 2009 the new central government indicated it would like to redeploy the army from towns and cities in Kashmir to the LoC, substituting civilian police. Pakistan had meanwhile moved troops away from Indian border areas to more western areas to counter the TTP.

In response to the Mumbai attacks, India took some measures to improve security. Home Minister P. Chidambaram (his predecessor Shivraj Patil resigned following the attacks) vowed to strengthen anti-terrorism laws. An Unlawful Activities (Prevention) Amendment, with provisions for an unprecedented 180-days detention without bail, was passed by parliament; a federal investigative agency, the National Investigative Agency, was formed; multi-agency centres for intelligence collection and assessment were beefed up; coastal security arrangements were strengthened and new arms and equipment were acquired for paramilitary and police forces, whose numbers were to be increased.

Other terror attacks in India over the past year highlighted the activities of home-grown jihadi groups. Eight near-simultaneous bomb blasts in Bangalore on 25 July 2008 killed eight people, and were followed the next day by 17 blasts in Ahmedabad, killing 53. Thirty people were killed in New Delhi by five explosions on 13 September. These attacks were carried out by the Indian Mujahadeen (IM) and indicated the radicalisation of a small section of India's Muslim community. IM leader Abdul Subhan Usman Qureshi and co-founder Mohammed Sadiq Israr Ahmed Sheikh were arrested, although others remained at large. On 29 September bombs also went off in Malegaon and Modasa in western India, killing six people. Eleven Hindu extremists from the radical group Abhinav Bharat, including a serving middle-ranking army officer, were arrested and charged. The most serious terror attack in the northeast, blamed on an Assamese insurgent group, took place in Assam on 30 October 2008 with nine bombs killing 83 people in crowded markets in Guwahati and three other towns.

Nuclear agreement completed

The completion of the landmark India–US civil nuclear deal on 10 October 2008 was an important achievement for Singh and his national security adviser M.K. Narayanan. Following several months of stalling, for fear that his government would fall, Singh finally pushed forward on the deal as the US November elections loomed. Although leftist parties which opposed the agreement had withdrawn support for his government on 8 July, Singh formally submitted an India-specific safeguards agreement to the International Atomic Energy Agency (IAEA) for approval – a requirement for US Congressional backing. Amidst hectic lobbying by India and the United States, the IAEA board of governors unanimously approved it on 1 August. A further requirement was a waiver from the 45-nation

Nuclear Suppliers Group. Although Austria, Ireland, New Zealand and China expressed reservations, the waiver was granted on 6 September. The US House of Representatives and Senate then voted by large margins to approve the agreement. On 8 October President George W. Bush signed the United States–India Nuclear Cooperation Approval and Non-proliferation Enhancement Act, and two days later US Secretary of State Condoleezza Rice and Pranab Mukherjee, then India's foreign minister, signed the accord.

Under the agreement India, for the first time since the mid 1970s, was permitted to acquire fuel supplies and equipment for its civilian nuclear reactors to counter growing energy shortages, in return for placing them under permanent IAEA safeguards. To implement the accord, India was required to submit a plan to increase the number of nuclear power reactors under international safeguards from 6 to 14, out of a total of 22. However, lengthy negotiations with Washington were expected on arrangements and procedures for reprocessing US-origin spent fuel. At the same time, delays in obtaining licences for dual-use nuclear and conventional technologies and equipment for India were apparent. Meanwhile, India signed nuclear-cooperation agreements with France, Russia and Kazakhstan, and in March received its first shipment of 60 tonnes of uranium ore from France.

The civil nuclear agreement was the culmination of a long period of substantial improvement in relations between Delhi and Washington, which had begun under President Bill Clinton after India's 1998 nuclear tests and continued under George W. Bush. It remained to be seen whether the momentum would be maintained by President Barack Obama, whose immediate regional focus was on forging a new policy to deal simultaneously with militants in Afghanistan and Pakistan – as well as to build a closer dialogue with China. A visit to India by US Secretary of State Hillary Clinton was scheduled to take place in mid July.

Delhi increasingly viewed China as a key security 'challenge and priority', a sentiment voiced by Mukherjee. The outgoing air force chief in May stated that India faced a greater threat from China than Pakistan, since the former's combat capabilities were little known. Indian plans to modernise, expand and equip its armed forces reflected a shift in Delhi's strategic focus beyond its immediate South Asian neighbourhood. At the same time, India remained keen to build economic and trade relations with China: Sino-Indian relations were expected to be determined by a judicious mix of cooperation and competition.

Sri Lanka: Civil War Ends

On 19 May 2009 the Sri Lankan military announced the defeat of the separatist Liberation Tigers of Tamil Eelam (LTTE), ending the conflict that had
wracked the nation for 26 years. Following a concentrated offensive against
the northern areas which had long been controlled by the Tamil Tigers, the
army killed LTTE leader Velupillai Prabhakaran and took control of the last
patch of territory held by the movement in Mullaitivu district in Northern
Province. Although there was jubilation amongst the majority Sinhalese
population, President Mahinde Rajapaksa said the war had not been against
the Tamil people and called for reconciliation. An estimated 70,000 people
had been killed since the conflict began in 1983, and at mid June 2009 over
280,000 Tamil civilians remain displaced from their homes.

Several factors accounted for the victory. The defection in 2004 of Colonel
Karuna Amman, a close aide to Prabakharan, had weakened the LTTE and
divided its command structure. In November 2005, Prabhakaran made a
strategic blunder by enforcing a boycott of presidential polls by Tamils in
Northern and Eastern Provinces. This deprived liberal United National Party
candidate Ranil Wickremesinghe of victory and enabled Rajapaksa, candidate of the more hardline United People's Freedom Alliance, to win with
50% of the votes to Wickremesinghe's 48%. Rajapaksa then failed to work
out a peaceful resolution of the conflict through peace talks with the LTTE in
March and October 2006, and resolved to defeat the LTTE militarily.

Another blunder by Prabhakaran and the LTTE was the closure of the
Mavil Aru reservoir sluice gates in July 2006, which deprived many farmers
and households in the eastern and bordering provinces of water. Following
a hard-won battle to reopen the gates, the Sri Lankan military continuously
engaged the LTTE in a series of battles, employing airpower and artillery.
In July 2007 the military took control of Eastern Province after 13 years of
LTTE control.

In addition, Sri Lankan diplomacy resulted in the closure of LTTE offices
abroad and greatly reduced funding from expatriate Tamil communities.
Following bans on the LTTE by India and the United States, the EU designated it as a terrorist organisation in May 2008. A number of Sri Lankan Tamils
in the United States were arrested and prosecuted on charges of attempted
arms procurement for the LTTE. Meanwhile, the Sri Lankan Navy neutralised the Sea Tigers in several clashes, ending LTTE arms supplies from the
sea and making it much easier to transport army troops to the north. China

meanwhile provided military aid and Pakistan provided crucial training and customised ammunition for precision-guided air attacks, while India provided non-lethal defence items such as radars and electronic support. Additional defence funding and recruitment of troops produced a rejuvenated military that was ready to carry out significant offensives.

Having won control over Eastern Province, the military focused on the north. It took control of the northern town of Kilinochchi, the LTTE's administrative headquarters, on 2 January 2009, pushing the LTTE into coastal areas. A week later, it captured the Elephant Pass, a strategic causeway linking the Jaffna peninsula with the mainland, and controlled the road to Jaffna for the first time since the late 1980s. On 14 January, it captured the last remaining LTTE stronghold of Chundikulam to take control of the entire Jaffna peninsula for the first time in nearly a decade. On 25 January it wrested control of the northern town of Mullaitivu after heavy fighting. LTTE fighters were then confined to a small zone in Mullaitivu district, bordered by a lagoon and the sea.

In the face of these defeats the LTTE carried out terror attacks, although they diminished in impact. On 6 October 2008 a suicide bomb killed 27 people in Anuradhapura, and on 2 January 2009 a suicide bomb attack targeted the air-force headquarters in Colombo, killing two people. An LTTE attack by two light aircraft on Colombo on 20 February failed when the first struck the main government tax office and the second was shot down near Colombo international airport.

Meanwhile, international pressure for a ceasefire mounted. On 4 February, Hillary Clinton and Britain's Foreign Secretary David Miliband called for a truce to evacuate casualties and allow provision of humanitarian assistance – a call rejected by Rajapaksa. Following an informal UN Security Council meeting on 27 March, the Sri Lankan government began a two-day ceasefire with the LTTE on 13 April but rejected the LTTE's offer to restart peace talks and negotiate a permanent, internationally backed ceasefire. On 30 April Miliband and French Foreign Minister Bernard Kouchner, visiting Sri Lanka, continued to press for a ceasefire to allow aid agencies to reach the tens of thousands of civilians trapped within a now only 5km-long, military-declared 'safety zone' near Mullaitivu. Sri Lanka refused, with Rajapaksa criticising the delegation for interfering in Sri Lankan internal affairs. Although Indian attempts to broker a ceasefire were also unsuccessful, they may have slowed down the pace of the Sri Lankan offensive.

Meanwhile, the final military offensive was under way in the Mullaitivu area despite mounting civilian casualties. While the UN accused the LTTE of using civilians as human shields, preventing the escape of civilians from LTTE-held territory, the government was accused of shelling the remaining LTTE-held area, including the safety zone. Each side denied the accusations made against it, which were difficult to verify as independent media were banned from the area.

On 18 May, the 25,000 troops involved in the operation took control of the last remaining LTTE stronghold, and 10,000 LTTE militants reportedly surrendered. According to a UN document, some 6,500 civilians had been killed in the first three months of the year. According to official Sri Lankan casualty figures, 6,261 security-forces personnel, policemen and paramilitary guards had been killed since August and 29,551 wounded, and 22,000 LTTE militants had been killed. However, the Sri Lankan government claimed that the Tamil Tigers' international network remained largely intact.

Bangladesh: Military-backed Rule Ends

Two years of military-backed rule in Bangladesh ended in December 2008 with the holding of general elections. The army had taken control ahead of elections due to take place in 2006 amid widespread allegations of corruption among the major political parties. It installed a caretaker government intended to create the conditions for elections.

One crucial step towards new polls was the caretaker government's reluctant release of the country's two main political leaders, despite outstanding corruption and extortion charges. Former premier and Bangladesh National Party (BNP) chief Khaleda Zia was freed on bail on 11 September after a year's detention while her arch-rival, former premier Sheikh Hasina, leader of the Awami League, returned to Dhaka from the United States in November, having previously been held in detention for 11 months until June 2008. A further essential step was the issue of computerised photo identity cards to 80m eligible voters to deter election fraud.

The 29 December elections, which saw 80% turnout, resulted in a landslide victory for the Sheikh Hasina-led left-of-centre Grand Alliance. The Awami League alone nearly quadrupled its seats to 230 in the 300-member Jatiya Sangsad (parliament). The victory reflected widespread anger and disillusionment with the corruption and misgovernance of the BNP, which saw its number of seats plummet from 193 to 30. The religious party, Jamaate-Islami, won only two seats. The trend continued in local council polls on 22 January 2009, in which the Awami League won 306 of 463 seats, though the elections were marred by intimidation and violence. Sweeping changes took place in the army and the intelligence services.

The first major challenge to Sheikh Hasina, who was sworn in as premier on 6 January, was a mutiny within the paramilitary border guard force, the Bangladesh Rifles (BDR). In a 20-hour siege on 25 and 26 February soldiers of the BDR killed at least 74 people, including 56 officers and their chief who were on secondment from the army. The mutiny spread from BDR headquarters in Dhaka to other paramilitary camps, including those in Chittagong, Sylhet and Rajshahi. Sheikh Hasina initially promised an amnesty to mutineers who surrendered, but subsequently changed her position and pledged severe punishment for those responsible for the killings. More than 3,000 BDR soldiers were arrested. An official report found no links between the mutineers and extremist groups, and blamed years of pent-up anger among BDR troops over pay, status and facilities.

The government's tough counter-terrorism policy saw successes against militant Islamic groups which were reported to be regrouping. On 23 March 2009 Maulana Sheikh Abdus Salam, a founder member of the banned terror organisation Harkat-ul-Jihad-al-Islami, whose Islamic Democratic Party, formed in September 2008, was not allowed to take part in the elections, was arrested. In a significant move, two former directors general of the powerful civilian intelligence agency, National Security Intelligence, were arrested on 16 May, allegedly for involvement in a ten-truck arms haul that had been seized in Chittagong port in 2 April 2004, apparently destined for northeast Indian insurgent groups.

Nepal: Arguments Obstruct Peace Process

Nepal had two coalition governments in the year to mid 2009 as political arguments obstructed efforts to implement the peace process that had ended a ten-year civil war, removed the monarchy and established a democratic republic.

On 15 August 2008 the newly elected constituent assembly elected the Maoist leader Pushpa Kamal Dahal, known as Prachanda, as prime minister with 464 votes to 351 for Nepali Congress Party candidate and former premier Sher Bahadur Deuba. Following lengthy power-sharing discussions, Prachanda headed a 20-party coalition government, led by his Communist Party of Nepal (Maoist) along with two other major parties, the Communist Party Nepal – United Marxist Leninist (CPN–UML) and the Madhesi People's Rights Forum. However, lack of trust and divergence of views among the ruling coalition partners, as well as between the government and the opposition Nepali Congress Party, made it difficult to implement the peace process, including steps to draft a new constitution. According to the coalition's Common Minimum Programme, a new constitution was to be written within two years, and former Maoist combatants of the People's Liberation Army (PLA) would be rehabilitated and reintegrated within six months.

The most contentious issue was the integration of some 19,600 former PLA fighters into the 70,000-strong Nepalese army, demanded by the Maoist Defence Minister Ram Bahadur Thapa ('Badal') but resolutely opposed by army chief General Rookmangud Katawal. On 10 March 2009 the defence ministry ordered the army to halt recruitment of some 3,000 personnel in view of its refusal to consider the recruitment of former Maoist combatants. The army defied the government and continued its recruitment drive. As a result, the defence ministry refused to extend the tenures of eight generals who retired on 16 March, but on 24 March the Supreme Court issued an interim order reinstating them. This two-month stand-off between the army and the Maoists took a dramatic turn when Prachanda sacked Katawal on 3 May for defying government orders, and appointed his deputy, Lieutentant-General Kul Bahadur Khadka, as acting army chief. However, President Ram Baran Yadav, in his role as supreme commander of the army, reinstated Katawal on the grounds that his removal was unconstitutional – though the new constitution was still being drafted. The desertion of major coalition partners, the CPN–UML and the Sadbhavana party, which opposed Prachanda's action, forced him to resign as prime minister on 4 May.

After considerable wrangling, Madhav Kumar Nepal, leader of the CPN–UML, was sworn in as prime minister on 25 May, leading a non-Maoist coalition of 22 parties with 350 of 601 assembly seats. Prachanda boycotted the ceremony, urging Maoist cadres to be ready for a revolution as the 'war' was not yet over. The new government revoked the retirement of the eight generals and extended their tenure by three years. While the new coalition included representatives from a wide range of parties, the country remained vulnerable to instability in view of ideological differences among the coalition partners, difficulties over integration of former rebels into the army, and the threat of violence – and with clashes continuing in the southern Terai where armed groups sought enhanced rights for Indian-origin Madhesis.

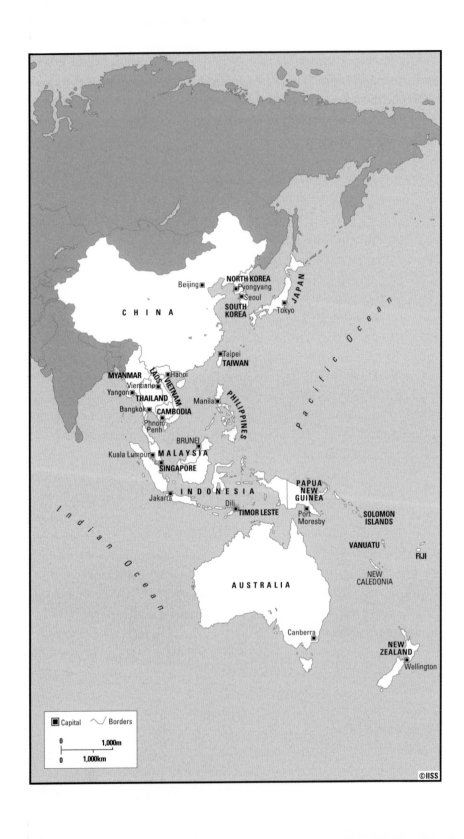

CHINA

NORTH KOREA
Beijing■
Pyongyang■
■Seoul
SOUTH
KOREA

JAPAN

Tokyo■

Pacific Ocean

■Taipei
TAIWAN

MYANMAR
LAOS
VIETNAM
■Hanoi
Vientiane■
Yangon■
THAILAND
Bangkok■
CAMBODIA
Phnom
Penh■

■Manila

PHILIPPINES

BRUNEI■
Kuala Lumpur■
MALAYSIA
SINGAPORE■

INDONESIA
Jakarta■
Dili■
■TIMOR LESTE

PAPUA
NEW
GUINEA
Port
Moresby■

SOLOMON
ISLANDS

VANUATU

FIJI

NEW
CALEDONIA

Indian Ocean

AUSTRALIA

Canberra■

NEW
ZEALAND
Wellington■

■ Capital   Borders

0   1,000m
0   1,000km

©IISS

Chapter 10

Asia-Pacific

China's continuing emergence as a global power was underlined by the financial and economic crisis, which highlighted its importance to the American economy and to the stability of the world's markets. The crisis badly affected other Asian exporters, and some countries, such as Japan and Thailand, were also caught up in domestic political wrangles. Recent diplomatic progress in negotiations with North Korea was reversed as Pyongyang ordered a nuclear test explosion and resumed other activities it had halted. Reflecting the changing strategic picture in the Pacific, Australia and New Zealand began to shift their defence postures.

China: Caution Tempers Rising Status

The year 2009 has seen several significant anniversaries for China. It is 60 years since the founding of the People's Republic of China (PRC) and the relegation of the Nationalists to Taiwan; 30 years since the normalisation of relations between the PRC and the United States; and 20 years since the massacre of pro-democracy demonstrators in Tiananmen Square. The events of the past year offered opportunities to reflect on the country's development since each of these landmarks.

Cross-Strait relations
In the six decades after the Chinese Communist Party saw off its civil-war rival, the nationalist Kuomintang (KMT), to a last foothold on Taiwan, the dispute between China and Taiwan festered but did not flare. The persistent

claim of the KMT that it alone, at the head of a Republic of China (ROC) only temporarily ejected from the mainland, held legitimate political authority over all China, was understandably irritating and threatening to Beijing. To outside powers as well, the assertion seemed over time to be increasingly fanciful. From the early 1970s, they saw no further strategic interest in participating in a political fiction: the PRC was assigned the permanent seat on the UN Security Council previously occupied by the ROC and diplomatic recognition gradually switched from Taipei to Beijing.

The evolution of Taiwan's political system, beginning in the 1980s, from authoritarian to vibrantly democratic was partly designed to anchor the island more firmly in international society. It was also intended to create bonds and affinities, based on values, that the PRC could not replicate, and which would to some extent compensate for the loss of formal diplomatic ties. Taiwan was only partially successful in this aim. Unflattering contrasts could certainly be drawn, especially in the United States, between the oppressive and occasionally brutal rule of the Communist Party on the mainland and the fervent – if somewhat feverish – democracy operating in Taiwan. And the interests of a fully fledged democracy of 20 million were not so easily ignored or traded away. But these things did not prove a counterweight to China's geopolitical heft. More worrying to Beijing was that doors were opening to political forces that favoured Taiwan's formal independence, which in 2000 succeeded in capturing the presidency for the first time. This ushered in eight years of increased tension across the Taiwan Strait, in which all parties to the dispute were nonetheless subject to powerful constraints, grounded in broad calculations of material interest, which prevented escalation to open conflict. In Taiwan, there was no consensus on whether independence from or reunification with the mainland should be sought, and an apparent preference for the ambiguity of the status quo; in China, the wish to assert sovereignty over the island was compelling, but had to be weighed against the costs a military confrontation with the United States over Taiwan might impose, and the (possibly permanent) disruption it would inflict on what could otherwise be a fairly smooth path to wealth and great-power status. The United States' principal objective was to help sustain a military balance between China and Taiwan that would predispose the two sides to a political resolution of their differences.

By 2009, however, the stalemate appeared, at least in a tactical sense, to be breaking in China's favour. The election in 2008 of a KMT government in Taipei determined to improve relations with Beijing paved the way for an open-ended, albeit somewhat insubstantial, confidence-building dialogue in which the dispute was at last seen to be managed, as Beijing wished, without the need for outside involvement. While reunification seemed as remote as ever, Beijing could allow itself to feel more relaxed and satisfied with cross-Strait relations than perhaps at any time since 1949. Chinese foreign policy was no longer dominated by, or captive to, diplomatic competition with Taiwan, nor by the need angrily to fend off perceived intrusions into the dispute by other powers. Beijing could refocus on its wider, now-global strategic and economic interests.

Expanding horizons

China was, if not exactly inducted into this wider world, at least introduced to it largely by the United States. The year 2009 marked the 30th anniversary of the normalisation of diplomatic relations between the two countries, an initiative soon emulated by many others. The consummation of contacts between Beijing and Washington came with President Richard Nixon's visit to Beijing in 1972 to meet the ageing but still shrewd Mao Zedong. The improbable flirtation was prompted more by an unsentimental coincidence of interests than by mutual sympathy. The United States had, after all, been reluctant to accept the outcome of the Chinese Civil War, and the two countries had fought each other during the Korean War; Beijing, meanwhile, had aligned itself squarely with Stalin's Soviet Union in opposition to the United States. Following Stalin's death in 1953, however, the competition always implicit in the Sino-Soviet relationship came to the fore. Beijing, challenging the legitimacy of Moscow's leadership of the communist world, soon found that vital economic and technical assistance from the USSR was withdrawn, and, amid a variety of territorial disputes, in time came to fear a Soviet military assault. It was understandable that China would, in such circumstances, seek room for manoeuvre through an accommodation with a United States whose Vietnamese predicament was deepening steadily and which was attracted to the possibility of exploiting Sino-Soviet tensions. Stronger ties with Beijing would not only provide Washington with means to resist Moscow internationally, but also with the greater credibility and leverage needed in pursuit of détente with the USSR.

In these larger US calculations, the importance of Taiwan receded. The switch of diplomatic recognition from Taipei to Beijing was made more palatable by the implicit willingness of Washington to come to Taiwan's defence against an unprovoked attack by China, and by its explicit willingness to provide the island with the means of self-defence. The logic of the Sino-American alignment proved compelling after the 1979 Soviet invasion of Afghanistan, which soon became the venue for a bloody and prolonged proxy war between the USSR and a wide array of enemies including the United States and China.

The accommodation with Washington and the stability and security it lent China's external relations gave Beijing the confidence to embark on the delicate business of internal economic reforms throughout the 1980s and beyond, designed to allow China to catch up with its much more dynamic East Asian neighbours and to strengthen the legitimacy of the Communist Party among a brutalised and fatigued population. The fall of the Berlin Wall in 1989 and the crumbling of the Soviet Union and its vassal regimes that followed, however, struck at the underpinning rationale of the relationship. Henceforward, the violent determination of the Chinese Communist Party to maintain its own monopoly on political power cast a long shadow.

> The appetite for change inside China was not self-evident

Twenty years after the June 1989 massacre of pro-democracy demonstrators in Tiananmen Square in Beijing, China has still not exactly been warmly welcomed into polite international society. But it has advanced a long way from the pariah status it attracted in the immediate aftermath of the bloodletting. This is partly a reflection of the lessons the Communist Party drew from the challenge it faced in 1989. One was the need to stifle, actively and fairly ruthlessly, actual and potential pockets of dissent; another was to remove grounds for dissent through the delivery of prosperity, to be obtained by an accelerated opening of China's economy to an outside world that could share in China's growth. Unlike Myanmar, whose ruling junta was no more brutal in its own suppression of dissent in 1988, but still finds itself isolated and widely sanctioned, China proved to be simply too large, too full of possibilities and too formidable in its diplomacy to be punished on a sustained basis. And economic engagement, bringing social change, held out at least the theoretical possibility of an accompanying alteration in China's political system in the direction of democracy.

The appetite for such change inside China itself was not self-evident, however. The 20 years since Tiananmen saw the emergence of a largely depoliticised generation enjoying much greater social and economic freedom than their parents could have imagined, and with reason to take more than a measure of pride in China's growing place at the centre of world affairs. This was symbolised by the highly successful Beijing Olympics of 2008. Whatever the failings of local authorities, the Communist Party leadership is for now at least credited with a dowdy competence. It has proved adaptive, portraying itself as the guardian of the poor and the struggling, yet also the only real vehicle for elite advancement. The party's challenge was to be equal to the accelerating complexity of China's society and the requirements for effective governance this imposed. It needed to be seen to be inducing and guiding positive change, rather than as overwhelmed by events. If economic growth were to falter, or the prospect of its continuation seen to be impeded by the peculiarities of one-party rule, the Communist Party's legitimacy would suffer. If the party could not satisfy the nationalist appetites it encouraged, its claims to power would be jeopardised. In mid 2009, however, it seemed much more secure than it might possibly have expected in June 1989, when it faced unrest at home, opprobrium abroad and the spectacle of the collapse of the communist world.

The party accomplished more than survival. Indeed, the international financial and economic crisis of late 2008 and the first half of 2009 seemed to confirm a shift in the centre of gravity of world affairs from a financially enfeebled West to Asia and, within Asia, especially to China. Recording reduced but enviably robust growth, expected to amount to over 6% in 2009, China appeared a bastion of economic stability. In late 2008 it unveiled a fiscal stimulus package valued at $585 billion, intended to offset the decline in external demand for Chinese goods, counter the drop-off in inward investment, and develop the physical infrastructure needed to sustain growth over the long term. Commentary in the international financial press often characterised China as the linchpin of global economic stability or, with intended irony, as the saviour of capitalism. It was seen as standing on the cusp of epochal change and geopolitical opportunity. Would China now take advantage of the problems of other major powers to exert, and compel international agreement for, a greater leadership role?

In the run-up to the April 2009 G20 summit in London, it was clear that China was to some extent testing the waters. Beijing implied heavily that its importance and interests should be more noticeably and formally reflected in the structure and operations of international financial institutions. The governor of the People's Bank of China, Zhou Xiaochuan, ruminated on the desirability of moving away from an overreliance on the US dollar as an international reserve currency. In truth, however, what the crisis principally revealed was the intense mutual economic reliance of China and the United States. The still-significant dependence of China on US consumer demand continued to predispose it to large holdings and further purchases of US treasury securities, a strategy intended to help suppress US interest rates and contribute to import demand, with low-cost goods from China helping to counter the inflationary implications of a loose monetary and fiscal policy in the United States, and Chinese demand for dollars offsetting the downward pressure on the US currency implied by ever-deteriorating US trade balances vis-à-vis China.

Cooperation and collaboration

At the height of the financial crisis there were calls for the United States and China to reflect this interdependence in a closer form of collaboration and joint international stewardship ranging over more than economic matters, a concept called 'G2' by former US National Security Adviser Zbigniew Brzezinski. The premise was that the G8, which formally excludes China, was unrepresentative of the actual distribution of global economic power; whereas the G20, which gathered in Washington in late 2008 and again in London the following spring, was too diffuse, cumbersome and consensual to provide anything more than lowest-common-denominator policies. Yet the G2 idea held little appeal for either the United States or China. Quite apart from the actual and material differences that separated China and America over wide areas of policy, Washington would presumably feel that any condominium would by implication confer on China enormous powers of veto over initiatives. It would certainly irritate Washington's allies and partners, as well as broader international opinion, which might otherwise be mobilised by Washington in existing multilateral forums to help effect desired changes in Chinese policy.

Beijing, while perhaps flattered by the idea and seeing it as confirmation of future superpower status, did not formally welcome it. The notion went against the grain of the psychology and practice of Chinese diplomacy. Beijing's preference, for the foreseeable future at least, was to avoid the controversies of a prominent leadership role and the burdens it could impose. It sought to move in broader, more consensual bodies, where international receptivity might be obtained for a leadership role that evolved gradually and, in its incrementalism, did not provoke anxiety. The international financial crisis, then, was not of a magnitude to persuade China's leaders to depart from an established strategic path that has served them well.

The relationship between Beijing and Washington was nonetheless subject to changes in rhythm and tone that flowed chiefly from the attitudes and policies adopted by the administration of President Barack Obama, which took office in January 2009. Although preoccupied in its early months by the travails of the global economy, the Obama administration also set about the enormous task of effecting sweeping change in US foreign policy to bring about a transformation in US strategic circumstances, a project which spread the international political capital of the Obama administration very thinly. In these circumstances, the administration's policy towards China proceeded from the conclusion that Beijing's strategic importance should not only be recognised but used in addressing security challenges common to both countries. It amounted, if perhaps by necessity, to a more relaxed view of Chinese power and influence than was prevalent during the Bush administration. Rather than merely requiring China to demonstrate its credentials as a 'responsible stakeholder' of the international system, the approach actively sought out instances where China could be encouraged to make useful contributions to the realisation of US objectives.

In practical terms this approach had several implications. During her first visit to Beijing as US secretary of state in February 2009, Hillary Clinton was criticised for allowing the impression to form, much more strongly than indicated by the rhetoric of the preceding administration, that the Sino-American relationship would not be held captive to long-standing disagreements about such matters as the poor observance of human rights in China or the treatment of Tibetans. The United States would continue to press its case on such matters, Clinton said, but not in such a way that could 'interfere' with collaboration 'on the global economic crisis, the global climate change crisis and the security crisis'.

Another feature of the Obama administration's policy was to encourage greater Chinese involvement in multilateral bodies and diplomatic endeavours, especially in Asia. This was made clear by both US Secretary of Defense Robert Gates and Deputy Secretary of State James Steinberg at the 8th annual IISS Shangri-La Dialogue, held in Singapore on 29–31 May 2009. The United States, as a 'resident power' in the Asia-Pacific region, would cleave tightly to its traditional bilateral alliances and partnerships with South Korea, Japan, Australia and others, but saw these as complementing rather than conflicting with the development of an inclusive, multilateral regional security architecture in which China would play a full role. Neither Beijing nor Washington articulated very precise prescriptions for such an architecture.

The United States, as the current preponderant power in Asia, was inclined to support the evolution of institutional arrangements that reflected and preserved existing power relationships, whereas China, as a rising power, had no interest in accepting formal arrangements that did not properly recognise its widening interests and potential. Yet both subscribed to the principle of multilateral consultative diplomacy and found a common espousal and practice of it both useful and reassuring to others in the region.

Bilaterally, the United States and China worked in the early months of 2009 to amalgamate and upgrade separate tracks evolved under the Bush administration into an enhanced mechanism, the US–China Strategic and Economic Dialogue. In this new approach, Secretary of State Clinton and Treasury Secretary Tim Geithner were to represent the United States, matched respectively on the Chinese side by State Counsellor Dai Bingguo and Vice-Premier Wang Qishan, in discussions that were to range widely and in detail over global affairs. And, again at the IISS Shangri-La Dialogue, Gates indicated his enthusiasm for inaugurating a parallel security dialogue dealing principally with questions of defence and strategy.

Yet the development of such a consultative infrastructure was a necessary but not a sufficient requirement for greater common action. At issue was whether real convergences of underlying assumptions and perceived interests would occur. China and United States differed on questions of international trade policy and exchange-rate management, and on how and by whom the phenomenon of climate change should principally be tackled, so that the prospects for the Copenhagen summit scheduled for December 2009 and a successor treaty to the Kyoto Protocol on greenhouse-gas emissions hung in the balance.

Conflicting interests

In security policy, basic divergences in the positions of Washington and Beijing remained. North Korea's test launch in April 2009 of a *Unha-2* intercontinental ballistic missile (based on the *Taepo-dong* 2) and second nuclear test in May confirmed that it had the potential to upset the strategic equilibrium of northeast Asia. Yet Pyongyang seemed to have strained rather than snapped Beijing's patience. Widely presumed to possess the greatest leverage over North Korea, by virtue of its importance as a supplier of energy and foodstuffs, China chose, despite US urgings, not to exercise its influence to an extent that would effect a meaningful change in Pyongyang's behaviour. If such pressure were to challenge the survival of the regime – made more fragile and unpredictable by questions over the succession to Kim Jong Il (see Korea, pp. 358–67) – possible consequences for Beijing would include a failed state on its border and a tide of refugees flooding into China. Wider calculations also bore on China's attitudes. At the heart of Pyongyang's desire for equanimity in its relations with the United States, based on an acceptance of its nuclear-power status, lies a wish for some strategic depth against its immediate neighbours, most notably China. For Beijing, whose long-term interests include a Korean Peninsula that strategically inclines towards China, confronting Pyongyang risks igniting anti-Chinese senti-ments present in the Korean nationalism to be found on both sides of the Demilitarized Zone. In these circumstances China was only willing to condemn North Korea's actions and support a new UN Security Council resolution reasserting sanctions and providing a mandate for more rigorous inspection of North Korean and other ships suspected of breaking them. The measures prompted Pyongyang to signal its intention to step up its nuclear and missile programmes.

With regard to Iran's nuclear programme, too, China tended to act as a brake on the application of pressure on Tehran. Echoing its attachment to the Six-Party Talks mechanism for North Korea, China preferred an open-ended diplomatic process. Beijing's stake in Iran differed from its stake in North Korea: Pyongyang was a local threat to stability, with nothing to offer except a withdrawal of that threat, whereas Iran's importance derived from its ability to supply China with the energy resources required to sustain economic growth. But China's essential strategic choice was the same. Its reluctance to join the United States and European powers in a vigorous effort to dissuade Iran of the desirability of a nuclear programme was based on the assumption that a confrontation of this kind would not only jeopard-ise Chinese energy interests in Iran but unsettle the Middle East as a whole. However, as Iranian nuclear capabilities developed it became clear to Beijing that regional stability would not be served by a policy that implicitly acqui-esced to the acquisition of such capabilities. In the light of China's default diplomatic position – playing for time in the hope that changes in the overall balance of factors might somehow avoid worst outcomes – it welcomed the Obama administration's greater willingness than its predecessor to engage Tehran. China's cautious instincts were reinforced by the political crisis that flowed from the disputed June 2009 Iranian presidential election, which appeared to some observers to have the potential to undermine the founda-tions of the Islamic Republic (see Iran, pp. 213–31). It seemed unlikely that

Beijing would lament the departure of President Mahmoud Ahmadinejad and his replacement by a loosely reformist figure who might be more acceptable to the outside world and less inclined to burn Iran's bridges.

Elsewhere in the greater Middle East, Beijing had as much interest as the United States in assuring the viability of Pakistan. Seen by Islamabad as a more constant ally than Washington, Beijing has traditionally viewed Pakistan as a useful counterweight to India. More recently, however, Pakistan has become an important component in a South Asian strategy designed to expand Chinese access to the Indian Ocean's trade and shipping routes, symbolised principally by the development of the Chinese port facility of Gwadar in Baluchistan. But Chinese interests were wider; Beijing would have much to fear from destabilisation of Pakistan, and was concerned over the degree to which the Taliban insurgency in Afghanistan was fed from inside Pakistan. The deteriorating situation in Afghanistan increased Beijing's fears of a strengthened challenge from Islamist Uighur militants operating in Xinjiang province in western China. As of mid 2009, however, no joint strategic approach between Beijing and Washington towards Pakistan had even begun to take shape.

> "Beijing would have much to fear from destabilisation of Pakistan"

There was some comfort to be drawn from the reduction in tensions between China and Taiwan over the course of 2008 and much of 2009, which removed one risk of irritation to Sino-American relations. Even so, there was no indication that the amelioration of cross-Strait tensions had an impact on China's assumptions about its own military requirements. Indeed, in the view of most US defence planners, China's thinking had moved beyond consideration of contingencies in its immediate locality. This was not wholly unwelcome.

In December 2008, for example, the People's Liberation Army Navy (PLAN) sent an anti-piracy taskforce to the Gulf of Aden. Consisting of two warships and a supply vessel, the anti-piracy flotilla became an ongoing deployment by the PLAN. Less welcome to Washington, however, was confirmation of Chinese interest in the development of an aircraft-carrier programme to provide greater expeditionary and power-projection capabilities. The Jiangnan Changxing shipyard near Shanghai was to be the home of the first domestically manufactured carrier, to displace 40,000–50,000 tonnes. The former Ukrainian carrier *Varyag* was meanwhile being converted by China into a training carrier. The Ukrainian government also provided the PLAN with its carrier-pilot training facility at Nitka in Crimea, as well as with T-10K training aircraft. Brazil was also to provide the PLAN with the use of its carrier, the *São Paulo*, for training purposes. China's increased desire for enhanced maritime capabilities to defend territorial and commercial interests went hand in hand with a greater sensitivity to US naval activities in its vicinity and a greater assertion of maritime territorial claims. The most serious incident occurred in March 2009, when Chinese fishing vessels, assumed to be operating with mandates from Chinese military authorities, harassed the USNS *Impeccable* off the southern coast of Hainan Island, in what the United States insisted were international waters. The Chinese boats approached to within close range of the US surveillance ship. It was forced to use water cannons to repel the harassment, which included efforts by Chinese crews to sever surveillance equipment towed by the *Impeccable*.

The tentative, largely informal contacts Beijing and Taipei developed after Ma Ying-jeou of the KMT was elected to the Taiwanese presidency continued fairly smoothly, and led to a willingness by China to see Taiwanese observers participate in World Health Assembly meetings for the first time. A kind of diplomatic truce evolved, with both sides looking to establish a modus vivendi in both bilateral relations and with regard to the relationships and affiliations Taiwan maintains internationally. Ma and Chinese President Hu Jintao advertised respective frameworks for future contact, initially emphasising forms of economic cooperation but with a view eventually to develop a more systematic political track. Both sides benefited from this relaxation in tensions, but perhaps not equally. Some of Ma's domestic political opponents charged that the engagement between China and Taiwan would over time increase Taiwan's dependency on China, narrow its options and weaken its hand in any hard bargaining that might arise over political and status questions.

In 2008 and 2009, China took an interest in two other international disputes involving separatist claims and disputed sovereignties. The Russia–Georgia War of August 2008, and Russia's diplomatic recognition of the breakaway regions of South Ossetia and Abkhazia, created some discomfort in relations between Moscow and Beijing. Russia plainly hoped for a degree of understanding for its actions, but as far as Beijing was concerned, Russia had simply extended a precedent set by Western recognition of Kosovo's separatist claims – a precedent it regarded as dangerous in the context of its own unresolved differences with Taiwan. Russia's behaviour gave China broader reason to doubt its strategic partner. Beijing could reflect on how its own patient diplomacy in Asia had created a degree of receptivity to China's re-emergence as a power and a sense that its rise was something from which others could benefit, in stark contrast to Moscow's tendency to alarm and antagonise its neighbours in Europe and the former Soviet space.

Elsewhere, China played a significant role in providing the Sri Lankan government with the means to inflict a final, brutal defeat on the rebel Liberation Tigers of Tamil Eelam, including economic assistance as well as ammunition, weaponry, fighter aircraft and other supplies (see Sri Lanka, pp. 320–22). Sri Lanka assumed greater significance for China after agreement on the construction of a port facility at Hambantota on the south coast of the island, which, it was assumed, was intended to both play a commercial role and provide refuelling and resupply capabilities for PLAN vessels, including those patrolling sea-lines of communication.

Hesitant power

The past year confirmed China's status as a power of considerable importance. It was treated – and, increasingly, accepted – as such by other major powers including the United States. Absent, however, was any indication that China at this stage was susceptible to the temptations of a greater, more overt international leadership role. In many respects China continued to keep its own counsel, and the world guessing.

Southeast Asia: Political and Security Questions

Instability and uncertainty continued to characterise the politics of several Southeast Asian states, most notably Myanmar and Thailand. Indonesia's democratic consolidation continued, with parliamentary elections in April 2009 bringing success to secular parties and a conspicuous (if largely unexpected) decline in support for Islamist candidates. Internal security remained a concern in Thailand, where the preoccupied authorities in Bangkok showed few signs of getting to grips with the insurgency in the south, and in the Philippines, where all-out conflict broke out anew between government forces and the Moro Islamic Liberation Front following the collapse of peace negotiations. Terrorism continued to recede as a pressing security concern, but inter-state tensions rose, with border clashes between Thailand

and Cambodia as well as signs of renewed competition between China and members of the Association of Southeast Asian Nations (ASEAN) over disputed boundaries in the South China Sea.

Myanmar: change in sight?

For Myanmar's military regime, managing the political scene in advance of the multi-party elections scheduled for 2010 has become a preoccupation. Following the new national constitution that the State Peace and Development Council (SPDC) junta announced in April 2008 and a referendum that approved the constitution in May 2008, the elections were supposed to be a key milestone in the seven-stage 'roadmap to democracy' that the SPDC adopted in response to domestic unrest including mass demonstrations in August and September 2007 as well as international pressure. The main consideration for the SPDC was evidently how to maintain the military's control despite the elections, and particularly how to circumscribe the likely popular appeal of Aung San Suu Kyi and her National League for Democracy (NLD). To this end, the constitution assigned a quarter of parliamentary seats to the armed forces, which would also retain control of the home-affairs ministry whatever the election's result, and disqualified from the presidency anyone who has married a foreigner (which includes Aung San Suu Kyi, whose British husband died in 1999). For its part, the NLD initially claimed that the SPDC's roadmap was fundamentally flawed and that the 1990 elections which it had won decisively had to be the basis for any political settlement. However, after their plenary meeting in Yangon in late April 2009, the NLD's leaders issued the Shwegonedine Declaration in which they said their party would take part in the elections if the SPDC reviewed the constitution and amended its undemocratic elements, released Aung San Suu Kyi together with all other political prisoners, embarked on a dialogue with the NLD, and allowed international observers to monitor the vote. The regime seemed unlikely to meet any of these conditions, except perhaps the last. However, any election in which the NLD failed to participate would almost certainly be seen as illegitimate, domestically and internationally.

The SPDC suffered renewed international criticism in May 2008, when Cyclone Nargis brought widespread destruction and death to Myanmar's Irrawaddy Delta and the military authorities initially resisted efforts by other governments and NGOs to provide emergency assistance. However, the SPDC did allow ASEAN to play a leading role in coordinating the international aid effort, and during June 2008 the junta began granting visas to

large numbers of UN staff and NGO personnel, who were able to reach the
worst-affected areas to assess the needs of the 2.4m survivors. Subsequently,
NGOs found that Myanmar's armed forces – implicitly acknowledging the
ability and resources that international agencies were able to mobilise –
largely allowed them to work effectively and independently. In February
2009, the SPDC extended the agreement allowing foreign access to the delta
region, but only to mid 2010.

Despite this openness to foreign involvement in disaster relief, external pressure on the regime to negotiate with the NLD proved ineffective.
In February 2009, UN special envoy Ibrahim Gambari made the latest in a
series of visits to Myanmar aimed at bringing the two
sides together; he met Aung San Suu Kyi as well as
several SPDC leaders, but was not allowed to meet
SPDC Chairman Senior General Than Shwe, and
was unable to report significant progress. In March
2009, the 14th ASEAN Summit meeting in Hua Hin,
Thailand encouraged Myanmar's government to
release political detainees and 'include all political
parties', but, notwithstanding the entry into force
of the ASEAN Charter in December 2008, the asso-
ciation proved as impotent as ever to influence a member state's domestic
political affairs.

> External pressure to negotiate proved ineffective

A new reason for regional and wider international disquiet over
Myanmar's domestic conditions emerged in early 2009. For the previous two
to three years, members of the Rohingya ethnic minority, who are Muslims
from Rakhine state in western Myanmar and have long been victims of discrimination and human-rights violations at the hands of Myanmar's military
rulers, had been fleeing their homeland in increasing numbers, many trying
to reach Malaysia by boat. In January 2009, allegations that Thailand's armed
forces had the previous month abused hundreds of Rohingyas en route to
Malaysia, towing many of them out to sea, provoked a senior Thai defence
official to say that the UN High Commission for Refugees should 'solve the
problem at source' by consulting with Myanmar. The March 2009 ASEAN
Summit delegated consideration of the Rohingya migration question to a
meeting in April of the Bali Process, a regional institution co-chaired by
Australia and Indonesia and intended to foster practical cooperation against
people-trafficking in the Asia-Pacific. However, the Bali Process failed to
make progress on the problem, with Myanmar's deputy minister for home

affairs, Brigadier-General Khin Yi, repeating SPDC claims that the Rohingyas were not citizens of Myanmar and that they were not persecuted.

Speaking at the IISS Shangri-La Dialogue in Singapore in late May 2009, Deputy Minister of Defence Major-General Aye Myint claimed that as a result of the SPDC policy allowing ethnic-minority insurgent groups to 'exchange arms for peace', 17 out of 18 armed groups had returned to 'the legal fold' along with factions of the Karen National Union (KNU), the only group that remained in open revolt. Aye Myint claimed that these ceasefires had 'established confidence between the government and the armed insurgent groups', allowing 'special development projects' to proceed, particularly in frontier areas. However, diverse sources suggested that the reality was more complex. While uneasy ceasefires endured with all insurgent groups apart from the KNU, by mid 2009 the SPDC's pressure on the insurgents to integrate with Myanmar's army as border militia forces and on their political wings to register as political parties in order to contest the 2010 elections appeared to be risking the resumption of open conflict. Groups such as the Kachin Independence Army, which already claimed an armed strength of 20,000, stepped up recruitment. Meanwhile, the 25,000-strong United Wa State Army – which the US Treasury Department in November 2008 branded 'the most powerful drug trafficking organisation in Southeast Asia' – had reportedly benefited from significant arms transfers from China, including artillery, anti-aircraft guns and surface-to-air missiles. While it continued to be the SPDC's main international ally, Beijing also maintained close links with the ethnic insurgent groups, which it saw as providing a buffer against potential future instability in Myanmar. Apart from arms, Beijing also provided development and investment in roads and other infrastructure in the border region.

With Aung San Suu Kyi's latest period of house arrest due to end on 27 May 2009, there was vocal international criticism when Myanmar's authorities brought her to trial in mid May on a charge of breaking the terms of her house arrest by not reporting to the authorities an uninvited American visitor who had swum across a lake to her residence, and by allowing him to stay there. Many observers saw the charge as a pretext to ensure that she would not be at liberty during the build-up to the 2010 elections, for fear that she would provide leadership for the political opposition as she had in 1990. In early June, the trial was suspended for a week while Aung San Suu Kyi's lawyer appealed for the reinstatement of three defence witnesses, all members of the NLD.

Thailand's political turmoil

Thailand's continuing political disarray, which one commentator likened to a 'national nervous breakdown', contrasted starkly with the image of stability and democratic consolidation that the country had presented earlier in the decade. Political controversy intensified in mid 2008. The well-funded, yellow-shirted People's Alliance for Democracy (PAD), the leaders of which included media magnate Sondhi Limthongkil and former Bangkok Governor Chamlong Srimuang, organised large-scale and persistent demonstrations against the government that took power under the leadership of Prime Minister Samak Sundarajev in February 2008 following the December 2007 elections. Samak was widely seen as a proxy for former Prime Minister Thaksin Shinawatra, who had been overthrown by a military coup in 2006 following earlier anti-government agitation by the PAD, and Samak's People's Power Party (PPP) was essentially a reincarnation of Thaksin's Thai Rak Thai (TRT) party. While the PAD found limited support from otherwise liberal intellectuals and academics concerned over Thaksin's alleged abuses, and had the backing of state enterprise labour unions, it was essentially an organisation with a hyper-nationalist, monarchist and (despite its name) fundamentally anti-democratic outlook. Despite initial avowals of non-violence, its supporters often used weapons including firearms during its protests in 2008, leading to widespread injuries and some deaths.

From late August to early December 2008, the PAD escalated its campaign of intimidation against two successive governments seen as representing Thaksin's interests. The PAD's modus operandi notably included the storming by massed supporters of key installations with symbolic importance. Because of a hugely negative media backlash, it quickly ended its occupation of the NBT television station it took over on 26 August. But the PAD also seized several airports in the south, and blocked major roads and highways. Sympathetic unions stopped train services throughout the country, and threatened to cut electricity and water supplies to opponents of the PAD. The occupation of Government House (the location of the prime minister's office), which began at the end of August and lasted for months, came to symbolise the PAD's lawlessness and impunity. However, it was the judiciary that removed Prime Minister Samak from power. Responding to complaints from Senators and the Electoral Commission that Samak's role as host of two television cookery shows represented a conflict of interest with his prime ministerial position, in early September the Constitutional Court (widely alleged to represent establishment political interests) ruled that these activities disqualified him from the premiership, forcing the PPP and its coalition partners to nominate a new leader in the person of Deputy Prime Minister Somchai, Thaksin's brother-in-law. The fact that Somchai won 298 parliamentary votes in support of his premiership against 163 for Democrat Party leader Abhisit underlined the democratic legitimacy of the PPP.

Somchai's election, however, only led the PAD to escalate its struggle to depose the PPP administration. In early October, thousands of PAD supporters besieged parliament in an attempt to prevent Somchai's government from announcing its programme within the mandatory 15 days of swearing-in. Clashes between PAD activists and police led to serious injuries and the death of a young woman protester, whose funeral the queen attended – thereby implicitly blessing the movement. The PAD accused the government and police of brutality and vowed 'bloody revenge'. In late November, the PAD's *Operation Hiroshima* involved hundreds of protesters seizing control of the terminal buildings and control tower of the country's main air hub, Suvarnabhumi International Airport outside Bangkok, closing down flight operations, stranding large numbers of tourists and cutting a key link with the outside world. Despite orders from Somchai's government, the army refused to support efforts to dislodge the PAD, which also took control of Bangkok's second airport, Don Muang. In an atmosphere of intensifying national crisis, which the PAD had apparently created to provoke another coup, on 2 November the Constitutional Court dissolved the PPP and two other parties from Somchai's coalition, citing the implication of party executives in voting fraud in the December 2007 election. The court banned 109 party leaders, including 29 MPs, from politics for five years. The PAD immediately ended its occupation of the airports.

Supporters of Somchai and Thaksin, who in October flew to London and subsequently claimed political asylum (though the British government later revoked his visa), claimed that the Constitutional Court's decision amounted to a 'silent coup' against the PPP administration. They initially expected that yet another reincarnation of the TRT – this time the Puea Thai party – could be the core of a new ruling coalition. The defection, though, of a bloc of former PPP MPs led by Newin Chidchob, a regional political power-broker from the northeast, made it possible for the Democrat Party under Abhisit to form a new government with military backing. The collapse of the PPP government stymied Thaksin's brand of dominant-party politics, while old-style Thai politics based on regional blocs dominated by political 'godfathers' willing to sell their support to the highest bidder seemed to have returned –

at least for the time being. Abhisit's Democrat-led government started with a relatively narrow 37-seat parliamentary majority, allowing Newin and other faction leaders considerable bargaining power – but by-elections in January 2009 gave it another 20 seats.

Thaksin claimed that he was ready to return to Thailand and fight his way back to leadership. The red-shirted United Front for Democracy against Dictatorship (UDD) group, which supported him, threatened PAD-style demonstrations. While Newin's defection, together with the depletion of the UDD's funding, initially seemed likely to constrain the group's ability to mobilise on the scale of the PAD, in March 2009 a video broadcast by

> **Protesters forced cancellation of the summit**

Thaksin claiming that a conspiracy led by former Prime Minister Prem Tinsulanonda was behind the 2006 coup and Abhisit's ascendancy galvanised large-scale UDD demonstrations in Bangkok. Thaksin called for a 'people's revolution' to overthrow rule by the traditional bureaucratic elite, and for three weeks protesters effectively forced the cessation of normal activities in parts of Bangkok. The focus of the demonstrations soon moved to the beach resort of Pattaya, 165km southeast of Bangkok, the site for

the fourth East Asia Summit conference (bringing together the leaders of the ten ASEAN states plus Australia, China, India, Japan, New Zealand and South Korea), scheduled for 11–12 April. Despite the presence of 8,000 soldiers and police personnel and the declaration of a local state of emergency, protesters broke through cordons that were supposed to protect the summit venue, forcing cancellation of the meeting and evacuation of some leaders by helicopter. Since the summit had been postponed once already (having originally been scheduled for Bangkok the previous December), this new indication of Thailand's disarray embarrassed Abhisit's government regionally and internationally. Meanwhile clashes between protesters and the security forces escalated in Bangkok, where the government also declared a state of emergency. On 13 April, troops used live rounds against demonstrators, many of whom were armed with Molotov cocktails and other improvised weapons. Local residents also clashed with UDD protesters. At least two people were killed and more than 120 injured. Against this violent backdrop, the government used censorship laws to close down pro-UDD radio stations. After troops tightened their cordon around the protesters on 14 April, however, UDD leaders – fearing large-scale loss of life – backed down, some surrendering to the police and others going underground. While this climbdown strengthened the prime minister's authority, one UDD leader, Jakrapob Penkair (a former minister under Thaksin), spoke of a continuing if covert campaign to unseat Abhisit's 'disguised dictatorship' over the following 6–12 months. Only three days later, PAD leader Sondhi Limthongkil was badly wounded in an assassination attempt that some (but by no means all) observers blamed on Thaksin and his supporters. By early June, the UDD was vowing to stage renewed demonstrations later that month.

Thailand's domestic political travails affected relations with neighbouring Cambodia. Following Cambodia's registration of the Preah Vihear temple with UNESCO as a World Heritage Site, in June 2008 the PAD used the long-running territorial dispute with Cambodia over the site as a weapon with which to undermine Samak's administration. In Cambodia, Hun Sen's Cambodian People's Party also exploited the issue while campaigning before the July 2008 parliamentary election. In mid July, cross-border tensions flared, with Cambodia alleging that Thai troops were on its soil. Both sides reduced their troop levels on the border during August, but tension escalated again in October, with the two sides' troops opening fire on each other on at least two occasions: one Thai and three Cambodian soldiers died. Further clashes in April 2009 killed another three Thai and two Cambodian troops. These skirmishes constituted the first clear-cut (if limited) armed conflict between two ASEAN member states and further undermined the regional grouping's credibility.

Indonesia's quiet success

In stark contrast to Thailand's disarray, as it prepared for its 2009 legislative and presidential elections Indonesia was much more peaceful, cohesive and stable than would have seemed possible at the beginning of the decade. Surprisingly, none of the more gloomy scenarios for Indonesia had come to pass. Serious economic and social problems remained, but this large and highly diverse country now displayed impressive stability, with relative calm and respect for due process prevailing in its domestic politics. Part of the reason for the improvement in Indonesia's circumstances lay in more effective and authoritative leadership since the 2004 elections brought to power a government led by Susilo Bambang Yudhoyono (widely known as SBY), a retired general. Among the SBY administration's achievements were a comprehensive peace settlement that granted autonomy to the previously rebellious province of Aceh, a nationwide exercise in political and fiscal devolution which empowered sub-provincial districts and largely undermined centrifugal forces, a highly effective counter-terrorist strategy supported by Australia and other regional and international partners, an anti-corruption campaign which has begun to make an impact, and a significant economic revival manifested in GDP growth of 5.5% in 2005 and 2006, 6.3% in 2007, and 6.2% in 2008 and the creation of millions of new jobs. Even in 2009, amid global recession, Indonesia's economy was expected to grow by around 2.4%.

Nevertheless, Indonesia remained a poor country by any standard, with almost half the population of 237m living on less than $2 a day. Indonesia is also the world's most populous Muslim country, and onlookers as well as some Indonesians expressed concern that it might be vulnerable to an Islamist takeover. A furore over the intimidatory tactics used by the militant group Defenders of the Islamic Faith (FPI), which claims a million members, against the minor Muslim sect, Ahmadiyah, in mid 2008 reinforced these fears, as did indications of increased popular support for the Justice and Prosperity Party (PKS), which is closely aligned with Egypt's Muslim Brotherhood. However, these fears were exaggerated. Seventy million adult Indonesians belong to one of two Muslim mass organisations – Nahdlatul Ulama (which is rurally based and traditionalist) and Muhammadiyah (urban and modernist) – which both espouse essentially moderate political and social outlooks. Moreover, a large proportion of Indonesian Muslims, together with the estimated 12–16% of the population who are non-Muslims (mainly Christians and Hindus), support secular political parties.

The result of the parliamentary election held in early April 2009 more than vindicated predictions that most Indonesians would continue to shy away from supporting Islamist politics. With 71% of 171m registered voters taking part, the election saw support for parties with an overtly Islamic outlook fall to 29% of the vote (from 38% in 2004). Fewer than 8% of voters backed the stridently Islamist PKS, which had aimed to secure 15% of the vote. Equally strikingly, the secular Democratic Party (PD) – which was formed in 2004 specifically to support SBY – dramatically increased its share of the vote to 21%, becoming the most popular party and indicating the president's widespread appeal. The other two leading secular parties – Golkar and the Indonesian Democratic Party of Struggle (PDI-P) – together took a further 28%.

The parliamentary election set the stage for the presidential contest on 8 July, which was to provide Indonesia with a national leader and a vice president for the following five years. Under the 2008 Presidential Election Law, candidates must have the support of a party or coalition that has won at least 25% of the popular vote or 20% of the 560 seats in the People's Representative Council (DPR), the national parliament). Of those who had indicated interest in running for president, only SBY – whose party secured 150 DPR seats – automatically qualified as a result of the 2009 parliamentary election. However, by 16 May, when presidential and vice-presidential candidates needed to register, there were three contesting teams. After Vice-President Jusuf Kalla announced in February that he would himself stand for election, SBY was forced to find a new running mate and chose Boediono, the Bank of Indonesia governor. The SBY–Boediono team had support from the four main Islamic parties, including the PKS, though they initially resented SBY's choice of a running mate from outside their ranks. Kalla chose former armed forces commander Wiranto as his partner; they had the support of Golkar and a number of smaller and mainly secular parties. The third team consisted of Megawati Sukarnoputri (who was president from 2001 to 2004) and Prabowo Subianto, a controversial former army special forces commander; this combination was supported by the PDI-P, Prabowo's Gerindra and other small parties. While public opinion polls during May and June 2009 registered overwhelming popular support for SBY, it was unclear whether the initial vote would produce an outright winner, and whether there would need to be a second round of voting in September. However, there seemed little doubt that SBY would ultimately emerge victorious, a prospect that reassured Indonesia's regional and international friends including Singapore, Australia and the United States, notwithstanding some reservations over the probable inclusion in the government of ministers drawn from the PKS.

Internal security and counter-terrorism

Internal security remained a concern in southern Thailand and in the Philippines. With Bangkok consumed with strife between pro- and anti-Thaksin factions, the southern Thai insurgency by Muslim militants, resentful of decades of neglect by the capital, festered with no progress towards a political solution. There was a decline in violence during 2008, partly as a result of increased and more offensively oriented Thai security force deployments resulting in the arrest or surrender of insurgent leaders, but also because of declining popular support for the insurgents. Nevertheless, bombings and drive-by shootings remained common. Despite the Democrat

Party's strong support in the south, Abhisit's new government failed to make a significant impact: indeed, after the relative lull during 2008, insurgent activity increased again in early 2009. Although the new prime minister promised in January to end emergency rule in the south soon, in April the government again extended these measures for a further three months.

In the Philippines, a Memorandum of Agreement on Ancestral Domain (MOA-AD) negotiated by the Moro Islamic Liberation Front (MILF) and the Manila government in July 2008 promised to bring an end to the long-running MILF rebellion and to entrench permanently the formal but fragile ceasefire which had been in place and supervised by a Malaysian-led International Monitoring Team since 2003. However, protests by Christian and indigenous communities on Mindanao over the expansion of the Autonomous Region of Muslim Mindanao under the agreement led the Philippine Supreme Court to issue a temporary restraining order in early August halting the signing of the MOA-AD. This exacerbated tension between MILF units under hardline rebel commanders and the Armed Forces of the Philippines (AFP), leading to escalating armed clashes on Mindanao. The MILF units seized 15 villages, prompting large-scale AFP assaults, with attack aircraft and helicopters providing close air support for army units. This intense fighting displaced more than 500,000 people, creating a major humanitarian crisis in Mindanao. In early September, Manila responded to the resumed fighting by dissolving its peace panel and ending talks with the MILF, saying that they would only resume when violence ceased. In mid October, the Supreme Court declared the MOA-AD 'contrary to law and the Constitution' because of the government's lack of proper consultation. Fighting continued during late 2008 and early 2009 as the AFP focused its operations – including more air-strikes – against three MILF commanders in central Mindanao that it held responsible for ceasefire violations. While casualties were relatively light, there was continuing large-scale displacement of civilians. In mid 2009, there appeared to be no credible prospect of peace negotiations resuming. The Supreme Court decision effectively necessitated a constitutional amendment to allow power-sharing between the Philippine government and any future Moro political entity. Because of President Gloria Macapagal Arroyo's long-established interest in exploiting constitutional change as a means of extending her term in office, no such change would be possible before the presidential election in 2010. And, even then, non-Muslim communities in Mindanao and the AFP would probably oppose any settlement. In the short term, a renewed ceasefire was the best that could be hoped for.

The Philippine government continued to argue that the insurgency of the New People's Army (NPA), the armed wing of the Communist Party of the Philippines, would be defeated by 2010. Despite AFP claims that its counter-insurgency campaign (which included a Social Integration Program aimed at encouraging rebels to surrender, as well as military offensives) substantially undermined the military strength of the Maoist group during 2008, the government's target seemed unrealistic given its acknowledgement that 5–6,000 armed NPA insurgents still operated across the country and had influence over almost 1,400 villages. Nevertheless, NPA claims in early 2009 that it had recently boosted its 'revolutionary mass base' substantially were also probably over-optimistic. The reality appeared to be that while NPA strength was gradually declining and the group was having difficulty funding its operations, it was hardly on the brink of extinction.

> **Islamist terrorism appeared to pose less of a threat than earlier in the decade**

Meanwhile, the Abu Sayyaf Group (ASG) continued to challenge the Philippine security forces in Basilan, Jolo and Zamboanga. The Philippine authorities claimed that the ASG was responsible for 27 kidnapping incidents aimed at raising funds during 2008, despite the success of the AFP in gradually reducing the group's strength and killing key commanders since mid decade. In a high-profile kidnapping in mid January 2009, the ASG took three International Committee of the Red Cross (ICRC) officials hostage; two were subsequently freed but one, an Italian, was still being held five months later. In early April, arrests of non-militant associates of the ASG, including policemen, revealed an apparently extensive criminal conspiracy that had facilitated the ICRC kidnappings. Nevertheless, the ASG took further hostages in April and May, and some were murdered.

Despite the persistence of the ASG, which had evidently degenerated over the course of the decade from an ideologically motivated extremist group into a criminal band, Islamist terrorism (as opposed to campaigns aimed at achieving regional autonomy) in general appeared to pose a considerably less serious threat in Southeast Asia than it had done earlier in the decade. This was mainly due to the continuing effectiveness of the Indonesian authorities' counter-terrorism efforts involving the pursuit, arrest, trial and sentencing of members of Jemaah Islamiah (JI) known to have been involved in violent activities. In November 2008, Indonesia executed by firing squad three JI militants – Imam Samudra, Amrozi Nurhasyim and Ali Ghufron –

found guilty of planning attacks on Bali nightclubs that killed 202 people (including 88 Australians) in October 2002. While there had been fears that the executions might provoke a new wave of JI attacks, the fact that there was no significant violent reaction indicated the inability of JI remnants to mount significant operations, or at least their unwillingness to risk an even tougher crackdown by the Indonesian authorities if they did so. However, key JI figures – most importantly the Malaysian-born bomb-maker Noordin Mohammed Top, who was implicated in the 2002 Bali attacks and bombings in Jakarta in 2003–04 – remained on the loose, and some JI renegades were believed to have taken refuge in the southern Philippines with the MILF and ASG. Moreover, the fact that JI detainee Mas Selamat Kastari (allegedly the former head of the Singapore branch of JI) was able to escape from custody in Singapore in February 2008, cross into southern Malaysia and remain there undetected for more than a year before his capture by the Malaysian police in April 2009 suggested that underground JI networks might still exist in Singapore and Malaysia. In addition, the conviction in April 2009 of ten members of a radical group in Palembang, Sumatra not directly linked to JI or other previously known terrorist organisations, on charges of murdering a Christian preacher pointed to the danger from autonomous groups of jihadists in Indonesia and possibly elsewhere in the region.

South China Sea tensions

The South China Sea continued to emerge as a locus of tension between China and several Southeast Asian states with territorial claims that conflicted with Beijing's in the Spratly Islands. There was growing concern in some Southeast Asian capitals that China's rapidly expanding energy demand together with its growing international confidence and ability to project power were encouraging it to assert its claims more aggressively. Reports in July 2008 that Chinese officials had warned ExxonMobil and other energy companies not to explore for hydrocarbon resources off the Vietnamese coast provoked a sharp response from Hanoi. In May 2009, Vietnam submitted a claim to the United Nations Commission on the Limits of the Continental Shelf (CLCS), effectively staking its claim to maritime natural resources beyond its exclusive economic zone; this time it was China that responded to what it saw as a violation of its sovereignty. One effect of continuing Sino-Vietnamese tensions over maritime issues was Hanoi's interest in developing closer security relations with partners in the Asia-Pacific region and beyond. In June 2008, during a state visit to the United States, Prime Minister Nguyen

Tan Dung became the most senior Vietnamese government official to visit the Pentagon since 1975. During the first half of 2009, a delegation of senior Vietnamese officers visited a US aircraft carrier in the South China Sea for the first time, and two Indian naval task forces paid port calls in Vietnam. In May 2009, Vietnam elevated its participation in the IISS Shangri-La Dialogue when Minister of National Defence General Phung Quang Thanh attended the summit in Singapore for the first time. Vietnam also continued efforts to modernise the maritime and air components of its own armed forces.

In the Philippines, there was a considerable domestic political backlash over the Arroyo administration's acquiescence in the 2005 tripartite Joint Marine Seismic Undertaking (JMSU) agreement signed by the state energy companies of China, the Philippines and Vietnam (which was alleged to have compromised Manila's claims in the Spratlys) and to Chinese pressure on Manila not to adopt new legislation relating to the Philippines' archipelagic baseline claims. In consequence, when the JMSU expired in June 2008, Manila announced that it would not be renewed. Moreover, on 10 March 2009, Arroyo signed into law the new baseline legislation, setting the Philippines' maritime boundaries and effectively reasserting Manila's claims to sovereignty over what it referred to as the 'Kalayaan Islands' and Scarborough Island in the Spratlys in order to meet a deadline set by the CLCS. Beijing protested that the new law violated China's 'indisputable sovereignty'. The passage into law of the Philippine baseline bill came only two days after an incident in the South China Sea south of Hainan in which Chinese vessels harassed the US ocean-surveillance ship USNS *Impeccable*, which was collecting intelligence on Chinese navy submarines. China's position was that it had the right to prohibit foreign naval vessels from operating in its exclusive economic zone.

Southeast Asian governments watched the new US administration's behaviour towards the region closely for indications of change in Washington's diplomatic and military posture. During the March crisis, they doubtless noted President Obama's telephone call to President Arroyo in which he reaffirmed the US–Philippines alliance. This seemed to provide evidence – if any was needed – that the US remained committed to Southeast Asian partners despite the major demands on America's attention and resources from the Middle East and Afghanistan. Indeed, US concern over China's growing naval capabilities, the potential vulnerability of US energy companies' interests and activities, and the threats to freedom of navigation seemingly implicit in Beijing's maritime posture collectively suggested that the United States, while avoiding any commitment to support Southeast Asian states' territorial claims, had its own reasons for taking a close interest in developments in the South China Sea.

Australia and New Zealand: Defence Policy Shifts

The year to June 2009 saw a sea change in the strategic thinking of Australia and New Zealand. In both countries, the balance of emphasis in armed forces structures began to swing back towards maritime power – sea-denial and strike capability – after years in which greater focus and resources had been devoted to land forces in peacekeeping, stabilisation and intervention roles.

In Australia, the focus has overwhelmingly been on China, viewed from two conflicting perspectives. The first is of an emerging industrial giant, vying with Japan to be Australia's largest trading partner, paying ever-higher prices for Australian raw materials and energy, shipping low-cost consumer goods, and (since the global financial crisis began in 2008) the main hope of an easy way out of recession. The second view of China is as the first new Asian economic power that is not also a US ally, but rather, in some ways, a challenger. Australians watched uneasily in 2008 as the Chinese Embassy and its consulates organised local Chinese residents to block anti-Beijing protests at Olympic warm-up events. A bid by Chinese state-owned firm Chinalco to buy a 20% stake in the mining giant Rio Tinto provoked an intense debate about foreign state investment in Australian resources. Australian Defence Minister Joel Fitzgibbon became embroiled in controversy over undisclosed trips to China paid for by a Chinese-Australian businesswoman; some of his own officials launched an investigation. In June 2009, he was forced to resign.

The changed perceptions of China were partly explored in a new White Paper on Defence commissioned by the Australian Labor government of Prime Minister Kevin Rudd soon after its election victory in November 2007. The first such paper in nine years, it committed Australia to a large expansion of the Royal Australian Navy over the next two decades, to a size that (except for aircraft carriers and ballistic-missile submarines) will be close to that of its ever-shrinking parent, Britain's Royal Navy. The decision to re-equip the Royal Australian Air Force (RAAF) with the fifth-generation F-35 *Lightning* was reconfirmed, along with associated force multipliers.

In New Zealand, a centre-right government under Prime Minister John Key came to power in November 2008, following the election defeat of the Labour Party and Prime Minister Helen Clark. The new defence minister, Wayne Mapp, announced a defence review panel to look at emerging needs to 2035, to be followed by a White Paper in 2010. The review was widely expected to take a new look at the need for maritime capability and conventional defence, downplayed since the Labour government cancelled acquisition of a third modern frigate for the Royal New Zealand Navy and scrapped the Royal New Zealand Air Force fighter wing a decade ago.

Behind these shifts in thinking about tangible military power was a sense of vast change in the strategic outlook for the Western Pacific and Indian Ocean. Australia's thinking was driven by concern that China's rising ability to project power would challenge the maritime dominance of Asian coastal approaches by the United States, and perhaps even further offshore, by the end of the period covered by the White Paper. New Zealand's thinking was yet to be formally set out, but according to Lance Beath, Victoria University of Wellington strategic scholar, the review signalled an end to two or three decades of a complacent view that 'New Zealand doesn't need a defence force to protect itself or its immediate environment' and a realisation that a 'standard range of military capability' was needed to protect the country's vast oceanic resources.

Australia's defence plans

Since the previous Australian White Paper in 2000, not only had the 11 September 2001 terrorist attacks in the United States changed the strategic outlook, but Australian forces had been committed to Iraq and Afghanistan and to stabilisation or disaster-relief missions in East Timor, Indonesia, Papua New Guinea, the Solomon Islands and Tonga. But the new White Paper also saw the beginnings of a fundamental shift in the Asia-Pacific power balance: 'Changes in the distribution of global power have become obvious in the past decade. China's rise in economic, political and military terms has become more evident. Pronounced military modernisation in the Asia-Pacific region is having significant implications for our strategic outlook.' High-intensity wars among the major parties were not likely, but could not be ruled out. The warning time for new military capabilities was shortening, and needed to be anticipated and planned for. Asian forces adding more sophisticated platforms such as advanced air-combat aircraft and submarines networked by new communications, command, computing, ISR and electronic-warfare systems; high-speed anti-ship cruise missiles and advanced torpedoes were two examples of this phenomenon.

While unlikely, a change in major-power relations in the Asia-Pacific region, particularly 'any diminution in the willingness or capacity of the United States to act as a stabilising force', would have a profound effect on Australia's strategic setting and require an even larger Australian Defence Force (ADF) than now contemplated as a significant 'strategic hedge'. Canberra did not see any other power having the military, economic or strategic capacity to challenge US global primacy out to 2030, but thought the United States might find itself overstretched and constrained to seek more active assistance from regional allies and partners. Economic growth in the Asia-Pacific region should help to build a sense of shared interests, supporting stability and security. But there were likely to be tensions between the region's major powers where the interests of the United States, China, Japan, India and Russia intersected.

Barring major setbacks, China by 2030 would become a major driver of economic activity, both in the region and globally, and would have strategic influence beyond East Asia. The White Paper noted that, by purchasing power parity calculus, China could overtake the United States as the world's largest economy around 2020, though in economic sophistication the US economy would remain supreme. The paper advocated the 'responsible-stakeholder' approach to China articulated by then US Deputy Secretary of State Robert Zoellick in 2005. China, however, would be Asia's strongest military power by a large margin, with growing power-projection capabilities commensurate with its economic size. It needed to reach out more to others to build confidence regarding its military plans, the paper said.

Looking at Southeast Asia, Canberra faced the strange picture of Indonesia as the most benign and progressive large presence in the region, while former pillars Thailand and Malaysia were slipping into political instability. As the Australian National University's Hugh White (who, as deputy defence secretary, wrote the 2000 White Paper) noted, 'in the 1970s and 1980s, Australian defence policy focused almost exclusively on one set of strategic risks – the possibility of conflict with Indonesia'. Although military training exchanges, chiefly between the Australian SAS and Indonesian Kopassus special forces, had resumed since the break over Timor Leste's independence vote in 1999, the weight of engagement had shifted to counter-terrorism work between the Australian Federal Police and the Indonesian National Police Detachment 88 against the Jemaah Islamiah movement. The

White Paper recognised that 'an authoritarian or overly nationalistic regime in Jakarta would ... create strategic risks for its neighbours'.

Beyond the primary strategic duty of defending Australian territory against direct attack, Canberra saw its next most important strategic interest as the security, stability and cohesion of the immediate neighbourhood, including Indonesia, Papua New Guinea, Timor Leste, New Zealand and the South Pacific island states. Many South Pacific island states and East Timor would continue to face stagnation and instability, exacerbated by climate change, and Australia needed to be prepared to respond directly with humanitarian and security assistance, including ADF deployments.

The third circle of Australia's strategic interest stretched from North Asia round to the Eastern Indian Ocean, centred on approaches to Australia and major trade routes in Southeast Asia. The White Paper saw the Indian Ocean, with growing traffic in energy supplies from the Middle East and Africa to Asia, becoming as central to Australia's maritime strategy and defence planning as was the Pacific, and envisaged a regional security architecture that included the United States, Japan, China, India, Indonesia and other regional states – an idea pushed since mid 2008 by Prime Minister Kevin Rudd. (see Strategic Policy Essay, pp. 64–74.) However, strategic stability was best underpinned by the continued presence of the United States.

Enhanced military capabilities

The White Paper saw Australia as a 'capable middle power that is able to contribute to global and regional security, including by way of military means'. In case of military contingencies, the appropriate Australian contribution 'might be our submarine force, special forces, surface combatants and air combat capabilities'. While force structures should be based on self-reliance in the defence of Australian territory, this did not preclude relying on the United States for intelligence and surveillance, communications, space systems, resupply and logistics.

Following on from these priorities, the Australian defence forces of 2030 were envisaged as having more punch in undersea warfare and anti-submarine warfare; surface maritime warfare (including air defence at sea); air superiority; strategic strike; special forces; intelligence, surveillance and reconnaissance; and cyber-warfare. The navy was to acquire 12 new submarines at a cost of A$35bn, with long range and endurance on patrol; three air-warfare destroyers to be equipped with long-range anti-aircraft missiles; and eventually a new class of frigates to replace the existing eight *Anzac*-class frigates,and 20 Offshore Combatant Vessels to replace the present fleet of patrol, anti-mine, hydrographic and oceanographic vessels. The navy was also to get, in the early part of the next decade, the two large Spanish-designed Landing Helicopter Dock (LHD) amphibious ships ordered by the previous government. The White Paper announced plans to acquire a strategic sealift ship of 10,000–15,000 tonnes and six new heavy landing craft.

Australia's army, already being expanded from six to eight deployable infantry, commando and mobile battalions, planned to combine combat and support units into ten battalion-sized 'battlegroups' able to carry out

> Critics thought hard decisions were avoided

a wide range of operations, backed by new MH-90 transport helicopters and Eurocopter *Tiger* recon-naissance-attack helicopters. A new fleet of about 1,100 'deployable protected vehicles' was to replace existing armoured personnel carriers. The Rudd government had earlier endorsed the previous government's decision to acquire for the RAAF a squadron of F/A-18F *Super Hornet* attack fighters as a bridging strike capability between the retirement in 2010 of the ageing F-111 aircraft and arrival of an expected 100 F-35 *Lightning* aircraft to replace older F-18 and the F-111 air-craft. Maritime-strike capability was to be provided by the *Hornet* and *Super Hornet* fleets using *Harpoon* missiles, with a new maritime-strike weapon to be acquired for the F-35. Air force networking would depend greatly on the successful delivery of six *Wedgetail* AEW&C aircraft, likely to be delivered six years late from 2011. Five KC-30A air-to-air refuelling aircraft were to be delivered from 2010, eight new maritime-patrol aircraft were to replace the current AP-3C *Orion* fleet, and up to seven large high-altitude, long-endurance unmanned aerial vehicles were to be acquired.

Although the White Paper proclaimed that Canberra was not taking the 'easy path of having elements of everything in our force structure', White and other critics thought Canberra had still shied away from taking hard decisions on capabilities unlikely to be deployed except in the most severe contingencies, when Australia's contribution would be mostly symbolic. These included the army's fleet of heavy *Abrams* tanks, acquired in 2006 by the previous government, and the two LHD vessels, which might have been substituted by a larger number of smaller ships suited to low-intensity oper-ations in the Pacific island ring.

The White Paper envisaged some A$20bn being cut from previously planned defence costs over the period to 2030, and the Rudd government's budget, for the 2009/10 fiscal year starting in July, saw the first A$5bn of cuts being achieved over the coming four years, mostly from changes to supply sources and maintenance. However, the defence budget allocation of A$25.1bn kept to the government's promise of a 3% annual real increase out to FY2017/18.

International operations continued to increase demands on Australian forces. In April 2008, Canberra decided to add 450 new troops to the existing 1,000-strong force in Uruzgan province, Afghanistan, with a cost estimated at A$1.3bn in 2009/10 – a commitment likely to last several more years. Keeping the 650-strong stabilisation force in Timor Leste would cost A$214m and the 110 personnel in the Solomon Islands about A$30m. With the withdrawal of a battalion-sized task force from southern Iraq in 2008, the only presence in Iraq was a detachment of 100 soldiers guarding the Australian Embassy in Baghdad.

New Zealand and the Pacific islands

New Zealand's defence review was to be carried out with much more modest fiscal and manpower resources. It was to be undertaken by retired Major-General Martyn Dunne, chief of the New Zealand Customs Service, leading accountant Rob McLeod, and the recent head of the Department of Foreign Affairs and Trade, Simon Murdoch. Among the capabilities to be studied were replacements for the ageing fleets of C-130 transports, P-3K *Orion* maritime-patrol aircraft and *Iroquois* helicopters; and additional strike components to the two Australian-built *Anzac*-class frigates and mixed fleet of patrol vessels. The review was also to study recruitment, the mix of regulars and reserves, and possible switches of the 4,500-strong regular army from its one-brigade, three-battalion structure into smaller battlegroups.

The troubling regional picture for which both Australia and New Zealand feel responsibility was underlined by continuing problems in a number of Pacific island states. For example, in Fiji, Commodore Frank Bainimarama, the army commander and prime minister who took power in a coup in 2006, reacted in April 2009 to a court ruling that his regime was illegal by sacking judges and abrogating the constitution. He promised elections, but only for September 2014 after replacing the complex system of electorates based on racial communities, which had been set up to protect ethnic Fijian rule since independence from Britain in 1967. International soldiering has been widely blamed for creating an institution too powerful for its domestic setting. With two battalions regularly stationed with United Nations forces in the Middle East, Fiji's defence force has become a major hard-currency earner, while creating a pool of about 24,000 serving and retired soldiers with experience in population control and urban warfare. In addition, about 2,000 Fijians serve with the British Army, and about 1,000 former soldiers work with private security firms in Iraq and Kuwait. As well as tightening sanctions imposed by the 16-nation Pacific Islands Forum after the Fijian regime refused to commit to holding elections by May 2009, Australia and New Zealand have lobbied the United Nations not to employ Fijian units in future UN operations.

Given these regional problems and frequent deployments of security forces, as well as the broader issue of the shifting power balance in the Asia-Pacific region, it is not surprising that the new governments in Australia and New Zealand have both embarked on reviews of their defence postures.

The Korean Peninsula: Diplomacy Derailed

Uncertainty loomed large on the Korean horizon in the year to mid 2009, clouding the outlook for denuclearisation of the peninsula, North–South relations, and the political and economic climate in both Koreas. The illness of Kim Jong Il and Pyongyang's nuclear and missile tests and announced abandonment of the Six-Party Talks contributed to growing international unease, while the South saw a sharp drop in economic growth and in the public-approval ratings of President Lee Myung-bak.

The North: leadership in question

A stroke reportedly suffered by North Korean leader Kim Jong Il in August 2008 threw the country's leadership into question. A French neurosurgeon who treated Kim confirmed in an interview with *Le Figaro* that he had undergone treatment, though not surgery, and was recovering. While Pyongyang's statements about Kim's activities for the rest of the year were meant to give the appearance of normalcy, they failed to dispel suspicions about his health since none of the activities were dated and only still photographs were released. Kim's reappearance in public in January 2009 at a meeting with senior Chinese envoy Wang Jiarui triggered a new phase of speculation, as observers closely examined pictures of the North Korean leader for the after-effects of his illness. Reports focused on the fact that his left hand appeared swollen and his face was worn. Speculation continued in the wake of his appearance at the April 2009 session of the Supreme People's Assembly, when pictures showed him to be noticeably thinner.

Speculation about Kim's successor intensified. Although there was no official confirmation by June, the leading contender was believed to be Kim Jong-un, his third and youngest son, who was educated in Switzerland and was said to be his father's favourite. Because Kim Jong-un lacked experience, there was also speculation that Jang Song-taek, the Dear Leader's brother-in-law and right-hand man, was a possible regent. Other internal political developments appeared to reflect preparation for a transition and generational change. By January 2009, it had become clear that North Korea had replaced up to one-quarter of its 37-member cabinet in recent months, and other reports suggested similar shakeups in the party and the army.

Short-lived nuclear progress

Like a train chugging uphill, negotiations with North Korea on denuclearisation and reconciliation had been making gradual progress in 2008 towards disabling Pyongyang's plutonium facilities. However, they were thrown into reverse by mid 2009.

In accordance with its obligation under an October 2007 accord to 'provide a complete and correct declaration of all of its nuclear activities', on 26 June 2008 North Korea gave China a 60-page declaration. It covered only the plutonium programme, although in a secret side letter to the United States, Pyongyang reportedly committed to disclosing its enrichment and proliferation activities, including assistance to Syria's clandestine nuclear reactor. Doubts were immediately raised about the accuracy of what was included in the declaration. Reportedly, North Korea had earlier told US diplomats it had produced 30kg of plutonium, but subsequently amended that in the declaration to 38kg, still at the lower end of US estimates. In an 8 August report to Congress, the US director of national intelligence estimated that 'prior to the [2006 nuclear] test North Korea could have produced up to 50 kg of plutonium, enough for at least a half dozen nuclear weapons'. The crux of the dispute was how much plutonium the North had separated before 1991. Before completing its own requirements under the second phase, the United States insisted on agreement on measures to verify the declaration. Although the declaration could not be deemed 'complete and correct' without verification, the problem was that the October 2007 agreement had said nothing about verification in the current phase of denuclearisation.

The day Pyongyang submitted its declaration, the White House reciprocally announced its intention to remove sanctions on North Korea under the Trading with the Enemy Act and to delist North Korea as a 'state sponsor of terrorism'. However, the White House repeated the caution issued by US Secretary of State Condoleezza Rice the previous week that the level of North Korean cooperation on verification would be assessed before the United States went through with the delisting. She also raised concern that traces of highly enriched uranium (HEU) had been detected on some of the 18,000 pages of operating records of its reactor and other plutonium facilities that Pyongyang had given Washington to help verify its declaration. The United States had long claimed that North Korea had a uranium-enrichment programme, but this was denied by Pyongyang. The traces could have come from centrifuges or other equipment that North Korea had acquired from Pakistan, but some officials were inclined to believe that the North was producing HEU.

> The US proposal was sweeping in scope

Reaction to the administration's announcement ranged from hostile in Tokyo to sceptical in Washington and Seoul. But the American position appeared to bear fruit. In a 12 July Six-Party Talks communiqué, North Korea agreed to establish a six-party verification mechanism and to allow visits to declared nuclear facilities, a review of documents, interviews with technical personnel, and other measures as agreed upon by all six parties. Key details including scope, sampling procedures, and the timetable for a verification agreement were deferred to working-level discussions.

The progress was short-lived. Japan and South Korea demanded a written protocol on verification. Hardliners in Washington wanted to start with a maximalist negotiating position and President Bush sided with them. In mid July the administration gave Pyongyang a Verification Measures Discussion Paper covering not only the plutonium programme but also 'records of all imports or exports of nuclear materials and nuclear-related equipment'. It was sweeping in scope, calling for 'full access to any site, facility or location that ... is related to elements of the nuclear program as declared or as determined by the relevant parties'. The United States said it would not delist North Korea as a 'state sponsor of terrorism' without a written protocol.

North Korean reacted harshly. On 14 August, it suspended the disabling of its plutonium facilities at Yongbyon in retaliatation for what it saw as backtracking on the October 2007 accord. That month it also apparently attempted to send missile components by air to Iran in a transparent resumption of the proliferation it had forsworn under the October 2007 accord. The effort was blocked when India denied the over-flight clearance of the leg of the journey from Myanmar. North Korea also began restoring equipment at Yongbyon and on 9 October it barred International Atomic Energy Agency inspectors from the complex.

With the past year's progress in disabling the plutonium facilities being reversed, US negotiator Christopher Hill met his counterpart Kim Gye Gwan in Pyongyang on 1–3 October, armed with a revised draft verification protocol more in keeping with what North Korea had earlier signalled it could accept. The North stopped short of committing to the protocol but did, according to a State Department announcement, orally reaffirm its commitment to verification in the dismantlement phase, including 'sampling and other forensic measures' at its declared sites at Yongbyon: the reactor, reprocessing facility and fuel-fabrication plant. When undertaken, those steps might have been enough to ascertain how much plutonium it had produced. If not, the North also agreed to 'access, based on mutual consent, to undeclared sites'. That was insufficient for Japan or South Korea, which wanted a formal six-party verification protocol closer to the tougher original draft. Nevertheless, Bush decided to proceed with delisting the North as a 'state sponsor of terrorism'. Rice's 10 October telephone call notifying Japan occasioned a heated exchange with Foreign Minister Hirofune Nakasone. Disabling of the Yongbyon plant resumed with nearly 60% of the 8,000 fuel rods already removed from the reactor, although the pace was slow.

About half the energy aid promised to Pyongyang in return for disabling in the October 2007 agreement had yet to be delivered. Japan had reached an agreement with the North in bilateral talks on 11–13 August to relax some sanctions in return for reopening Pyongyang's investigation into the fate of Japanese citizens abducted by North Korean agents three decades earlier, only to have North Korea call off the deal upon Japanese Prime Minister Yasuo Fukuda's resignation on 1 September. Tokyo insisted that without progress on abductions it would not contribute its share of energy aid.

These issues came to a head at the seventh round of Six-Party Talks on 8–11 December. The United States, Japan and South Korea threatened to suspend their energy aid unless Pyongyang agreed to a written verification protocol. Russia and China made clear they intended to fulfil their energy pledges. As the United States had already delivered all the heavy fuel oil that it owed, South Korea was left in the hot seat. North Korean envoy Kim Gye Gwan made it clear Pyongyang would retaliate for any backtracking on the October 2007 agreement: 'We'll adjust the speed of our disablement work if it [energy aid] doesn't come in'.

Rocket and nuclear tests

In January 2009, just after the new administration of Barack Obama entered office, North Korea began assembling a long-range rocket for launch at its east-coast Tonghae Satellite Launching Ground. The North had long been developing the *Taepo-dong*-2 missile, but had only test-launched one, in July 2006, which failed 40 seconds after takeoff. Pyongyang portrayed the planned launch as a peaceful attempt to put a satellite in orbit. On 12 March, it announced its accession to the 1967 Outer Space Treaty, which provides for 'freedom of scientific investigation in outer space'. The North for the first time gave notice to international civil aviation and maritime agencies about the timing of the planned launch and the flight path. The United States and others urged Pyongyang not to test and warned that if it did, they would seek additional sanctions under UN Security Council Resolution 1718, adopted after the North's October 2006 nuclear test, which demanded that North Korea suspend all activities related to its ballistic-missile programme. There was tough talk in Tokyo about attempting to intercept the launch if it were directed at Japan. China and Russia, in contrast, contended that the rocket was a space-launch vehicle and that UNSCR 1718 was not applicable.

In the run-up to the launch, US officials were torn between wanting to keep open the possibility of resuming negotiations and the desire of Japan and South Korea to deter missile testing. Picking up public hints that Pyongyang was interested in resuming missile talks, US Secretary of State Hillary Clinton told an 11 March news conference that 'we need to have a conversation about missiles, and it wasn't in the Six-Party Talks'. On 3 April, Ambassador Stephen Bosworth, newly named special representative on North Korea policy, told reporters that the North would face 'consequences' for defying UNSCR 1718. Asked about the agenda for talks he mentioned not only denuclearisation, but also 'what might be required to normalize the relationship between the DPRK and the United States' and 'how we can facilitate North Korea's integration into the region'. He added that Washington was open to bilateral talks: 'I am prepared to go to Pyongyang whenever it appears to be useful'. He did not mention that the North had been told he could come in early March only if it called off its launch. Asked what leverage was available to pressure North Korea not to launch, he answered, 'in my experience in dealing with North Koreans, pressure is not the most productive line of approach'.

On 5 April, North Korea launched its rocket. The first stage, identical to the first stage of the *Taepo-dong*-2, worked. The second stage, thought to be a Soviet-designed SS-N-6 body, separated and flew about 3,200km – further than observers had anticipated, but short of the zone announced beforehand by Pyongyang. The third stage separated but failed to ignite, dropping the purported satellite into the Pacific Ocean. The partial success of the launch not only put the North on a trajectory to acquire a missile capable of carrying a one-tonne payload to nearly intercontinental range (capable of hitting parts of the United States) but also gave it marketable missile technology and added to its leverage in negotiations.

North Korea's motives for the test and its timing were unclear. Many saw the launch as driven by internal politics in the North, since it came just before the Supreme People's Assembly convened to re-elect Kim Jong Il as chairman of the ruling National Defence Commission. North Korean media portrayed the launch as part of its campaign to 'open the gate to a powerful and thriving nation' by 2012, the centenary of the birth of Kim Il Sung, Kim Jong Il's father.

The UN Security Council condemned the launch as a contravention of Resolution 1718, closing a loophole covering space-launch vehicles some saw in earlier resolutions. It demanded an end to launches and called on member states to implement sanctions. Although it did not adopt a new sanctions resolution, the council took action to designate three North Korean missile-related firms as subject to sanctions under Resolution 1718.

North Korea's sharp reaction was seen by many as disproportionate to the relatively mild nature of the Security Council statement. Rejecting the council's action as an infringement of its sovereignty, Pyongyang expelled international inspectors at the Yongbyon nuclear facility and vowed 'never' to return to the Six-Party Talks or 'be bound to any agreement'. Pyongyang also said it would restore the Yongbyon facility to 'the original state for normal operation', and had begun to reprocess the 6,500 spent fuel rods removed during disabling, a step which could extract about a bomb's worth of plutonium. Two weeks later North Korea threatened to conduct more nuclear and long-range missile tests, build a light-water reactor plant and start the development of fuel for it, which meant producing enriched uranium that could also be used to build nuclear weapons – unless the Security Council promptly apologised.

Pyongyang quickly carried out the first of those threats, conducting its second nuclear test. Unlike the 2006 test, this one did not fizzle, although the yield of 2–4 kilotonnes was rather low for reasons that were not clear. The Security Council's response was swift and concerted, evidence of China's unhappiness with North Korea's behaviour. Resolution 1874 extended the arms embargo to ban all arms transfers to and from the North except for its imports of small arms, which were subject to prior notification of the DPRK Sanctions Committee. It called on all states to conduct port inspections of ships suspected of carrying banned cargo and seize such cargo, and to allow inspections of their flag vessels at sea, but it stopped short of authorising boardings without consent of the flag carrier. It extended the measures imposed by Resolution 1718 to freeze North Korean assets and withhold financial support for trade that could contribute to proliferation. Pyongyang responded by saying it would 'weaponise' its stock of plutonium and repeated its threat to enrich uranium. A more urgent concern was the possibility that it could refuel and restart the Yongbyon reactor to generate more plutonium.

The diplomacy of denuclearisation and reconciliation was back to square one. With tensions mounting, two US journalists working for an Internet news outlet were detained by North Korean authorities in mid March for allegedly crossing the border from China. In a closed trial in early June they were convicted of illegal entry and unspecified 'hostile acts' and sentenced to 12 years in a labour camp.

South Korea

The suicide of former President Roh Moo-hyun on 23 May 2009 sent shockwaves through South Korea's political system. Hundreds of thousands of mourners thronged his funeral cortège in Seoul. Roh, who had run as 'Mr Clean', came under investigation for a $1.6 million gift from a businessman to his family. He was the latest in a long list of former presidents whose reputations had been tarnished by prosecutors. Instead of focusing on corruption, however, public opinion turned against Roh's successor, President Lee Myung-bak.

Lee was already in trouble over economics. He had campaigned as the 'economy president' on a '747' platform that promised a 7% growth rate, per capita income of $40,000, and the world's seventh-largest economy. However, the country's export-driven economy was severely affected by the global financial crisis. Capital flight caused sharp declines in the won and stock market. GDP contracted by 5.1% in the fourth quarter of 2008, though it then grew by 0.1% in the first quarter of 2009. Slowed growth fuelled a public backlash against globalisation. Ratification of a free-trade agreement with the United States negotiated by Roh stalled in the National Assembly, where the ruling Grand National Party had a bare majority of seats. Lee's decision to lift a ban on US beef imports, imposed after a 2003 outbreak of mad cow disease, led nearly a million Koreans to join a candlelight vigil in Seoul on 10 June 2008. Yet, as protests mounted, Lee withstood them with the help of timely regulatory concessions from Washington. Bush soon reciprocated Lee's stance on US beef by easing visa restrictions, an important issue for thousands of Koreans studying in and visiting the United States.

North–South tensions

Relations between North and South Korea deteriorated rapidly over the past year. Lee moved to put his policy of strict reciprocity into effect by slowing the flow of food aid to the North. After the South Korean leader showed little interest in implementing two summit agreements negotiated by his predecessors, the 15 June 2000 and 4 October 2007 summit declarations, Pyongyang reacted. It had never accepted the Northern Limit Line (NLL) drawn by the allies at the time of the 1953 armistice, but agreed at the 2000 summit to abide by it until a peace treaty fixed a permanent boundary. The 2007 accord went further, committing the two sides to establish a joint fishing area in the West Sea and negotiate naval confidence-building measures. On 28 March 2008, in a pointed reminder of what was at stake in failing to implement the accord, the North fired two ship-to-ship missiles into the area. It launched another on 7 October.

The fatal shooting of a South Korean tourist at the Mount Kumgang resort in the North on 11 July raised new tensions. Hours after learning of the incident, Lee went ahead with a scheduled address to the National Assembly in which he expressed willingness 'to engage in serious consultations on how to implement the inter-Korean accords' and offered 'to cooperate in efforts to help relieve the food shortage in the North as well as alleviate the pain of the North Korean people'. Pyongyang's expression of regret over the shooting did not mollify Seoul, which demanded a joint investigation. Pyongyang curtailed access to the resort by officials, and Hyundai Asan, the South Korean company that operated the resort, suspended tours. The North then curbed official access to the joint development zone just across the Demilitarized Zone near the city of Kaesong and impeded cross-border traffic. Pyongyang denounced Lee's proposal to condition substantial aid on denuclearisation and economic and political reform as a ploy to undermine its regime. It further jeopardised commercial relations in the Kaesong Industrial Zone, first in late March when an employee of a South Korean firm was arrested and accused of a 'hostile act' for allegedly saying something unflattering about the regime, and then later in the spring when in talks with the South it demanded a fourfold increase in rent and pay for North Korean workers.

On 17 January 2009, the Korean People's Army (KPA) joint staff said it was adopting 'an all-out confrontational posture' in response to annual joint US–South Korean military exercises. It also said it would no longer be bound by the NLL. As the crabbing season began, both sides braced for a clash at sea. Pyongyang further escalated tensions after Seoul announced that it would participate in the Proliferation Security Initiative. South Korea had long held back from joining the initiative, which is intended to impede shipments of materials and technology related to weapons of mass destruction. The Lee government announced its decision immediately after the North's 25 May nuclear test. Denouncing the decision as a violation of the Korean armistice, the North Korean army issued a statement declaring it would not longer be bound by the 1953 armistice agreement.

At the same time Pyongyang was coping with other domestic difficulties, although how severe these were remained open to debate. Although the South Korean government estimated that the North's economy shrank by 2.5% in 2008, others say that overall industrial production grew. The primary reason seemed to have been refurbishment of equipment, development assistance, and the provision of heavy fuel oil as part of the Six-Party Talks and of raw materials for light industry from South Korea. Efforts to legitimate and support markets that had sprouted all over the country seemed to have been postponed. The food situation was unclear. Surveys taken by the United Nations pointed on the one hand to falling output for the third year in a row and a possible shortfall of 836,000 tonnes of grain between November 2008 and October 2009. South Korea's Rural Development Administration, on the other hand, suggested that North Korea had one of its best harvests in years in 2008, with grain output rising by 7% to 4.3m tonnes, although that was still 15% short of what was needed for self-sufficiency. The United States said in May 2008 it would provide North Korea with 500,000 tonnes of food aid, with half to be handled by non-governmental organisations and the rest by the World Food Programme (WFP). While the NGO effort moved ahead, the WFP effort stalled in disputes with the North Koreans. Both programmes ended before completion in early 2009, probably because of the intensifying disputes between Washington and Pyongyang.

Although prospects at mid 2009 on all fronts on the Korean Peninsula seemed grim, all sides understood that negotiations would be the only way out of the nuclear crisis, however uncertain the outcome. If Kim Jong Il meant what he said when he held out the promise of a 'prosperous' as well as 'strong' North Korea by 2012, the 100th anniversary of his father's birth, he would need a political accommodation with the United States, South Korea and Japan to make it possible. From an outside perspective, acquiring nuclear weapons would not seem to contribute as much to the North's security as would turning the three former foes into friends. But whether the North would turn towards accommodation, particularly if it required Pyongyang to give up its new nuclear status, looked doubtful.

Japan: Politics Overshadows Security Issues

Domestic political uncertainties tended to dominate Japan in 2008–09, as the fourth prime minister in as many years took office. Japan also faced uncertainties in its key relationships with China and North Korea, and concerns over a drift in US–Japanese ties towards the end of the George W. Bush administration. These surrounded Tokyo's efforts to maintain its support for the Bush administration's 'war on terror' through the despatch of the Japan Self-Defense Forces (JSDF), and disaffection with the United States over concessions made to North Korea in the denuclearisation process. From early 2009, however, Japan's security policy regained momentum. This was in part due to renewed confidence in the US–Japan security relationship under the new Barack Obama administration, but also to the re-emergence of traditional security concerns involving North Korea and China. Japan exerted a stronger security presence, despatching the JSDF overseas for anti-piracy missions and responding to North Korea's ballistic-missile and nuclear tests in April and May.

Domestic politics: persistent instability

Japan's domestic political instability was highlighted by the resignation on 24 September 2008 of Prime Minister Yasuo Fukuda, who had managed to stay in office only 364 days, precisely one day less than his predecessor Shinzo Abe. Fukuda had been touted as a competent, if uninspiring, choice for prime minister, capable of uniting the factions of the governing Liberal Democratic Party (LDP), forging compromises with its coalition partner New Komeito, and possibly conciliating the main opposition Democratic Party of Japan (DPJ). He found himself, however, entangled in the same policy problems as Abe, and in the end lacked the political backbone to fight his corner. Fukuda's administration was lambasted for perceived failures in pension reform and health-insurance programmes for the elderly, and for the re-imposition of unpopular petroleum taxes, all in the context of concerns over growing inequalities in Japanese society and the slide of the Japanese economy into recession by late 2008 – Japan's GDP contracted by an extraordinary annual rate of 12% in the last quarter of the year.

Fukuda's problems were compounded by the continuing efforts of the DPJ and its leader Ichiro Ozawa to use control of the House of Councillors (the upper chamber of the National Diet) to impede legislation originating in the lower House of Representatives, which was controlled by Fukuda's coalition. The DPJ was trying to force early general elections for the House of Representatives, otherwise due in autumn 2009. Fukuda could only push his legislative agenda by using the two-thirds 'supermajority' of the LDP and New Komeito in the House of Representatives to override the upper chamber. In the meantime, the approval rating of Fukuda's cabinet declined to the low twenties by summer 2008, and threatening to fall to the low single-digit level not seen since Prime Minister Yoshiro Mori in 2001.

Fukuda's precarious domestic political situation meant he had little appetite for controversial foreign- and security-policy initiatives, and he was preoccupied for a large part of his premiership in preparing for the Tokyo International Conference on African Development-IV (TICAD-IV) in May and the G8 Toyako Summit in July. At TICAD-IV Fukuda pledged that Japan would double its official development assistance to Africa by 2012, a clear attempt to counter China's rising resource diplomacy in Africa and to secure African support for Japan's candidacy for a permanent seat on the UN Security Council. Fukuda then used his chairmanship of the G8 to push for renewed support for the UN Millennium Development Goals, especially in relation to Africa. Fukuda's other key objective was to promote a Japanese

'Cool Earth' climate-change plan and to carry negotiations forward to the UN climate conference in Copenhagen in 2009. The aim of the Japanese plan was to reduce global greenhouse-gas emissions by half by 2050. It employed a sectoral-target approach in an attempt to bridge the differences between the United States' market-based emissions-cutting approach and the EU's binding-target-based approach.

Fukuda's chairmanship of the G8 proved relatively successful, securing agreement in principle for halving of emissions, but it failed to translate into a bounce in domestic popularity. A cabinet reshuffle at the start of August had no significant effect on his stagnant poll ratings, and he felt additional pressure because it was necessary to seek renewal of the Replenishment Support Special Measures Law (RSSML) at the end of the year to maintain the Maritime Self-Defense Force (MSDF) mission in the Indian Ocean in support of *Operation Enduring Freedom*. Fukuda seemed intimidated by the prospect of once again having to ram the legislation through the Diet in the face of DPJ opposition, and his New Komeito coalition partner was also beginning to express doubts about the impact of the mission on its electoral prospects. In the end, mindful that failure to renew the RSSML would demonstrate his administration's inability to maintain its promises of security cooperation with the US and the international community, Fukuda succumbed to the pressure and suddenly resigned.

> Aso was soon embattled by the same domestic problems as Fukuda

His departure triggered a contest for the presidency of the LDP and the premiership. The front-runner was Taro Aso, the former foreign minister, whom Fukuda had defeated for the premiership in 2007. Other LDP factions, concerned that Aso (despite his hawkish credentials in foreign affairs) represented a retreat towards old-style pork-barrel domestic politics, fielded four other candidates. Aso's relatively high public profile, though, was thought to be an electoral asset, and was enough to secure him 351 out of 525 votes in the National Diet and local chapters of the LDP. After Aso assumed the premiership, there was speculation he would call a snap election to capitalise on his early poll lead over Ozawa and the DPJ. Instead, he chose to concentrate on passing a ¥12 trillion supplementary budget to respond to the looming global economic crisis.

Aso was soon embattled by the same domestic policy problems as Fukuda, and his populist image was damaged by revelations of his expensive (albeit paid for out of his own family's considerable fortune) dining habits during a recession and by his generally arrogant, but at times strangely indecisive, leadership style. Aso's poll ratings, and those of his party, steadily slipped behind those of Ozawa and the DPJ, and by the end of 2008 they were nearly at the level suffered by Mori. By early 2009, it appeared that the other LDP factions, fearing electoral defeat under Aso, were close to revolt. Yoshimi Watanabe, a popular former minister for administrative reform, split from the LDP in January in frustration at Aso's failure to continue reform efforts. He looked to form a new political alliance with fellow reform-minded LDP and DPJ members. Even former Prime Minister Junichiro Koizumi re-emerged on the political stage, openly criticising Aso for contemplating renationalisation of the Japan Post Service (privatisation had been the election issue upon which Koizumi had won a landslide victory in the lower chamber in 2005) and encouraging other LDP politicians to turn against their leader. The Aso administration plumbed new depths by mid February, when Finance Minister Shoichi Nakagawa was forced to resign after showing signs of apparent intoxication during a press conference at a G7 finance ministers' meeting in Rome.

By late February, however, the Aso administration began to show signs of recovery. The DPJ's lead in the polls reversed after a scandal involving the receipt by Ozawa's chief secretary of illicit political funds from the Nishimatsu Construction Company. Toshihiro Nikai of the LDP, the minister of economy, trade and industry, was also caught up in the scandal, but its main impact was on the DPJ, which had portrayed itself as a clean alternative to the LDP. The DPJ argued that the timing of the scandal in the run-up to possible elections was politically inspired and its top leadership rallied around Ozawa. Although he avoided a personal corruption investigation, the scandal sapped his credibility, and doubts emerged over whether his leadership could continue into the next general election. The popularity of Aso and of the LDP received a further boost from the government's announcement in April of its intent to pass an extra stimulus budget worth at least US$100bn. Aso was able to exploit changing international circumstances to portray himself as an international statesman and to strengthen his domestic standing. In the end, Ozawa concluded that clinging to the leadership was damaging the party's electoral prospects, and he resigned at the start of May. Yukio Hatoyama, a DPJ veteran close to Ozawa, was elected in his stead in mid May, and immediately began to slow the DPJ's decline in opinion polls and to place new pressure on Aso's premiership.

Japan–China relations

Fukuda's other main diplomatic preoccupation before his fall from power was to inject more substance into the so-called 'mutually beneficial strategic relationship' with China, initiated under Abe in 2007 in an attempt to repair the damage inflicted on bilateral relations during Koizumi's premiership. An important step forward in this regard was the visit of Chinese President Hu Jintao to Tokyo in May 2008, the first visit by a Chinese president to Japan for a decade, which had been delayed by Sino-Japanese disputes over the safety of imported Chinese food products and because of China's problems with Tibet. Fukuda and Hu issued a joint statement pledging annual visits by the two leaders, mutual visits of defence ministers, and cooperation on food safety, energy, African development, North Korean denuclearisation and the environment. Fukuda did not press Hu on the Tibet issue, apart from requesting that China open the province to the international media as soon as possible, and Hu chose not to push Japan over issues of colonial history. In a separate document, Japan extracted positive Chinese recognition of its climate-change strategy, and Fukuda engaged Hu further on climate change at the G8 summit in July.

The two countries were unable to agree over the East China Sea in time for the summit. Since 2005 a dispute over China's development of gas fields adjacent to, and even within, Japan's exclusive economic zone had become one of the most contentious issues in the bilateral relationship. However, in mid June Japanese and Chinese diplomats announced a new agreement on joint development, stating that China would welcome the participation of Japanese enterprises in its development of the Shirakaba/Chunxiao gas field. Japan would invest in exploration for an unspecified return from the field. Beijing and Tokyo also agreed to designate an area just south of the Asunaru/Longjing field as a 'joint development area', with expected equal investments and returns; and to continue consultations on the development of the Kashi/Tianwaitian and Kusonoki/Duanqiao fields. Japanese analysts and the media questioned the substance of the agreement, unsure of the exact meaning of 'participation' and how far China would allow joint exploitation of the gas fields. Japanese policymakers, however, expressed relative satisfaction with the deal. Japan had come late to the development of the East China Sea, and the remoteness of the fields made them difficult for Japan to exploit on its own. Just as importantly, Tokyo could claim that China had in effect recognised the status quo in acknowledging Japan's right to share in the gas fields, and had thus yielded on its assertion of exclusive sovereignty in the area.

Sino-Japanese relations continued to improve throughout spring and summer 2008. Japan provided significant humanitarian assistance to the victims of the Sichuan earthquake. The Japanese and Chinese governments at one point even agreed that the Japanese Air Self-Defense Force (ASDF) might transport aid supplies, which would have been the first despatch of the Japanese military to the Chinese interior since the 1940s. But nationalist popular sentiment in China forced the mission to be aborted. Japan instead sent the destroyer *Sazanami*, carrying relief supplies, to the port of Zhanjiang in Guangdong province at the end of June, marking the first visit by a Japanese naval vessel to China in the post-war period.

> "Aso had openly described China as a threat"

From autumn onwards, however, familiar tensions began to reappear. Japanese leaders and the public welcomed the striking progress in Chinese development marked by its holding of the Olympic Games, but also took umbrage at China's rising power and nationalistic sentiment. Japanese suspicions of China's military intentions were raised by the MSDF's detection of what was thought to be a Chinese submarine in Japanese territorial waters in mid September (China denied any connection to the incident). The *Defence of Japan* White Paper released in September again emphasised Japanese anxieties over the lack of transparency around China's double-digit increases in defence spending and build-up of new submarine and ballistic- and cruise-missile technologies. Tokyo continued to wrangle with Beijing over demands that the latter be more forthcoming on food-safety issues. Moreover, Fukuda's resignation at the end of September and the succession of Aso, who in the past had openly described China as a threat, raised doubts about the continuing improvement of ties.

Aso visited Beijing in October to attend the Asia–Europe Meeting (ASEM) and deliver a speech on the 30th anniversary of the Japan–China Treaty of Peace and Friendship. He reassured Chinese leaders that he would maintain the pragmatic policies of Abe and Fukuda to strengthen bilateral ties. Aso then hosted Chinese Prime Minister Wen Jiabao and South Korean President Lee Myung-bak at the first Trilateral Summit in Kyushu in mid December. Japanese–Chinese relations were destabilised, though, by renewed problems over the East China Sea. Japan was forced in January to make an official protest to China regarding the latter's continuing development of the Kashi gas field, in contravention of Japan's understanding that the next steps for this and other fields were subject to bilateral consultations. In response Chinese officials simply asserted their exclusive sovereignty over the territory.

Relations were tested further by China's continued insistence on sending 'survey' ships into waters around the disputed Senkaku/Diaoyu islands, leading Aso in February to reassert strongly that the Senkakus were Japanese and that he expected the United States to assist Japan, if necessary, to repel aggression in this area. He was forced to postpone a scheduled visit to China in late March due to need to prepare for the G20 summit in April. In March 2009 Yoshikazu Hamada did pay the first visit by a Japanese defence minister to China for five years, but the main focus of the Japanese media covering the trip was on the remarks by his Chinese counterpart that Beijing did not rule out acquiring aircraft carriers, a concern reinforced by the release the same month of the Pentagon's annual report to Congress on China's military power, which predicted it would acquire multiple aircraft carriers by 2020. Even though Japan under Koizumi's successors had made important strides in its relationship with China, the problems of energy and maritime security continued to hamper the relationship.

Japan and the Korean Peninsula

In early 2008 relations between Japan and South Korea seemed at their most propitious for many years. Fukuda had taken advantage of Lee Myung-bak's accession to the presidency to reboot bilateral relations, which had suffered under Koizumi over issues of the colonial past and the territorial dispute over the Takeshima/Tokdo islands. Fukuda's conciliatory style seemed to fit well with the new South Korean president's desire for more pragmatic diplomacy, focused less on contentious issues of colonial history and more on cooperation to push forward North Korean denuclearisation, and for the restart of negotiations for a Japan–Korea Economic Partnership Agreement (JKEPA).

Relations were soon, however, afflicted once again by issues of history and territory. In mid July reports surfaced that the Japanese Ministry of Education was planning to insert a new emphasis on the Takeshima islands as Japan's 'inalienable' territory into guidelines for school teachers. This drew official protests from Seoul, and Fukuda was forced to restrain the ministry to avoid endangering ties. Fukuda's replacement by the more combative Aso did not seem to augur well for the bilateral relationship, not least because of his past nationalist views on the benefits of Japanese colonial rule in East Asia and his family's use of Korean forced labour in its Japanese mines during the Second World War. But Aso continued with shuttle diplomacy, visiting Seoul in January 2009 for talks with Lee; the two had met every month since November, at the Asia-Pacific Economic Cooperation forum (APEC), the G20 and the Trilateral Summit. Aso and Lee pledged greater bilateral cooperation to influence the incoming Obama administration's policy on North Korea; and were drawn together by the need to combat the growing financial crisis, with Japan increasing support for the South Korean currency through the ASEAN+3 Chiang Mai process.

Tensions continued to arise in 2009. At the end of February Seoul protested when Shimane Prefecture celebrated Takeshima Day to reassert its claim to administrative sovereignty over the islands, and the JKEPA negotiations remained suspended due to South Korean concerns over Japan's potential penetration of its manufacturing markets and lack of reciprocation in agricultural imports. Nevertheless relations, whilst still fragile, were not subject to the types of downward spiral seen under previous administrations, and the two sides strengthened diplomatic cooperation over the North Korean missile and nuclear tests in April and May.

Japan–North Korea ties seemed to hold some prospect of improvement in mid 2008. Fukuda tried to back away from Abe's hardline policy of diplomatic pressure and unilateral economic sanctions on North Korea over the unresolved abductions of Japanese citizens and the North's ballistic-missile and nuclear tests in 2006. Instead, he looked for opportunities to re-open dialogue, mindful that the Bush administration was intent on driving towards a nuclear deal with North Korea in its final months, and that Japan's inability to improve bilateral ties with the North meant it risked isolation in the six-party process.

In mid June Japan and North Korea held bilateral talks which produced an agreement by the North to reinvestigate the fate of Japanese abductees; Pyongyang had argued previously that the abductions issue had been fully resolved. Japan in return promised to consider lifting some of its bilateral sanctions on North Korea. In mid August the two sides held working-level talks which established agreed terms for the reinvestigations. However, Japan–North Korea relations ground to a halt when Fukuda resigned. Pyongyang announced it would suspend the reinvestigations until it was able to evaluate the new prime minister's stance towards bilateral ties. Aso had been one of the key architects of economic sanctions towards the North. He predictably took a harder stance, and at the end of September extended Japanese sanctions on the North for another six months.

Japan's diplomatic leverage vis-à-vis North Korea risked serious erosion towards the end of 2008. Although Japanese policymakers put a brave face on the decision by the United States in mid October to remove North Korea from the list of state sponsors of terrorism, in truth they felt abandoned by Washington, and found it hard to restrain themselves from publicly railing against the Bush administration.

Japan's position was only saved by North Korea's failure at the reconvened Six-Party Talks in mid December to agree a mechanism for verification of denuclearisation, thwarting a final nuclear deal with the Bush administration and producing a hiatus in US policy during the transition to the new administration. Japan's hardline stance was then strengthened in early 2009 as it discovered a new convergence with the Obama administration on security policy, and as North Korea shifted back to brinkmanship with its attempt in April to launch what it claimed was a civilian satellite – Japan regarded this from the start as most likely a test of the *Taepo-dong*-2 ballistic missile.

> Japan readied itself to intercept the rocket

Japan prepared for the North Korean launch by deploying, for the first time, its ballistic-missile defence (BMD) system. North Korea had given pre-warning that the trajectory of the rocket would mean the first stage landing in the Sea of Japan, and the second stage passing over Iwate and Akita prefectures in the north of Honshu before splashing down in the Pacific Ocean. Japan readied itself for an intercept in case the rocket or any of its jettisoned debris threatened to stray off course. Amidst tremendous media coverage, the ASDF deployed two PAC-3 interceptor batteries to Iwate and Akita and a further PAC-3 unit to the Ministry of Defense compound in central Tokyo, and the MSDF deployed two BMD-capable *Aegis* destroyers to the Sea of Japan and one *Aegis* destroyer to the Pacific Ocean. The United States deployed five BMD-capable *Aegis* cruisers around Japan. Japanese anticipation of the missile launch reached near fever pitch as the projected date window of 4–8 April for the test approached, and tensions were raised further when the government issued a false launch alert on 4 April. When the rocket was launched on 5 April the first two stages landed as planned in the seas either side of Japan, though the second stage fell short of the zone predicted by Pyongyang.

Japan's Ministry of Defense concluded that the launch had indeed been a *Taepo-dong*-2 test. The ministry's analysis, in conjunction with that of the

United States, revealed that the test had partly failed because a third stage of the rocket had apparently not separated. However, the test was seen as a linear step in the upgrading of North Korea's missile technology. The Ministry of Defense and JSDF felt relatively encouraged by the functioning of the BMD system on its first active deployment, despite the embarrassing false alarm the previous day. Japan's sensor systems, although still dependent on US early-warning satellites, were able to track the missile's trajectory with some success. The fact that Japan did not actually have to use the system kept its relatively untested deterrence credibility intact, whilst affording valuable experience for future deployments; and the public's heightened awareness of BMD helped legitimise the vast expense of the system.

In the immediate aftermath of the test Tokyo argued it was a violation of UNSCR 1695 and sought, along with the United States and South Korea, a condemnation from the Security Council. Aso's administration also tightened some financial sanctions on the North and extended the period of sanctions to one year. Though Japan's hardline stance appeared to have been vindicated, its attempts to seek a binding condemnatory resolution at the UN were thwarted by an agreement among China, Russia and the United States that a statement by the president of the Security Council was sufficient punishment for Pyongyang.

Japan's leaders only felt vindicated by North Korea's nuclear test at the start of the following month and again stepped up calls for a hardline diplomatic and even military response. Japanese, US and South Korean policymakers pressed Russia and China hard to cooperate in the drafting of UNSCR 1874. Japan planned to introduce new legislation to enable the Japan Coast Guard to inspect in international waters shipping suspected of carrying missile and nuclear components, and agreed with the United States to tighten financial sanctions on the North. In the meantime, Japanese leaders openly debated the need to acquire a new cruise-missile capability to enable strikes against enemy ballistic-missile bases and to complement the BMD system.

Japan–US relations: waiting for Obama

The US–Japan alliance threatened to drift in 2009. Japan's participation in George W. Bush's 'war on terror' had appeared to be weakening under Fukuda and Aso. The Japanese government resolved in July 2008 to withdraw the ASDF from logistical-support operations in Iraq and Kuwait by December; and Fukuda's resignation in September cast doubts on Japan's willingness to maintain the MSDF Indian Ocean mission. Japan also failed to respond to Bush administration requests to expand support for *Operation Enduring Freedom* by despatching the Ground Self-Defense Force (GSDF) and ASDF to Afghanistan to provide helicopters, transports and other logistical support to the Coalition. Fukuda's administration raised US and NATO hopes in mid 2008 by discussing the possibility of passing a new permanent despatch law to avoid slow and damaging political battles in the National Diet over every individual overseas mission for the JSDF. Afghanistan was considered one of the key destinations for the JSDF, but Fukuda dashed international hopes by shelving plans for the law as it became clear that the risks of combat in Afghanistan meant that despatch of forces was politically unacceptable.

The relationship drifted further over the slow progress of US base realignments (first agreed under the 2006 Defence Policy Review Initiative, particularly the relocation within Okinawa of the US Marine Corps (USMC) air station from Futenma to Henoko, and the relocation of USMC units outside Okinawa to Guam. In the first case, the Japanese government, after a 15-year search for a solution to the Futenma issue, continued to vacillate about whether it should accept Okinawa Prefecture's request for a change of location for the planned V-shaped runway at Henoko on safety and environmental grounds or whether it should stick to the plan agreed with the United States. In the second case, Tokyo and Washington negotiated long and hard over the financial costs and conditions for Japan to fund the construction of new base facilities in Guam.

Japanese policymakers anticipated that the incoming Obama administration would be more pro-China in orientation, even more conciliatory towards North Korea, and would emphasise economic more than security issues in the relationship with Japan. But they were pleasantly surprised by the early importance accorded Japan by the Obama administration. In February US Secretary of State Hillary Clinton chose Japan for her first overseas trip after assuming office, and Aso was honoured by becoming the first foreign leader to visit Obama in the White House the same month. Obama and Clinton have repeatedly described Japan as the cornerstone of US security strategy in East Asia. Aso began to show some determination to strengthen alliance ties. In contrast to Fukuda, he did not hesitate to use the LDP's super-majority to ram renewal of the RSSML through the Diet in December. The agreement on funding for the relocation of bases to Guam was concluded during Clinton's visit, and both sides' militaries cooperated closely on BMD and the response to North Korea's rocket launch in April.

Japanese policymakers continued to harbour doubts, though, about the dependability of the Obama administration. Suspicions remained that the US might not press North Korea particularly hard on the abductions or ballistic-missile issues, and that once its comprehensive review of strategy towards China was complete it might yet shift to a more pro-China position. Such suspicions were not one-way. Ozawa was strongly criticised in February for his suggestion that the US military presence in Japan could perhaps be limited to the Seventh Fleet, suggesting that a future DPJ administration might look to downgrade alliance ties.

Japan's foreign and defence posture

Japan sought other ways to push forward its security relations under Fukuda and Aso. In Tokyo in June 2008, Fukuda and Australian Prime Minister Kevin Rudd concluded a Comprehensive Strategic, Security and Economic Partnership. The agreement was designed to complement the Japan–Australia Joint Declaration on Security Cooperation signed the previous year, and to expand cooperation in areas such as maritime security and peacekeeping. Japan and India signed a similar joint declaration on security in October, and Japan intended to steadily build links with other democracies in the region to quietly counter China's rise. Japan has also tried to re-engage with Russia to provide additional leverage against Chinese influence. However, bilateral relations have not been immune from the fallout of the conflict in Georgia, and Japan was forced to cancel a joint search-and-rescue exercise in September because Russia would have used the same Japanese ports as US vessels. Nevertheless, Japan has pressed ahead with attempts to improve relations. Aso and Russian President Dmitry Medvedev held their first summit in February, looking to expand cooperation on energy development in particular.

Japan made one major new external military commitment in 2009, sending naval vessels on an anti-piracy mission. Tokyo had hesitated over whether to join Combined Task Force-150, the international naval task force in the Gulf of Aden, despite repeated pirate attacks on its own shipping, because the MSDF lacked a clear constitutional mandate for anti-piracy activities. In the end, Japan's hand was forced by China's announcement in December that it would send destroyers to join the coalition effort, highlighting Japan's inactivity. Aso decided in January to despatch the MSDF to the Gulf of Aden by early March with the mission of defending Japanese-related shipping, but also submitted an anti-piracy law which would allow the MSDF to defend the ships of other countries as well. Two destroyers began their anti-piracy mission in the Gulf of Aden in early April, and they were joined in May by MSDF P-3C maritime surveillance aircraft operating out of Djibouti. Japan thus used the anti-piracy mission to expand its naval presence in the Indian Ocean and Arabian Sea.

In 2008–09 Japan continued to quietly add to its overall military capabilities. The ASDF successfully tested its BMD PAC-3 system in New Mexico in September 2008; and the MSDF conducted a second test of the *Aegis* BMD system near Hawaii in November, which (though not entirely successful) was deemed sufficient to confirm deployment of the system. The MSDF commissioned the first of its two *Hyuga*-class light helicopter carriers in March 2009. The ASDF was pledged under the Oslo Convention to dismantle its stockpiles of cluster bombs in December, but was compensated by the procurement in the 2009 defence budget, for the first time, of Joint Direction Attack Munitions. Meanwhile, Japan's search for a new F-X fighter aircraft continued. Tokyo had been hopeful that the Obama administration would release the F-22, but the Pentagon's declaration in April that it intended to shut down the programme threw this further into doubt. In the meantime, Japan decided to postpone a decision until the new National Defense Program Guidelines and Mid-Term Defense Program, in preparation by the Ministry of Defense for the end of 2009, which would set the trajectory of its defence posture for the next five years. Finally, in May Japan passed a new Basic Space Law which opened the way for the explicit use of space for defensive military activities, and which should lead to the long-term strengthening of Japanese military satellite capabilities. In April and May the Prime Minister's Office and the LDP called strongly for Japan to embark on a major programme of procurement of infrared early-warning satellites to strengthen BMD sensor capabilities.

Uncertain outlook

Aso showed a greater propensity than had Fukuda to push forward Japan's international security commitments. However, Aso's position remained highly precarious, and Japan's strategic outlook similarly remained uncertain in line with domestic political uncertainty. But whenever the parliamentary elections due by autumn 2009 were to be held, and whatever the result – an LDP–New Komeito reduced majority government, a grand LDP–DPJ coalition, a DPJ-led coalition or outright win – there were unlikely to be opportunities for any great change in strategic orientation. Any government would still face the problem of dealing with North Korean provocations and a rising China, and would likely be compelled towards greater security cooperation with the United States. The Obama administration's unfolding regional strategy might, in the end, overcome Japan's domestic impasse over security and create momentum for an expanded international security role.

Chapter 11

Prospectives

Following President Barack Obama's historic election and the onset of the world's gravest economic crisis for generations, the questions on many people's minds were of a dramatic character. Will the world move to a more egalitarian political order where the United States is less apparently supreme? Would there be lasting geopolitical change as a result of shifts in the financial balance of power? Might the economic crisis further weaken fragile states and make the challenge of conflict resolution even more daunting?

Clearly the US share of 'global power', however measured, is in decline, but the very interest in Obama's election and the inclination he showed early on to strengthen America's international relationships suggested that US leadership could still be effective if buttressed by strong alliance policies. An important aim of Obama's foreign policy is clearly to limit through strong diplomacy the challenges to American interests and to seek to defend them through artfully constructed bundles of cooperation with the powers that are central to resolving any particular issue of concern. Still, the model of private capitalism championed by the United States is in retreat, and the state capitalism more typical of modern authoritarian regimes is on the advance. The leverage that the United States previously had on others is reduced because of relative American economic weakness. While the Obama administration displayed considerable international energy in its early months, the need to focus on re-ordering the US domestic house will place regular limits on its appetite for foreign affairs.

China's financial power has been thrown into sharp relief by the economic crisis. Its regional ambitions in the political, military and economic fields are substantial, and its ability to woo regional favour is considerable, given the weight it carries. Still, many states in the Asia-Pacific remain wary

of China's ambitions and the numerous formal and informal regional political, economic and security structures serve to encase China's efforts as much
as possible within a multilateral format. Beyond the region, China's national
interests are well defined and advanced in the commodities field, but its contribution to discussions about global-governance issues and the provision of
international public goods remains limited and basic. Its ability to shape the
global agenda is therefore not as considerable as its growing powerful assets
might imply. While there remains a good deal of fascination in the US–China
Group of Two (G2) idea, by which the true global balance of financial power
would be primarily managed by these two countries, it remains the case that
for most international issues, the United States has greater opportunities to
gather coalitions around its point of view than does China.

In general, the United States must confront the many international challenges it faces aware of its domestic priorities. It says that it will address
the important, the urgent and the long-term, and that it sees contemporary
international policy as 'multi-tasked'. Yet there are bound to be places that
receive more rhetorical than practical attention, including perhaps Latin
America and Africa, where the United States will avoid being heavily drawn
without very strong reason. Here, the injunction to find regional solutions to
regional problems is inspired at least in part by an awareness of the limitations on US power. The corresponding obligation in these parts of the world
to establish more regionally enforceable norms of conflict containment and
resolution is therefore high. Unfortunately, this is at a time when territorial
disputes, international competition over natural-resources access, domestic tensions over indigenous rights, governance crises, trade in contraband,
insurgencies and destabilising migration movements all conspire to retard
the political and economic development that would make the regional negotiation of such norms and enforcement mechanisms more realistic in Africa
and Latin America.

In areas where US strategic interests are more intense and challenged,
the administration is evidently seeking to build coalitions of the relevant
to advance shared interests. What some have styled 'mini-lateralism', the
tactic of composing the best number of relevant states to address a particular
issue, is now being pursued on various themes and in different theatres. The
meetings of the G20 thus have assumed more importance, even if they have
not yet achieved significant outcomes. Ad hoc meetings of countries key to
solving climate change are being convened. The United States has called for a
nuclear summit in 2010, which would involve the relevant powers that have

something direct to contribute to this dossier. Increasingly, the United States is pulling together regional states central to the management of a regional problem with the hope both of alleviating conflict-management burdens and ensuring that solutions have the necessary regional accent to allow them to be accepted. Over the course of the next year, it will be important for the United States to build those regional constituencies, if it is to succeed.

The US ability to do this is heavily affected by how it can meet other countries on their terms and trade interests successfully to mutual advantage. In this sense, the Obama administration tried early on to resurrect good old-fashioned diplomatic practices. With Russia, the United States showed itself quite willing to accept nuclear-warhead and missile limits that would go beyond the ceilings imposed by expiring arms-control treaties. That willingness recognised a Russian need greater than a US interest insofar as Russia would have difficulty in successfully maintaining higher levels. The offer of cuts was a proper consequence of Obama's earlier declared commitment to eventual nuclear disarmament, but was equally consistent with the administration's aims to get on better terms with Russia so that Russian cooperation could be gained on matters of interest to the United States. In this respect, while no formal linkage was claimed and none would be admitted, it is clear that the United States expected that progress on nuclear arms control would lead to better cooperation on other issues of importance to the United States, and in particular on the Iran nuclear file. While Russia and the United States will continue to have a number of important differences, and even some irreconcilable disputes, the prospect of cooperation in areas in which the two share strategic interests is heightened by the pragmatic approach adopted by Obama.

That said, relations could still sour again in 2010, if Russians come to the conclusion that they have helped the United States on matters that are of most interest to Washington – Iran, North Korea, re-supply in Afghanistan – while not gaining any ground on regional issues sensitive to Russia, notably security arrangements in Europe and missile defence. That is why more than pro forma discussion would need to take place on President Dmitry Medvedev's proposals to revise European security architecture. The answer so far provided by the West to the proposal is that it is vague; the cleverer response would be to invite the Russians to refine it with North Americans and Europeans in a consensual manner. Acknowledging a Russian sphere of influence in its neighbourhood, which the Russians would dearly like, is for the West retrograde and therefore inconceivable. The trick is to find what informal tribute can be paid to Russia's size and residual power in the discussions of European security futures. The paradox is that Russia might be easier to deal with if it truly saw itself as a global power, for then, the prospect of cooperating on wider global issues would serve as a useful tonic in the relationship. But as Russia's primary interests have become so resolutely regional, the points of diplomatic contact are potentially forever sore.

Raw nerves are most dangerous perhaps in the Middle East, and balancing progress on the Arab–Palestinian front with advances on the Iranian issue requires imagination. Most Arab states share with Israel the assessment that the Iranian regime acts frequently as a potentially destabilising force. But that congruence of strategic interest cannot easily find public expression because the unsettled Israeli–Palestinian issue leaves Arab states unable to ally themselves with Israel. An argument that in private moves certain Israelis is that the main strategic purpose of arriving at a two-state solution would be to legitimise Israel in the eyes of moderate Arab public opinion. That in turn would permit Arab states, in normalising diplomatic relations with Israel, to work alongside Israel against such continuing threats from Iranian-supported regional groups or even Iran itself that might persist. A two-state solution may not lead to immediate peace; there would still be radicalised groups wanting to punish Israel. But it would create the political legitimacy for Israel that would allow certain Arab states to support Israel against radical groups that also threatened those same Arab states.

In dealing with the Iranian nuclear challenge, it would therefore make sense to find some mechanism for involving key Arab states in the diplomatic engagement with Iran to find a solution. In summer 2009, that diplomacy, if revived, would involve principally the so-called E3+3: the UK, France and Germany plus the United States, China and Russia. In contrast to the Six-Party Talks with North Korea, no regional states are involved. In the future, it may be too diplomatically burdensome formally to add a group of regional states to any diplomatic negotiation, but some linkage would be strategically advantageous and sensible. First, regional states would have the most immediately to lose if Iran were to acquire nuclear weapons. They have an incentive to prevent an Iranian 'break-out' capacity. Secondly, many regional states fear that, being excluded from the negotiations, they could become 'part of the package' in some grand bargain by which Iran were to renounce its interests in nuclear matters but somehow be given a greater role in regional security. However unlikely such a result, it is a regional perception that needs to be managed. Thirdly, some regional states, such as Turkey,

Saudi Arabia and Egypt, are cited as potential proliferators if Iran were to have a confirmed nuclear military capacity. It would be best to involve them in the diplomacy to tie them into a non-proliferation outlook. Fourthly, if diplomacy were to fail, these and other states would be key elements of a regional policy to contain Iran's power. They would be more amenable to joining the West in a containment policy if their overtures to Iran had also been rebuffed. Fifthly, and to return to the earlier argument, by involving regional states more on the Iran file, it would demonstrate to Israel that Arab states were engaged in *their* strategic interests. This might permit outsiders to be more forceful in their encouragement of Israel to accelerate towards a two-state solution that would allow for more full-blooded regional security cooperation. As the Obama administration weaves its diplomatic web in the Middle East, its special envoys and others should find clever ways to connect diplomatically these complex strategic questions.

Certainly if there is to be any chance of resolving the North Korean proliferation file, more attention needs to be given to the general regional security environment. The United States is resolute that it will not acknowledge North Korea's nuclear status. It equally does not wish to resurrect the Six-Party Talks only to see the North Koreans seek further incentives to promise again to roll back their programme, a promise for which 'payment' has already been made. China has become genuinely concerned that North Korea's nuclear programme is a danger. In the past, China has been concerned that putting too much pressure on North Korea could lead to such regime instability that refugees might flow over the Yalu River. A North Korean collapse would deprive China of a strategic buffer state. The failure of another one-party state might have an uncomfortable 'demonstration effect' for Beijing and give rise to domestic pressures. But these fears are being diminished by the stark prospect of North Korea becoming a de facto nuclear state, and therefore inspiring nuclear revisionism in South Korea and Japan as well as strengthening US arguments for regional missile defence. China's emerging strategic calculus may be that North Korea's value to China is questionable in these circumstances. What is needed to strengthen this calculation is more direct, if discreet, talks between the United States, Japan, South Korea, Russia and China on regional security outlooks in the event of Korean unification. Such five-party talks would be aimed at defining measures to be taken were there to be a sudden collapse of the North Korean regime, including the handling of refugees. China would be assured that a unified Korea would mean a reduced US presence, but a continuation of the US alliance that could help to keep a unified Korea non-nuclear. In the past, China has feared that placing too much pressure on the regime in the north could lead to its collapse. If the consequences of a collapsed North Korea and a unified peninsula appeared less worrying to China, Beijing might be persuaded to impose the sort of sanctions on the North that could persuade it to concede its nuclear position.

In sum, to address the proliferation problems in both the Gulf and East Asia, the Obama administration will need to encourage more 'mini-lateralism' amongst the regional states to define a political-security architecture within which these issues can be more comfortably addressed.

That approach is also necessary in addressing the one conflict, Afghanistan, in which the president has invested most effort. Having campaigned against the Iraq War, and having stuck to the view that a drawdown of the US military presence is necessary, Obama must hope that the political situation there does not reverse, as he concentrates US effort on the now restyled 'AfPak' conflict. Public support for the Afghan mission remains reasonably strong amongst states contributing to the political-military effort there. However, sustaining that support is dependent not just on progress, but on keeping the mission to ensuring that Afghanistan is not a safe haven for those who would conduct external terrorist activity. While that has always been the core purpose, the understandable efforts to create the 'good governance' necessary to embed security successes has created the impression that the 'mission creep' in Afghanistan extends to building a democratic nation recognisable to Western publics. That clearly is too ambitious an aim. The link with Pakistan having been strategically recognised, and the growing appreciation in Pakistan that the neo-Taliban constitute a direct threat also to Pakistan, has resulted in genuine intelligence cooperation in Kabul among Afghans, Pakistanis and others on how to address this AfPak security dilemma. Further cooperation with other regional states will continue to be important to sustain regional consent for the mission. Measuring the balance between the continued application of military force and the negotiation of political compromises, the latter at some point entailing discussions with 'reconcilable Taliban', will be one of many complex tasks confronting the Coalition in Afghanistan.

Moving into 2010, many of the ambitious foreign-policy agendas and practices established by Western powers in the previous decade and a half appear in retreat. What appetite will there be for the 'nation-building' projects that were thought at once strategically necessary and morally desirable? The efforts in Iraq are bound to become modest. Those in Afghanistan, especially as the economic crisis continues and the magnitude of the challenge becomes ever more evident, will naturally become minimalist in comparison to the original design. New projects seem unlikely to be undertaken and would have trouble garnering public support except in the most exceptional of circumstances. What appeals for humanitarian intervention will be answered? The so-called 'Responsibility to Protect' has been advanced as an international imperative, though often with Western impetus, in the face of acts of genocide or equivalent natural tragedies. It is to be hoped that a sense of natural human charity persists even in times of grave economic crisis. But tragedies in Sudan, the Democratic Republic of the Congo and elsewhere have not resulted in the concerted international action for which so many campaigners have pleaded. The static or declining military budgets of European powers place limits on expeditionary capacities already stretched by operations thought to be of strategic vital national interest. Rising powers in Asia, and elsewhere, are still more reluctant to 'interfere in the internal affairs' of others. The survivability of these doctrines will depend on countries outside the West adopting them more fully than has heretofore been evident.

The intellectual habit in the West has recently become to align national or alliance strategic interests with the delivery of a global public good. It may be that budgetary constraints and the disillusions of recent experience may inspire more political leaders to move from the poetic towards the more prosaic end of the strategic spectrum: defining goals more crisply in terms of clear national interest rather than acts of wider strategic charity. Emerging countries may need to move in the other direction, and find some way to define the advance of a wider public good as in their national interest. Rising powers, if they are truly to rise, will only achieve genuine prominence if they are to shape the wider order in which they live. This rebalancing will take time, and may not have wholly beneficial effects. In some areas, like climate change, it may be that Western powers will continue to provide the impetus for an effective global regime, though one will not emerge without key participation from the bigger rising powers. But other causes will need champions from emerging power centres. As time passes, the limitations on Western and US foreign and security policy may become more evident. Domestically Obama may have campaigned on the theme 'yes we can'; internationally he may increasingly have to argue: 'no we can't'. That is why in the next year or two, the greatest demand on US talents and power will be to persuade more to become like minded and adopt greater burdens. Even in retreat, extroversion is necessary. Successfully managed, an imaginative US foreign policy in these straitened times could delay or even reverse the narrative of decline on which others have seized with perhaps too much relish.

Index